UTB 3125



UTB

**Eine Arbeitsgemeinschaft der Verlage**

Böhlau Verlag · Köln · Weimar · Wien
Verlag Barbara Budrich · Opladen · Farmington Hills
facultas.wuv · Wien
Wilhelm Fink · München
A. Francke Verlag · Tübingen und Basel
Haupt Verlag · Bern · Stuttgart · Wien
Julius Klinkhardt Verlagsbuchhandlung · Bad Heilbrunn
Lucius & Lucius Verlagsgesellschaft · Stuttgart
Mohr Siebeck · Tübingen
Orell Füssli Verlag · Zürich
Ernst Reinhardt Verlag · München · Basel
Ferdinand Schöningh · Paderborn · München · Wien · Zürich
Eugen Ulmer Verlag · Stuttgart
UVK Verlagsgesellschaft · Konstanz
Vandenhoeck & Ruprecht · Göttingen
vdf Hochschulverlag AG an der ETH Zürich

JODY SKINNER

# Anglo-American Cultural Studies

UTB basics

A. Francke Verlag Tübingen und Basel

**Jody Skinner** lehrt angloamerikanische Landes- und Kulturwissenschaft an der Universität Koblenz.

Abbildungen Umschlaginnenseite: United Kingdom Map: Teleatlas/EU © European Communities, 1995–2009; US Map: National Atlas of the United States.

Bibliografische Information der Deutschen Nationalbibliothek

Die Deutsche Nationalbibliothek verzeichnet diese Publikation in der Deutschen Nationalbibliografie; detaillierte bibliografische Daten sind im Internet über http://dnb.d-nb.de abrufbar.


Dischingerweg 5 · D-72070 Tübingen
ISBN 978-3-7720-8283-2


Gedruckt auf chlorfrei gebleichtem und säurefreiem Werkdruckpapier.

Internet: http://www.francke.de
E-Mail: info@francke.de

Einbandgestaltung: Atelier Reichert, Stuttgart
Fotokomposition mit Bildern von fotolia: victoria p., paylessimages, ruscello, Harry Macias
Satz: Informationsdesign D. Fratzke, Kirchentellinsfurt
Druck und Bindung: CPI – Ebner & Spiegel, Ulm
Printed in Germany

ISBN 978-3-8252-3125-5 (UTB-Bestellnummer)

# Contents

**Introduction** . . . . . . . . . . . . . . . . . . . . . . . . . . . . . . . . . . . . . 1

**Part I: Specific Topics in Anglo-American Area Studies** . . . . . . . . . . . 5

1 The Where (geography) . . . . . . . . . . . . . . . . . . . . . . . . . . 6
2 The When (history) . . . . . . . . . . . . . . . . . . . . . . . . . . . . 31
3 The ABCs of British and American Life (special issues) . ► utb-mehr-wissen.de
4 Uniform-ity and Plural-ity (education) . . . . . . . . . . . . . 67
5 Queendom and Republicracy (political life) . . . . . . . . . 87
6 The Pound Stops Here for a Commonwealth for All? (economics and international relations) . . . . . . . . . . . . 108
7 Who, Where From, and Where To (minorities and immigration) . . . . . . . . . . . . . . . . . . . . . . . . . . . . . . . . . . . 129
8 Weddings, Baptisms, and Funerals in The City on the Hill (religion) . . . . . . . . . . . . . . . . . . . . . . . . . . . . . . . . . . 156
9 From National Parks to Natural Disasters (environmental concerns) . . . . . . . . . . . . . . . . . . . . . . . . . 184
10 Paper, Waves, and Bytes (media) . . . . . . . . . . . . . . . . . . ► utb-mehr-wissen.de
11 Bread and Circuses (the arts, leisure time activities and sports, food). . . . . . . . . . . . . . . . . . . . . . . . . . . . 201

**Part II: Ways of Looking at Anglo-American Cultural Studies** . . . . . . . 227

12 Identity: Who's the Us, Who's the Them? . . . . . . . . . . . 229
13 Power: Those Who Got It and Those That Ain't . . . . . . 242
14 Gender: Wo-Men . . . . . . . . . . . . . . . . . . . . . . . . . . . . . 256
15 New Media Was, Is, and Always Will Be the Message?. 270
16 Culture with a Big "C" and with a Little "c" in Anglo-American Cultural Studies . . . . . . . . . . . . . . . . . 283

**Conclusion** . . . . . . . . . . . . . . . . . . . . . . . . . . . . . . . . . . . . . 307

**Recommendations for Further Reading**
**(a partly annotated bibliography)** . . . . . . . . . . . . . . . . . . . . . . . . 312

**Index** . . . . . . . . . . . . . . . . . . . . . . . . . . . . . . . . . . . . . . . . . . . 319

**List of Illustrations** . . . . . . . . . . . . . . . . . . . . . . . . . . . . . . . . . 329

Very special thanks go to three very special readers of the drafts of this book. **Susanne Fischer** combined encouragement and close reading to become more than just the perfect copy editor. **Beate Körner** inspired me with her astute critical eye and her voracious curiosity. **Edward Martin** generously provided expert advice based on his innate love for language and his meticulous attention to detail.

This book is dedicated to my amazing students of the past and the present…

*…für Robo – ohne Dich hätte ich es nie geschafft.*

# Introduction

Let's begin this introduction with a few words about the title of our book. I use ***Anglo-American*** as an adjective to refer to both the United Kingdom and the United States. Why cover both the UK and the US? Especially since you can often just skim the surface in a book of this size? It's always a question of what's better: being able to cover a lot more by skimming the surface like a surfer or diving into the waves like a deep sea diver but at the cost of not seeing enough of the whole. I hope you'll find it satisfying to see more of the surface and then use this UTB Basics book as a springboard to take your deep sea dives in places that you hadn't thought of before.

both US and UK?

Through comparison I think we can gain more interesting insights than just by covering one country. Covering American Studies alone would leave out the interesting comparisons with Britain, which is closer to Germany and part of the European Union. Covering British Studies alone would leave out America, which, for better or worse, is a force to be reckoned with. American culture in the broadest possible sense can be seen as a symbol of freedom, as a monstrous threat, or as a glorious promise, but you would probably need less energy to try to understand America than to try to ignore it. And there are unfortunately no introductory books currently in print on American issues written in English especially for German university students.

I've written this book for different audiences. If you're pursuing a degree in English and are taking courses where information about the United Kingdom and the United States is either taught or is presupposed, you can read any of the chapters in Part I for an overview, which you'll hopefully find entertaining and will help you prepare for examinations on topics about American and British life.

intended audiences

I'm also writing for interested people with a German background who want to understand aspects of American and British life that they find puzzling. I assume that you're not interested in reading a tourist guide that only emphasizes positive things about both countries. While I hope that my enthusiasm is contagious, I'll also try to encourage you to develop a critical perspective with the goal of a deeper understanding of things American and things British.

cultural studies

And what about the ***Cultural Studies*** part of the title? The subject called "cultural studies" has become very popular in publishing, teaching, and in research at universities in Britain and in the US since the 1960s and now too in other parts of the world. In Part II we'll be looking at some of the same information covered in Part I from a different perspective, giving you the chance not only to review the "facts" but also to see how newer ways of looking at culture have changed our attitude towards these "facts." In Part II we'll be seeing how key words like "identity" and "power" and "gender" can lend a new light to things British and American. I hope that students doing degrees in English or sociology at German universities will find Part II of our book useful as a springboard to dive into the depths of cultural studies.

America?

A few words about terminology. You'll notice that I often refer to the United States either informally as the *US* (without the periods) or as *America*. When I use the term *America* to refer to the United States, I'm of course aware that the United States makes up only about a third of the area of the continent of North America. Even noting that almost 75% of the population of the entire continent lives in the United States wouldn't justify ignoring Canada and Mexico. Perhaps another English noun will gradually come to be used as a substitute for *America* in the meaning of *the United States*. Or perhaps if Spanish continues to gain in importance, a new term will come into existence that will clearly indicate the US without perhaps offending Latin Americans.

Britain?

The terminology connected with Britain is so complicated that it deserves its own chapter as you'll see in just a few pages. But for now I'll just say that I use *Britain* to refer to the *United Kingdom of Great Britain and Northern Ireland*.

me

You'll perhaps be surprised about the style of writing, which, while perhaps startlingly informal in comparison to academic books in Germany, is actually not so uncommon at all in the Anglo-American academic world. Perhaps you're used to reading academic books in German in which the author is invisible and the reader is not addressed. Academic writing in the US and in Britain often involves the first person. The author chooses the material he or she thinks is relevant and important. This choice is always partly subjective. Not using "I" wouldn't make the choice any more objective. And since subjectivity and identity play a very important role in cultural studies, I've taken the liberty of making my identity more explicit than you may have expected for reasons that I hope to make clearer in the second part of the book.

you

You'll have also noticed that I address you the reader in the 2nd person. By addressing you directly I hope to encourage a dialogue that on the pages of this book must remain one-sided but can become a true dialogue on the companion website at utb-mehr-wissen.de. And you'll have noticed that I've also used contractions throughout in order to set an informal tone. Those who are aware of some of the differences between American and British English will also notice that I've almost always chosen the American equivalent. You'll no doubt notice some other differences between this book and other academic books intended for a German audience. You might find it useful to make a note of the differences – I'll be mentioning some of them in Part II.

sources?

You may ask yourself about which sources I've used for the information in the chapters. First of all: Almost nothing in this book is original except the way it's written and my combination of *Landeskunde* facts in Part I with cultural studies approaches in Part II in one volume. And even the way it's written isn't original in the Anglo-American academic world. Since the books in UTB Basics are intended as an introduction for students, almost all of what you read in this book is based on commonly accepted facts and insights. You can find more detailed information about sources on the companion website, which I'll be updating far more frequently than is possible for this book. I assume that neither digital immigrants like myself nor digital natives like some of you still rely on printed bibliographies alone to provide you with up-to-date tips on what to read. But I have included recommendations of books that I find useful for further in-depth reading so that you can start your deep sea diving without having to log on to the companion website.

Although you can find an index at the end, this book isn't meant to be a substitute for a cultural dictionary or an online encyclopedia, which you would turn to for quick factual answers. My goal isn't to provide you with an overload of quick facts but to present fairly common basic knowledge about a wide range of specific topics about life in Britain and America in addition to an introduction to the exciting world of cultural studies.

it rings a bell

You can find many cross references marked with a bell they are supposed "to ring a bell" for you. If this were an online book, you could click on the bell and be whisked away to another page. But while you don't have to read this book chapter by chapter, I'd hope that you find the book interesting enough to read chapterwise and ideally from start to finish since I've incorporated a narrative with elements of surprise and a few intentional traps that work best if you follow a first-chapter-first order. You'll note that many – but not all – of the chapters follow the same pattern. The first three chapters are appetizers. The many individual items about American and British geography, history, and special issues are all fairly small as good hors d'œuvres are supposed to be. I hope you're hungry enough to proceed to chapters 4 through 11, which mostly deal with classic *Landeskunde* topics. After we've digested these topics, we'll then be ready for an after-dinner discussion of cultural studies in Part II.

goals for you and me

If you find this book to be interesting and thought-provoking enough to continue your own exploration of things American and British, then I will have achieved my goal. If you also discover new subversive ways of approaching Anglo-American cultural studies, then you'll make me blissful. "Subversive?" you may ask in surprise. But let's take things one step at a time and begin by using the song "Starting Here, Starting Now," which my favorite singer, actor, and director Barbra Streisand sang on her tour of Europe in 2007 (music by Daniel Shire, lyrics by Richard Maltby Jr):

**Now take my hand**
**For the greatest journey**
**Heaven can allow**
**Starting love**
**Starting here**
**Starting now**

# Part I: Specific Topics in Anglo-American Area Studies

Contents


| | | |
|---|---|---|
| 1 | The Where (geography) | 6 |
| 2 | The When (history) | 31 |
| 3 | The ABCs of British and American Life (special issues) | ► utb-mehr-wissen.de |
| 4 | Uniform-ity and Plural-ity (education) | 67 |
| 5 | Queendom and Republicracy (political life) | 87 |
| 6 | The Pound Stops Here for a Commonwealth for All? (economics and international relations) | 108 |
| 7 | Who, Where from, and Where to (minorities and immigration) | 129 |
| 8 | Weddings, Baptisms, and Funerals in The City on the Hill (religion) | 156 |
| 9 | From National Parks to Natural Disasters (environmental concerns) | 184 |
| 10 | Paper, Waves, and Bytes (media) | ► utb-mehr-wissen.de |
| 11 | Bread and Circuses (the arts, leisure time activities and sports, food) | 201 |

# 1 The Where (geography)

Let's cover geography and history in the form of easily digestible appetizers. You may be familiar with some of what you'll taste, other things may be somewhat new for you. We'll be using the insights and facts gained from our survey of geography and history in the chapters to come. When you see a bell, imagine that your host is ringing a bell signaling a main course (in a different chapter). You can then either go right to the main course or you can simply ignore the bell and continue with the hors d'œuvres. Bon appétit!

Our first very short question and answer: Where should we begin? On an island or on a continent? Let's take the bigger one, the continent, first.

## Does the term "continental US" make sense?

The first question is very easy to answer: No, the term "continental US" doesn't make any sense. Since we decided to start with a continent, you may be somewhat surprised by a question that seems to imply that the United States is a continent. While the US is very big, the continent of North America is even bigger and includes the second largest country in area in the world, Canada, and according to some geographers all of Central America, meaning from Mexico to Panama too, and even Greenland.

lower 48

If "continental US" doesn't refer to an entire continent, then it would make sense to understand the term as referring to all states of the United States on the continent of North America, thus including the lower 48 below Canada as well as Alaska, the largest state in area and separated by Canada from the lower 48 but still squarely on the North American continent. But unfortunately the commonly used term "continental US" almost always refers just to the lower 48 as if Alaska wasn't even part of the continent. Even though the term doesn't seem to make any sense, it at least could remind us of the fact that Alaska (number 49) and Hawaii (number 50) are the two "newest" states of the Union, each barely fifty years old. And the use of the term lower 48 could remind us of the special status of Washington DC, which isn't a state at all even though – or because – it's the capital of the entire country, a country that while absorbing mil-

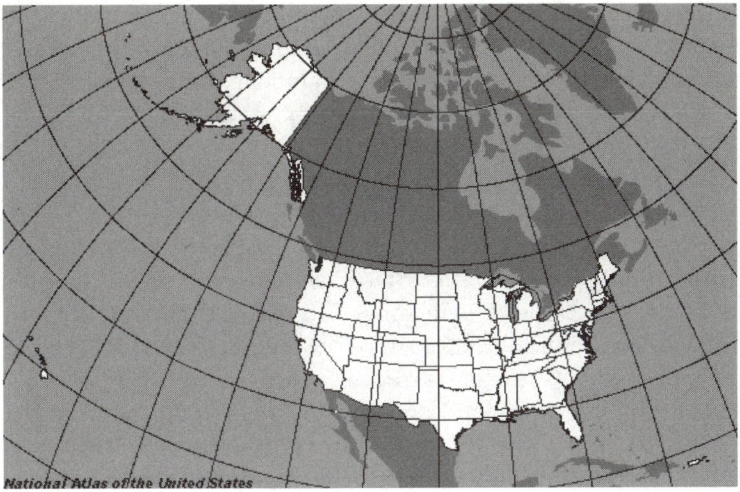


|Fig. 1.1
*Continental US?*

lions of immigrants presented challenging physical barriers for the trip from east to west.

## How have physical barriers affected the settlement of the US?

oceans, mountains, plains, rivers, deserts

An easy answer would be "a lot" since physical barriers have both restricted and defined settlement from the very beginning. We're supposed to be answering geography questions here, you might object, not history, so let's keep the answer short and just list the barriers from east to west starting with the Atlantic Ocean, the Appalachian Mountains from New England to the south, the Great Lakes if you stay north after crossing the Appalachians, then the Great Plains – which you wouldn't need climbing skills to cross but which require a great deal of perseverance: the Great Plains are thousands of kilometers of nothing but very plain Plains. But to get across the Plains you would have to swim across the Mississippi and its tributaries first (and during flooding, the Mississippi can be several kilometers wide). Only after surviving the great sameness of the Great Plains would you be faced with the sheer faces of the Rocky Mountains, which are rocky indeed with more than 60 peaks easily dwarfing Germany's Zugspitze. But even after crossing the Rockies, settlers then have a few deserts to traverse, including one of the hottest places on the planet, Death Valley. Travelers now would have to resist the temptations of recreation at one of the largest man-made lakes in the world, Lake Mead, and the temptations of gambling in one of the largest man-made cities in one of the least habitable places on Earth, Las Vegas, before finally arriving in the Promised Land of California. But the American drive towards the West wouldn't stop at the coast but continue into the Pacific to one of the most isolated islands in the world, Hawaii, and even further to one of the United States' few territories, the island of Guam, the most extreme western point of the United States, which is so far west that it's almost in the Far East, being only a couple of thousand miles (or a few more thousand kilometers: 1.6 kilometer = 1 mile) from Japan, where it's already tomorrow since Guam is on the other side of the International Date Line. We've now moved from the East coast all the way across the country and much of the Pacific Ocean and thus duplicated partly the original movement west, a movement that has been thought of in some periods of American history as a sign of divine will (6).

## How does the size of the US compare to European countries?

The answer can be simple and easy: the US is a lot lot bigger than any European country taken individually. The US is roughly sixteen times larger than France, the largest country in the European Union. On the other hand, the US is only about five times larger than Greenland, which although politically connected to Denmark isn't part of the EU. But the US is twenty-seven times bigger than Germany and almost forty times bigger than the United Kingdom. But at least Germany is bigger than almost any of the states of the United States taken individually. Only the states of Alaska, Texas, California, and Montana are each bigger than Germany.

how big exactly?

Well, you may ask, just how big is the US? Would you prefer the US Census Bureau's figure of 3,537,438,44 square miles or the CIA World Fact Book's figure of 9,826,630 square kilometers or the United Nations' figure of 9,629,091 square kilometers? If you have a hard time imagining what these numbers mean, then what about comparing how long it would take you to drive from the East coast, say from New York, the largest city in the US, all the way across the country to the second largest city, Los Angeles, on the West coast? Well, if you drove according to the old national speed limit of 55 miles per hour (which converts to a wonderfully leisurely 88 kilometers per hour), it would take more than 44 hours non-stop driving – from the Big Apple to the City of Angels, comparable to driving from the Cologne Cathedral southwest all the way through France and Spain right down to where Europe ends at Gibraltar and then back again including a final one-way trip to Frankfurt Airport. But what would you see in the US on the 44-hour marathon from the east to the west?

## What are some interesting and unusual physical features of the US?

mountains, valleys, canyons, lakes

Do you like outdoor recreation? What about the wide open spaces? Wet or dry, cold or hot? Some of the same barriers we just heard about that made the settlement of the continent so difficult are now some of the top tourist attractions in the country. Interesting features might include the Great Lakes if you enjoy water recreation; the Rocky Mountains if you enjoy climbing, hiking, and skiing; Death Valley if you enjoy being at one of the lowest points on Earth (the part of Death Valley called Badwater is actually the lowest point in North America). Unusual physical features would certainly include the Grand Canyon in Arizona formed by the Colorado River over millions of years, one of the natural wonders of the world. The Grand Canyon National Park is one of the oldest in the US and extends from one man-made lake, Lake Powell, formed by the controversial Glen Canyon Dam in the mid 1960s, to Lake Mead, one of the largest man-made lakes in the world formed by one of the largest dams in the world, the Hoover Dam, which when built in the mid 1930s was the largest concrete structure in the world. Of course there are also natural lakes; some of the largest in the world make up the Great Lakes, which partly form the border between Canada and the US and which have the illustrative names Lake Superior (the biggest as the name implies), Lake Huron (named after the Huron Indians), Lake Michigan (which forms part of the border of the state of … Michigan of course and is the only one of the five completely within the US), Lake Erie (named after the Erie Indians), and Lake Ontario, the smallest and most easterly, which has the same name as the Canadian province on its northern banks. All five lakes taken together make up an area larger than the UK. What "lies" or better "falls" between Lake Erie and Lake Ontario? The most famous waterfall in the US: Niagara Falls (the word stress in *Niagara* is on the second syllable unless you're speaking German).

rivers

Although the Grand Canyon wouldn't exist without the Colorado River, the Colorado isn't even half as long as the Mississippi. (Remember to pronounce the "a" in *Colorado* like an "ah"; Germans commonly mispronounce the name. And if you can't remember how many s's and p's are in *Mississippi*, then just call it Ol' Man River, its name in a famous song from the musical *Show Boat*.) The Mississippi River's origin lies in the far north of Minnesota fairly close to the Canadian border, and when joined on the west by the Missouri and on the east by the Ohio, it drains most of the vast Great Plains in the center of the country before expanding into a delta area in New Orleans and flowing into the Gulf of Mexico.

sameness

Americans not only crossed the enormous Great Plains on their movement westwards, they also managed to turn these vast open areas into fertile grazing and farming land and to exploit the mineral resources – in spite of extreme temperatures and lack of rain, which in the worst of times can lead to conditions found in the Dust Bowl, a part of the southern Great Plains where extensive farming led to extreme soil erosion. Perhaps the most interesting and unusual physical feature of the US compared with Western Europe is the sameness of the landscape, clearly evidenced in the Great Plains: you can drive for hours and hours through Texas and not see anything else than fields so flat that on a clear day and with good eyesight you can almost persuade yourself that you can experience the curvature of the earth by staring into the distance (and since much of Texas is "dry", meaning you can't legally purchase alcohol, you'll probably even be sober).

And if this book were only about interesting and unusual features, then we could continue westwards and describe in detail the Rocky Mountains, Death Valley, Mount Saint Helens, the Hawaiian Islands …, but let's leave that to the tourist brochures and films and turn our sights to some of those aspects not usually on the ordinary tourist's route.

## What effects has civilization had upon America's physical features?

A lot of environmentalists might be tempted to respond immediately with "certainly not any good effects", but dam builders might respond with "fantastic examples of feats of human engineering" providing millions of Americans with electricity and water and recreation and gambling opportunities. You can probably find one example of environmental damage for each and every triumph of man over nature, and we'll be looking at a few examples in more detail later (🔔 9).

## How do the latitudes of major American cities compare with European cities?

further south than you think

Comparing the size of the US with European countries probably wasn't very surprising since almost everyone knows the US is a really big country, so why not try and fool your friends with this question: If you were to draw a very straight line from Mainz (which conveniently lies directly on the 50-degree line of latitude) due west, which American city would be the first one you'd hit? Answer: Regina (which curiously enough has almost the same population as Mainz) but only if you interpret the word "American" to mean "North American" and thus include the Canadian province of Saskatchewan with its capital city of Regina. Mainz and of course all other parts of Germany north of Mainz are further north than the entire continental US. Pick an American city, say New York or Washington, DC or Miami. What are the corresponding European cities? New York is on the same line of latitude as Madrid, Washington DC's equivalent is Athens, and Miami's equivalent would either be slightly south of the Canary Islands in the West Sahara desert or if you insist on a "twin city of latitude" for Miami, then you'd have to choose Dubai.

If most of Germany lies farther north than the entire lower 48 states of the United States, then why is it not only much hotter but also much colder in the US than in most of Germany? A very good question!

## How could you briefly describe the climate of the US?

In a word: varied. In two words: extraordinarily varied. In a long sentence: Because the two main mountain ranges of the US, the Appalachians in the east and the Rockies in the west, run north to south, cold Arctic air from the north has no natural barrier and can flow into the very heart of the country, making places in the Great Plains much colder in winter than other places on earth with the same latitude. The southeastern region can also be hot and humid, with Florida's peninsula extending a bit into the subtropics, with milder winters than the northeast region, which can experience heavy snowfall even close to the coast. Parts of the west coast are the only areas comfortably habitable without energy needed for central heating and air-conditioning.

## And how have Americans learned to live with climatic extremes?

wonders of technology?

The answer in two words: amazingly well. The explanation for how and why Americans have managed to live with climatic extremes is a bit more complicated. Perhaps part of the American character involves the kind of resilience that can be seen in all the building and rebuilding of homes or buying new mobile homes until the next tornado blows them away: this ability to continually start afresh and start anew seems very American. Technological advances like central heating and air conditioning, the use of snow plows, the development of weather forecasting with special networks devoted to nothing else than descriptions of the next storm have enabled millions of Americans to spread across a continent which in amazingly large parts isn't fit for comfortable human habitation. Of course you could also wonder why electrical wires aren't run underground so that hurricanes, tornadoes, and ice storms wouldn't interrupt electricity as often. Maybe politicians are to blame? Speaking of politics…

## How is the United States divided for political purposes?

states and districts

If you quickly peek at the map we'll be using to show population change a little later (figure 1.3), you can instantly see one way in which the US is divided for political purposes, namely into 50 states. Each state is made up of congressional districts, each of which elects its own member to the House of Representatives.

There are a total of 435 districts and with a total US population of roughly 300,000,000 each district should represent roughly 700,000 people. Since people tend to move a lot within the country, some areas lose population and others gain. Every ten years a national census takes place partly to see which districts need to be redrawn so that all districts more or less represent the same population. What sounds complicated sometimes turns out to be extremely complicated, especially when some politicians try to redraw districts so that their party can gain a majority (🔔 5). What's much easier is the division for the Senate: each state has two Senators regardless of area or of population and regardless of what the state actually looks like on the map!

state boundaries

And what do you notice about the way state boundaries look on the map (figure 1.3)? When you look at the boundaries in the western two-thirds of the US west of the Mississippi, you can easily see that mostly straight lines form the borders between the states, evidence that the vast western part of the United States was settled in a different way than the area east of the Mississippi, which was settled earlier. And although as you can see on the map, the area of the United States is already nicely divided up entirely into 48 sections, some say that there could be future states added to the Union.

## What do you think will become the 51st state?

additional states

Now that we've reminded ourselves of the fact that there are 50 states in the US – and have been since the admission of Alaska and Hawaii around 50 years ago – we can ask the question: Will there be a 51st state? Additional states are certainly possible if both the inhabitants of the areas that want to apply for statehood and the Congress of the United States agree. There has been a movement for Washington DC to gain statehood status now for several decades even with a suggested name: New Columbia. Since a change in the status of DC would require an amendment to the Constitution (🔔 5), Washington DC or New Columbia probably wouldn't be as likely to become the 51st state as would Puerto Rico, for example (🔔 6). And there's always the problem of how to add an additional star to the flag … But let's leave the states and turn to another political division in America, the city.

Log on to utb-mehr-wissen.de for information about the most interesting American city.

## And what about Washington DC?

capitals state and national

Whenever you're asked to associate a country with a city, you probably usually think of the capital. Washington isn't on the list of the ten largest cities (unless you take the metropolitan area into account), which may surprise you. But then many state capitals are, strangely enough, not the most populous or the most famous cities in the state either. To name just a few: Austin, Texas; Harrisburg, Pennsylvania; Lansing, Michigan; Sacramento, California; Tallahassee, Florida; and Topeka, Kansas. Washington DC, of course, isn't in any state, it's the capital of the entire United States of America. While Washington DC had the more or less unofficial status of the most dangerous city in the United States for a number of years, the official status of Washington is that of a district (DC stands for District of Columbia) and not a state although Washington could become the $51^{st}$ state as we saw a bit earlier. More than two hundred years ago the US Constitution designated land to be set aside for the official capital of the newly-founded nation partly in order to solve conflicts among states that had fought to have the capital located in their states. The capital had been temporarily well-known cities like New York and Philadelphia but also smaller places like Princeton in New Jersey and Annapolis in Maryland.

contrast rich and poor

Originally Washington DC had the shape of a square made up of land taken from the two states of Virginia and Maryland until Virginia took some of the land back. The citizens of DC (who call their hometown "DC" for short) lacked any sort of representation until Congress decided to grant them the chance to elect one member to the House of Representatives, a member who had no voting rights. At least DC inhabitants gained the right to vote for the president when the $23^{rd}$ Amendment to the Constitution was ratified in the 60s and can also now vote for their mayor and city council. Reasons for the long lack of representation and power for DC residents include the fact that the daytime population is almost double the number of actual residents, the fact that 20% of all residents live below the poverty level, and the fact that an astonishing one third of all residents are illiterate. The contrast between rich and poor, between those with power and those with little power, can be seen as starkly in DC as anywhere else in the US. And speaking of anywhere else …

## Where do most Americans live?

We've already had the top ten list of the cities with the highest population, and we can use this information to come up with the major population centers with the help of the US Census Bureau's wonderful map of population density.

megalopolis

The dark areas are those with the most people per square kilometer (or per square mile if you like). You can thus probably identify fairly easily the major megalopolises (a fancy word for large urbanized areas, the Rhine-Ruhr area is a good example in Germany): BosWash from Boston south to Washington in the northeast, ChiPitts from Chicago to Pittsburg, thus from the Great Lakes eastwards to Pennsylvania, and SanSan on the west coast from San Diego northwards through Los Angeles and ending in San Francisco.

US population movement

We learned a bit earlier that the movement of population can cause changes in one level of American government, the congressional districts, as long as each member of Congress always represents roughly the same number of people. We can easily see the movement of population within the US by comparing the number of members in the House of Representatives between the 1990 and the 2000 census. The lighter colored states lost one or two seats in the House between 1990 and 2000 and the dark states gained one or two.

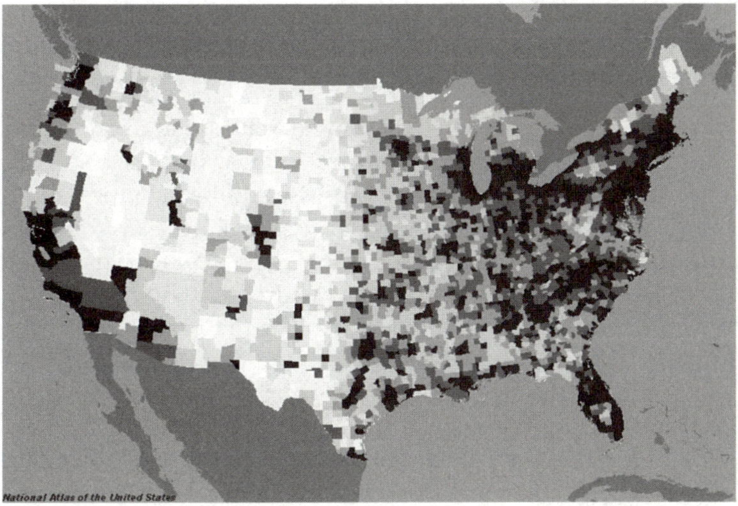


Fig. 1.2
*Population density*

Fig. 1.3 | *Population change*

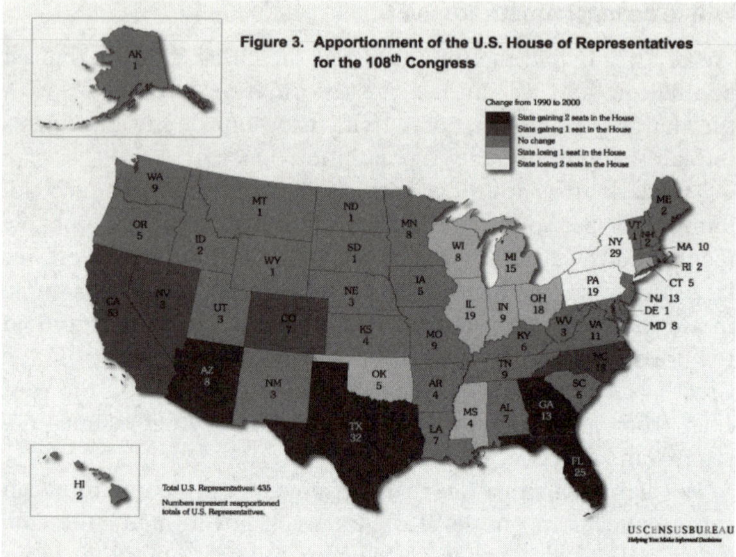


Perhaps it's not so surprising that people have been moving from parts of the country with uncomfortable climate conditions and economic problems like those in the northeast or around the Great Lakes, an area sometimes called the Rust Belt, to parts of the country with sunshine and jobs like those in the south and southwest, areas that have become known as the Sun Belt.

## And what about the entire population of the US in comparison to European countries?

US population density

You might think that since the United States is so much bigger than individual European countries in area, it must also have a far higher number of inhabitants. Not quite. Let's first of all compare the population density of a few European countries with that of the US. The most densely populated country in the European Union is the Netherlands with almost 400 people per square kilometer, the UK has about 250, and Germany has just a little less. The US as a whole is much less densely populated. If you round up the size of the US in square kilometers (look at a previous item for the answer) and know that in 2006 the US Census Bureau's estimate of the population reached the 300 million milestone, (7) then you can very easily figure out that the current population density has to be around 30 people per square kilometer. Not only does the EU have a population density more than three times higher than the US, considerably more people live in the EU (around 500 million) than in the US.

state populations

If we compare American states to European countries, the most populous state California with 35 million has almost as many inhabitants as Poland, the sixth-largest EU country in population. And the others?

<table>
<tr><th colspan="3">top ten largest states in population compared to EU countries</th></tr>
<tr><td>1st</td><td>California 35 million</td><td>Poland</td></tr>
<tr><td>2nd</td><td>Texas 23 million</td><td>Romania</td></tr>
<tr><td>3rd</td><td>New York 20 million</td><td></td></tr>
<tr><td>4th</td><td>Florida 19 million</td><td></td></tr>
<tr><td>5th</td><td>Illinois</td><td rowspan="6">US states from fifth to tenth place in population can each be compared roughly with Portugal, Belgium, or the Czech Republic (between 9 and 12 million)</td></tr>
<tr><td>6th</td><td>Pennsylvania</td></tr>
<tr><td>7th</td><td>Ohio</td></tr>
<tr><td>8th</td><td>Michigan</td></tr>
<tr><td>9th</td><td>Georgia</td></tr>
<tr><td>10th</td><td>North Carolina</td></tr>
</table>

## And what languages do all these people speak as their mother tongues?

US languages spoken

The easiest answer to this question is: Almost all languages known to humankind. Such an answer should come as no surprise to those who know the United States as a nation of immigrants from around the world (7). While there has never been an official national language, some states have declared English to be the official language – mostly as a response to some of the recent Spanish-speaking immigrants' insistence on keeping their own language while considering themselves to be American. Since the Spanish-speaking minority is the fastest growing, the bilingual parts of America where English and Spanish are spoken also continue to grow. Those who want a few more facts can use the US Census Bureau's official data from 2005 to see the top five languages spoken at home: In first place is English (no surprise). Spanish or Spanish Creole comes in second (shouldn't be a surprise). A very distant 3rd place is Chinese. French and Tagalog (the language spoken in the Philippines) are almost tied for 4th place, and Vietnamese is 5th. But – and this is perhaps the real surprise – German is officially the sixth most common language spoken at home in America after English.

And on this proud note (at least for German speakers), let's leave the continent and travel across the ocean to our beloved island kingdom, which is actually a kingdom made up of more than 5,000 islands.

### Is it easy to distinguish between the terms Britain, the British Isles, England, Great Britain, and the United Kingdom?

big and small islands

No, as you can imagine, it's not easy to distinguish between these terms and some of them will seem just as illogical as the term "continental US" (as you may remember from the beginning of this chapter). But as with "continental US" all these terms about Britain are commonly used even though they're problematic. We could start with the term "British Isles"; after all I just promised you more than 5,000 islands although you were probably only expecting two: namely the larger island called Great Britain and the somewhat smaller island called Ireland. What about the Hebrides, Orkneys, or Shetlands (the northernmost point of the UK), which lie off the coast of Scotland? Or the island of Anglesey off the coast of Wales, which became a center of Druidism. Or the Isles of Scilly (pronounced "silly"), which weren't silly to the captains of the many ships that were wrecked off the rocky coasts. The Scilly Isles contain the southernmost point of the UK and the southernmost and westernmost extremity of England, more than 50 kilometers further south and west than Land's End in Cornwall. Want even more islands? The Isle of Man is midway between the English/Scottish coast and the coast of Northern Ireland at the geographical center of the British Isles. And in spite of its central position, the Isle of Man neither belongs to the United Kingdom nor even to the European Union but is something called a Crown Dependency. Other Crown Dependencies are not at all at the center of the British Isles but far to the south just off the coast of France: the Channel Islands of Guernsey and Jersey (6).

(Great) Britain, United Kingdom

So far so good. But the situation becomes more complicated when you start to use some of commonly known terms. You can even insult some of the inhabitants of Wales and Scotland if you say "England" and mean "Britain." Compare the name "Great Britain" with "Britain" – which is bigger? Since you probably think this is a trick question, you'll probably guess "Britain" and you'd be right. The confusion is basically one of using geographical and political terms interchangeably. "Britain" is widely used to refer to the formal political term "The United Kingdom of Great Britain and Northern Ireland," which because of its length only the most serious politicians use – and have used only since 1922 (2). "Great Britain" isn't bigger than "Britain" (in the meaning of the UK) when you use the name Great Britain to refer to the island made up of the three countries of England, Wales, and Scotland. England is the largest country of the three in area and also has by far the largest population (we'll come to the numbers a little later) – and maybe that's why foreigners like Germans or Americans sometimes say "England" when they mean "Britain" or at least "Great Britain." (Even Deutsche Bahn made this mistake on the packages of chocolates given to passengers during the World Cup in 2006: The English St. George's flag filled up the entire map of the island of Great Britain. You could read that England had a population of 60,441,457 and an area of 130,395 square kilometers, which is very exact and very wrong – unless you change the name of the UK to England.)

Maybe a summary can help to "un-confuse" you while at the same time making you aware of the complications connected with names from a political and from a geographical perspective.

British? Isles

Maybe the easiest term to understand at first glance (but only at first glance) is the British Isles, a geographical term that includes not only the biggest island, Great Britain, but also the second biggest, Ireland, and many more. Unfortunately what seems to be a clearly geographical term is also a political term: the Irish could very well object to having their Emerald Isle called anything British or English, and as we'll see later in the history chapter, there are lots of good reasons for this. The British Isles also include the little Isle of Man, located in between the two bigger islands, as well as the Channel Islands, which would belong to France if distance played a role: the Channel Islands are much much closer to France than to the "precious stone set in the silver sea" as Shakespeare famously described England (but meaning of course "Great Britain"). The Channel Islands and the Isle of Man are part of the British Isles although they aren't part of the United Kingdom. But we're getting too complicated again, so let's drop politics until a later chapter (6).

| **names and terms** | |
|---|---|
| political | geographical |
| ***British Isles***<br>a politically loaded term used by those who don't consider Ireland as British | ***British Isles***<br>a politically neutral term referring to the island of Great Britain, the island of Ireland, and many other islands;<br>other terms less commonly used:<br>***Britain and Ireland,***<br>***British-Irish Isles*** |
| ***United Kingdom of Great Britain and Northern Ireland***<br>often referred to as<br>***Britain***<br>or as<br>***Great Britain*** | ***Great Britain, Ireland***<br>the entire island ***Great Britain*** and the northeastern part of the island ***of Ireland*** |
| ***England*** | |
| ***Scotland*** | |
| ***Wales*** | |
| ***Northern Ireland***<br><br>***Republic of Ireland*** | ***Ireland***<br>as an island with the countries of Northern Ireland and of the Republic of Ireland |
| ***Isle of Man*** as a Crown Dependency | ***Isle of Man*** as an island in the Irish Sea |
| ***Channel Islands*** as Crown Dependencies | ***Channel Islands*** including the islands of ***Guernsey***, ***Jersey***, and other smaller islands off the coast of France |
| and many other geographical islands considered as part of the political entities Scotland, Wales, England | |

## How has the geographical location of Britain affected its history?

You may ask here just as with our second American geography appetizer: What's history doing in the geography section of our overview? So, let's keep it short. Britain, as we've just seen, can be looked at geographically as a group of islands, the biggest of which, Great Britain, only barely makes the top ten of the world's largest islands in terms of area (but at least is number 1 in Europe). Since Great Britain is more than twice as long as it's wide and has a highly indented coastline, any given point on the island is at most only around 125 kilometers from the sea. And the sea here means the North Sea (which in spite of its name is east of Great Britain) or the Atlantic Ocean. Heading counter-clockwise we come to the narrow North Channel, the Irish Sea, and St. George's Channel in between the islands of Great Britain and Ireland, (to the west of the island of Ireland lies the Atlantic Ocean), the Celtic Sea off the coasts of Wales and Cornwall, the Atlantic Ocean off the southwestern extremities of the Isles of Scilly, and the English Channel in between England and France with its narrowest point at the Strait of Dover, which separates the English Channel from the North Sea.

island life

Life on an island can be idyllic – if you like sunny weather and choose an island in the Pacific – or can contribute to a sense of identity if the island is small enough or can lead to increased emigration if the inhabitants suffer from claustrophobia. Life on an island can encourage the inhabitants to develop special talents useful for emigration or colonization like shipbuilding. We'll be seeing examples of insular mentality throughout the book. Since this geography question deals just a little with history, maybe it's useful to remember that Great Britain hasn't always been an island. Around 10,000 years ago the narrow English Channel was so narrow as to allow people to walk across. After the ice of the last Ice Age melted and turned what had been a peninsula into the island of Great Britain, crossing the Channel meant either sailing or rowing or swimming until …

## What are some of the effects of the Channel Tunnel on Britain?

still an island?

One linguistic effect of the Channel Tunnel, inaugurated by Queen Elizabeth and the French president Mitterrand in 1994, was the invention of the new word Chunnel. While plans for a tunnel to connect the island and the continent can be traced back at least a couple of hundred years, engineering challenges weren't the only reason why it took so long. Britain had been an island for a long time, longer than most of its inhabitants can trace back their roots, and the tunnel changed this special island status. It might be difficult for non-islanders to imagine the psychological impact of such a change. Easier to quantify are the results of the Chunnel: distance, speed, and economic aspects including the enormous cost of the Chunnel. The organization running the Chunnel has been on the verge of bankruptcy now for almost as long as the Chunnel has been open. While some of the British might welcome the closing of the tunnel, it looks as though the connection between Europe and Great Britain is here to stay – at least until either the next Ice Age or global warming changes the geographical face of north-west Europe.

### How does the size of the UK compare to European countries?

We've already found out that the United Kingdom covers all of the island of Great Britain plus a smaller part of the island of Ireland, Northern Ireland (plus a few hundred smaller islands). Using rounded numbers in square kilometers (in spite of the British preference for miles): United Kingdom 250,000; England 130,000; Wales 20,000; Scotland plus lots of islands way up north 80,000; Northern Ireland 15,000. A comparison: Germany is considerably larger than the United Kingdom at more than 350,000 square kilometers and France as well as Spain are individually more than twice as big as the UK, which ranks as number eight in area but makes up only about 5% of the entire area of the EU. But as we learned above, the island of Great Britain is the largest in Europe (if we conveniently ignore Greenland …) and more than twice as big as Iceland (and considerably more pleasant climate-wise as we'll be seeing a little later on).

### What are some interesting and unusual physical features of the UK?

witch on a pig

With a little bit of imagination you might agree with the American travel writer Paul Theroux, who famously described the outline of Britain on the map as a witch riding a pig (with the witch's head in Scotland and the pig forming the Welsh coastline).

mountains, hills, coasts

For those who like hiking, the Pennine Way was Britain's first official trail and follows the Pennine Mountains, often said to form the backbone of England, which stretch from the Peak District (also the name of a national park) up past the border to Scot-

|Fig. 1.4
*Outline map UK*

|Fig. 1.5
*Witch on a pig*

land. But don't let the word "mountains" mislead you: the highest peaks in the Pennines are barely 900 meters, less than a third of the Zugspitze. If you want higher mountains, you have to go northwest to the Highlands of Scotland, where you can find the highest point in the United Kingdom, called Ben Nevis, which is however still less than half as high as the Zugspitze. And the highest mountain in Wales is Snowdon (in the national park area called Snowdonia) at just over 1,000 meters. While the Highland zone might be the favorite for mountain climbing tourists, most British people live in the Lowlands, which comprises all the land that isn't part of the Highlands and includes most of England. While some of the Lowlands is hilly, some is flat with the lowest point in Britain in the Fens on England's east coast. We'll be finding out more about some of the more famous areas of Britain that have been set aside as National Parks later (9). The Jurassic Coast isn't a national park but is England's first natural World Heritage Site and offers a geological walk through time along the southern coast of England. There aren't any dinosaurs, but if you're not careful, you could get caught by the tides coming in. Another famous attraction along the coast and another World

Heritage Site off the coast of Northern Ireland is Giant's Causeway, a collection of basalt formations shaped like columns left over from volcanic eruptions many millions of years ago, formations which appear to be stepping stones leading from the coast into the sea. Giant's Causeway is one of the most popular tourist attractions in Northern Ireland and belongs to the National Trust (🔔 9).

Returning to England you can find yet another unusual physical feature that sometimes poses an even greater danger of getting caught in the tides than along the Jurassic Coast. The Severn Bore may sound "boring" but is actually very dramatic and is caused by unusually high tides that race up the Severn River. Speaking of rivers …

## Can you name three important and interesting rivers in Britain?

Thames, Severn, Tweed

Most probably the one river that almost everyone would immediately think of – but might not be able to pronounce correctly – is the Thames, which in spite of the spelling is actually easy to say if you remember one syllable only and no difficult "th": tems. While the Thames may be the most famous and was one of the reasons that the Romans established a camp they called Londinium at the place where this important river was narrow enough to build a bridge, the Thames isn't the longest river in the UK. But you now know of another river that partly forms the boundary between Wales and England and that can be surfed on if the Severn Bore is high enough. The Severn River is a bit longer than the Thames but still is only a fourth as long as the Rhine. We've now mentioned two important rivers in England, one of which also flows through parts of southern Wales. What about an interesting river in Scotland? If you think of a particular kind of material when you hear the word Scotland, then you'll find it easy to remember a beautiful but not very long river that flows in the Borders area between northern England and Scotland, the River Tweed. Although this item only asked for three rivers, hopefully no one will mind if we mention just one lake, the biggest lake in the UK, Lough Neagh in Northern Ireland.

## Can you briefly describe the historical and contemporary importance of some of the forested areas in Britain?

If you hear the words "England" and "forest," you might immediately think of Robin Hood and Sherwood Forest, but there are other forests left in the United Kingdom although Britain is one of the least-forested countries in the EU with roughly 12% forest. Germany has more than double that percentage. Large parts of England were once covered by huge oak forests, but wood was needed not only to build ships – essential for island people who want to travel – but also to build and to heat castles and later to build and heat factories. Forests were also useful for the monarchs for hunting and other aristocratic activities. Nowadays tourists make "non-consumptive" use of British forests.

The New Forest

The New Forest in heavily populated southeast England just across from the Isle of Wight (one of the many other islands of the British Isles) is a good example of how forested areas have changed over the last thousand years or so. The New Forest belonged to William the Conqueror and was first recorded in the Domesday Book (2). It was used for royal deer hunting and also as a source of timber for the royal navy and was later used as a training area in World War II. The New Forest is one of the newest national parks in Britain (9).

## How could you briefly describe the climate of the UK?

rain? and palms?

Let's dispel right from the start a myth about English climate. No, it doesn't rain more in England (or in Wales or in Scotland) than anywhere else (except maybe the Sahara). In fact Milan, Italy, has more rainfall annually than London. Why then does English weather have such a bad reputation? Although, as we've learned, Great Britain is the largest island in Europe with ten degrees of longitude from north to south, there are only at the very most four degrees of latitude from east to west, making Britain a long rather skinny island. One result of this narrowness and the lack of mountains near the coast to stop the winds is the changeability of weather. So if you don't like the weather, just wait and it'll change. And the changeable weather makes a great conversation topic. Even if it seems to rain every day – and often does – it doesn't often rain for days on end. Those who think of Britain as

Fig. 1.6 | *Exeter palm*

cold and wet probably wouldn't expect palm trees, but in the southwest of England from Devon to Cornwall all the way west to the Isles of Scilly you can find palm trees and other vegetation usually only associated with tourist countries of the Mediterranean.

Keeping in mind how far north Britain is by remembering what we learned about comparing US and European latitudes earlier in this chapter, you might ask yourself why it's not colder there. Something called the Gulf Stream is responsible for the British Isles having such a mild climate. Without the influence of the Gulf Stream, the fishing industry wouldn't be nearly as successful as it is (🔔 6).

## How is the United Kingdom divided?

Perhaps the most obvious political division in the United Kingdom of Great Britain and Northern Ireland is between the four countries (from largest to smallest in population): England, Scotland, Wales, and Northern Ireland. Each country has varying degrees of power over education and taxes (🔔 5). If we were to zoom up from Britain, we could say something about the Commonwealth as perhaps the largest element of political division (and imagine its historical size by keeping in mind the famous saying that "the sun never sets on the British Empire"), but let's save the Empire and the Commonwealth for a later chapter (🔔 6) and be satisfied for now just with those divisions that are relevant just for the UK.

constituencies, counties, shires, ...

Just as the US is divided into congressional districts with one district sending one representative to the House of Representatives, Britain is also divided into constituencies with each constituency sending one member to the House of Commons in Westminster. There are also older divisions into counties or shires, some of which like Essex, Sussex, and Kent go all the way back to

Anglo-Saxon times (🔔 2). In the Midlands area of England especially you can see the old name for county "shire" in the county names of Leicestershire (don't let the spelling keep you from the easy correct pronunciation: only three syllables les-tuh-shuh), Nottinghamshire, where Robin Hood came from, and Worcestershire (hard to spell, easy to pronounce in only three syllables: wu-stuh-shuh), where the sauce still comes from. The British government has attempted to reform the complicated local government system and has created new "unitary authorities" or "unitary councils," which haven't always been accepted by people used to old county names. You can still often connect old cities with their corresponding counties: Gloucester with Gloucestershire, Nottingham with Nottinghamshire, and Leicester (les-tuh) with Leicestershire of course. The connection between city and county names is thus actually quite simple although the political divisions of power and responsibility are enormously complicated.

and boroughs

There are also divisions within larger cities, the most famous perhaps are the boroughs of London like the Royal Borough of Kensington and Chelsea or Westminster. Actually the City of Westminster is also a borough in spite of its name and in spite of the signs you can still find in London. Keep Westminster in mind; you'll be hearing about it again in several different contexts later.

**Fig. 1.7**
*Westminster sign*

Log on to utb-mehr-wissen.de for information about the most interesting British city.

Speaking of cities …

## And where do most British people live?

Remember the population density of Britain from a previous item comparing the US population with European countries? While the UK as a whole is only slightly more densely populated than Germany, England with 380 people per square kilometer is one of the most densely populated countries in the world. And as you might expect, some areas of London far exceed this figure with more than 13,000 people per square kilometer.

conurbations

Let's look at conurbations, which are similar to American megalopolises; they include cities but aren't cities themselves. Although just where conurbations begin and end isn't clearly

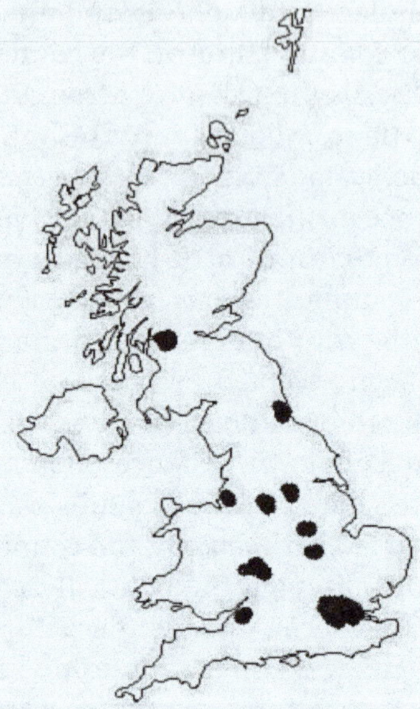

**Fig. 1.8** *Population urban density UK*

defined, everyone agrees that the vast majority of the population of Britain lives in heavily urbanized areas, which we can see represented as black dots on the map.

In the northwest lies the urbanized area around Scotland's largest city, Glasgow. Continuing south on the east coast we have Newcastle, which isn't on any of the top ten lists of cities according to population but which we heard about as one of the ports on the northeast coast of England. In the middle part of England, in the region called the Midlands appropriately enough, we have the dark spots indicating the large metropolitan areas which grew during the industrialized 19th and 20th centuries and which now form a belt across England (here given alphabetically): Birmingham, Bradford, Leeds, Liverpool, Manchester, Sheffield. You can also see in the southwest indentation the Bristol urban area and in the southeast the largest spot, Greater London, where roughly 20% of the entire population of England (about 15% of the entire UK) lives. London with around 8 million inhabitants is also the largest city in the European Union and is roughly the same size as the largest American city New York, give or take a few hundred thousand.

## And what's the entire population of the UK in comparison to European Union countries?

UK number three in the EU

After all the problems with trying to come up with reliable figures for cities, we now have a much easier task. If we use very rounded inexact numbers, then we have Germany in first place among EU countries followed by a three-way tie for second between France, Italy, and the UK.

If you want the exact numbers and trust your sources, then Germany is number one, France number two and the UK number three with 60,587,300 inhabitants at the end of 2006 according to an estimate by the Office for National Statistics (ONS), which conducts a national census every ten years. The ONS, as we just saw, was very complicated when it came to deciding how many people live exactly in which urban area, and the ONS presents us with a problem here too. The figure of roughly over 60 million includes the population of those areas of the UK that are not part of the EU, but since neither the Isle of Man nor the Channel Islands are heavily populated, the UK's third-place position isn't threatened no matter which figures you use.

We won't have a top ten as we had with American states because there are only four countries in the United Kingdom and the sequence is easy. As you noticed from a previous question but probably could've guessed anyway, England is number one with 50 million inhabitants and thus roughly 85% of the entire population of the UK. Scotland is second with 5 million; Wales is third with 3 million; and Northern Ireland is fourth with a bit more than 1.7 million. Why does England have so many more inhabitants than the other three countries? One reason: population movement.

## Give two terms to describe population movement in Britain

North-South Divide, Celtic Fringe

Both terms describe the same movement towards the southeast of Great Britain: the North-South Divide and the Celtic Fringe. The North-South Divide is a political and economic division in England between the older industrialized north including most of the darker dots on our population density map and the richer services-oriented southeast. Just as with the Rust Belt and the Sun Belt in the US, such divisions tend to encourage population movement: people move to where the economic conditions are better. The Celtic Fringe is a term sometimes used negatively to describe the areas in southwest England, like Cornwall, and Wales and Scotland, areas that are actually much larger than the word "fringe" indicates. But fringe refers not to geographical areas but to parts of Britain characterized by economic troubles and decreasing population. While there was considerable movement from north to south between the 70s and the 90s, some of the movement has been reversed since the turn of the millennium. People have started to move away from heavily urbanized areas, perhaps due to much higher property costs or new jobs in other parts of the country or simply the desire to escape the hectic life in crowded cities.

## And what languages do all these people speak as their mother tongues?

UK languages spoken

Just as for the US, here too we could get away with an easy one word answer: "all." But there are a few other interesting comparisons and contrasts to make. While only the languages of the American Indians could be looked at as indigenous languages in the US and most of them have become extinct, there are a few comparable indigenous languages still spoken in Britain, and they are still very much alive in defining identity. We just mentioned the Celtic Fringe as a sometimes critical term for some parts of Great Britain. But there is evidence for a revival of Celtic identity, culture, and music including increased awareness of the Celtic languages. The increase of political power in Wales and especially in Scotland (5) has been mirrored in more people learning Welsh, an official language in Wales, or to a lesser extent Scottish Gaelic or even Cornish, the ancient language spoken in Cornwall, or Manx, another Celtic language spoken on the Isle of Man.

Of course we could mention the very many mother tongues of the immigrants to Britain, (7) we could also mention the mother tongues of the emigrants from Britain and we could find remnants of English regional accents of the 18th century in one of the most popular places to emigrate to a few hundred years ago – namely the New World. And it's the New World that we want to turn our attention to now.

But for those who'd like review tasks before continuing.

### Exercises

1. Find, download, and print out an outline map of the US and sketch in all the physical features, cities, and other aspects mentioned in this chapter.
2. Find, download, and print out an outline map of the UK and sketch in all the physical features, cities, and other aspects mentioned in this chapter.

# The When (history) 2

Now that we've covered things spatially by answering some geography questions, let's turn to the "when." After a few geography appetizers, we can now try some history appetizers. We'll begin with American history (it's shorter), and just as with the geography appetizers we'll be using the insights and facts gained in the chapters to come. The bells should signal to you that you can continue the topic in another chapter. Hope you're still hungry…

First question: When should we begin? At the very beginning, of course.

## America: Early and Colonial Period 2.1

### And when was the very beginning?

when to start?

We could start with the earliest traces of human habitation in what is now the United States (but then probably American history wouldn't be shorter) – if only someone really knew when that was. It used to be commonly accepted that the first Americans came from Asia crossing a land bridge that later became the water (the Bering Straits) that now separates Russia from Alaska around 10,000 or maybe 20,000 years ago. This view was based on the old bones and tips of spears archaeologists love. Nowadays DNA comparisons have generated other theories suggesting that the first inhabitants could have come from Asia across the Pacific or even from Western Europe across the North Atlantic, which was partially frozen back then. And a Stone Age Columbus (to use the title of a BBC documentary) could have arrived from southern Europe more than 20,000 or 30,000 years ago.

1492?

We could begin with the one date that probably every American school child knows: 1492, when the non-Stone Age Columbus "discovered" the New World. Unfortunately there are at least three problems with this date. Firstly, 1492 is very late, and secondly Columbus didn't actually set foot on any of the land that was later to become the United States (unless Puerto Rico becomes the 51$^{st}$ state). Thirdly, if we started with 1492 and Columbus, we run the risk of not paying tribute to those people who later would become known as the Native Americans.

## Who were some of the original inhabitants of what is now the USA?

Indians and Indians

You don't have to be a Karl May fan to have heard about Indians, but knowing German has one advantage: having two words for two different peoples. Columbus thought, according to popular legend that the inhabitants of America were those of another continent many thousands of kilometers further westward. The word "Indian" in English still refers both to all those people who originally lived in North America as well as to the inhabitants of a former British colony and now the second most populous country in the world, India, which we'll be reading about in other contexts later (🔔 7).

## And who were some of the first European settlers in the New World?

Spanish, French, Dutch, ...

Countries like Spain, France, the Netherlands, Sweden, and England actively encouraged settlement and colonization as part of their policy of enlarging their territories and increasing their power. While everyone has heard of Christopher Columbus, fewer people have heard of the Spanish explorer Ponce de León, who arrived just a few years later and actually landed on what was to become much later the United States, establishing in St. Augustine, Florida, the oldest European settlement.

Other Spanish explorers came for God (Christianizing the natives) and gold. For example, Coronado discovered the Grand Canyon and explored what would later become part of the southwest

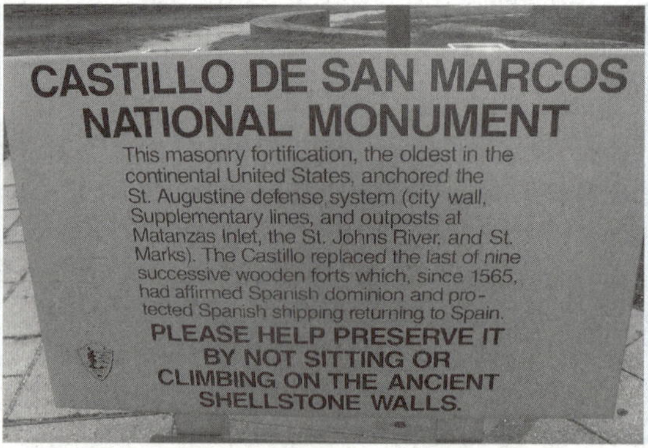


**Fig. 2.1** *Fort San Marcos in St. Augustine, Florida. Note the use of "continental United States" (🔔 1) in the description.*

US; De Soto discovered the Mississippi River. French explorers and traders settled around the Great Lakes; De Cadillac founded a fort that he called Detroit. And Cadillac became the name of an American luxury auto built in Detroit a few hundred years later. The Dutch West India Company claimed a chunk of what would become the states of Connecticut, New York, New Jersey, and Pennsylvania, and named it New Netherland. The famous Dutch colonial governor Peter Stuyvesant conquered the small neighboring colony of New Sweden but later was forced to surrender the entire colony as well as the settlement called New Amsterdam to the English, who then renamed it New York.

But more than fifty years earlier, Sir Walter Raleigh, an adventurer and explorer for Elizabeth I, founded the first English settlement on Roanoke Island off the coast of what would later become North Carolina. When a successor to Raleigh returned to Roanoke after being delayed by the Spanish Armada, the "Lost Colony" had mysteriously vanished. The first permanent English settlement that didn't disappear was made a few years later in Jamestown further north along the coast in an area which later would become the state of Virginia.

... and the English

## What were some events leading to the American Revolution?

13 colonies

We have just heard about three different English settlements: the Lost Colony, Jamestown, New York (in chronological order). For the century and a half after the founding of Jamestown in 1607, colonies were established up and down the east coast, from the Massachusetts Bay Colony at Plymouth in the northeast founded by the Pilgrims, a group looking for religious freedom, to Georgia in the far south, a colony founded for prisoners from England. The English colonies were far from the mother country and relations began to become strained after the colonists began to resent having to pay taxes to the mother land where they had no voice in Parliament. The protest slogan "no taxation without representation" became common from the middle of the 18th century. The increasingly violent nature of the conflict was echoed in phrases like the passionate patriot Patrick Henry's "give me liberty or give me death." What later became known as the "shot heard round the world" was fired near Boston and the beginning of a war that was to last for eight years.

Life, Liberty, Pursuit of Happiness

After the first couple of years of armed conflict, some of those who later were called the Founding Fathers decided for a complete break with Britain and signed the Declaration of Independence, a document with the bold claim: "We hold these truths to be self-evident," truths that were revolutionary at the time: "That all men are created equal, that they are endowed by their Creator with certain inalienable Rights, that among these are Life, Liberty, and the Pursuit of Happiness." At the bottom of the document is the huge signature of John Hancock – legend has it that Mr. Hancock signed extra large so that King George wouldn't need spectacles (an old word for "glasses") to see the signature. The main author of the Declaration was Thomas Jefferson, who was later to become the third president. The Declaration of Independence is the most famous of the many documents that paved the way for the establishment of the United States of America. The date of the official signing of the Declaration of Independence, 4 July 1776, became known as Independence Day and is celebrated as the most important patriotic American holiday. The term American Revolution can be used to refer not just to the War of Independence but also to the time before and after the thirteen colonies became the United States of America. While the thirteen colonies at first seemed in favor of a loose confederation instead of a strong union, the group known as the Federalists, one of whom was the important "founding father" George Washington, eventually convinced the states to sign the Constitution of the United States, which took effect in 1789 (5).

## 2.2 | Territorial Expansion

### What was the Louisiana Purchase?

Fig. 2.2 | *Sacajawea dollar coin*

The territory originally recognized as being part of the United States of America extended from the Atlantic coast in the east to the Mississippi River in the west. We've already heard that France was present in the New World almost from the start and settled the area around the Great Lakes. The French also claimed large portions of the interior of the continent along the Mississippi River, lost these to Spain, and then won them back again. To solve his financial problems Napoleon decided to sell the vast area called Louisiana, which Jefferson agreed to buy. The Louisiana Purchase was a very good buy, doubling the size of what was then the United States. In 1804 the deal was signed, and, not long after, two explorers named Lewis and Clark set off to see exactly what the new land was like and also to find a way through the mountains to the Pacific, assisted by a Shoshone Indian woman named Sacajawea, who would embellish a US dollar coin two hundred years later.

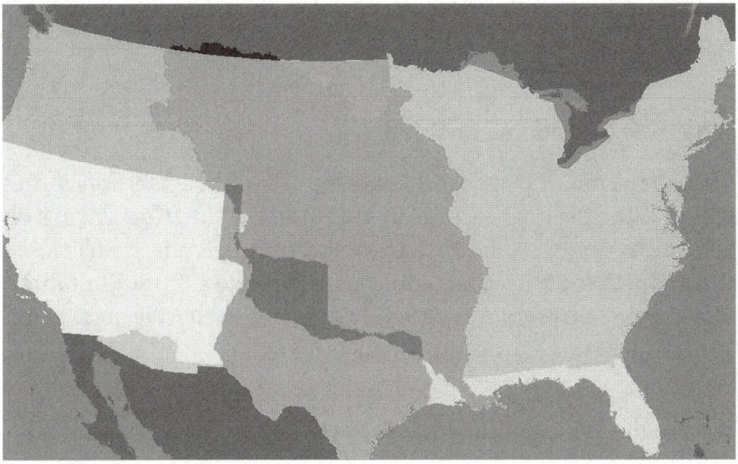

Fig. 2.3
*Territorial expansion map*

The area in the middle of the map is the Louisiana Purchase. (The area that would later become the state of Louisiana is only a small part of this great expanse of land.) Other shaded areas show land areas that were to become part of the United States by acquisition such as Florida, acquired from Spain twenty years after the Louisiana Purchase, or large portions of the west taken from Mexico. The famous term "manifest destiny" was used in the middle of the 19th century to justify first the annexation of Texas during the Mexican-American War and then the gradual turning of all land right up to the Pacific Ocean into American territory and then into American states (🔔 6). But we're getting ahead of ourselves now. Let's return to 1812.

## What were some of the effects of the War of 1812?

The War of 1812 is sometimes called the Second War of Independence; the US, still a very young nation, was again at war with

another War of Independence?

Britain. Washington DC, the new national capital was burned to the ground. The bombardment of Baltimore inspired the young poet Francis Scott Key to write the "Star-Spangled Banner," which would much later become the national anthem of the US. Although neither the US nor Britain won the war, which lasted until 1815 in spite of its name, Americans did develop a greater sense of national identity and were able to pursue both expansionism across the country as well as increasing isolationism towards Europe, a prime example of which is the Monroe Doctrine.

### What was the Monroe Doctrine?

James Monroe, the fifth US President, described the policy that would later become known as the Monroe Doctrine during an address to Congress in 1823: the western hemisphere was closed to any further European colonization, but the US wouldn't interfere either in the colonies already existing in the Western hemisphere or in any European conflicts (6).

### What were some political and social reforms of this time period?

Jacksonian Democracy

While the young nation was beginning to expand across the North American continent, other movements indicated expansion of another kind. Andrew Jackson was the first president to have come from humble roots in the backwoods of the Carolinas. Jacksonian Democracy is a term used to summarize the changes that took place during his two administrations. He came to be associated with the spoils system, rewarding loyal party members with government positions, and is seen as the maker of the modern presidency. Although Jackson was popular as a president of the people, his enemies called him King Andrew I for his autocratic style. He was also a famous military officer in the War of 1812 and played a critical role in driving the Indians westwards (7). In addition to the political reforms of Jacksonian democracy, the seeds for future reforms were being sown in other areas too.

Seneca Falls Convention

One important meeting which raised issues that would be relevant for women for the next hundred years and more took place at a Wesleyan Church chapel (8) in a small town with the idyllic name Seneca Falls in upper New York State. The Seneca Falls Convention took place in a year that most Europeans would connect with revolution: 1848, and one result of the Convention was the Declaration of Sentiments, which sought to have the same effect as the Declaration of Independence and which echoed the famous line "all men are created equal" with an important addition: "all men and women are created equal" (14). While the founding mothers of feminism didn't live to see women gain the right to vote, which came more than seventy years after the Seneca Falls Convention, one woman who did live to see some of her attempts succeed was Dorothea Dix, who became famous for her attempts to improve conditions in prisons, hospitals, and insane asylums.

Fig. 2.4
*Dorothea Dix postage stamp*

But all the reformers weren't only women, there was a man too, whose name conveniently enough was Mann, Horace Mann, the first very important reformer of the American school system, who believed in equal and free education for all children (4). Mann wasn't only an important reformer in education, he was also an ardent supporter of women's rights and the abolition of slavery but died before the abolitionist movement really became an important force.

The 19th century wasn't only a century in which the US expanded across the continent with reforms taking place in many areas of life, it was also the century in which the bloodiest of all American wars was fought on two issues – the right to secede from the union and the right to own slaves. These issues threatened to tear apart the United States before the country could even celebrate the first full century of its existence.

## The Civil War | 2.3

### What was the Underground Railroad?

neither underground nor railroad

The Underground Railroad was neither literally underground nor a railroad but instead a metaphor for a network of abolitionists with the goal of freeing slaves by establishing escape routes from slave states to free states. The "conductors" were those abolitionists who helped the "passengers," the runaway slaves, to escape to freedom. Those involved in the Underground Railroad could be imprisoned since they were in effect breaking the Fugitive

Slave Law, which was passed as part of one of many compromises between the North and the South in the years leading up until the beginning of the Civil War. This strict law was supposed to help slave owners to more easily re-capture their "property" but in effect resulted in increased support on the part of Northerners opposed to slavery.

## Name some important, interesting, and influential people

two Harriets

Fig. 2.5

Fig. 2.6

Two famous Northerners who became "conductors" shared the same first name Harriet. Harriet Tubman was a former slave who escaped and received the name Moses for her role in helping many other slaves "travel" along the Underground Railroad to freedom. She has become an American icon and a living bridge from one era to another, partly due to her age: she lived for almost a half century after the Civil War ended.

The other Harriet was a small white lady with the full name Harriet Beecher Stowe, who wrote one of the most famous novels in American history, *Uncle Tom's Cabin*, which portrayed graphically the cruelty of slavery. According to legend, President Abraham Lincoln famously greeted Stowe with the words: "So you're the little woman who wrote the book that started this Great War!" Whether or not Lincoln actually said these words, most historians believe that Stowe's novel was one of the causes of the Civil War and that her book convinced many Northerners of the wrongs of the slavery system.

Brown, Howe, Douglass

Other famous people of the period include the radical abolitionist John Brown, who with his supporters had the hope of starting a revolution with freed slaves. Although he was hanged for treason, his actions are also thought to have helped to begin the Civil War. His name became immortalized in connection with the "Battle Hymn of the Republic," the rousing anthem adopted by Union forces during the Civil War. The author who wrote the lyrics to this well-known song that would later be sung during the Civil Rights movement was Julia Ward Howe, yet another abolitionist. In contrast to the former slave Harriet Tubman, Harriet Beecher Stowe, John Brown, and Julia Ward Howe were all white. A famous black abolitionist, author, journalist, statesman, and reformer was Frederick Douglass, whose life began in slavery. Douglass became one of the greatest public speakers in American history, wrote one of the classic American autobiographies, participated in the Seneca Falls Convention and supported women's rights, founded a weekly newspaper, and became a well-known journalist. Just like Harriet Tubman, Frederick Douglass has also been portrayed on two American stamps.

One person who hasn't yet been portrayed on an American stamp but who had a huge effect on American history was yet another slave, whose story however didn't have the same happy ending like Frederick Douglass and Harriet Tubman.

Fig. 2.7

Fig. 2.8

## What were some of the results of the Dred Scott decision?

slaves as property

The word "decision" is a clue that we're talking about the Supreme Court here (🔔 5). Dred Scott was a slave whose master traveled quite a bit including stays in free states where slavery was illegal. After Scott's former owner attempted to sell him to a new owner, Scott sued for his freedom, first at the state and then the federal level and finally before the Supreme Court, which ruled that not only did Dred Scott have no claim to freedom but also that no other slave or any other person descended from Black Africans even had the right to sue in court, much less the right to freedom. Slaves were property and not citizens. Although Scott's new owner voluntarily freed him, the most famous slave in the US lived for less than a year in freedom, dying in 1858. The results of the Dred Scott Supreme Court decision were to long outlive the man himself. The sense of outrage at the Court's decision also led to the growth of the Republican party, which had been founded as an anti-slavery party a few years earlier with a strong belief that slavery should not be allowed in the new states that were being added as settlers moved westwards.

## What problems were caused by admission of new states to the Union?

A main problem caused by admission of new states to the Union was upsetting the balance in the Senate, where each state is represented by two senators (🔔 5). As long as the number of slave and free states was equal, a balance of power between the two groups in the Senate was maintained. To maintain this balance states were usually admitted in pairs starting with the Missouri

Compromise in 1820 and extending through the Compromise of 1850. The balance was finally lost in the 1850s.

not USA but CSA

Finally states of what was (and still is) called the Deep South, spreading from South Carolina to Texas, seceded from the Union and proclaimed themselves to be part of a new union, no longer the USA but the CSA, the Confederate States of America. Some border states were torn between their loyalty to preserving the Union and their laws, which allowed slavery. After Virginia seceded from the Union, part of the state seceded from Virginia to become the state of West Virginia.

slavery, tariffs, right to secede

We've now heard about some individual causes of the Civil War starting with the abolitionist movement including John Brown's raid, the heroism of the conductors on the Underground Railroad like Harriet Tubman and Frederick Douglass, the shock caused by Harriet Beecher Stowe's portrayal of slavery in *Uncle Tom's Cabin* and by the Supreme Court decision *Dred Scot v. Sandford*. All these aspects are connected to the slavery issue. We can add two larger issues that also separated the two parts of the US. The southern states relied on agriculture and the need for low taxes on imported goods versus the northern states' industrialization and their need for protection against imports from abroad. And there was one question that the North and the South answered very differently: Did one state have the right to secede from the Union? South Carolina believed it had the right to secede, and that is exactly where the first shots of the Civil War were heard.

## Name some interesting names, places, and events associated with the Civil War

Fort Sumter

If we start with the first shots, we'd have to begin at a small island in the harbor of Charleston, South Carolina, with a fort manned by Union, that is, Northern forces, who refused to give up the fort. The first shots fired at Fort Sumter at the beginning of 1861 are seen as the start of the war.

Emancipation Proclamation

Two years after the beginning of the war, the President of the Union, Abraham Lincoln, issued the Emancipation Proclamation. The Proclamation wasn't supposed to free all slaves at once and everywhere – Lincoln was an astute politician who wanted more than anything to restore the Union – but only in those Confederate states that didn't return to the Union by a certain date, in effect an attempt at political blackmail. Perhaps slavery would've continued if the southern states had given in to Lincoln's demands and returned to the Union. But no Confederate state was willing to take up Lincoln's offer, and so slavery was forbidden as of 1 January 1863 in all Confederate states not then under Union control. Interestingly enough it wasn't until the passage of the 13th Amendment after the end of the Civil War that slavery was also prohibited in the slave states that had not seceded from the Union.

Gettysburg Address

Almost three years after the first shots at Fort Sumter in a small town in Pennsylvania near the bloodiest battlefield of the entire war, Gettysburg, President Abraham Lincoln made history with an address that was to be given the same name as the battlefield. The Gettysburg Address was only a few lines long and began with the beginning of the nation a mere 87 years earlier "four score and seven years ago," then echoed the Declaration of Independence that "a new nation, conceived in Liberty, and dedicated to the proposition that all men are created equal," now being tested by a "great civil war" if "it can long endure." Lincoln concludes by dedicating himself to the "great task" remaining, "that these dead shall not have died in vain – that this nation, under God, shall have a new birth of freedom – and that government of the people, by the people, for the people, shall not perish from the earth."

Appomattox

Although the Battle of Gettysburg was considered the turning point of the Civil War with Union forces defeating the Confederacy, the Civil War was to continue after this bloodiest battle for almost another two years until Confederate General Robert E. Lee surrendered to Union General Ulysses S. Grant near the small town with the somewhat strange-sounding name of Appomattox Court House. The formal ceremony of surrender involved no cheering. The American Civil War, the bloodiest in the nation's history, ended in April 1865 not with a celebration but with an act of mourning. The war was over; the reconstruction of the Union was, however, just beginning.

## 2.4 | From Reconstruction to Closing of the Frontier

### Why did the Constitution have to be changed?

slavery abolished, rights gained

If you remember the Dred Scott decision and know that Supreme Court decisions can only be changed by new decisions or by changes to the Constitution, you'll see the need for the first amendments in more than sixty years. The 13th abolished slavery; the 14th overturned the Dred Scott Decision and ensured that almost all those people born or naturalized in the United States had the full rights of citizens. (Native Americans weren't yet included.) The 15th Amendment guaranteed that no (male only!) citizens of the United States could be denied the right to vote because of "race, color, or previous condition of servitude."

### Who were the winners and losers at the end of Reconstruction?

blue beat gray

At least one winner and one loser of the Civil War is easy to determine: the Union forces (color blue) of the North beat the Confederate forces (color gray) of the South. The other winners and losers aren't as clear. The former slaves were freed in name but often were faced with poverty and harassment. Former slave owners became bitter extremists; the grand plantations lay in ruin. While the sense of loss remained in the South – I can remember hearing as a boy in the Deep South the saying "the South will rise again" one hundred years after the end of the Civil War – the United States had remained united, the Union that Lincoln had sought to maintain would not be questioned again.

The very end of Reconstruction is tainted by a political deal that mirrored in many ways the political corruption that had come to be associated with so many aspects of the decade after the war. In the 1876 presidential election the Republican Rutherford B. Hayes, who didn't win the popular vote, gained support in the electoral college (5) from three states in the South in exchange for the promise to withdraw federal troops from the former states of the Confederacy, thus ending Reconstruction and also delaying the attempts of many supporters of Reconstruction to give fully equal rights to the newly-freed slaves. The promise of equal rights for African Americans was put on hold for nearly one hundred years until the Civil Rights movement of the 1960s.

## What was the Homestead Act?

Go West! ...

Those of you who are keeping track of chronology might ask yourselves what the Homestead Act is doing in a section entitled Reconstruction since the first Homestead Act was passed at the height of the Civil War, namely in 1862. The greatest impact of this legislation, however, wouldn't take place until almost a half century later when a vast amount of land was literally given away by the government. You may have heard the saying "Go west" in other contexts; the full sentence, "Go west, young man, and grow up with the country" was first made popular by the journalist and politician Horace Greeley and symbolized the promise of a new beginning that some thought the open plains would provide.

## What event is associated with Promontory Summit?

... and take the train

After beginning our glance at the Civil War with the Underground Railroad, what better way to end a section on the closing of the frontier than with the union of two real railroads. President Lincoln started the project during the Civil War and was perhaps hoping that uniting the country by railroad would also lead to a re-uniting of the divided country. The Union Pacific and the Central Pacific railroads met in northern Utah near a place called Promontory Summit a few years after the end of the Civil War. Even if the term "transcontinental railroad" doesn't actually apply to a railroad that only linked Nebraska with California, the event at Promontory Summit in 1869 was an important symbolic closing of the frontier, a frontier that was already being divided into parts separated by barbed wire, invented at this time as the only cheap way to establish borders in the vast grasslands that had been previously been open for all to cross. The growth of the railroad across the country was an important economic factor as well as a last encroachment of the white man into Indian territory with the locomotive: the "Iron Horse" winning ultimately against the Indian buffalo and deciding the fate of the remaining Indians (🕮 7).

## 2.5 | From the Gilded to the Jazz Age

If we set the closing of the frontier at 1890 with the Census Bureau's decision to stop tracing westward movement and with the last Indian battle at Wounded Knee, then we could start our next era in American history just before the beginning of the $20^{th}$ century. The "Gilded Age" was definitely not a "Golden Age," at least not for the vast majority of Americans but certainly for a selected few either praised as captains of industry or damned as robber barons. These selected few had famous names like Astor, Carnegie, and Vanderbilt. The name Gilded Age, by the way, comes from the title of a novel by Mark Twain, which sarcastically criticized the greed of the era. While the term Gilded Age has a negative connotation, the name Jazz Age is more positive and is also based on the title of a work of fiction, F. Scott Fitzgerald's collection "Tales of the Jazz Age."

inventions and inventors

Many of the technological advances that have forever changed the way human beings around the world live and work were first invented in the US during this time, also known as the Age of Edison, named after one of the world's greatest inventors Thomas Alva Edison, who invented the light bulb and who also significantly improved the telephone, invented a few decades earlier by Alexander Graham Bell. The elevator was invented earlier in the mid $19^{th}$ century but improved by Werner von Siemens and made safer by Charles Otis in the late $19^{th}$ century. Henry Ford invented the Model T Ford automobile and also changed the way the world worked with his assembly line method of production. The Gilded Age was the age of inventions and of hard work and of the riches earned by those who worked hard or by those who exploited others (6).

### What was one reaction to the power of the newly rich industrialists?

Square Deal

Theodore Roosevelt became known for his Square Deal and as a Trust Buster and even lent his name to a stuffed animal which millions of children go to bed with each night. But Teddy Roosevelt wasn't a teddy bear to some of the powerful captains of industry and robber barons. He initiated government action to limit some of the power that monopolies and trusts had acquired and proclaimed: "We must treat each man on his worth and merits as a man. We must see that each is given a square deal, because he is entitled to no more and should receive no less." Teddy Roosevelt was also known for his love of the open expanses of the west and his support of national parks (🔔 9).

## What was the Plessy v. Ferguson decision?

Remember the Dred Scott Decision, a decision by the Supreme Court that contributed to the beginning of the Civil War? About fifty years later at the very end of the 19th century, the Supreme Court ruled in another controversial decision, Plessy v. Ferguson, that separate facilities (in this specific case separate railway cars for blacks and whites) weren't per se unconstitutional as long as the facilities were of equal quality (🔔 7).

## What did "Remember the Maine" and "Remember the Lusitania" refer to?

a little and a big war

Both phrases refer to two ships and two wars, a little and a very big one. The little war took place at the very end of the 19th century between the US and Spain with the sinking of an American ship, the Maine, in Havana harbor. "Remember the Maine and to Hell with Spain!" became the battle cry. The US gained Puerto Rico and the Philippines (🔔 6).

A much bigger war began about a generation later: World War I, which the US entered late. One reason for American involvement was the sinking of yet another ship, this one a passenger ship called the Lusitania. Another reason for the US to enter the "Great War" was the publication of the Zimmermann telegram, an attempt by the German Foreign Secretary to persuade Mexico and Japan to attack the United States. After the US and the Allies won World War I, President Woodrow Wilson received the Nobel Peace Prize for his attempts to create "a peace without victory" and "to make the world safe for democracy" although the US chose not to join the League of Nations.

## What is suffrage?

"Suffrage" doesn't have to do with "suffer" except for those people who don't like politics at all; "suffrage" now simply means having the right to vote. Women didn't gain the right to vote until the 19th Amendment was passed in 1920 (14). Not only did women gain the right to vote, but they also began to do other shocking things, like cut their hair, smoke, and dance the Charleston in the age that had become the Jazz Age.

### What was Prohibition?

The Jazz Age wasn't only characterized by new music, new rights, and new dances but also by people who thought nothing was more evil than alcoholic beverages and who amended the Constitution to prohibit "the manufacture, sale, or transportation of intoxicating liquors." Prohibition was repealed less than fifteen years later with yet another Amendment, passed after the event that is usually considered to have ended the Jazz Age: the stock market crash in 1929 and the ensuing economic collapse that became known as the Great Depression. But wouldn't it be better to end the Jazz Age with a bottle of champagne to celebrate the repeal of Prohibition than with a Great Depression?

And while you're enjoying your champagne, log on to utb-mehr-wissen.de for information on Contemporary America.

## 2.6 | Britain: Early and Norman Period

when to start?

When to start British history could be as easy – or as difficult – as the decision about when to start American history: When you use the term "British," you need to begin with the birth of Britain as a union of England plus some other "less important" countries also present on the British Isles. After our first British geography appetizer we know how complicated the mere term "British Isles" can be.

### And what about the beginning of English history?

Well you could start with 1066 (the year is pronounced "ten sixty six," by the way) as indicated in a wonderful parody of schoolbook history first published in the 1930s: *1066 and All That: A Memorable History of England, comprising all the parts you can remember, including 103 Good Things, 5 Bad Kings and 2 Genuine Dates*. We don't have room for all the 103 good things here and will need a few (but only a few) more dates. We could begin history when Britain became an island, around a few thousand years ago although remains of human settlement in the area that was connected to Europe have been dated back several hundred thousand years.

## Mention some evidence of Britain's early population

stones, mounds, jewelry, weapons

If I can give you the hint to start with the Stone Age, then you might immediately think of perhaps the most famous monument in the UK: the odd-looking collection of huge stones arranged in somewhat circular fashion in the southern part of England. But Stonehenge isn't the only or even the largest monument built at least partly by people from the Stone Age. Not too far from Stonehenge is another less well-known but even larger monument: the stone circle at Avebury. And there are hundreds more scattered all over the British Isles. In addition to stone circles, mounds of earth are also testimony to the inhabitants of ancient Britain. Beakers, drinking vessels made out of pottery, point to the fact that a prehistoric people found throughout much of Western and Southern Europe had also found their way to Britain. And finally beautiful gold jewelry and coins as well as weapons made of iron or bronze are silent testimony to the Celts as inhabitants of Britain. You can still find not silent but very much spoken testimony to the Celts in Scotland, Wales, and Cornwall as well as in Ireland as you learned from our last geography appetizer ( 1).

## Mention some evidence of the Roman conquest of Britain

place names, roads, walls

The Roman conquest first provided us with written records about the inhabitants of Britain. As we've just seen, pre-Roman inhabitants left stone circles, hills of earth, and jewelry but no written records. Famous Romans like Caesar and Tacitus wrote about the natives. We can see other evidence just by glancing at any given map of Britain and noting down the names of towns and cities like Colchester (claims to be the oldest town in Britain), Chester (with its medieval city walls), Gloucester (a test of your knowledge of English pronunciation – two syllables only!), Cirencester, Lancaster (we'll come back to this place later, keep "rose" in mind), Manchester (we'll come back to this place later, keep sports in mind). The suffix *caster* or *chester* is derived from the Latin word *castrum*, meaning camp or fortification. The suffix also helps us to see that the Romans were pretty much everywhere in England and built roads to get to everywhere. Those who'd like to see remnants of one of the largest stone walls built in the whole Roman Empire just need to head north towards Scotland to Hadrian's Wall, parts of which are still standing today more or less along the present border between England and Scotland. Hadrian's Wall makes up the northwestern part of a UNESCO World Heritage Site called Frontiers of the Roman Empire, which includes the Limes walls in Germany. For those who like dates, Caesar first arrived in Britain in 55 BC and the Romans left Britain in the early $6^{th}$ century AD; for those who don't like dates, just say the Romans were in Britain for around 500 years.

## Mention some evidence of the Anglo-Saxons (and don't forget King Arthur)

place names

You could argue that the history of England begins with the Anglo-Saxons since they gave England its name. The Anglo-Saxons were various tribes who came from the continent, many from present-day Germany, and after some time together gradually began to call themselves English; the reintroduction of Christianity, which had first arrived while the Romans were still in Britain, was another unifying factor. Other than giving England its name, the Anglo-Saxons are also still present in the county names that end in *shire* from Buckinghamshire in the southeast to Wilshire in the south (where Stonehenge is) to Worcestershire (as you might remember from our spicy geography appetizer) in the West Midlands. And then there are the regions Essex (still a county name), Wessex (no longer a county), and Sussex (still used in the county names of East and West Sussex) named for the East, the West, and the South Saxons in England.

legend of King Arthur

You've probably heard of King Arthur and his round table and of the sword Excalibur, the tragic knight Lancelot and the love-torn Guinevere, the search for the Holy Grail. You might wonder what a question about King Arthur is doing in a section on British history since historians have as of yet found no evidence that King Arthur was a real person. This survey of British history isn't supposed to be a strictly historical one in the same way that a historian might describe things. Legends are often more important than historically sound facts in the formation of a nation's identity, and King Arthur plays a big role as a defender of the

Celts in post-Roman Britain in their struggle against the Saxon invaders. Perhaps you've also had the chance to see one of the many film or stage versions of the King Arthur legend ranging from the popular stage musical and film *Camelot* to *Monty Python and the Holy Grail*. For those who don't like dates, just remember that the Anglo-Saxons ruled in Britain just about as long as the Romans did, roughly 500 years.

## What do you associate with Alfred the Great?

Alfred the Great

While Alfred the Great was definitely a king, in contrast to the legendary King Arthur, a lot of people associate a particular legend with Alfred. A peasant woman who didn't recognize Alfred asked him to watch some cakes while she was away. Alfred was, however, more concerned about the many problems his Kingdom of Wessex was facing and let the cakes burn. When the woman returned, she scolded Alfred but then apologized when she discovered who he was. Alfred said that he was the one who should apologize. For those of you who don't really see the sense in this story, which is commonly known in Britain and was supposed to show the humility of Alfred as king, just rely on the facts: Alfred was the first king to unite large parts of what was to become known as England and defend it successfully against the Scandinavian invaders including the much feared Vikings. He's the first – and only monarch so far – to have been given the title "the Great," partly based on the scholarship which made his court famous. He was also the first in England to use ships (in his fight against the Vikings) and thus is considered to be the founder of the English Navy, an important part of the armed forces for an island country! And for those who like dates, Alfred conveniently died just one year before 900.

## Describe the causes and effects of the Norman Conquest

William the Conqueror: French and feudal

From the only king with the title "the Great" to the only King with the title "the Conqueror" and a foreigner – there'll be many others later – who assumed the throne. And the one date that practically everyone who has ever heard anything about English history knows and all readers who digested the first history appetizer now also know how to pronounce: ten sixty-six. In the century and a half between Alfred and William there were many monarchs with short reigns and all with similar-sounding names like Edward and Edmund and Edgar. There were a couple of Danish kings who ruled England named Sven and Canute although Alfred had done his best a century before to rid the island of all Danes. The last and most important of the Edwards, named the Confessor, had Westminster Abbey completed in time for his burial. Unfortunately Edward didn't leave any clear choice of heirs to the throne. The result of all the confusion was William's victory near Hastings in 1066 and his coronation shortly thereafter as the first king of England of the Norman dynasty. The effects of William's conquest were enormous. He severed England's ties with Scandinavia in favor of close ties with his homeland France, he promoted church reform, strengthening the power of the monarch. French became the language of the nobles, the government became hierarchical and feudal. His effective and efficient taxation was based on the information about property given in the Domesday Book, a detailed description of property and livestock, which provided William information he could use for taxation and which still provides valuable details about life at the beginning of the Norman dynasty.

## 2.7 | From the Plantagenets to the Roses

Dynasties or royal family trees have coats of arms, sometimes without the typical aggressive military symbols you might often associate with such things. The name Plantagenet comes from the Latin name for a plant which became the symbol for the dynasty.

Fig. 2.9 | *Planta genista*

### Describe the importance of Henry II's reign

In two words: Church, State. In his attempt to increase the power of the church over that of the state Henry quarreled with the Archbishop of Canterbury Thomas Becket, who was then murdered in his own cathedral supposedly at Henry's request. While Henry didn't succeed in subjugating the church, he did succeed in reforming the legal system and laid the groundwork for modern English common law. His reign is also seen as the beginning of English rule over parts of Ireland. And what about Henry's sons? Henry's son Richard I, famously known as the Lion-Hearted, spent most of his time on Crusades in the Holy Land. Richard's younger brother John eventually became King but also became so unpopular that the barons forced him to sign one of the most important documents of what would become the British Constitution, the Magna Carta (5). John's nickname was Lackland because of all the land he lost in his failed expeditions, and John is one of the few monarchs whose name wasn't used again. Both John's father, Henry II, and his son, Henry III, had the far more popular royal name Henry (there will be more to come), and John's grandson was one of many Edwards.

## What about Scotland and Wales during the reign of Edward I and II and afterwards?

the Hammer of the Scots and the Prince of Wales

One of Edward I's nicknames was Hammer of the Scots because of his battles with Scotland. He was also able to conquer most of the little kingdom to the west of England, Wales, and he almost succeeded in conquering the larger kingdom to the north of England, Scotland. According to a famous legend, his answer to the Welsh who complained about having to accept a ruler who spoke English was to hold up his baby son, who was born in Wales, and proclaim: My son, the Prince of Wales, was born in Wales and doesn't speak a word of English and is thus fit to be the Prince of Wales. The eldest son of each monarch has thus been called Prince of Wales ever since.

Welsh hero Owen Glyndwr

Fig. 2.10

Even after Edward I had practically annexed Wales, the Welsh rebelled again and again, most famously under Owen Glyndwr, who also claimed the title Prince of Wales about a hundred years after it was given to Edward II. While Owen Glyndwr didn't ultimately succeed in freeing Wales from English control, he was also never captured by the English and thus did succeed in becoming a great Welsh hero. You can see a statue of what one sculptor thought Glydwr could've looked like in Cardiff's City Hall. You may remember from one of our geography appetizers that Cardiff is the capital of Wales and thus a fitting location for the greatest Welsh hero.

Speaking of heroes, we need to return to the Edwards and their attempt to conquer Scotland. Movie-goers probably know a lot more about English and Scottish history now than before Mel Gibson's film *Braveheart* became popular. Neither Edward I nor the II was able to do much more than win a few and lose more battles against the Scots. Under Edward III the Scots finally more or less asserted their independence and peace was more or less achieved, but the hatred between the English and the Scots would continue.

### What were the effects of the Black Death?

ong war, short lifespan

Edward III is also associated with a very long war with France, which became known as the Hundred Years War and lasted even longer than Edward III reigned. Edward III along with Henry III, whom we just passed over, and George III, whom we'll be meeting soon, were among the longest reigning monarchs. Edward III managed to live so long in spite of an epidemic that cut short the lives of many of his subjects: an epidemic called the Black Death or the Bubonic Plague, which dramatically reduced the population within just a few years. Since the Plague destroyed people and not possessions, those left alive were wealthier; the few workers left could also demand higher wages although these demands led to revolts. The power of the Roman Catholic Church was shaken since the Church was unable to provide help; the persecution of the Jews and other minority groups, who were often blamed for the outbreak, increased. Just as the horrors of the Black Death were beginning to subside, the quarrels between the two Houses of York and Lancaster were beginning.

### What were the effects of the Wars of the Roses?

House of Lancaster v. House of York

We began this section with the plant for which the Plantagenets were named, and we'll end with a much more beautiful flower, but one that has thorns. There were Henrys and Edwards and a Richard too, who belonged either to the House of Lancaster with a red rose or the House of York with a white one, who both claimed the right to the throne. Those who are really interested in the complicated times in the mid 15$^{th}$ century will no doubt enjoy Shakespeare's eight plays dealing with all the intrigues and complications or any of the many filmed versions of the plays. We just have to mention one battle and one wedding here. At the Battle of Bosworth Field Henry Tudor defeated Richard III. Henry Tudor from the House of Lancaster wisely married Elizabeth of

York and thus not only ended the wars but also strengthened the crown since many of the nobles had been killed in all the battles. Henry Tudor, who became Henry VII, started a new dynasty: the Tudor dynasty.

## From King Henry to Cromwell

2.8

Although two men form the bookends for this section, women actually played at least as important a role. One of the great ironies of English history deals with Henry VIII's desire to have a son, a desire so strong that he was busy marrying, divorcing, beheading wife after wife most of his life. His only son, the weak and sickly Edward, barely reigned before dying and leaving the throne to Henry's two daughters, Mary Tudor and Elizabeth. And yet another Mary from a different dynasty, the Stuarts, was also to play a role far more important than many of the males of the time. Sounds like a great soap opera? I remember being hooked as a child on the very popular BBC series *The Six Wives of Henry VIII* (with six episodes, one for each wife) and *Elizabeth R* (with a dazzling Glenda Jackson as the first Elizabeth); thirty years later another hit television series *The Tudors* made history come alive for audiences in the UK, the US, and in Germany.

### Who won the struggle between the Catholic Church and the English monarch in the mid 16th century?

monarch as Head of Church

The easy answer: the monarch. England had changed from a Roman Catholic country to a country whose monarch became the head of his own church. One of the most prominent victims of this change was Thomas, who was beheaded when he refused to sign the Act that would make Henry VIII Supreme Head of the Church in England. Henry rewarded those who supported him by granting them much of the property and goods he and his minister Thomas Cromwell had confiscated from the monasteries. The Parliament passed the Act of Supremacy, which then regulated the power struggle between Church and State that had begun with one bishop being murdered in the Cathedral (as we saw with Henry II and Thomas Becket) and ended with many more executions 350 years later.

## What role did religion play for Mary Tudor and Mary Stuart?

Mary Tudor, Queen of England; Mary Stuart, Queen of Scots

Religion played a very important role in family life for Henry, his first wife Catherine of Aragon, and their first daughter Mary Tudor. When Mary Tudor became Queen Mary, she attempted unsuccessfully to introduce Roman Catholicism again after her father had made himself head of the church. Her marriage to the Catholic King Phillip of Spain didn't result in any children. Mary Stuart was also Catholic but belonged to a different dynasty and ruled two different countries. One way to distinguish the two 16$^{th}$ century Marys: Mary Tudor became known as Bloody Mary (perhaps a bit unfairly since the rest of her family – father and sister included – probably executed just as many as she did); Mary Stuart is also known as Queen of Scots because she became Queen of the Scots in addition to Queen of France (at least for a little while). Since Mary Stuart had a justifiable claim to the English throne and was probably involved in some of the unsuccessful plots to overthrow her cousin Elizabeth, Mary Stuart was imprisoned for many years and then finally beheaded. Another irony of this period: Mary Stuart's son, James, later became king since Elizabeth, the Virgin Queen, had no children.

## Why was Elizabethan England glorious?

Elizabethan Golden Age

In the long reign of Elizabeth I the full glory of the Tudor dynasty became evident with theatre (Shakespeare, Marlowe, Jonson), music (both Henry VIII and Elizabeth were accomplished musicians themselves), architecture (the building of great houses began to rival that of great churches) and exploration. We've already heard about Walter Raleigh as one of Elizabeth's explorers who founded the mysterious Lost Colony off the East coast of North America. But Walter Raleigh wasn't the only adventurer and explorer sailing – and plundering – for the Virgin Queen. Francis Drake was also involved in the defeat of the Spanish Armada.

## But what does the Spanish Armada have to do with English history?

Spanish Armada

In a previous "don't forget" item from earlier English history we dealt with a legendary figure, King Arthur, whom the English are very proud of. Here we have another legend, which is historically

Fig. 2.11

*The Armada Portrait of Elizabeth by George Gower. You can see the Armada in the background; her hand resting on a globe signifies victory.*

documented and has also become part of national identity: the Defeat of the Spanish Armada. The Armada was a great fleet of ships built by Phillip II of Spain (who had been married to Mary Tudor, Elizabeth's half sister, who had become Queen Mary, as you may remember) to invade England not only to avenge the death of the Catholic Mary Queen of Scots but also to fight against the English pirates supported by Elizabeth. The skill of English sea captains but also to a great degree bad weather and bad luck defeated the Armada and thus banished the Spanish threat of an invasion of England. The defeat increased national pride, cemented the role of the Protestant religion, and helped to make the English navy famous. You could say that the Spanish Armada was just the legend England needed to assume the role that sailors on an island need: that of invincibility.

union of the crowns of Scotland and England

Elizabeth was to reign for another fifteen years after the defeat of the Spanish Armada and as a "Virgin Queen" had no children. Her nearest relative was James, who as we've just heard was the son of Mary Stuart, Queen of Scots. It was this James who became James I of England after already being crowned James VI of Scotland and thus became the first monarch ever to rule both Scotland and England. James was also the first king of a new dynasty: the House of Stuart. After the problems with religion had been more or less solved with the monarch winning and the Roman Catholics losing, the next conflict began to get worse: the conflict between the monarch and parliament, which was to lead to a Civil War during the reign of Charles I, James' son.

### Describe the causes and results of the Civil War

Charles v. Cromwell

You may be surprised to have this question in the British history section since perhaps you had only heard of the American Civil War. I can remember seeing the movie *Cromwell* as a young boy and being horrified by the scene of the beheading of Charles I.

And now you already have one grisly result of the Civil War: Charles I was the first European monarch to have been formally tried and then executed as a traitor. Causes of the Civil War were Charles' rule without the consent of Parliament and illegal taxation and the increasing power of the opponents led by Oliver Cromwell. Cromwell led the Parliamentarians against the King, who were called Roundheads because of their short haircuts, which were a sign of their devout Puritan status in contrast to the long ringlets of the Cavaliers, the supporters of Charles and the monarchy. After Charles' execution a republic was declared, called the Commonwealth of England, which then became a "Protectorate" – but who was being protected from whom? Cromwell began acting more and more like a king and dictator. The English soon had enough of the Puritan tradition started by Oliver Cromwell and continued by his less competent son, Richard, and longed for a monarchy again.

### What about Ireland?

Ulster Plantation

Remember Henry II? He had conquered a part of Ireland and established English rule over the Irish. Five hundred years later in the middle of the $17^{th}$ century Oliver Cromwell continued the English policy of confiscating land and encouraging English and Scottish Protestants to settle especially in the northern part of the island (only a narrow North Channel separates northeastern Ireland from southwestern Scotland), which had already become known as the Ulster Plantation. Ulster, originally an ancient name for the northernmost part of Ireland, is still today used informally as a synonym for Northern Ireland and as an indication of the long history of Protestant settlement. Cromwell was and still is hated in Ireland for the brutality with which he subjugated the Catholic Irish. The violence between the Irish Catholics and the Protestant emigrants was to continue for another few centuries (7).

## From Restoration to the Hanovers | 2.9

### What effects did the Plague and Great Fire have on London?

We've already heard about an earlier disease that plagued the island of Great Britain – and much of Europe too – in the middle of the 14th century. In 1666, one year after another, less serious plague had ravaged London, the Great Fire not only destroyed the carriers of the plague but also a great part of London. Sir Christopher Wren, England's greatest architect of the time, was in charge of rebuilding the city and not only left his mark in St. Paul's Cathedral but also in modernizing London with broad streets and stone houses instead of the medieval walls, narrow lanes, and wooden houses that had characterized London before (11).

### What role did religion play in the reign of James II?

Catholic problem again

We've already seen how religion wreaked havoc in the lives of the Tudors. Charles II (son of Charles I) restored the monarchy after Cromwell's so-called Republic, and his brother, who later became James II (grandson of James I), seemed at first Protestant enough. After James' first wife died, he married a Catholic and openly converted. Parliament wasn't able to prevent James from becoming king, and when James' first son was born, the danger that the monarchy would then have a Roman Catholic succession became great. James had also alienated enough of his supporters for a very different kind of revolution to begin.

### What was the "Glorious Revolution"?

William and Mary

Revolutions usually have something bloody about them – lots of executions or at least a good battle or two. The winners of the Glorious Revolution invented the name – a bit unfairly perhaps since there was some bloodshed involved but not a lot. We can already guess who's involved from the last question. What happens to monarchs in Britain who seem a bit too much Catholic? Well, either they have to gain power and execute their enemies as Mary Tudor did or they have to leave the country fairly quickly as James II was forced to do. Britain had already suffered as a so-called "Republic" and wanted to have no more of that, but what can a country do if there are no royal Protestant relatives in the immediate family? Well, why not look around and see what the rest of Europe has to offer? And since James II's first wife was Protestant and their oldest daughter, Mary, had conveniently married a Protestant, King William of Holland, Parliament invited Mary and William to take the throne in 1688. With the threat of the Dutch navy and army breathing down his neck and with no support in Parliament, James II gave up the throne and fled to France, where he lived most of the rest of his life except for one last attempt to regain power. In the famous Battle of the Boyne in Ireland, William defeated James II. As part of the Glorious Revolution one document of what would become known as the British Constitution was passed, the Bill of Rights, not to be confused with the part of the United States Constitution with the same name that was written exactly one hundred years later (5).

## What was the effect of George I on English politics?

German George with Walpole as first prime minister

George I was proof of how much the English hated Catholics. Although neither William nor Mary were called "Virgin" like Elizabeth, they also had no children. And Anne, Mary's sister, who became queen after William's death, also died with no heirs to the throne. Since the nearest relatives were Catholic, Parliament came up with an Act of Settlement, which in effect passed on the throne to some distant German cousins, who all were Protestant and had to remain Protestant if they wanted to become English kings or queens. The first import was someone called George, or more precisely Georg Ludewig von Braunschweig-Lüneburg, who also started the House of Hanover (note the different spelling in English). Since Georg's English wasn't the best, he didn't particularly enjoy attending meetings of his ministers and turned over much decision-making to one of his ministers, the highly capable Robert Walpole, whose long years as minister helped change the structure of the way Britain was ruled and created in effect the position of the prime minister (🔔 5).

## Briefly outline the rebellion led by Bonnie Prince Charlie

many James, many Charles, one Bonnie Prince, one last battle at Culloden

"Bonnie" is an old-fashioned word (can still be used in some Scottish dialects) for "pretty" and nicknames can be helpful in distinguishing the many Charles and James in English history. The first James, called James I of England (who happened to be James VI of Scotland), had a son who later became Charles I (who was beheaded as you might remember). Charles I had two sons, whom he named Charles and James. The oldest one, Charles, became Charles II when the monarchy was restored (after Cromwell) and was known as a "Merrie Monarch" in contrast to the Puritan lifestyle of Cromwell. When Charles II died with no legitimate children, his brother James II became king (later exiled because of his Roman Catholic faith as we just heard). James II belonged to the Stuart dynasty and in addition to his daughter Mary (who married William and became the only couple ever to jointly rule England) had a son, whom he named … yes, I'm sorry but the English monarchs seemed to have been very conservative in giving names to their children … James. This James became known as the "Old Pretender" to the throne by those who thought he had no right to claim the throne and had a son named … not James … but Charles; and it is this very Charles who became known as "Bonnie Prince Charlie" and who led the last attempt by the Catholic Stuarts to regain the Protestant British throne. This movement, by the way, was called "Jacobite" after the Latin form of the name James. What would you call the son of an "Old Pretender" if you thought he too had no right to the throne? The "Young Pretender" of course, and Bonnie Prince Charlie, the Young Pretender, tried to regain Britain and with some help from Scotland came with an army to Culloden, a town close to Inverness in the Scottish Highlands, where the last battle on British soil was fought. The forces of George II defeated Bonnie Prince Charles' army and thus ended all Stuart hopes of regaining the throne. George II as you can imagine was the son of George I, the German we just met, and one of many Georges to come – a relief after all the James and Charles we've had to

**Fig. 2.12**

*Portrait of Bonnie Prince Charlie*

deal with. But before we leave all the James and Charles for good (or at least up until the present Charles, Prince of Wales, who may become Charles III if he ever becomes king), you may perhaps ask about Bonnie Prince Charles' nickname. Evidently Bonnie Prince Charles was so pretty that disguised as an Irish maid he was able to flee George's troops, who chased him all over Scotland.

### What are some results of the Industrial Revolution in Britain?

workshop of the world with inventions and innovations

We've just looked at one unsuccessful rebellion after one Glorious Revolution. Before ending this section called from Restoration to the Hanovers, we need to glance at yet another revolution that started roughly in the middle of the 18th century and continued throughout the next century, which began in the northern part of England and ultimately not only changed Britain but also the entire world. The Industrial Revolution made the North of England the manufacturing center of Britain and for a while at least "the workshop of the world." During the 19th century this area led the world in many industrial fields: iron, steamships, railway engineering, bridge-building, industrial machinery, iron and steel production as well as textile production. The first railroad connection between Liverpool and Manchester allowed goods and people to be transported at speeds not known before to mankind. Scotland and Wales also played a part: Glasgow as a "dear dirty city," the valleys of iron and steel in south Wales. Production grew rapidly as the economy changed from an agrarian handicraft economy to one dominated by industry and manufacturing. An increase in population led to increased demand. Inventions like the steam engine and spinning machines greatly increased efficiency. Innovations included substituting inanimate for animal sources of power, machines for human skills and strength, new methods of making iron and steel, organization of work in large factories and mills. The Industrial Revolution brought an increase in wealth and commercial and political supremacy to Britain but also included destruction of the environment, the growth of slums in industrial cities, bad conditions for factory workers, and child labor. The positive effects of the Industrial Revolution are the reason for it being honored on a new £ 50 note to be issued in 2010 with the Scottish engineer who designed the Steam Engine, James Watt, and his business partner Matthew Boulton.

## Describe the importance of the Acts of Union up to 1801

union of England and Scotland

The very attentive reader might have noticed that the words "England" and "English" and "Britain" and "British" seem to be used almost interchangeably. But there are big differences, as we learned in our very first geography appetizer. We can trace one big historical difference back to the passing of the Act of Union in 1707, which united the Parliaments of the previously independent kingdoms of Scotland and England and created the new country of Great Britain. As we now know, England and Scotland had shared the same monarch since James created the Union of the Crowns. Each monarch after James thus wore two crowns, one for Scotland and one for England. England and Scotland agreed to an Act of Union not so much out of sympathy for the poor monarchs having to wear two heavy crowns but more because of the practical need for England to safeguard itself from possible Jacobite attacks (no one could know that the Battle of Culloden would indeed be the very last failed attempt of the Catholic Stuarts to regain the crown) and Scotland's need for economic assistance. England promised free trade, Scotland agreed to be ruled in future by Protestant Hanoverian monarchs. The Scots were allowed to keep their own church, their own school system, and their own legal system. Since Anne (the last of the Stuarts, younger sister of Queen Mary, who ruled England with William III, as we've already heard) was the queen both before and after the Act of Union of 1707, she was thus the last Queen of England (and Scotland) and the first Queen of Great Britain. But perhaps because the phrase "Queen of England" or "King of England" is so much easier to say, it's been used ever since although actually between 1707 and 1801 the correct term would have been "Queen or King of Great Britain."

union of Britain and Ireland

"Queen of England" certainly is much easier to say than "Queen of the United Kingdom of Great Britain and Ireland," which became the proper title in 1801 in another Act of Union when Ireland was forcibly joined to Great Britain against the will of many Irish Catholics. The unification of the two main islands of the British Isles provided the largest free-trade area in Europe with no internal borders or local tariffs and contributed to the spread of the Industrial Revolution.

early forced union of England and Wales

But we also need to mention the first Act of Union, the origins of which go back to the time of Edward I and his son, the first Prince of Wales. It wasn't until King Henry VIII, with whom we began this section, that England and Wales were officially united by the Act of Union of 1536 or rather Wales was (forcibly) united with England. You can still see the lack of importance of Wales in the Union Jack flag. While both Scotland and Ireland are represented through crosses and colors, the Welsh dragon simply doesn't appear. It's doubtful if the Welsh took comfort in the fact that the House of Tudor was of Welsh origin. After all these dates and acts and forcible unions, let's finally end this section on a positive note. After so much bloodshed based on religion, in 1829 – just one more date for now – the Catholic Emancipation Act – just one more act – was passed.

### What was the Catholic Emancipation Act?

If you look back a few hundred years and go back a few pages to the section "From the Plantagenets to the Roses," you can see that one of the early struggles between Church and State started with Henry II. Struggles between Catholics and Protestants characterized the section "from King Henry to Cromwell" and resulted in many a death. While religion still seems to play a violent role in Northern Ireland, we can look at one government act as the end of most of the violent problems between Catholics and Protestants in England, Scotland, and Wales. One of the most influential figures of the 19th century and a British (now we can use the term "British") prime minister, the Duke of Wellington, persuaded Parliament and a reluctant King George IV to pass an act that gave Irish and English Catholics all political rights including the right to almost all government posts, except to the monarchy, which was still in the hands of the Protestant German Georges.

## 2.10 | From Victoria to Churchill

We had a previous section of British history with male bookend names: Henry and Cromwell. And we started with a look at some of the important women of the time – the queens. Our penultimate section begins with a queen, the longest reigning queen of all time (unless the current Elizabeth continues to reign for just a few more years), whose name became that of an entire age, the Victorian Age. But let's start with a man: not with Winston Churchill, who'll come later, but with Benjamin Disraeli.

## Describe Britain's foreign policy during the Disraeli era

colonial expansion

Benjamin Disraeli doesn't sound like your common English name, and Disraeli wasn't your common Englishman. His name reveals his Italian-Jewish descent, but his family converted to Christianity at an early age. He was first elected to the House of Commons in his thirties; as Conservative party leader and later prime minister he was instrumental in extending the right to vote to the working classes and in passing legislation that improved housing and working conditions for the poor. His greatest triumphs were in foreign policy. Disraeli enhanced Britain's imperial power, helped Britain control the important trade route through the Suez Canal, and convinced Parliament to declare Queen Victoria "Empress of India." But Disraeli wasn't only a politician, he was also a novelist and at least at the beginning of his political career was better known in literary and social circles than in political ones. After Disraeli's death but before the end of the Victorian era, Britain's foreign policy was characterized by aggressive colonial expansion with "Great Imperialists" like Joseph Chamberlain and Cecil Rhodes and colonial acquisitions in Rhodesia, South Africa, and Nigeria in a "scramble for Africa" among the European powers Britain, France, and Germany. At home in Britain and partly due to some of the results of the Industrial Revolution – a dramatic rise in population and of the middle class – important intellectuals began to look for ways to solve the problems of the rich and the poor.

## Describe the beginnings of socialism and the founding of the Labour Party

founding of the Labour Party

At the beginning of the 19$^{th}$ century political authority was in the hands of landowners, merchants, and aristocrats in Parliament, but by the end of the century much had changed. We've just read about Disraeli's extension of the franchise (the right to vote) to the working classes. Another reform was the legalization of trade unions. The Fabian Society, founded by a group of influential socialists like the authors H.G. Wells and George Bernard Shaw, believed that the whole community should own a country's land, natural resources, and wealth. The growing power of the workers led to the founding of the Labour Party around the turn of the 20th century with its goals of moderate socialism under the guidance of Parliament. Before we leave the 19th century for good, we have to return to a topic that has been a leitmotif throughout British history.

## Mention some of the important events in Irish history

Great Famine and Home Rule

Perhaps the one event that most people would associate with Ireland and the 19th century is the Great Famine, which resulted in the deaths of over a million people and mass emigration especially to the US (🔔 7). Many Irish lived on farms owned by British landlords. The Irish sold their grain and cattle to pay the rent, leaving potatoes as their only food. When a disease destroyed the crop in the 1840s, people began to starve to death; but the British government was slow to react. Prime Minister William Gladstone attempted to resolve the Irish question by a Home Rule Bill, which would give an Irish Parliament the right to appoint a leader.

Irish Free State

The Easter Rebellion in Dublin occurred after World War I and eventually led to Ireland's independence, at least for most of the southern and western parts of the island. British Parliament then gave the part of Ireland that became known as the Irish Free State the status of a dominion, an independent country within the British Commonwealth of Nations with the British monarch as official head of government. The counties in Ulster in Northern Ireland remained part of what then became the United Kingdom of Great Britain and Northern Ireland. The Irish Free State later declared itself independent, was neutral during World War II, officially left the Commonwealth in 1948, and became the Republic of Ireland.

Hanover becomes Windsor

What happened to the German-sounding monarchs in Britain? Queen Victoria had died in 1901, just one year after the turn of the century, and was the last monarch of the House of Hanover.

Before she died, she married off most of her many children and grandchildren to various other European royal houses and thus became known as the "grandmother of Europe." Her son, Edward VII, began the very short-lived House of Saxe-Coburg-Gotha. This dynasty with its very German-sounding name – due to the fact that, as we learned earlier, German and British nobility had been intertwined for centuries – lasted only until World War I. Because of anti-German feeling, the name was changed to Windsor, the name of the largest inhabited castle in the world and home to English and British kings and queens for almost one thousand years. In spite of the name change, the faces remained the same, including the face of Edward VIII and his very romantic entanglements (8). But unfortunately we have no time for romance now but must proceed with the two wars that would define the 20th century as the bloodiest in all of human history.

## Name a few British leaders during the two World Wars

The first two British leaders aren't nearly as famous as the last two. But H. H. Asquith is not only worth mentioning because he was the prime minister during the first half of World War I but also because of his success in limiting the power of the House of Lords (5) and in laying the framework for what would become the welfare state with the help of his successor as prime minister, David Lloyd George, who admired the German system of insurance benefits (3). Lloyd George is even better known for his part in the Treaty of Versailles and ending World War I and for his helping to end British repression in Ireland. Perhaps Lloyd George, whose native language was Welsh, was more understanding of the Irish than earlier leaders because of his own Celtic background. You can find one statue of him in a dramatic pose in the capital of Wales, Cardiff, and another in London not far from the most famous prime minister, whom we'll meet at the end of this section.

**Fig. 2.13**
*Statue of David Lloyd George, Cardiff*

If you've read the previous pages carefully, you should've come across the name of someone who was instrumental in expanding the British Empire, a man named Joseph Chamberlain. The key word "appeasement" could make you think of Neville Chamberlain, Joseph's son, who returned from a meeting with Adolf Hitler in Munich and promised the British "peace with honour" and "peace for our time." As we all know, Chamberlain wasn't able to prevent the world war he so desperately wanted to avoid. After the first year of the war brought no victories for the UK, Chamberlain was forced to resign, handing over to probably the most famous of all the more than fifty prime ministers in British history.

blood, toil, tears, and sweat

Winston Churchill's rhetorical flourishes have echoed through the years. In his very first speech as prime minister, he famously claimed: "I have nothing to offer but blood, toil, tears, and sweat." Other stirring speeches were to follow, evidence of Churchill's skills as an orator and as a writer. While you may not be surprised at Churchill being a Nobel Prize winner, would you have expected him to win the Nobel Prize for literature? If you think about another British prime minister mentioned at the beginning of this section, you might even think literary accomplishment was part of the job. Instead of "from Victoria to Churchill" we could've named this section just "Churchill" since his public service spanned the period from the reign of Victoria to the Cold War and since he lived to the ripe old age of 90. Churchill was voted the greatest Briton of all times in a BBC poll and regularly appears at the top of lists of the most effective prime ministers. One of the many statues you can find of him across Britain is not far from David Lloyd George directly across the street from Parliament in London.

**Fig. 2.14** | *Statue of Winston Churchill*

Where can you find this last section? On utb-mehr-wissen.de of course!

The prime minister who succeeded him, Clement Atlee, certainly isn't as famous but could be judged to have had an even greater impact on contemporary Britain. Why? To answer that question, we need to begin our last section in British history.

As with our geography appetizers, two review tasks:

**Exercises**

1. Create a timeline with all the people mentioned in American history and underline the presidents.
2. Create some royal family trees, one for each dynasty.

# Uniform-ity and Plural-ity (education) | 4

Never let your schooling interfere with your education.
attributed to Mark Twain

… open to people, places, methods, and ideas from the Mission of the Open University <http://www.open.ac.uk/opencetl/>

Probably you've all experienced some aspects of education in the United Kingdom and the United States even if you've never set foot in an American or English school. We've all no doubt seen pictures of cute British school students in uniforms smiling into the camera just as we've all seen pictures of American school students with their multitude of ethnically different faces illustrating the many different minority groups in America. We can look at the educational system as a whole in both countries as being astoundingly uniform with primary, secondary, tertiary, and continuing education playing a very similar role both in Britain and in America. We can also see an astonishing number of different types of schools and universities, at times representing different attitudes towards and motives behind getting an education in both countries.

When you finish the chapter, you should be able to say something about

- kinds of schools, colleges, and universities in the UK and US
- kinds of exams and degrees given at all levels
- those in charge of education
- differences between Britain, the US and Germany
- controversial topics in British and American education.

## Education in Britain | 4.1

While you might have heard of "reception" only in connection with hotels or formal parties, the word also refers to the beginning of primary education in an English educational context. And while you might know "infant" as a synonym for "baby," infant schools are for children aged four to seven. The British school system can be complicated, so to keep things simple, let's first divide schools into two types based on funding: state and independent. And also to keep things simple, we'll have to just concentrate on England and unfortunately mostly ignore Wales, Scotland, and Northern Ireland where the educational system ranges from somewhat to very different from the schools, colleges, and universities in England.

state primary school

Children aged between three and four years old can receive part-time nursery or preschool education before they begin the reception year. These first two years taken together comprise the Foundation Stage during which learning is done through play. The six years of primary school that follow are divided into two Key Stages during which students are taught English, history, science, mathematics, and other subjects. Two important state-run tests called National Curriculum assessments (also called Standard Assessment Tests: SATs) are as the name implies part of the National Curriculum (which we'll be looking at a little later) and are taken during primary school, which in England can also be referred to as infant school (usually the first two years) and junior school (usually the last four).

state secondary school: tripartite to comprehensives

Usually at the age of twelve in Year 7 students begin secondary school and continue until age sixteen when compulsory education ends. The five years of secondary school are like primary school divided into two Key Stages during which students take courses in many subject areas with important assessments at the end of each Key Stage. The final two years of compulsory secondary education also include courses with external exams leading to the General Certificate of Secondary Education (GCSE). Students can also receive National Vocational Qualification (NVQ) in certain specific occupations like engineering, health service, and manufacturing among many others. We've dealt so far with state schools, which have no tuition fees and are open to everyone and must follow the National Curriculum (at least in England and Wales). Before we turn to independent schools, let's take a brief look at history. You may remember the name Rab Butler from our history chapter (🔔 2). The Butler Education Act radically changed the system of state education towards the end of World War II, making education until the age of 16 free and available for all and setting up a tripartite system (similar to one version of the German school system) with grammar schools, secondary modern schools, and technical schools. Students took an examination called the Eleven Plus at the end of primary school to determine which school type they could attend. Most students went to grammar and secondary modern schools as there were few technical schools established. Over the next half century elements of the Butler Act were changed. Dissatisfaction about the system led to comprehensive schools open to all students, which have become the school type for the vast majority of students.

National Curriculum

A National Curriculum was also introduced in the attempt to ensure that all state schools in England and Wales were meeting the same standards. We've already heard of the National Curriculum in the brief summary of primary and secondary education, which is divided not only into years but also into Key Stages with exams after each Stage based on the subjects taken. The core subjects are English, math, and science; foundation subjects include art, music, geography, history, ICT (information and communication technology), and physical education. The most recent foundation subject Citizenship provides us with one interesting example of what's taught at school. Citizenship should give students a sense of topical political, spiritual, moral, social and cultural issues, problems and events. Students should learn to identify the role of the legal, political, religious, social and economic institutions and systems that influence their lives and communities. Sounds almost like the goals of this book! But it's not always easy in a multicultural country to agree on what important spiritual and moral issues should be covered (🔔 7).

religion in schools

An additional subject required in all state schools is religious education, which covers all religions but reflects the predominant status of Christian religion. Parents have the right to withdraw their children from taking this subject and can also withdraw their children from the collective worship that is usually part of assembly, when all students meet – often at the beginning of the school day. The issue of whether faith schools, schools which are state funded but run by religious organizations, should be financed by the state is one of the controversial topics in Britain as a multicultural and multi-religious country. While the vast majority of schools in Britain are either secular or associated with the Church of England, there is a small but growing number of Jewish, Muslim, and Sikh faith schools with at times restrictive policies regarding student intake and teacher qualifications (🔔 8).

In addition to controversies over the role of faith schools in British society, the National Curriculum itself has been criticized for exerting increased pressure on students throughout primary and secondary school. Pressure on teachers includes what some see as an overemphasis on "teaching to the test" and more work. The original purpose of the Curriculum along with the change-over to comprehensive schools was to provide quality education for all regardless of class differences. And who exactly is in charge of checking to see if quality education is being provided for everyone at state schools?

who's in charge: Ofsted and LEA

As is usually the case in life, the people who pay are the ones in charge. And since the government funds state schools, the government decides what's to be taught and who's to be hired. When we say the "government" and want to be more specific, we usually need an authority, an office, or a ministry. Starting at the top there was at first a Ministry of Education, which changed to the Department for Education and Science, then to the Department for Education and Employment, then to the Department for Education and Skills, which as the result of yet another cabinet reshuffle (🔔 5) was then divided into two ministries: Department for Children, Schools and Families; and the Department for Innovation, Universities and Skills. Easier to understand is the Office for Standards in Education, Children's Services and Skills (Ofsted), which inspects schools. Local Education Authorities (LEA) are responsible for funding and hiring teachers for all the schools in their area, or for almost all of them. In an attempt to improve education, other types of school administration have been created. Foundation schools, for example, are state schools mostly independent of the LEAs. Foundation schools can hire their own teachers as can the state faith schools. As you can see, there are varying degrees of government control in state schools. But let's turn to a completely different type of school.

public schools

Independent schools can be either expensive (private schools) or extremely expensive (called "public schools," which are prestigious private schools with long traditions). And although fewer than 10 % of all English students attend independent schools, if you were asked to name a few English schools, you'd probably be able to name a few of the most exclusive public schools like Eton, where Prince William and Prince Harry went to school, or Harrow, which Winston Churchill attended, or Westminster, where Peter Ustinov went to school. Although you might notice I've listed only famous male graduates (Eton are Harrow only ad-mit boys), some – but not all – public schools are co-educational and a few are only for girls. Tuition fees for public schools are extraordinarily expensive, a bit ironic considering that many famous schools were originally founded in the Middle Ages often by kings and queens as charitable institutions to provide free instruction for poor boys, thus the name "public" in contrast to the private fee-paying schools of the time. Both the high fees and the better chances public school graduates have in gaining places at prestigious universities and then getting positions of power in government and business provide evidence for the existence of a continuing class system in British education.

grammar schools and academies

Parents who are dissatisfied with the quality of education at state comprehensive schools can choose independent schools that aren't as prestigious or as expensive as the old famous public schools. Some of these independent schools are grammar schools left over from the original tripartite system mentioned above. Grammar schools, originally intended for students planning to attend university, can select students based on achievement. There are also independent schools that charge no fees and are funded by the government and by industry like City Technology Colleges or Academies. The goal is to improve education by allowing schools more independence from government control and from the LEAs.

uniforms

One aspect both state and independent schools share is the obligatory school uniform. Uniforms serve the purpose of encouraging a sense of school spirit and community and also of attempting to eradicate class differences. But recent conflicts between school loyalty and religious identity shown through clothes (use of veils and religious jewelry, for example) have become more common and will no doubt keep the old topic of traditional school uniforms in the news.

sixth form and A-Levels

Obligatory secondary schooling, whether state or independent, ends at age sixteen. What follows is called post-secondary education or further education or the sixth form. You may wonder why the equivalent of the German *Oberstufe* is called the sixth form in Britain although it actually involves two years: 12 (lower sixth) and 13 (upper sixth). The term makes sense if you know that in the past the word "form" was used for each year of the five years of secondary school. The sixth year of secondary school was called the lower sixth and the seventh the upper sixth, and in spite of all the other changes, the term sixth form is still used for the last two optional years of education, which are often also called "further education" and lead to Advanced Subsidiary and Advanced Level examinations. Some state schools and most independent schools have a sixth form. Students can also attend special sixth form colleges or further education colleges. We've already heard about the Key Stages in primary and secondary school. In the old days learning about which examinations were common in English schools was as simple as A and O. O stood for Ordinary Level examinations taken at the end of obligatory education at the age of sixteen; those who continued through the sixth form took their A-Levels or Advanced Level examinations and were thus qualified to apply to university. But who wants to say they're only "ordinary"? With the sweeping reforms in education in Britain in the 80s the O-Level was changed to the GCSE mentioned earlier. At the turn of the millennium the A-Level was split into two parts, the Advanced Subsidiary during the first year of sixth form and the A2 Level during the second year, both together forming the General Certificate of Education Advanced Level, which students need to apply to university.

colleges and colleges and colleges

Before we look at universities in Britain, we need to clarify some very confusing terms. We've already read about City Technology Colleges (CTS), colleges of further education (CFE), and sixth form colleges. Some public schools are called colleges like Eton College. But there are also colleges of higher education (CHE) that provide courses at the university level. And there are also institutions called university colleges that provide courses but aren't recognized as full universities and can't award degrees. Yet another use of the word college points to one of the differences between Oxbridge and other universities. Colleges at Oxford and Cambridge are names for communities of students and teachers who work together. And although "school" usually refers to pre-university education, there are exceptions like the famous London School of Economics, which is part of the University of London. The terms "college" and "school" in British English (and as we'll see later in the chapter in American English too) can thus refer to very different institutions!

Oxbridge to redbrick to plate glass to New Universities

But at least the word "university" has only one meaning although there are quite a few different kinds of universities in Britain. If you look at most introductions to Britain and read the few pages devoted to university education, you'll most probably find the classic terms used to describe different types of universities. The terms are easy to learn and easy to teach and used to indicate basic differences. First there was "Oxbridge" (a word that linguists call a blend), which is not a real university at all but just a short way to refer to the two most famous institutions in the land: Oxford and Cambridge. These medieval universities – among the oldest in Europe – were the only ones in England until much later in the 19th century when a growing population and industry in the Industrial Revolution (2) increased the need for an educated populace. The result was the founding of what came to be called redbrick universities, which don't always have buildings made of redbrick. These universities were founded in the large industrial cities like Birmingham, Leeds, and Manchester and still specialize in engineering. The plate glass universities, which aren't always made up of glass and chrome, were founded a century later in the 1960s to meet increased need for more university educated employees in places usually outside of towns with room for expansion like Essex, Sussex, and York. Plate glass universities specialize in the new social sciences. Institutions called polytechnics (very similar to German Fachhochschulen) gained university status in the early 90s and are now sometimes called appropriately enough New Universities. The enormous growth in universities in the last few decades has resulted in more than one hundred individual universities with many larger towns and cities having two or more.

Open University

In addition to Oxford and Cambridge another British institution of higher learning has gained an international reputation and is one of the largest and most successful universities in the world. Maybe you read the play *Educating Rita* at school or perhaps enjoyed the film version with Michael Caine and Julie Walters and noticed the role of the Open University in the film, an institution that gives working-class hairdresser Rita the possibility of higher education. The Open University was founded in the 70s and is open to all interested students in Britain with no previous qualifications required. It also has many branches abroad with three centers in Germany, for example. Most courses are done via distance learning and the programs are open to students who have to work in addition to their studies. The philosophy of the Open University shows a stark contrast to the elitism found in the public school system. The cost of studying at the Open University varies depending on the type and length of courses and the place of residency – those who live in Britain pay less. Speaking of costs in general...

tuition fees

While the debate about university tuition fees in Germany was just beginning, tuition fees in England and Wales were introduced by the Labour government and have risen continually in the past decade up to more than 3,000 pounds per year. Attempts to create extra revenue for universities and apply fees that take into account differences in student income have resulted in a new system that delays payment until after graduation. The Welsh government pays part of the tuition fees for Welsh students at Welsh universities, and the Scottish government pays all fees for Scottish students at Scottish universities. English students must pay just like EU students to study at some of the ancient prestigious universities in Scotland that we can mention now in passing: St. Andrews, Aberdeen, and Edinburgh.

qualifications and degrees

And what do you get for your money and if you pass the courses and examinations? While there used to be a limited number of names for qualifications, now there is a daunting variety ranging from certificates and diplomas to the new Foundation degrees. To keep it simple, let's just stick to the major university degrees awarded in England and Wales (Scotland uses a different system). The first one is the bachelor's degree, which can be abbreviated in many ways based on the subjects studied: a BA for example is a degree with a specialization in the arts or humanities, a BSc is for specialization in the sciences. Students who have gotten very good grades can receive their degree with first-class honours, followed by a 2:1 (for upper second-class honours) or a 2:2. In most cases a master's degree follows the bachelor's degree for those who wish to specialize more. The highest degree granted in Britain is the doctorate, usually abbreviated as PhD for doctor of philosophy, even when you didn't study philosophy but instead English or German or history. In the Middle Ages philosophy was the name for all subjects other than theology, medicine, and law. There's the possibility of receiving something called a "higher doctorate" from some universities in Britain (in medicine you can receive an MD degree or in law an LLD, for example), but since it generally takes around three to four years for a bachelor's degree, another couple of years for a master's, and another three to five years for a doctorate, we should move on now to the US and go back almost two centuries.

## Education in the US

4.2

German connections to American education

Perhaps you remember Horace Mann as one of the reformers in 19th century America from a history appetizer. Mann, the "Father of American Public Education," founded the first state board of education in Massachusetts in the 1830s and believed that the government should provide education that was free of charge and available to children of all religious, social, and ethnic backgrounds, and that children should be taught by professionally trained teachers, education being central to becoming good citizens. Although you might think because of his name Horace Mann had German ancestors, Mann's most important connection to Prussia wasn't family background but his belief that some of the aspects of the education system in Prussia should be adopted in America. Although Mann wasn't German, Margarethe Schurz was. She was the German wife of the German-born and influential American statesman and reformer Carl Schurz and is credited with setting up the first American kindergarten in the mid 19th century.

## And the situation today?

kinds of schools US

Today while a variety of schools exist, the system of education in the US is more homogeneous than in the UK although there is no national curriculum and each individual state is responsible for most educational matters. Since all schools in the US are organized in a very similar pattern called the K-12 system, we won't look at schools chronologically except to note that as in Britain you can find two levels: elementary school, which usually lasts for the first four or six years and begins with kindergarten (the K of the K-12 system), and continues with first grade. Secondary school is called high school (often divided into junior and senior high) and continues until the age of 18 and twelfth grade (the 12 of the K-12 system).

public and private, church and state

The school system is similar across the US with twelve grades and mostly similar subjects in all states. The vast majority of schools in America are public schools with those students attend-

Fig. 4.1 | *American education*

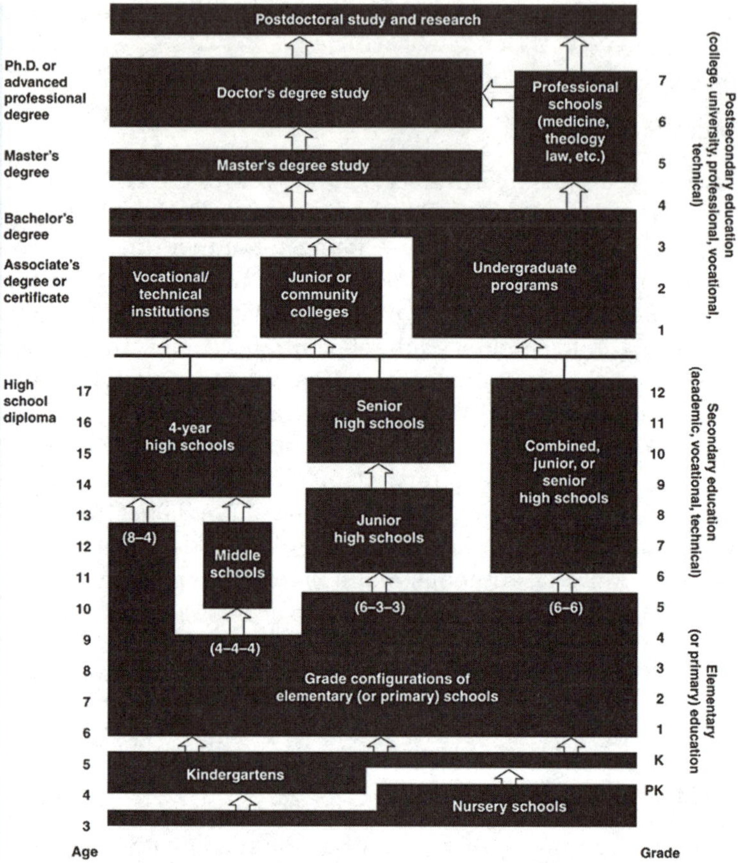


ing who live in the area. The basic distinguishing factor is public, financed by the state (and to a much lesser degree also by the federal government), and private, mostly religiously oriented and privately funded at least partly through tuition fees. The name "parochial" often refers to schools run by the Catholic Church. We'll be dealing with the role of the separation of church and state when we turn to religion in chapter 8. While prayers at school have been continually declared unconstitutional by the Supreme Court and thus are forbidden, the debate on the role of evolution and Creationism or Intelligent Design is still going on. Mostly Christian evangelicals or fundamentalists who believe in a literal interpretation of the Bible have been trying to convince school boards – who decide about which subjects are going to be taught among other issues – to put Creationism on the same level as evolution, seeing both as non-provable theories of the origin of the world and of life.

who's in charge

Public education in the US as in Germany is a matter of the individual states. The states set the general curriculum and standards; the states are divided into school districts run by elected or appointed school boards, which have varying degrees of control on the running of the public schools in their districts. You may remember a famous Supreme Court decision that involved one of these boards (2). Parent teacher associations (PTAs), which can also be found in Britain, can also have a say in school policy. Federal funding of schools is very limited. Most of the money necessary to run schools comes from the state and local governments with property tax playing a major role in many school districts. Districts with high value property thus have more income to be used for schools than poorer districts. This inbuilt inequality isn't the only thing that is controversial: some people also find paying property tax for school funding unfair if they don't have children in school or if they send their children to private schools. Vouchers are sometimes used as an alternative.

vouchers and home-schooling

School vouchers were introduced in the 60s as a way for white families to avoid sending their children to integrated schools. The state government gave certificates to parents who chose private schools. This use of vouchers was ruled unconstitutional. Those who support vouchers point to parental choice and how free market competition could improve public schools. Opponents claim that offering free education is a responsibility of the state and that using public money for private schools would result in the financial ruin of the public school system. Since many private schools are religiously run, providing money for vouchers would in effect provide money for religious schools, a violation of the separation of church and state guaranteed in the Constitution. The issue of vouchers points to the tension between state responsibility and individual choice. One extreme of individual choice is homeschooling where parents or tutors hired by the parents educate children at home often for religious reasons (8). While homeschooling is legal in all states, the rules governing homeschooling vary considerably across the country. Critics claim that students educated at home lack contact with peers and the social opportunities that only regular schools can provide. Research has not proven consistently lower scoring in standardized tests of students taught at home, and homeschooling is a trend that has been increasing in the past couple of decades.

magnet and charter schools

There is already some parental choice within the state school system. Magnet schools are public schools that should function as magnets, drawing not necessarily those children who live near the school but those children who share the same talents. Charter schools aren't bound by all the same regulations that apply to traditional public schools and have more control over their curriculum and how they spend funding but must prove an increase in quality in exchange. Reminds you of a similar school type in England? If you said "foundation school," then you'd deserve a good grade. And speaking of grades…

assessments and qualifications US

Courses at American schools are assessed through many factors including tests and assignments. Students receive a grade for each course and for each term. Report cards are issued after each school term, the length of which varies from school district to district, and some parents can also access their children's grades online. These report cards, also called high school transcripts, are important for applications to college. Letter grades from A–F with A as best are transferred into numbers in the grade point average (GPA), a number that indicates overall achievement with 4.0 being a perfect grade in all courses. All states require students to pass courses in English, science, history, and mathematics. But there is no national curriculum that prescribes these requirements as in England and Wales. And the variety of courses students can choose from (called "electives" in contrast to the required courses) is huge, with everything from photography to music to driver's education. Some of these courses have similar content as the important extracurricular activities offered outside of and after class in the afternoons. Most American schools have schooldays that last from the morning until the mid-afternoon and have three-month long summer breaks usually from June until late August or early September.

high school diploma

Whether American young people go to state-run public schools, to church-run private schools, to Catholic parochial schools, or are taught at home, the goal is always the same: graduation with either a high school diploma or an equivalent after 12 years of school. While high school diplomas used to be granted to all students after having passed a certain number of courses, some states have instituted a centrally administered high school exit examination. People who have dropped out of high school can also earn a high school diploma by passing the General Educational Development (GED) tests. A large majority of students who graduate from high school decide to continue their education at college or university. Before we turn to American higher education in detail, we need to glance at two aspects that have become characteristic of American education both at the school and at the university level.

violence

In 1999 Columbine High School near Littleton, Colorado, became associated with one of the worst school shootings in American history with more than a dozen people dead. The Virginia Tech massacre, the deadliest shooting on an American college campus with more than two dozen deaths, occurred almost exactly eight years later. Both these acts of violence along with the many other examples of shooting sprees (8) at American schools and colleges since the 1960s have led to an increased debate about gun control and about security issues involving the use of metal detectors and security guards. The director Michael Moore used Columbine as an example of American violence in his award-winning film *Bowling for Columbine* (3).

extracurricular activities

Extracurricular activities are all those activities that take place outside the classroom and in American schools and universities. In accordance with the general belief that education especially at school is supposed to turn children into good citizens, extracurricular activities are an important part of school and include many different kinds of activities to increase a sense of community and school spirit like playing in the band, working together on the school newspaper or website or radio station, and especially playing team sports like football or basketball (11). We'll be looking at one unique aspect of extracurricular activities at American universities, fraternities and sororities, just a little later. Now we need to turn our attention to the application process all prospective American students have to go through to be admitted to college.

applying to college

Since the high school diploma doesn't give students the right to study and since the quality of secondary education varies widely from school to school, students who wish to attend college must apply. In order to give colleges and universities the chance to compare applicants' intellectual abilities, most institutions of higher education require results from standardized tests like the Scholastic Aptitude Test (SAT) as well as additional information provided by essays or by interviews or recommendations.

colleges and schools and colleges

As in Britain, the word college has many different meanings in America. First of all community colleges, also called junior colleges, are small public colleges serving the local population with courses in a wide variety of areas (similar in some ways to German *Volkshochschulen* or to British colleges of further or higher education). These colleges also offer two-year general education or vocational degrees. Liberal arts colleges are four-year public or private institutions that award mostly four-year degrees. A college can also be part of a university. Parts of large universities are often called the College of Arts and Sciences or the School of Medicine, for example. As you can see, "school" is yet another word with multiple meanings. The term "graduate school" refers to an institution that provides courses and support for students who have already earned their undergraduate degree. This term has been translated literally into *Graduiertenschule* and is now used as part of the reformed German university system. This use of the word "Schule" for postgraduate study at a university might sound strange in German, but Americans often informally use the word "school" when they mean "college" and "college" when they refer to "university." Not only are there several names for post-secondary education, there are also several types.

from community college to Ivy League universities

Technical and community or junior colleges provide vocational and general education courses. State universities are an example of the influence of the federal government, which granted federal land to the states (hence the name "land-grant") to found and fund colleges and universities for more people. For those of you who like the names of specific government acts: it was the Morill Act. Both the time – middle of the $19^{th}$ century – and the motives were similar to those for the founding of the redbrick universities in Britain. And while we're comparing American to British institutions: the American equivalent of Oxbridge is the Ivy League with eight very prestigious and wealthy and expensive universities like Harvard, Yale, Princeton, all located in the northeastern part of the US. Two big differences between the Ivy League and Oxbridge: the American universities have much more money and generally fewer students than the old English universities.

tuition fees

You've probably all heard about how expensive American university education can be. Students can transfer credit for courses from inexpensive community colleges to other more expensive colleges in order to spend less time at the more expensive colleges and thus to save money. In the US, education is looked at as a consumer good, and the consumers – the students and their parents – consider education as a service. Often parents open a savings account for their children upon birth so that the costs can be met twenty years later. The costs can be very high and have been increasing rapidly in the past couple of decades. However, state residents of state universities pay less than students coming from other states, and the majority of students attend institutions that charge less than $10,000 per year. Even though Harvard charges more than $40,000 per year, it also provides 70 % of all students with financial aid. Education isn't limited just to the wealthy or to those who've been able to save enough. Student loans and scholarships are available, and a majority of all American college students receive some kind of government or privately funded financial aid. Both American and British universities and colleges have to face the global financial crisis, which began in 2008. The full effect of the reduction of savings combined with fewer students being able to afford high tuition rates isn't yet clear but may change the landscape of American higher education in the years to come.

helicopter parents

University administrators have recently noticed that some parents have started to take a strong interest in their son's and daughter's educational career and needs, hovering over them like helicopters, always ready to help or to intervene if necessary. This new attitude can be connected to the increased cost of a college education, to the role of parents as consumers, who want to make sure that their investment is paying off, and to the fact that college education has become more and more a mass phenomenon and has become more an extension of high school. A bachelor's degree is no longer seen as a ticket to a guaranteed future career as was the case in the past.

college sports

Along with increased career options and higher lifelong earnings, Americans consider the social aspects of college life to be very important. Extracurricular activities are as important a part of college as they are of high school life. Intramural sports – sports done "within the walls" or just within the college – are popular but not as lucrative as intercollegiate team sports such as football or basketball played in competition with other college and university teams. Such games not only lure alumni back to their alma mater (we'll be dealing with these Latin-looking words soon), but also generate lots of money from broadcasting rights. The debate about whether these revenue-generating sports are good for universities or can lead to corruption and to abuse of college athletes, who due to poor academic records can't graduate, will no doubt continue.

fraternities and sororities

We just mentioned Latin-looking words used at American colleges. There are also student organizations with Greek letters for names: fraternities are social organizations for mostly undergraduate men, and sororities mostly for women. These organizations have been part of American college life since colonial times, when Greek and Latin were common subjects at college. Also called Greek-letter organizations, fraternities and sororities serve social and academic functions. You may have seen some of the popular American comedies or parodies or American television programs that depict wild parties or silly or dangerous initiation rites. Perhaps due to the general image in such films, social Greek-letter organizations have been criticized in the past for hazing – the abuse of new members – and for encouraging binge drinking. While some colleges have banned all fraternities, some serve a useful function in providing both inexpensive accommodations in residence halls as well as a network of support for young people living away from home and from their parents for the first time. In addition to social fraternities, there are also other kinds of societies open to men and women that are limited to students who do very well academically such as the famous honor society called Phi Beta Kappa. Other fraternities are professional and limited to those studying and working in a certain field such as Phi Delta Phi for those studying and working in the legal field.

degrees

We've already learned the names for university degrees in the United Kingdom. The names are the same in the United States even if the time required to earn a degree differs somewhat. A uniquely American degree is the Associate of Arts (A. A.) or Associate of Science (A. S.) degree that students can receive after two years of college at a community college by passing general courses in the humanities and in the sciences. Just like in Britain,

American students can receive a bachelor's or master's degree with the highest degree being the doctorate. And you can find yet another German influence in education (remember kindergarten and Prussian influences on the American school system?): the American bachelor's degree, which is based on Wilhelm von Humboldt's belief that the first step in education is general all-round education. While a British bachelor's degree is more specialized, an American bachelor's degree isn't meant to qualify graduates for any kind of job; the first college degree is supposed to be proof of a good education. Training comes later in the job, or for those who decide to pursue an academic career in the graduate master's and doctoral degrees. Neither Americans nor British people put as much emphasis on titles as people in Germany do. The teaching profession isn't as highly esteemed either. An old saying goes: "If you can't do, teach" and could continue with "if you can't teach, become a professor" to indicate the social status of academics in some parts of the Anglo-American world. American and British universities have, however, been using evaluations of teaching at the university level for promotion and granting tenure for many years.

on the tenure track to publish or perish

Perhaps you looked up the word "tenure" just used in the degrees section and thought we'd be turning back in history to feudal England. No, the tenure in this chapter doesn't have to do with land but with job security. Academic tenure is job security with the right to academic freedom and is supposed to ensure that professors aren't afraid of doing research that could offend those in power. Tenure track positions at American colleges are those that lead to guaranteed life-long employment and involve up to seven years of teaching, researching, and appraisal. Those who aren't given tenure must leave the university. Since tenure can be often based on the number of articles and books published, the slogan "publish or perish" is used to account for the pressure on academics in tenure track positions. When you are given difficult articles to read as part of your studies, have a little bit of pity on the authors. What else would you expect from a system that rewards quantity over quality? And although with electronic publishing much electricity is needed to keep all those servers around the world online and cooled off, at least there's not the same waste of trees for paper journals as in the past.

alumni and the alma mater

Two very Latin-sounding words play a very big role in American universities. The graduates from universities are called alumni – the Latin root is related to nourishment and support – and the universities they graduate from are often called alma mater, meaning literally the mother who nourishes or supports. Universities provide students with support and then expect the alumni to support their alma mater. And the ties between graduates and their universities can be similar to the ties between a mother and her child. The common spirit and sense of community that should develop during "time at school" – as Americans often refer to their studies at college and university – should also last after graduation. Alumni can thus connect their professional and personal lives after graduation with the time as students. Universities arrange homecomings with special football games or other sporting events designed especially to welcome back graduates, who not only are a source of financial support but who can also provide helpful networks for current students. These personal ties are perhaps especially important in such a highly mobile society where graduates move to other parts of the country or the world but still have the need to keep connected with their past. Both British and German universities are learning that the investment in developing structures that encourages a closer relationship between alma mater and alumni can pay off later. It may seem a bit odd to German students who are accustomed to free university education that first Americans are expected to pay high tuition fees and then after graduation expected to support their alma mater further. But Americans also demand service and support from their universities as service institutions. This very different kind of attitude towards education often leads to lifelong ties between students, parents, and their colleges and universities, ties which can be beneficial for all. When I first came to Germany as an exchange student, I was at first surprised at the poor quality of service: restricted library hours, unfriendly administration personnel, boring lectures and seminars. But then I thought "you get what you pay for" and remembered Mark Twain's advice about not letting such aspects interfere with real education outside the classroom.

But in order to continue our education in this book, we now need to leave schools and colleges and turn our attention to another classic item on the menu of American and British Studies:

the powers-that-be in the political institutions on both sides of the Atlantic.

## Exercises

1. How do the words "uniformity" and "plurality" in the title of this chapter fit the content?
2. What are SATs?
3. Pick a special kind of American college and name a famous graduate based on information you've found elsewhere in this book (hint: look in chapter on gender in Part II).
4. Look for a picture with the name of an English university somewhat hidden (hint: look in the geography chapter about UK climate) and then try and categorize the university.
5. What was the Butler Act?
6. What could be confusing about the following pictures?

Fig. 4.2–4.5

Challenging and interesting projects:

Go to a school or college in Britain or America and compare the average day with the info given in this chapter. Write down all the things you notice that you didn't find in the chapter. (Maybe you'll need a new edition of this book ...)

Imagine what subject you'd like to study and where you'd like to go for a few years. Choose to do either an undergraduate degree or a graduate degree if you'd like to finish your first degree in Germany first. Then by doing some web research, find out exactly what courses you'd need to take and how much your degree program would cost in the UK or in the US. List the benefits you'd have that you don't have as a German university student.

And finally the if-you-can-do-this-you-deserve-an-automatic-PhD tasks:

Devise a school system for England that satisfies those who wish their religious beliefs to be part of the curriculum, a system that is also acceptable for those who think a secular education is best, and a system that encourages achievement but doesn't lead to further class distinctions.

Show the similarities and contrasts between a compulsory, state-run authoritarian educational system like that in Prussia and the public school system that developed in the US. How do both systems show causes and effects of totalitarianism and democracy?

And further topics not dealt with in this chapter... for those with time and passion either as undergraduates, graduates, postgraduates or retirees:

schools and universities in Wales, Scotland, and Northern Ireland; bilingual education; the No Child Left Behind Act as a classic example of the US federal government intervention in education; accreditation of schools and universities in the US and the UK; the importance of life-long learning, ...

# Queendom and Republicracy (political life)

5

I cannot lead you into battle, I do not give you laws or administer justice but I can do something else, I can give you my heart and my devotion to these old islands and to all the peoples of our brotherhood of nations.

Queen Elizabeth II's first televised Christmas broadcast in 1957

We hold these truths to be self-evident, that all men are created equal, that they are endowed by their Creator with certain unalienable Rights, that among these are Life, Liberty, and the Pursuit of Happiness.

Opening words of the Declaration of Independence

Sometimes we take things for granted and don't ask really obvious questions that can lead us to new insights: Why, for example, is the Queen often called the Queen of England even though she's just as much the Queen of Wales, Scotland, Northern Ireland and head of state for a dozen other countries around the world? And why should Americans have to choose between two political parties that at least as far as their names are concerned – the Republicans and the Democrats – both represent political views that not only most Americans but probably most Western Europeans (even those with a king or queen as head of state) would want to support?

When you finish the chapter, you should be able not only to answer these "obvious" questions but also to say something about

- the British monarch and Parliament
- the British Constitution
- devolution and the future of the United Kingdom
- British and American political parties
- the American system of checks and balances
- the American presidential election process.

from power to ceremony

We could begin our look at British political life a long time ago with the unpopular King John (one of the sons of one of the many Henry's – Henry II to be exact) being forced to sign something called the Magna Carta at the riverside meadow Runnymede. Although the Magna Carta is often described as one of the milestones on the way to sharing of power between the monarchs and subjects, it actually doesn't have many of the rights later to be famously described in the American Bill of Rights, which we shouldn't confuse with the Bill of Rights that another king, a William, (2) was more or less forced to sign six hundred years later and that further reduced the actual power of the monarch. But without going into more historical detail, let's begin with the political situation today in Britain and with someone we all know: the Queen. While the monarch's powers are largely ceremonial, the current monarch Queen Elizabeth II holds two very interesting records on the throne: she's number three on the list of the longest-reigning monarchs (only Victoria and George III reigned longer) and is already the oldest living monarch in British history.

from ceremony to royal prerogative

"The Queen reigns but does not rule" is a good summary of both the power of the Queen as a symbolic figure and the personification of a tradition that has now lasted for more than a thousand years. She has the right to be consulted and regularly meets with the prime minister, whom she officially appoints after each Parliamentary election, but in effect she really only has to choose the leader of the majority party in the House of Commons. This power of appointing the prime minister is one of the powers summarized in the term "royal prerogative," which also includes other powers such as dissolving Parliament and calling new elections and also giving Royal Assent to acts of Parliament. Theoretically the Queen could refuse to choose the leader of the majority party to be prime minister or could make her own choice if there's no party with a majority, but a "hung parliament" is rare in British politics. She could refuse to give her Royal Assent to bills passed by Parliament, but such a refusal would no doubt bring about a constitutional crisis and hasn't happened in the last two hundred years. Almost all of the rights associated with the royal prerogative have passed from the monarch to the government or specifically to the prime minister. The royal prerogative also includes the right to sign treaties like the one that Edward Heath signed that made the UK a member of the European Community. The royal prerogative also includes the right to declare war as Margaret Thatcher did on Argentina over the Falkland Islands. Tony Blair asked for parliamentary approval before the invasion of Iraq and thus set a precedent. In the past few years both the Conservative and the Labour parties have indicated a desire to move some of the power and the responsibility implied in the royal prerogative from the prime minister to Parliament.

| Fig. 5.1
*The Queen on her way to work from Buckingham Palace to greet the President of Mexico as part of the 2009 London Summit*

But the Queen also has many other real duties not delegated to the prime minister. The monarch is also head of the Church of England (🔔 8) and head of the armed forces. As head of state she performs many ceremonial functions such as opening Parliament and entertaining foreign heads of state (and in the fifty years of her reign she's gotten to know very many of them). As head of nation she travels throughout Britain, attending hundreds of events like opening hospitals or museums, unveiling plaques, attending film premieres, giving speeches, or meeting with people. The entire royal family helps the Queen fulfill these many ceremonial functions. In spite of all the family problems she's had in the last few decades including divorces and scandals and the death of Princess Diana, the British tend to see in her a symbol of unity for the entire country. The Queen has seen herself in this role from the start as the quote from her first televised Christmas greeting given at the beginning of this chapter movingly shows. In a more cynical way, we could of course mention the value of royal scandals in selling copies of tabloid newspapers (🔔 10) or the attractiveness of the palaces and traditions of the royals to many tourists, perhaps especially to tourists from countries like Germany and the US, which don't have the same grandeur associated with a real Queen.

Head of Church, of State, of Nation

Somewhat similar to the royal family assisting the Queen in her duties, the prime minister also has help from ministers in the cabinet although – just as the word "prime" implies – the prime minister is the most powerful figure in government. The word "cabinet" used to refer to a little room or chamber that the monarch used to meet with his (or sometimes her) most important group of advisors. Now the British cabinet meets in a larger room at 10 Downing Street, the official residence of the prime minister. The cabinet has more than twenty members, who are almost always chosen from the House of Commons, and meets

cabinets

**Fig. 5.2 and Fig. 5.3**
*The monarch's entrance to Parliament may be a bit disappointing, but the entrance for non-royals is even less majestic tucked under the famous tower of Big Ben as the most visible part of the Houses of Parliament, also known as the Palace of Westminster.*

regularly. Most cabinet members have the title secretary of state and are responsible for various departments like defense, education, and environment among others. The most important cabinet posts are the chancellor, the foreign secretary, and the home secretary. Sometimes those who want to become prime minister work their way through the cabinet. Gordon Brown, for example, held the post of chancellor for ten years before finally becoming prime minister after Tony Blair resigned in 2007. The role of the cabinet in actually determining government policy depends on the style of the prime minister. Margaret Thatcher and Tony Blair were often described as "presidential" in making decisions without consulting the cabinet. The prime minister chooses the members of the cabinet and has the power to reshuffle the cabinet if he (or sometimes she) thinks that such a change would help to make a government more popular or to reward important politicians.

House of Lords

In addition to the monarch and the prime minister with his or her cabinet, there are also some other players in the British political system. The phrase "the Crown in Parliament" emphasizes the importance of Parliament, made up of the House of Common and the House of Lords. The power of the House of Lords has been continually reduced over the centuries, and hundreds of hereditary peers – those members of the House of Lords who inherit their titles and seats – were thrown out in 1999. Plans to further reform the House of Lords are still being discussed. The House of Lords now exercises a legislative function in discussing and revising bills, they also can delay bills already passed by the House of Commons. Currently, besides the remaining hereditary peers, there are life peers, people of varied occupations who are appointed by the Queen on the recommendation of the prime minister; lords spiritual, archbishops and bishops of the Church of England; and Law Lords, important judges, who will be moving as part of another big political reform in Britain into a new Supreme Court separate from Parliament. The House of Lords, where the opening of Parliament takes place, has red benches and is more lavishly decorated than the plainer House of Commons with its green benches.

**Fig. 5.4**
*The Ministry of Justice is one of the newest parts of government and the Secretary of State for Justice is a new cabinet post first created in 2007.*

House of Commons

The House of Commons currently has fewer members than the Lords with 646 members representing one constituency each (🔔 1). Members are called MPs for Member of Parliament; don't get them mixed up with the PM – the Prime Minister, who also happens to be an MP. The House of Commons has much more power than the Lords since in effect it comprises not only the elected representatives of the government including the prime minister but also the opposition. The election procedure in Britain is actually quite simple. Candidates from the various political parties campaign within each constituency and citizens (technically speaking "subjects of the monarch" since the United Kingdom is a constitutional monarchy) are given the chance to choose one candidate on election day, generally a Thursday.

first-past-the-post

Each constituency can only elect one MP in a system called first-past-the-post in which the one candidate with the most votes wins. In races with more than two candidates, the winner could gain less than 50 % of the total votes but would still be sent to Westminster – I don't mean the London borough here (🔔 1) –

but the famous palace on the Thames in London with both the House of Commons and the House of Lords. You can understand the term "race" here literally since the first-past-the-post term comes from horse racing. But while the post is usually fixed in horse racing, the position of the post in parliamentary elections depends on just how many people vote. With only two candidates the post would be at 51% of the total votes. With three candidates, the post could be at just 34% of the total votes in a very tight race. In any case the winner takes all and is the only one sent to Parliament. While the disadvantage is that the votes of many people aren't represented, one advantage is stable government with usually one clear winner and one opposition party that forms something called the shadow government.

hung parliament

Maybe you noticed the strange term "hung parliament" mentioned above – the case when no one party has a majority in the House of Commons. Hung parliaments are much more common in proportional parliamentary systems like that in Germany and result in a coalition government made up of several parties together. In Britain with its two-party system, hung parliaments are rare and usually result in new elections being called.

parties

In spite of the fact that almost always just one party has governed Britain in the last century, there are actually three major parties. The Conservatives – also known informally as the Tories – are one of the oldest parties in the world. The Labour party was founded about a hundred years ago to represent the interests of workers (2). The Liberal Democrats are the third-biggest and also the youngest party, founded in the late 80s, and could perhaps become part of a coalition government in Britain if Labour or the Conservatives were not to gain a clear majority. Differences among the parties used to be clearer than they are now. Prime Minister Tony Blair, whose Labour party won after two decades of government by the Conservatives, helped to create what was called New Labour, the symbol of which had become the new red rose of the (New) Labour party. The new philosophy of government was often described as a "third way" with a combination of belief in the free market system, a typically Conservative doctrine, with some limited government intervention. The Conservatives themselves traditionally support capitalism and free enterprise. The Liberal Democrats have not surprisingly been in favor of reforms to the first-past-the-post system since a proportional election system would allow them significantly more representation in Parliament. The LibDems (as they're often called) are also opposed to government intervention in personal affairs and strongly in favor of the UK having a more important role in the European Union. They're also in favor of a written constitution and a bill of individual rights. "But doesn't Britain already have a constitution and a bill of rights?" you might ask.

unwritten Constitution?

Often you can read that the United Kingdom has an "unwritten Constitution" – a very strange thing when you think about it. If the Constitution is unwritten, how does anyone know what's in it? And usually sources that claim in the first sentence that the British Constitution is unwritten will then go on in the second sentence to list parts of the Constitution that are very much written: ancient documents like the Magna Carta or the Bill of Rights (2). The British Bill of Rights didn't contain some of the individual rights mentioned in the American Bill of Rights or what we would expect today from a Bill of Rights. This Bill of Rights, passed during the Glorious Revolution in the 17$^{th}$ century, was instead yet another step towards the present-day British government: a constitutional monarchy in which the real power lies with Parliament. The Bill of Rights prevented the monarch from making laws or raising an army and also stated that no monarch was allowed to be Roman Catholic and all monarchs had to swear an oath to maintain the Church of England before being crowned (8). The "unwritten Constitution" also contains written reports of Parliamentary proceedings and even written laws from the European Union in Brussels. The word "unwritten" isn't a very good choice. A more accurate description would be "not written down in just one document that anyone can consult easily" or, in one word, "uncodified" and thus very different from the codified German Basic Law or the much shorter codified American Constitution. Although some groups – like Unlock Democracy, an organization that developed out of the Charter 88 (founded understandably enough in 1988) – have strongly advocated the creation of a written constitution, the UK's uncodified one may retain the organic form it has developed over many centuries. Some see this organic form as evidence of flexibility. The question remains whether the flexibility of an easily changeable constitution can offset the dangers of abuse of power by Parliament, which can in effect change the Constitution with each and every

Act of Parliament. Since Britain became part of what was to become the European Union, EU law is supreme over individual member state's laws.

constitutional monarchy and parliamentary democracy

But regardless of how the Constitution develops, the government of Britain can best be described as a constitutional monarchy, constitutional because of the very important role of the Constitution even if it's uncodified, and monarchy because of the very important role of the monarch. Another name for the British type of government is parliamentary democracy, parliamentary because of the very important role of the Parliament, and democracy because the members of the House of Commons at least are elected and thus the people (the "demos" part of "democracy" comes from a Greek word meaning "people") can at least theoretically exercise their power. And it's the power of the people in Scotland, Wales, and Northern Ireland that has had a huge effect on politics in Britain in the last few years.

devolution

While there hasn't been a revolution in British politics in the last couple of centuries, the process of devolution is changing the face of government in Britain in radical ways. Devolution is the procedure of transferring power from a central government to regional governments and is in effect the reversal of what had been going on in British history in the past thousand years or so: that of gradually expanding power from smaller to larger areas. Remember the various Acts of Union through which England "grew" into Great Britain and finally into the United Kingdom of Great Britain and Ireland (2) and then began to shrink, first with the establishment of the Irish Free State and then the Republic of Ireland (2).

Scottish Parliament

The desire of some of the people in Scotland for more power increased in the 90s, partly due no doubt to the increased revenues of North Sea Oil (6), and resulted finally in a referendum with a large majority of Scots voting for the establishment of a Scottish Parliament in Edinburgh. The MSPs (Members of Scottish Parliament) in the Pàrlamaid na h-Alba, as it's called in Scots Gaelic (1), have power to raise taxes and make laws affecting Scotland in areas such as health, education, transport, and the environment.

Welsh Assembly

The Welsh also voted for a Cynulliad Cenedlaethol Cymru, as the National Assembly for Wales is called in Welsh. The AMs (Assembly Members) don't have the same powers as the MSPs to raise taxes, but Welsh cultural identity is perhaps more important than political power (the percentage of Welsh in favor of devolved power was considerably lower than the percentage of Scots who voted for a Scottish Parliament). The Welsh political party Plaid Cymru has been fighting for extended powers of the Assembly, called the Senedd in Welsh, which is located in the Welsh capital, Cardiff.

Fig. 5.5

*The Senedd building houses the Welsh Assembly and was opened in 2006. On the left you can see part of the Welsh Millennium Centre (🔔 2).*

Northern Ireland Assembly

Northern Ireland had its own parliament from the time of the formation of the Irish Free State in the 1920s up until the early 70s when the "Troubles" started between the pro-British Protestant Loyalists and the mostly Catholic Republicans in favor of a united Ireland. The parliament was abolished and direct rule from London established. As a result of the Good Friday Peace Talks, the Northern Ireland Assembly was reestablished in 1998 but suspended several times afterwards when the political parties in Northern Ireland couldn't agree on forming a government. The Assembly meets in Stormont Castle, the same building in the Belfast suburb of Stormont that was built to house the first Northern Ireland Parliament.

proportional representation

All three devolved institutions in Scotland, Wales, and Northern Ireland are elected under a system of proportional representation, which, as we've seen, is not the case for elections to the British House of Commons with its first-past-the-post system. One interesting result of the combination of devolution with regional parliaments and the House of Commons is that while the Scots and the Welsh MPs in London have a voice in affairs that affect England, English MPs don't have any say in internal matters in Scotland and Wales. Other than the establishment of a London Assembly that gives the city more power in dealing with London affairs, attempts have failed to give regions in England similar devolved institutions like in Scotland, Wales, and Northern Ireland. The debate about how to deal with fair representation in a partly devolved United Kingdom is sometimes called the West Lothian Question. One radical answer to this question is total independence of the four countries, in effect a total dissolution of the United Kingdom, in effect the untying of the Acts of Union made in the last five hundred years.

an Untied Kingdom?

The probability has increased that in the next few years the flag you can see on the cover of this book might be changed – if Scotland indeed withdraws from the United Kingdom and thus the Scottish cross is erased from the Union Jack. At least then the expression "Queen of England" would no longer be as inaccurate for a future Kingdom of England. The key to the future will probably be found in the extent to which a common national identity as British can transcend and incorporate the national Scottish, Welsh, and English identities. American minorities have been successful in creating hyphenated identities; it remains to be seen if the Brits will continue to be successful in their United Kingdom.

Speaking of Americans, what about the American flag on the cover of this book? If you remember one of our geography appetizers about a possible 51st state (1), you might expect a new American flag at some point in the future too. But there are none of the radical historical changes taking place in American government that currently make watching British government such an unusually exciting hobby. There are, however, enough other fascinating aspects about a Government By the People, For the People, and …

UK – US comparison

Let's do a brief review of the situation in Britain. In the United Kingdom the head of the government, the prime minister, is the executive and has far-reaching powers. The prime minister is also a member of the legislative branch, the House of Commons. And the judiciary, the Law Lords, also sit in the legislature, the House of Lords, one of the few important bodies left in any modern industrialized country that isn't elected in any way. But the Law Lords may be moving soon to their own Supreme Court, a new building planned to show the separation of the judiciary from the legislative aspects of government. In one important way the political system in the US is simpler than that in the UK: the three branches are much more clearly defined. Since the first-past-the-post system is the same system used in America, where it's described as the winner takes all, we won't have to mention this kind of election system at all. And the two-party system is also similar, just with different names and different symbols.

Democrats and Republicans

In the past, parties had names like the Democratic-Republicans, the American Republicans, the Gold Democrats, the Silver Republicans; there was even a party nicknamed the Know Nothings (🔔 7). Even those who know nothing (or next to nothing) about the history of political parties in the US can still easily learn quite a bit about the situation today, which is much simpler than in the past. America has had a system with just two major parties for most of its existence starting with the founding of the Democratic-Republican party by Thomas Jefferson, which later became the Democratic party. You may remember that we've already heard about the founding of the Republican party as an anti-slavery party, a party that became famous with the election of President Abraham Lincoln in the mid 19th century (but confusedly enough can trace its name back to the … Democratic-Republican party) (🔔 2).

donkeys and elephants, blue and red states

The two names Democrats and Republicans don't indicate, however, that the Democrats aren't in favor of living in a republic (which we could simply understand as being a government form different from a monarchy) or that Republicans aren't in favor of a democracy (belief that the people should have the power to influence their own government). One interesting difference between the two parties has a German connection. Thomas Nast, an influential political cartoonist who was born in Landau in the Palatinate region, first used the symbol of the donkey for the Democrats and the elephant for the Republicans. The donkey is supposedly based on the insult critics of the first president of the Democratic party used to describe Andrew Jackson: "jackass" (🔔 2) – an insult that the Democrats changed into a compliment as a humble, smart, and loveable animal just as the Republicans look at the elephant not as pompous and conservative but dignified and strong. While the donkey and elephant are still used to represent the Democratic and Republican parties, the colors blue for Democrats and red for Republicans are now even more common. You might be familiar with "red" as being the color for socialists and left-of-center parties and might remember reading a few pages ago about the red rose symbol for Britain's Labour party. The British Conservative party is often associated with the color blue, by the way. Thus you might be a bit confused about the American choice of colors since American Democrats would be closer to British Labour in terms of their policies and Republicans closer to the Tories. But perhaps because of an American lack of interest in other political systems, the exact opposite color-party connection has become commonly used in American media since the 2000 election. If you think of "r" for "red" and "Republican" and "d" for "donkey" and "Democrat", then you can easily remember the symbolic distinctions between the parties. The color purple is becoming common to refer to those states that are more or less split between the Democrats and the Republicans. These states are also called "swing states" and have made the difference in close presidential elections, which can seem complicated at first glance – so we'll have to devote an entire section to the procedure.

presidential elections: first caucuses and primaries

While Germans might have a hard time understanding the process of electing a president (and the system is so complicated that probably not so many Americans fully understand it), one requirement of the long haul to becoming president is that each candidate goes through a grueling test that determines who can survive. We can basically see the presidential election as made up of four important parts: primaries and caucuses, party conventions, general election day, and the Electoral College. The primaries and caucuses give Americans the right to be involved in the political process from a very early starting point. The system that the Democratic and Republican parties use for selecting their candidates puts small states like Iowa (with caucuses) and New Hampshire (with a primary) with their early decisions in January and February on the domestic political map – and also in the headlines in Germany. Caucuses are meetings of party members in schools, town halls, in gymnasiums, or at private homes with the goal of deciding on how many votes which candidate should receive. Caucuses vary from state to state but share the same sort of small-town democracy that Americans like to say forms the basis of their government. Primaries are much like regular elections but can also vary from state to state; in some states only registered party members are allowed to vote, in other open primaries any registered voter is allowed to vote regardless of party affiliation.

Some political commentators have suggested primaries for Germany. Such a suggestion ignores one basic difference between the two political systems – American voters choose an individual (or at least believe they do, the election for president is an indirect one); Germans choose a party, although the personality of the politicians in our media age is becoming more and more important. Another important factor that has changed the way politics is done in the US is the internet, which Barack Obama was able to use to his advantage not only in generating small donations but also in building grass roots support in his campaign to win the Democratic party's nomination in 2008.

then party conventions and general election day

The results of the caucuses and primaries are used in the National Conventions that each party organizes in late summer and during which the party nominees are officially chosen. The atmosphere in these conventions is very different from most political conventions in Germany – the music, the flags, the enthusiasm seem more appropriate for a real party and not just a political one. This kind of atmosphere is evidence that one important characteristic of American politics is its entertainment value. All American voters then have the chance to vote for the candidate they wish on the first Tuesday after the first Monday in November, the date prescribed in the Constitution for election day. Usually by midnight Eastern Standard Time at the latest the whole world then knows who won. As one of very many people across Europe I too shed tears of relief and joy early in the morning on 5 November when it became evident that Obama had won enough states to be elected president – although the last official step to becoming elected president doesn't take place until January when the Congress counts the votes of the Electoral College.

Electoral College

We can now add one more meaning to the word "college," that troublesome word with so many different meanings (4). The Electoral College doesn't grant any one a college degree, neither is it a place for students to live. The function of the Electoral College is to officially choose the president. Originally the Electoral College was supposed to choose the president in the times when it took weeks for communication to reach all citizens and when there was some doubt that regular citizens had the necessary skills to elect the president. The Electoral College nowadays is made up of the same number of electors as each state has representatives in Congress (1): each state is represented by two senators in the Senate and by at least one representative in the House of Representatives, thus each state has at least three votes in the Electoral College. States with larger populations have more representatives (1). Currently there are a total of 538 electors in the Electoral College, who then meet every four years to vote for the President a month after the general election. The electors from each state are expected to vote for the candidate who received the most popular votes in the state. In an important way the presidential election isn't thus one election nationwide but in effect 51 separate elections in each of the states and in the District of Columbia, which also has three votes in the Electoral College (1).

2000 presidential election

A few times in presidential election history the candidate who received the most popular votes nationwide didn't receive the most votes in the Electoral College, most recently in the controversial 2000 election. Although the Democratic candidate Al Gore received nationwide almost half a million more votes than the Republican candidate George W. Bush, Bush won the majority of popular votes in more individual states and thus 271 electors, one more than needed for the majority in the Electoral College. The controversy over who had really won the most votes in the state of Florida – and thus Florida's 25 electoral votes – lasted for more than a month and was finally decided by a Supreme Court decision. George W. Bush won reelection in 2004 with both a majority of the popular vote and a larger majority of the electors in the Electoral College. But if John Kerry, the Democratic candidate in 2004, had gained just a few thousand more votes in Ohio (where the results were almost as close as in Florida in the 2000 election) and had thus won Ohio's 20 electoral votes, he would have become president in spite of the fact that he hadn't won the majority of votes nationwide and would have thus been the second president in a row to have won the majority of electoral votes but not the majority of the popular vote. Then maybe the method of using the Electoral College would've been changed. One very big obstacle to reforming the Electoral College, however, lies in the most important document in American politics, the Constitution of the United States.

Constitution and Bill of Rights

The Founding Fathers wanted to create a document that would be permanent enough to unite a nation of individual states and yet flexible enough to adjust to the future. After the Americans won the Revolutionary War and thus could have called themselves American for the first time, they were more likely to call themselves New Yorkers or Virginians or Carolinians than Americans. The thirteen original colonies we learned about in the American history chapter had become more or less thirteen independent countries. It soon became clear that thirteen weak and bickering little countries would never last for long, and so the weak Articles of Confederation became the strong Constitution, which provided for a central federal government with clearly defined rights and responsibilities and state governments that also assumed powers not given to the federal government. We'll be looking at the branches and at the checks and balances of this system shortly. This compromise of creating a document that would stand the test of time and at the same time would be flexible can be seen in how the Constitution can be changed or amended. The very first Amendments came with the document itself, the Bill of Rights, which guaranteed the individual rights and freedoms that the government couldn't take away like freedom of religion and of the press and the right to bear arms (3). Since these first ten Amendments, only seventeen further Amendments have been ratified, a sign of the wisdom of the Founding Fathers and evidence of how difficult it is to change the Constitution, which requires a two-thirds majority in both Houses of Congress followed by ratification in three-quarters of all states.

checks and balances

The American Constitution is the oldest existing constitution in the world and is an astonishingly brief piece of writing, only 7500 words and thus shorter than this chapter! The organization of the Constitution matches the organization of the government in the United States. Article I describes legislative power, II executive power, III judicial power, IV the relationship between state and federal power, V the process of amending the Constitution, VI establishes the Constitution as the Supreme Law of the Land, and VII regulates the ratification procedure. Using the structure of the Constitution, let's take a look at the various branches of the American government and keep in mind two important principles of American government: the separation of powers, which as we've already seen is much clearer in the US than in Britain, and the systems of checks and balances.

lame ducks and presidential coattails

The president is head of the executive branch but is not alone; just as in Britain the executive leader can rely upon a cabinet. The president is both head of state and commander-in-chief of the armed forces. He (so far every president has been male) has the power to sign or veto laws passed by Congress. You may remember the longest-serving president from the American history chapter. Hint: he was second of the two Roosevelts (2). After FDR died shortly after beginning his unprecedented fourth term of office, an Amendment was added to the Constitution to limit the terms of the president to just two. Since then no one can be reelected more than once to the presidency. This restriction can turn a reelected president into a "lame duck," a term often referring to politicians whose term of office is due to expire. The president's power can sometimes start even before Inauguration Day in January. Remember that all important elections are held in the US on one day as stated in the Constitution, namely the second Tuesday after the first Monday in November. So every four years the President, the entire House of Representatives, and one-third of the Senate are elected together. If larger numbers of Representatives and Senators are elected who belong to the same party as the winning presidential candidate, you might hear the phrase "presidential coattails" as a sign that the presidential candidate is seen as being powerful enough to sweep in members of the same party "on his coattails." This was the case in the presidential election of 1980 when the Republican Ronald Reagan not only defeated the incumbent president Jimmy Carter resoundingly, winning 44 states to Carter's mere 6 states, but also when Reagan's party, the Republicans, gained control of the Senate for the first time in more than twenty years. Again in 2008 Barack Obama not only won the presidential election but his Democratic party also won a majority of seats in both the Senate and the House of Representatives.

separation of executive and legislative branches

While often a victorious presidential candidate may also have majorities of the same party in both the Senate and in the House, remember that there aren't the same ties between the executive and the legislative branch in the US as is the case in the UK and in Germany. Often the president belongs to one party and the majority of both Senate and House belongs to another one. Bill

Clinton, for example, began his first term with Democratic majorities in both Houses; in the midterm election of 1994 after Clinton's first two years in office, the Democratic party lost the majority in both Houses and the Republican party had a majority in both Houses for the first time in more than forty years. The Republican party maintained their majority in both Houses even though the Democrat Clinton was reelected president. The Republican majority continued until the last half of the Republican president George W. Bush's second term of office when in 2006 the Democrats regained both the House and the Senate and Nancy Pelosi became the first female Speaker of the House.

Another example of checks and balances between the executive and the legislative branches was when Congress passed the War Powers Act of 1973 curtailing the power of the president to send troops abroad without a formal declaration of war. And a last example that has been possible from the start: presidential impeachment. The word "impeach" doesn't mean to remove an official from office but is only the first step to removal from office, namely to put a public official on trial. Impeachment is one powerful check that the legislative branch has on the executive branch.

Congress

You've already heard about the Senate and the House of Representatives. Let's put them both in the context of the legislative branch. Elections to Congress, the name for the legislative branch, take place every two years, meaning that when the president's elected, Congressional elections also take place. The Congress is bicameral and consists of the Senate and the House of Representatives, but the two parts are unequal. The Senate has 100 members, making two per 50 states, so states with a smaller population have proportionately as much influence as states with a large population. Senators are elected every six years, but to maintain continuity only one-third of the Senate is up for election every two years. The House of Representatives is much larger with 435 members: the number of representatives per state is based on the population of the state. What's the state with the largest population? If you remember the map that helped us trace the movement of population in our survey of American geography, then you should know (1). The state with the largest population, California (with somewhat less than half the population of Germany), has 53 representatives and two senators. Alaska is the largest state in area (five times bigger than

Germany) but is third to last in population (as many people live in Frankfurt am Main, for example, as in the entire state of Alaska). Alaska has only one representative and two senators.

The word "legislative" implies for those who know a little Latin "laws" and that's what the legislative branch is concerned with: creating bills that with the president's signature can become law. If the president refuses to sign or vetoes the bill, then Congress can override the president's veto with a two-thirds majority. While you might expect lawmaking to be a normal activity connected with the legislature, there are a few other activities that are a bit more unusual.

gerrymandering and filibustering

What sounds like some kind of rare disease is actually two historically based aspects dealing with the two chambers of Congress. Gerrymandering has to do with the way Congressional Districts are divided up. We've already learned that the number of Representatives in the House is based on the population of the state. The citizens of each state as a whole elect the two senators; the representatives (in states that have more than one representative of course) aren't elected statewide, each is elected in his or her Congressional District. The districts should be roughly equal in population, but as we saw Americans like to move, meaning some areas lose inhabitants and others gain (1). In order to take this movement into account and to keep the size of the districts more or less roughly equal, redistricting takes place, usually every ten years after the census determines the current population of each state and of each district. As you might imagine, there are many different ways to divide up a district. And the Democrats and Republicans are both interested in drawing the line so that the population of the new district is tilted towards one party – so lengthy discussions take place and sometime even end up in court. A 19th century politician called Elbridge Gerry (a signer of the Declaration of Independence and also the fifth vice president, by the way) was notorious in trying to force redistricting in his favor, creating a district that had the strange shape of a salamander on the map or what Gerry's critics called a "gerrymander." "Filibustering" wasn't named for an obscure American politician but originates from a Spanish word for pirate and is something that can only happen in the Senate. Senators can namely speak for as long as they wish until a majority of three-fifths or 60 out of 100 senators, votes to end discussion. Filibustering, which has increased in the last few years, can postpone a vote favored by a majority and thus protect minority rights but has also been criticized for slowing government decision making.

constituency versus party affiliation

You might remember that we used the word constituency to refer to the political districts in Britain which are each represented by one MP (Member of Parliament). While a rough equivalent of a constituency in the US as we've just seen is "congressional district," the word "constituency" is also used in American English to refer to the voters who elect politicians, voters who are far more important to representatives, who must be reelected every two years, or to senators, who must be reelected every six years, than the views of the party. Often party alignment plays a lesser role so that Democrats from the south may have more conservative views on cultural issues like abortion or gun control or gay marriage than liberal Republicans from west coast states. Remember that there isn't the same force tying a representative to his or her party in the US as there is in the UK or especially in Germany.

the Supreme Court

The third and last branch mentioned in the Constitution is the judicial branch, made up of the Supreme Court, the highest court in the land, the court that decides if laws passed by Congress and acts signed by the president are unconstitutional. To avoid a misperception – the Supreme Court doesn't actively check all the laws passed, they only act on their own in a very limited number of cases. Most of the cases that reach the Supreme Court have to go through all the lower courts of appeal to finally reach the nine justices who have their jobs for life. We've already mentioned a few major Supreme Court cases in previous chapters, and we'll be hearing more about the role of the Court in future chapters. Justices are nominated by the president but must be confirmed by the senate, another example of the principle of checks and balances.

federal and state

The 10th Amendment to the Constitution and the last part of the Bill of Rights leaves all power not explicitly given to the federal government to the states. Not only are the states responsible for education but also for laws dealing with abortion and capital punishment and gun control (3). You've now already learned about the political division into three branches at the federal level as well as how the House of Representatives in the legislative branch reflects the division of states into congressional districts. If you remember one topic from our British geography appetizer

(🔔 1) then you already know the term used to designate smaller political divisions than the states in the US: counties. The counties in Britain often have names that refer to much older historical areas like kingdoms (🔔 1, 2). In contrast, counties in the US are much more prosaic and are the basic political and geographic subdivision of a state with responsibilities in police enforcement, highway maintenance, and increasingly health care and social services.

But it's time now to zoom up from the county level through the state back up to the national and return in history to that moment in the late 18th century when the US Constitution was created.

Benjamin Franklin, perhaps the most famous of the Founding Fathers, famously responded to the question about which form of government the Constitutional Convention had decided on: "A Republic, Madam, if you can keep it." After more than two centuries the United States has kept the republic. In idealistic terms we could look at the development of American government as slowly extending rights from the early landowners in the late 18th century to all those over the age of eighteen with the 26th Amendment to the Constitution in the 1970s. In the light of the draconian restrictions on individual rights made after 9/11 this view of the extension of rights and of keeping the republic may seem overly optimistic. But even if the promises made in the opening words of the Declaration of Independence – that all men are created equal and have the right to life, liberty, and the pursuit of happiness – haven't yet been fully granted, the sheer audacity to guarantee the pursuit of happiness as a human right has remained unique and is perhaps one of the keys to understanding the American spirit both inside and outside of government.

## Exercises

1. What important aspects of this chapter is its somewhat strange title supposed to make you aware of?
2. Why is the Queen of England an inaccurate term? (Hint: you might need to do just a little bit of historical research to answer this question. Have a look at the British history chapter again.)
3. What evidence do you have that the British Constitution is very easy and the American very difficult to amend? (hint:

the last Amendment to the American Constitution mentioned in this chapter extending suffrage to all those over 18 is the next-to-last amendment.)

4. How can you compare congressional districts with British constituencies?
5. Find examples in this and previous chapters that show the importance of the federal and state government division of power.
6. What do you notice about the photos used in this chapter? Any explanations?

---

Challenging and interesting project:

First describe and then try and explain the unique atmosphere in British Parliament and during the American Democratic and Republican National Conventions. If politics is supposed to be so boring, then why do Americans seem to have so much to do during the conventions with the ambitious task of deciding who will be the nation's next president? And why do British MPs seem so raucous in the hallowed halls of Parliament?

And finally the oh-my-god-if-you-can-do-this-you'll-be-elected-President-automatically-or-maybe-even-become-Queen tasks:

Advise the British government and monarch on how to reform the British Constitution so that traditions are kept while at the same time allowing for a modernized House of Lords.

Advise all the branches of the American government on increasing political participation of all citizens with the aim at improving the reputation of politicians.

And further topics not dealt with in this chapter… for those with time and passion and imagination to consider what life would be like as the next president or the next king or queen:

The structure of local government in both America and Britain; some of the more interesting and strange smaller political parties in both countries; details about political scandals; details about the legislative procedure in both countries; the Patriot Act as an example of quick response under pressure showing cooperation between the legislative and the executive branches or of a knee-jerk reaction with terrible consequences for American individual civil rights and for world peace; …

# 6 | The Pound Stops Here for a Commonwealth for All? (economics and international relations)

The buck stops here.
sign on President Harry S. Truman's desk

I want my money back.
attributed to Prime Minister Margaret Thatcher in negotiations over a special rebate for the UK from the EEC budget

We're beginning this chapter with several puns. "Buck" can mean "dollar" in informal American English, probably originally related to the value of "buckskin," the hide of a male animal like a deer (also called a buck), which was traded between Indians and settlers. With "buck" in this sense we also have one main focus of this chapter: the economy.

"The buck stops here" is a well-known phrase in American English meaning "I'm the one responsible for making decisions." One of the other meanings of "buck" supposedly comes from the card game of poker where the "buck" was a marker that symbolized whose turn it was to pass out the next cards. If a player didn't wish to deal, he (in frontier days only men played poker) "passed the buck" onto the next player. "Passing the buck" became known as a synonym for "not assuming responsibility." Truman, the US president responsible for the decision to use the first atomic bombs in history on the Japanese cities of Hiroshima and Nagasaki, had a sign with the slogan "the buck stops here" on his desk throughout the seven years of his presidency. International relations (which thankfully aren't only expressed through war and bombs) are the other focus of this chapter. And we'll learn that common wealth for all isn't necessarily the same as a commonwealth, a term that we'll see has several different meanings.

Of course there are areas where the economy and international relations intersect; Prime Minister Margaret Thatcher has been famously somewhat misquoted in negotiations between the UK and the European Economic Community (the predecessor of the EU). She really said: "But it is not asking the Community for money; it is asking the Community to have our own money back..."

When you finish the chapter, you should not only be able to quote Thatcher correctly but also be able to describe

- some interesting aspects of the American economy
- some captains of industry or robber barons in American history
- some American territories around the world
- expansionism and isolationism as principles of American foreign policy
- some interesting aspects of the British economy
- the role of the Commonwealth in Britain today
- the relationship between the UK and Europe
- the special relationship between the US and the UK.

Before we start to look at some interesting and perhaps surprising aspects of the American economy, let's go back in history to the Gilded Age (🔔 2) to see what could be considered the roots of capitalism. Whether you consider men like Astor, Carnegie, Ford, Mellon, Morgan, Rockefeller, or Vanderbilt as "captains of industry," great men who contributed positively to American society at the end of the 19th and beginning of the 20th century, or as "robber barons," selfish and greedy men who exploited many of the poorer people during the country's vast intake of immigrants, depends at least partly on which facts you choose from these famous people's biographies. You could even use the expression "so-called" (which often has a negative connotation) correctly (Germans tend to overuse it) if you wanted to express your doubts about the following "so-called captains of industry."

Astors, Carnegies, Vanderbilts

The Astor family can trace its roots back to before the American Revolutionary War and is considered to have started America's first business monopoly with the American Fur Company. John Jacob Astor was well-known for building grand hotels like the one that later became the Waldorf-Astoria, the name of which reveals where the Astor family originally came from: Waldorf near Heidelberg. The Astors earned their millions through real estate and donated large sums to the Metropolitan Museum of Art. While one Astor was accused of being a slum landlord in New York, later generations engaged in philanthropic activities. Andrew Carnegie came from Scotland, created an empire out of iron and steel, became one of the richest men in history (if you measure personal wealth as percentage of the total economy of the time), and left many millions of dollars to found libraries, universities, and to Carnegie Hall, one of the most famous music halls in the US. His reputation was publicly tarnished through his involvement in one of the most violent strikes in American history: the Homestead Strike. The Vanderbilts originally made their millions through shipping and railway companies but also founded Vanderbilt University.

from laissez-faire to Reaganomics

One reason for the success of these families was an economic and political policy with the French-sounding name laissez-faire, literally "let do" meaning "let things alone," especially the things that prohibited the industrial giants from enlarging their businesses and their wealth. As in Britain (2) the combination of natural resources with the belief that wealth was a sign of God's blessing led to an enormous increase of wealth, which was, however, very unevenly distributed. The belief that the government should have a role in controlling the very powerful in business started in the 20th century. American governments today tend to vary in their degree of intervention into economic affairs with Democratic administrations like Clinton being more involved and Republican administrations like that of Reagan or Bush less so. Reagan's economic policy in the 1980s was based on the belief that the government should reduce taxes and thus give citizens more money to spend. Increased spending would result in increased investment and economic growth and would eventually "trickle down" to those who didn't have much. The government should cut spending on social programs and should deregulate industry. This view of the role of the government became known as Reaganomics. The deregulation of the finance industry resulted in 2008 in one of the worst crises since the Great Depression. One of the ironies of political life is that as a result of the crisis a Republican administration under George W. Bush proposed one of the most massive interventions by government ever. The Democratic administration under Barack Obama has expanded government spending and responsibility to levels not since the days of FDR's New Deal (2). Whether Obama will be able to restore America's role as an economic leader remains one of the unknowns and will no doubt become an important and interesting chapter in early 21st century history.

After this look at some of the big names of the past, names that you'll still encounter in the present US and in the near future too, let's turn to some interesting and surprising aspects of the American economy in general.

old belts and new agribusiness

We can start with farming. Earlier generations of English teachers had it easier when nice fairly clearly-cut agricultural belts divided American agriculture into easily teachable and learnable sections with a limited amount of new vocabulary: corn belt, cotton belt, wheat belt, dairy belt (with the chance for a joke: "No, they don't grow cows there"). But these belts no longer fit. Modern farming in the US involves much more land and more diversification. Even the name for farming has changed to represent this shift from the small plots of land first settled in colonial America and then given away by the government in the Homestead Acts (🔔 2) to the combination of farming and high technology today: agribusiness. Farmers who cultivated the prairie in the late 19th century used barbed wire and improved mechanization to harvest and later the development of transportation like nationwide trains to sell their crops. The government encouraged the development of the science of agriculture by founding and funding large state universities (🔔 4). Nowadays those who work in agriculture make up only 1 % of the population although around 20 % of the total land area of the United States is suitable for growing crops. The term "agribusiness" we just mentioned is often used to describe the large scale commercial farms that combine technology and industry with crop growing. The United States remains the world's leading single exporter of agricultural products although the EU taken together as one political entity exports four times more.

services, services, services

In spite of the fact that one of the iconic images of America is no doubt the vast expanses of crops in the Great Plains, America's economy today – like other western post-industrialized countries – is driven by the services sector, in which more than three-quarters of all Americans are employed. As early as the 1950s white-collar workers (service sector, public employment) outnumbered blue-collar workers, leading to a postindustrial society. In the sheer numbers of paid employees, health and social services is the largest sector today followed by manufacturing and retail trade – not surprising when you consider that the American economy is driven by the consumer. When consumers buy less, then the American economy begins to have big problems. Visitors to America are often struck by the role advertisements play and the emphasis on consumption in the media. This consumer culture also started as early as the 50s.

vacation? job security?

One difference that surprises and puzzles many Europeans is the short vacations of most American employees, a similar shock that Americans experience when they find out how long German vacations are. When I first arrived in Germany, I asked myself how any economic system could function when the vast majority of workers had four to six weeks of vacation a year in addition to the many state holidays. Most Americans have far fewer vacation days with no national government law guaranteeing a minimum number of paid days off. One group lobbying for minimum guaranteed leave has called the US a "no vacation nation." Opening hours were also vastly different between the US and Germany until the liberalization of the law in Germany, and many stores in the US are open on Sundays in spite of the importance of church-going in America. The convenience for the consumer is offset by the forced availability of the employees, yet except for some resistance to opening on Sundays years ago (the laws forbidding businesses from opening on Sundays were called Blue Laws because they were written on blue paper) Americans accept long opening hours and longer working hours as a given. Americans also seem to accept the hire-and-fire mentality of many employers. I remember being amazed at the level of job security in Germany but also bemused by the hurdles job seekers had to face in getting part-time work. While Americans certainly aren't immune to the fear of losing their jobs, there are always other jobs to be had – albeit of the McJob variety: low-skilled and low-paid.

What can Americans do about low-skilled jobs? Get a better education, many would say. We've already looked at tuition fees in the education chapter (4). Since colleges and universities aren't normal businesses with easily quantifiable production costs, fundraising is very important, as is being able to provide financial aid to students who can't afford high tuition fees. But many Americans consider the investment in a college education to be necessary for future economic success.

from the Rust Belt to Silicon Valley

Although most employment opportunities are to be found in the services sector, as we've just seen, you can still find remnants of America's industrial past in modern America. While we've just learned that traditional agricultural belts aren't a very accurate way of mapping agriculture today, there is one "belt" that is still commonly used to describe certain parts of the US stretching from Pennsylvania through Ohio and Michigan – the Rust Belt, those areas that are facing problems because the great textile, automobile, and steel industries of the past have now closed down. And to add one more physical feature term used nowadays to describe economic activity: probably most of you have heard of Silicon Valley, which isn't a real valley – although it encompasses the real Santa Clara Valley in northern California – where you can find silicon growing (a common chemical element found all over the world used for making the chips that make our computers work). The abundance of jobs in the computer and other technical industries has given Silicon Valley its name, a name that has inspired other names around the world as a designation for the concentration of jobs in the technological industries.

American isolationism and expansionism

Just as we started our look at the US economy by going back in history, let's go back now and apply some of what we covered in the history chapter to a look at two seemingly diametrically opposed ways of explaining America's role in the world: isolationism and expansionism. If we had an entire chapter to devote to this issue (and there have been enough books to fill a small library about it), then our chapter title would be: "From Two MDs (the Monroe Doctrine and Manifest Destiny) to the World's Policeman – Isolationist and Expansionist Tendencies."

Manifest Destiny and Monroe Doctrine

Remember the use of the term Manifest Destiny, which we heard about earlier in one of our history appetizers? Manifest Destiny nowadays sometimes refers to the sense of responsibility that some Americans and some American governments assume: spreading American-style democracy or more generally American ideals of personal liberty all over the world is not only good but also God's will. As we have no doubt all heard, this belief can be both attractive in its genuine perhaps naïve sense of wanting to better the world and repugnant in its naïve sense of being inherently arrogant (God's chosen people) and at the same time ignorant of other cultures. We can also see Manifest Destiny as one example of expansionism, usually offset by isolationism, an example of which could be the Monroe Doctrine, originally written a generation before the term Manifest Destiny was first used, as an example of American isolationism or at least as a warning on the part of the still young nation to the much older nations of Europe to stay out of not only the territory of the United States but also the entire western hemisphere. One aspect of the Monroe Doctrine that would later become more important was the implied right of the US to interfere in the internal affairs of countries in the western hemisphere. The Monroe Doctrine also defined what would be considered as the right of the US to establish a sphere of influence throughout both American continents and thus can be seen as an example of expansionism too.

We saw in the history chapter that the US entered World War I late; another sign of the isolationist side of American policy was the refusal to join the League of Nations (2). The Nobel Peace prize-winning American President Woodrow Wilson had dreamed of the US joining the League of Nations to ensure that the First World War was indeed "the war to end all wars." His failure to convince Congress of the necessity for the United States to join the League was Wilson's – and perhaps America's – biggest mistake.

from General MacArthur ...

Another example of American isolationism was waiting until 1941 to take sides actively in World War II and then only entering after the shock of the Japanese attack at Pearl Harbor in Hawaii. One of the heroes of World War II was General Douglas MacArthur, the commander of the Allied Forces in the Pacific during the war and one of the few men to reach the rank of five-star general. MacArthur served in the Philippines, which the US had taken from Spain during the Spanish-American War at the end of the 19th century (2) and originally planned to defend the islands against the Japanese threat. When President Franklin Delano Roosevelt ordered him to withdraw from a losing battle against the Japanese, MacArthur uttered the famous words "I shall return" and did indeed return to retake the islands in the Pacific that the Japanese had conquered. MacArthur was ready to lead forces to invade Japan itself before Japan surrendered after the US had used the first atomic bombs to destroy the cities of Nagasaki and Hiroshima. Why mention MacArthur in the context of expansionism? Later in the early 1950s MacArthur was appointed leader of UN forces involved in the Korean War and was in favor of expanding the war to China, which had sent troops to support the North Koreans. President Harry S. Truman, who was concerned that such an expansion would result in a nuclear war, relieved MacArthur of his command.

... to Senator McCarthy

While General MacArthur was still head of the occupation forces in Japan, a young Senator from Wisconsin claimed to have the names of many top-ranking government officials who were secretly members of the Communist party. Although he wasn't able to substantiate his accusations, Joseph McCarthy was able to exploit the widespread fear of communism that had become rampant in the wake of the Korean War and the fear of Soviet domination. McCarthy became chairman of a Senate Investigations Subcommittee and continued his highly public accusations of officials. After lengthy televised Senate hearings on McCarthy's methods, which gave the general public the chance to see his extremist behavior, his influence began to diminish, and the Senate formally condemned him for acting "contrary to senatorial ethics." Although McCarthy died only a few years later, the term "McCarthyism," which was already coined during his lifetime, has been used ever since to critically describe the persecution of innocent people and attempts by those in power to enforce conformity. In 2005 George Clooney wrote, directed, and acted in the critically acclaimed film *Good Night, and Good Luck*, which portrayed the television journalist Edward R. Murrow, whose televised programs helped to discredit McCarthy's tactics.

Cuban Missile Crisis

While you could see McCarthy as being a good example of the fear of communism rampant in the 50s, sometimes called the Red Scare, there was another scare in the early 60s that showed how important international relations had become. In October 1962 the US received evidence of the building of Soviet nuclear missile sites on Cuba. The Cuban Missile Crisis would later be dramatically called "thirteen days" or "the week the world stood still"; never before had the world been so close to nuclear war. Kennedy was able to persuade Soviet Premier Khrushchev to withdraw the missiles in return for a promise that the Americans would not invade Cuba. The successful resolution of the Cuban Missile Crisis is regarded as the first thawing in the Cold War.

We've already looked at one other war that was definitely not cold (🔔 2), but in the context of international relations we need to briefly look at the buildup to the first war that America was to clearly lose. In the mid 1950s parts of the former colony of French Indochina were divided into two countries: North and

South Vietnam. Believing that communism presented a threat to security and peace, Americans began supporting South Vietnam in the struggle with the communist North Vietnam as early as the early 1960s, at first with only advisors and then later with an increasing number of combat troops. The general belief, which became known as the domino theory, was that if South Vietnam fell to the North Vietnamese, who were interested in establishing a communist government for a reunited Vietnam, other countries in Asia would also become communist just as the fall of one domino piece causes all other dominos to fall too. Since the United States never officially declared war on North Vietnam and since the buildup of troops proceeded at first gradually, opposition to the war didn't develop until the late 1960s. We've already glanced at the results of the Vietnam War on American society in our history chapter (2).

9/11 as a second Pearl Harbor?

Before we conclude our brief survey of American international relations, we have to at least mention one defining moment that every reader of this book experienced. Just as the news of the bombing of Pearl Harbor at the start of American involvement in World War II and much later the assassination of John F. Kennedy were defining moments in the lives of many people of different generations in the US as in Britain and Germany, the news or the experience via live television of the attacks on the World Trade Center in New York created such a defining moment. The loss of human life and property on that fateful day in September is incomparable with the loss of life and property in American actions following 9/11 however one might judge them as being justified or not. But no American "victory" in Afghanistan or in Iraq – both conflicts can (but don't necessarily have to) be seen as direct results of the 9/11 attacks – has had the symbolic power of the Twin Towers crumbling on live television shown around the world. The US and the world changed with 9/11, and its repercussions will no doubt affect our lives for a long time to come.

While US territories are strictly speaking not a topic for international affairs since they belong to the US, some of them are far enough away from the continental US to justify being mentioned in this part of our chapter on international relations. Let's begin with one of the closest territories, one that shares the name of this chapter – but in a totally different use of the word – the Commonwealth of Puerto Rico.

Commonwealth of Puerto Rico as 51st state?

Puerto Rico also has a special status, which you can't see as clearly in its official English name Commonwealth of Puerto Rico as you can in its Spanish name: Estado libre Asociado de Puerto Rico, which stresses the fact that Puerto Rico, originally ceded to the US by Spain at the end of the Spanish-American War in 1898, became partly autonomous fifty years afterwards (2). Now Puerto Ricans are US citizens who can travel and move to the United States but who don't pay all the taxes that other US citizens pay. Puerto Ricans can't vote in the presidential election but can vote in the primaries to choose the Democratic or Republican nominee. While Puerto Rico has no representation in Congress, it is able to send a non-voting member to the House of Representatives, just like Washington, DC. Confusing? In the referenda held in the last fifty years, Puerto Rico has consistently and sometimes narrowly voted for maintaining its commonwealth status. Most Puerto Ricans have opposed the chance for full independence in the past, but they are also very proud of their Spanish heritage and thus reluctant to apply to become the 51st state of an English-speaking America (1). But with the growth of the Hispanic minority in the US, Puerto Rico could decide to apply for full statehood in an America that has changed a lot in the past fifty years (7). The US Census Bureau has already begun a special Community Survey for Puerto Rico for the next census in 2010 similar to the surveys the Census Bureau conducts in the fifty states and Washington DC.

**Fig. 6.1**
*The Puerto Rican flag became official and legal with the birth of Commonwealth of Puerto Rico in 1952.*

And if Puerto Rico doesn't become the 51st state, what about Washington, DC (1)? While this is unlikely because of constitutional reasons, DC is more likely than some of the other possibilities: Sometimes but almost always humorously or cynically the United Kingdom or Canada are referred to as candidates for the 51st state as a sign of the influence the US has/should have/shouldn't have on both countries. But actually there are some other candidates for the 51st star on the flag, less likely than Puerto Rico or DC but more likely than the UK or some Canadian province.

exotic territories from Guam to Guantamo

Those geography buffs who read the first chapter carefully might remember the name of one of the islands so far from the mainland that it's practically on the other side of the world from the continental US. If you said Hawaii, you'd be right in the context of US territories, but only until 1959 when the territory of Hawaii became the 50th and so far last state. When you check the geography appetizer again (1), you'll see that the territory I mean here is the island of Guam, one of those ceded by Spain at the end of the 19th century as a result of the Spanish-American War, just like Puerto Rico. The inhabitants of Guam, like the Puerto Ricans, are American citizens, and Guam like Puerto Rico also sends one non-voting member to the House of Representatives. Otherwise Guam is much smaller than Puerto Rico in area and in population. Guam forms part of the Mariana Island group, and the Northern Mariana Islands are another American commonwealth. All the Mariana Islands are located strategically in the western Pacific. One other island group on the other side of the world from the Marianas and much closer to the American mainland is the American Virgin Islands, just east of Puerto Rico where the Atlantic Ocean meets the Caribbean Sea. The US Virgin Islands are popular with tourists and weren't taken as the spoils of war like Puerto Rico but actually bought from Denmark during World War I. One part of an island not at all popular with tourists or with many people inside and outside the US is Guantanamo Naval Base at Guantanamo Bay on the southeast coast of Cuba, which those of you with political interests will no doubt have expected in this section. But the area isn't a territory: Cuba leased it "perpetually" as part of an agreement signed between Cuba and the US – yet another result of the Spanish-American War. As one of the first acts as president, Barack Obama announced the closing of the Guantanamo Bay Detention Camp. Maybe one day the entire Naval Base will be closed, and this leased territory finally be returned to Cuba – an island incidentally that Americans weren't allowed to travel to until the late 1970s. Americans who violate the American embargo against Cuba are liable to prosecution, as the filmmaker Michael Moore experienced and documented in Sicko (3).

Speaking of islands… we need to return to our United Kingdom and to the lady we (mis)quoted at the beginning of the chapter.

features of Thatcher's government

Margaret Thatcher was the first female prime minister of the United Kingdom and head of the government and of the Conservative party for about 12 years and thus longer than any other prime minister in the 20th century. Some of her critics claimed she "reigned" with an iron hand; in any case she was very proud of her nickname "Iron Lady." She followed a strict anti-union policy resulting in the defeat of the miner's strike of 1984–85, and she privatized many traditional government-owned industries with British in their names like British Telecom, British Steel, British Gas, and British Airways. Thatcher's emphasis on a free-market economy greatly increased economic output and decreased the high inflation rates of the 1970s. But Thatcherism, the term used to describe Thatcher's ideology, is also said to have increased the gap between the haves and the have-nots and to have contributed to a society of two nations, one wealthy and one poor. She is also – depending on your political perspective – either credited or blamed with dismantling some of Britain's post-war welfare state. Many compare her with the American president whose term of office almost exactly coincided with hers: Ronald Reagan.

In addition to Thatcher, some other interesting aspects about the British economy? Questions with "interesting" are always good in examinations since they give you the chance to argue your point and there are no right or wrong answers: after all, what's interesting is subjective. We already answered a similar question about the American economy above, and what's true for the US could also be relevant for the UK.

from farming to fishing

Just as in our look at the American economy, we could begin here with farming to help you compare the importance of agriculture in the two countries. About a quarter of all land in the UK is arable or suitable for growing crops, and is thus considerably less than in Germany but a bit more than in the US. The amount of land available for farming in the UK is of course in absolute size far less than in the US, which is as we've learned (1) almost forty times bigger than the UK. Most of this land is used as grassland and for crops or grazing. The UK has the lowest percentage of workers employed in agriculture in the EU, just more than 1 %, less than in Germany. In spite of the low number of farmers, some world-famous breeds of livestock can be found like Hereford and Aberdeen Angus. But it wasn't these breeds that made international news in the last decade; the tongue-twisting disaster bovine spongiform encephalopathy, more pronounceable as BSE or mad cow disease, and the unappetizing foot and mouth disease made the headlines and caused a crisis in British agriculture and tourism. Whether genetically modified (GM) crops should be grown at all is a current controversial issue that makes headlines regularly; land reserved for organic farming increased rapidly in the 1990s but still only makes up roughly 4% of all the land used for crops, wheat and barley being by far the most common crops grown.

Speaking of food, what was once Britain's favorite food but is no longer? Fish 'n chips. While the EU is taking measures to stop the depletion of certain kinds of fish like Atlantic cod by restricting fishing, aquaculture or fish farming is growing in Scotland, accounting now for half of all Scottish food exports. Even though chicken tikka masala has displaced fish 'n chips as Britain's favorite food, a lot of fish still have to be caught to satisfy the deep-seated desire for seafood, understandable in a land where no point is further than … ( 1) as you remember from one of our geography appetizers.

my home is my castle

But no matter how far you are from the sea, you'll have to pass many user-owned homes of all kinds on your way there. Britain has one of the highest percentages of home ownership in Europe, much higher than in Germany. Not only is the desire to own your own home much stronger in the UK than in Germany, the way of financing property is also very different. Most British mortgages are financed by variable interest, meaning any interest rate changes immediately affect how much money any British homeowner has to spend. When the interest rates are low, they don't have to pay as much to finance their homes or their castles, and the more money they have for vacation (or as the Brits say "for holidays").

vacation

While employees in the newer computer industries may have the reputation for working long hours, those in the agricultural or construction industries work the longest statistically per week. At least the number of paid vacation days granted to workers in Britain has increased to 24 days a year, considerably more than the average American and a little less than the average German. We already know that few people work in agriculture in Britain. Most British people work in the services sector: public administration, education, and health form the largest group followed by distribution, hotels, and restaurants.

North Sea Oil

The services sector requires energy, and as with all industrialized countries energy is often gotten from oil. After North Sea oil was first discovered off the shore of Scotland and northeastern

England in the late 1960s, oil production soared, reaching a peak in the late 1990s and declining ever since. For a couple of decades, however, the UK was not only independent of the oil-exporting countries for its energy use but also had become one of world's top ten producers of oil in the mid 90s. As early as the mid 70s the boom in North Sea oil production was having political consequences too. The Scottish National Party (SNP) used the slogan "it's Scotland's oil" to force the central government to grant Scotland more power. The process of devolution (5) had begun although it would take another twenty years before Scotland gained its own parliament. North Sea oil has made it economically feasible for Scotland for the first time since the Act of Union united Scotland and England at the beginning of the 18th century (2) to seek an even greater break from the rest of the United Kingdom.

With the concept of devolution we've already begun to shift our view in this chapter from the economy to international relations, but before we leave the island economically, let's take a drive to Silicon Valley – but not back to California.

Silicon Fen, Gorge, ...

While the term Silicon Valley was first used for a part of northern California, Britain has since gained its share of Silicon names and also its share of high-tech and research industries. Sometimes the Cambridge Cluster or area around Cambridge University is called Silicon Fen (the Fens is the name of a flat geographic area in east England). Silicon Gorge is an area between Bristol, Swindon, and Gloucester in southern England with many research companies. Wales also has its Cwm Silicon (cwm is the Welsh word for valley) at the end of the Silicon Corridor. And southern Scotland, too, has an area called Silicon Glen (glen is the Scottish Gaelic word for valley) in which many high technology and software companies have their headquarters. Silicon Corridor is sometimes used as a nickname for the M4 motorway connecting London with Wales.

former Empire now at the steering wheel

What you won't see as many of on the Silicon Corridor are what were once exclusively British automobiles. Any Jaguars, Rolls Royces, or Land Rovers that you may see are reminders of the demise of one traditional British industry. Jaguar was the name of the company and is still the name of a luxury car originally built in Britain. The company privatized by Thatcher (one of many privatizations as we saw earlier in this chapter) was later bought by the American Ford Motor Company and then by Tata Motors of India, a nice example of how the former Empire is now taking over some of the businesses once owned only in the homeland.

from the sun never sets to island(s) on the edge?

Speaking of the Empire, ...you could say that the British Empire began to decline when the American colonies declared their independence, but you could also claim that the creation of the United States of America from the English colonies on the east coast of North America was more than compensated by the growth of the British Empire on the other side of the globe in Australia, an Empire that then a century later was expanded into Africa "from the Cape to Cairo" (2). We've already read about some of those in the Victorian era who helped the British Empire grow into the largest empire in the history of the world, and most of the 19th century could be called Britain's Imperial Century. The sun never set on the British Empire, which extended from the Cape to Cairo in Africa, from Cairo to Calcutta in India, and all the way around the world past Australia to Canada and back to the motherland. And then what happened?

**Fig. 6.2** *Map of the British Empire at its greatest extent after WW I. The different shades indicate differences in status: colony, dominion, or mandate.*

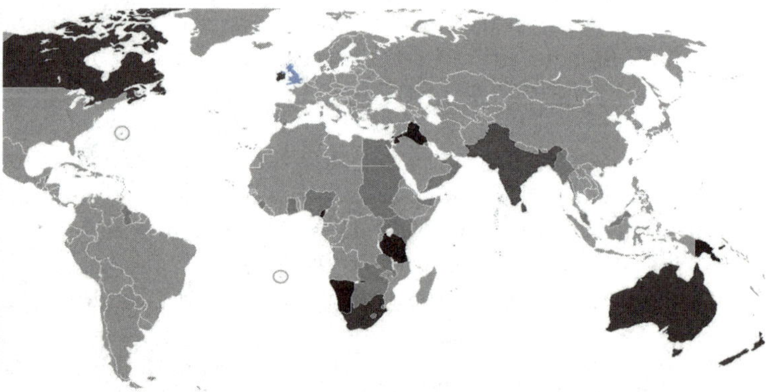

**Fig. 6.3** *Map of the Commonwealth of Nations in 2008. Do you notice any big differences?*

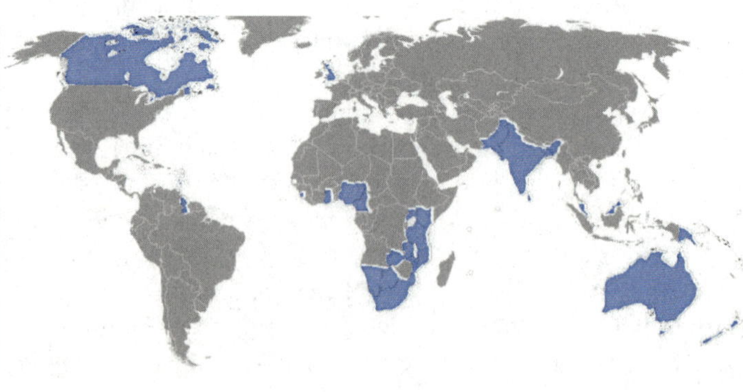

Ever heard of Westminster (🔔 1; 3; 5; 8)? While there are enough bells now ringing in this paragraph to make you think you might be in Westminster Cathedral, we're actually talking about the Statute of Westminster in the context of the British Empire or rather Commonwealth. At the beginning of the 1930s the Statute of Westminster established the British Commonwealth of Nations as an association of independent countries which had previously been part of the British Empire. After World War II as the former colonies of the Empire were beginning to gain their independence, the word British was dropped, leaving the Commonwealth of Nations, the name this association still has. The Commonwealth counts around fifty member nations more or less. The "more or less" has to do with the countries that were a part, then weren't, then rejoined like South Africa (left in the 60s, came back in 90s), Pakistan (left, then rejoined, was suspended and readmitted twice), Zimbabwe (suspended), or to countries that left and never came back (Ireland), or that no longer exist (like Newfoundland – now part of Canada – or Tanganyika – now part of Tanzania). The countries range from very large in population (India, Pakistan, Bangladesh, and Nigeria) and very large in area like the continent and country of Australia to very small in area and in population like the island of Grenada. But there are other islands too, some of which we've already heard of that aren't members of the Commonwealth but that we could associate with Britain, some which have even provoked a war.

Commonwealth of Nations

**Fig. 6.4**
*The flag of the Commonwealth of Nations was adopted in the 1970s. If you count the spears that form the C, you'll come up with a number that was never true for the number of nations of the Commonwealth but that is supposed to indicate the many facets of Commonwealth work.*

**Fig. 6.5**
*This photo is taken from inside the Commonwealth Cemetery, which is part of Cologne's Southern Cemetery and is one example of exterritoriality, an area in one country that officially belongs to another: here is British soil just a few kilometers from the Cologne Cathedral!*

UK territories?

The question mark indicates that we're going to mention not only the clear-cut territories like the Falkland Islands, a small group of small islands in the South Atlantic that have far more sheep than inhabitants. The Falklands were the islands that were the cause of a war, which we'll be hearing about a bit later. We can also mention some strange political units like the Channel Islands and the Isle of Man, which you might remember having had as one of our geography appetizers, and which are neither part of the Commonwealth nor part of the UK or even part of the EU but are called Crown Dependencies.

The current Commonwealth is only partly concerned with a common wealth for all since economics plays only one role among many in Britain's relationship to the countries that had been part of its huge Empire. How Britain deals with its two roles, a leading country in the Commonwealth and a member of the European Union, will be a guide to Britain's changing place in the world.

Speaking of the EU …

the UK in the EU

The relationship between the UK and the EU can be briefly described as stormy with patches of friendliness but with lots of mistrust. Let's just look at a few of the stops on the bumpy road of Britain's integration into Europe. First Britain applied for membership in what was called the EEC. After being turned down twice by the French leader Charles de Gaulle, Britain was finally accepted and became a member in 1973. A referendum was held two years later and the majority of the voters confirmed Britain's membership. Britain was one of the poorer countries in the EEC in the 70s and 80s. Britain also had relatively few small farms, and most EU spending was on farm subsidies, so most of the funding from Europe went to other countries. Thatcher won a special rebate from the EEC and has been misquoted on this issue since then (see the opening quote in this chapter). And the rebate has been continued by the EU, which in effect returns some of the money that Britain pays to the EU every year. These financial aspects aren't a clear-cut case with the UK being either the winner or the loser, and there are many other vested interests in other countries and their agriculture too. The EU has done repeatedly what it usually does with complicated financial debates: postpone a final decision about ending the special rebate and reforming some of the controversial agricultural funding in many EU countries.

pound sterling only please

Another financial connection between the EU and the UK is much easier to explain and is something that every tourist knows who crosses the Channel. In spite of signing the Maastricht Treaty in the early 90s, which founded the European Union and established the euro as a future currency of all member states, the UK negotiated an "opt-out" clause, which allows the UK to postpone adopting the euro. While there have been discussions again and again about Britain becoming part of the Eurozone, the British government has postponed any formal decision again and again due to the feared unpopularity that such a move would have among the British. It certainly seems that for the near future at least, all European tourists will have to continue to exchange euros for pounds. With no euro, no participation in the Schengen passport-free travel zone, and with the growth of the UK Independence Party (UKIP) (5), Britain remains a very skeptical member of the EU, looking often not eastwards towards "Europe" or the "Continent" but westwards towards the US. And one aspect of Britain's role in the world is its special relationship to the US, the final topic of this chapter.

Britain and America's special relationship

One of the quotes that we could've started this chapter with is usually attributed to the playwright George Bernard Shaw: "England and America are two countries separated by a common language." And although the US and the UK were allies in both World Wars, there have been some interesting differences in foreign policy that would've perhaps resulted in conflict if the Anglo-American ties hadn't been so long-lasting. But at least for the first fifty years of the US's existence, the special US-UK relationship was one based on war and on conflict: the War of Independence and the War of 1812. Britain supported American attempts to limit Spain's influence in the western hemisphere through the Monroe Doctrine and didn't side with Spain against the US (as most European countries did) in the Spanish-American War. American support for Britain and the other Allies in World War I, though late, cemented a relationship that was also based on common institutions, traditions, and a common language – in spite of some differences that Shaw was making fun of in his famous quote.

tests from Suez to the Falklands

Of course American support of Britain and later involvement in World War II further strengthened a sense of common goals: there were one and a half million American troops stationed in

Britain during the war, a "friendly invasion." Churchill, whose mother by the way was American, used the term "special relationship" to describe American-British relations shortly after World War II. And this special relationship was able to survive postwar political disagreements like the Suez Crisis in the 50s when Egypt nationalized the Suez Canal, provoking Britain and France to attack Egypt. After both the UN and the US took a firm stance against the attack and thus against Britain, the soldiers were withdrawn. The British response in the Falklands War in the early 80s could have been interpreted as having violated the Monroe Doctrine, yet the US remained neutral. Guess who was prime minister during the Falklands War? Margaret Thatcher. Her response to Argentina's invasion of the small group of islands called the Falklands in the south Atlantic was to declare war on Argentina, and two months later British forces had won. This victory boosted Thatcher's popularity and helped the Conservative Party to win the next general election in 1983. That same year the UK along with the UN condemned a US invasion of Grenada, a Caribbean island and independent member of the British Commonwealth, which you may remember reading about earlier in this chapter as an example of a very small member of the Commonwealth. In spite of these tests of Anglo-American friendship, the special relationship has stood the test of time.

British-American friendships

Along with historical and traditional connections, personal connections are further evidence of the special relationship. Millions of Americans claim British descent, and the first woman elected to the House of Commons wasn't only an American but had a name you might recognize: Nancy Astor of the famous Astor family with whom we began this chapter. Two important prime ministers, Churchill and Macmillan had American mothers. The much publicized and much criticized close friendship between George W. Bush and Tony Blair is an example of the important British support of the unpopular American involvement in the Iraq War. And one last example is the close friendship between President Ronald Reagan and Prime Minister Margaret Thatcher, both of whom we've read about in this chapter and both of whom provide a fitting final connection between the two topics of this chapter: economics and international relations.

## Exercises

1. Name one member of one of the most illustrious families who made it all the way into the House of Commons.
2. Can you distinguish MacArthur from McCarthy?
3. Name a few concrete places mentioned in the chapter and try and relate them to the topics of economics and international relations.

Challenging interesting projects:

Try and meet some American tourists travelling in Germany and engage them in a conversation (not usually difficult since American tourists tend to be very friendly and talkative). Ask them to describe what they consider important about the American economy. Ask them how much vacation they have each year and how much their friends have. Then tell them the facts about the average length of German vacation and note their response.

Try and meet some British tourists travelling in Germany and engage them in a conversation (perhaps explain you're a student doing research for an important project). Ask them to describe the most characteristic aspect of the British economy. Then ask them as tactfully as possible if they think Britain should have a closer relationship with the US or with the EU. (The answers may depend on whether you have a recognizable German accent or perhaps an American or neutral accent.)

And finally the oh-my-god-if-you-can-do-this-you-could-become-a-21st-century-captain-of-industry-or-maybe-even-Head-of-the-UN tasks:

Come up with an economic policy that allows for the free markets that Americans know and love and at the same time doesn't allow for the kind of financial crashes that America – and then the world – had to endure in the 20s and again at the end of the first decade of the 21st century.

Devise a future foreign policy for Britain that allows it to maintain its close ties to the Commonwealth, an important part of its history and tradition, while at the same time assuming a role in the European Union that reflects its importance as a nation in and for Europe.

Think of an American foreign policy that doesn't veer wildly from isolationism (no assumption of international responsibility such as refusing to join the League of Nations or defying the United Nations' mandates) to expansionism (playing the world's policeman in naively trying to impose democracy on countries with little experience of this form of government) but does attempt to export the American dream of promise and decency and equality. You could look in detail at foreign policy under Secretary of State Clinton in the Obama administration to see if it fulfills these high goals.

And further topics not dealt with in this chapter... for those with time and passion and an interest in bucks, pounds, diplomacy, and such:

the American banking system with its risks; reasons for why socialism and communism never took hold in the US; the importance of labor unions in the US and even more so in the UK; MI-15, MI-16, James Bond and other spies like Guy Burgess, Anthony Blunt etc. and their role in international affairs; America's war against terror as an encore of a failed foreign policy; Britain as a former world power; America's exceptionalism as a better key to understanding foreign policy than the traditional dichotomy between isolationism and expansionism (8) ...

# Who, Where From, and Where To (minorities and immigration)

7

"Give me your tired, your poor,
Your huddled masses yearning to breathe free,
The wretched refuse of your teeming shore.
Send these, the homeless, tempest-tost to me,
I lift my lamp beside the golden door!"

The Statue of Liberty "cries with silent lips" in the last stanza of Emma Lazarus' poem "The New Colossus" engraved at the base of the Statue of Liberty

Life in the United Kingdom – A Journey to Citizenship
title of the official test book and study guide for those who wish to take the obligatory citizenship test in order to be given the right to stay in Britain

Who am I? Where did I come from? Where will I end up? These are maybe the three most common and serious questions that we can ask ourselves as human beings... and perhaps the most difficult too. If we were doing philosophy in this book, we'd have to spend at least a couple of thousand pages discussing categories and identity and logic and probably have to go back to Aristotle and maybe not even have any answers after all the time and trouble. But while we've already touched upon the complicated and fascinating issue of identity and will be doing so right until the very end of this book, we can make the job easier for ourselves if we agree at the beginning to limit our view of minorities to those groups which are also closely connected to immigration.

When you finish the chapter, you should be able to say something about

- the beginning and the waves of American immigration
- the main immigrant and ethnic groups in the US
- American Indians, African Americans, and Hispanics
- metaphors used to describe American society
- the beginnings of British immigration
- problems with the naming of immigrant groups in Britain
- Indians, Pakistanis, Bangladeshis, Afro-Caribbeans, Black African, Chinese in Britain
- the future of immigration in Britain.

We began with the British in the chapters on education and political life; let's start with the Americans in this chapter not only because immigration to America started earlier than to Britain in one important sense. Immigration has also been a much more important and integral part of American identity from the start. But the challenges of immigration in the United Kingdom are becoming increasingly important and changing the face of this country before our very eyes.

US immigration: where to begin?

You may remember that we had the problem of where to start in our history appetizer chapter. We have the same problem with immigration. If we define immigration as the movement of people from one place to another, then we could theoretically start with the first human beings who moved to what would later become the United States, whether these first humans were from Siberia or from the Pacific Islands or even from the European continent. We could also start with Christopher Columbus or any of the other famous and infamous European settlers who made their way across the ocean. Although the descendants of the people who were there when the Europeans arrived make up only a very small percentage of the population of America today, the American Indians – the real natives you could say – still form part of American consciousness in general and thus deserve their own part of this chapter. But before we have a look at the Indians and a few other minority groups in more detail, let's do a quick summary of immigration to the US and learn some commonly used terms when describing immigration in general.

waves of immigration

The image of waves gradually extending throughout an entire continent could be a useful way of imagining the first human beings having crossed the Bering Bridge from Asia to Alaska and then throughout both American continents although there are now other theories about where the very first Americans came from (2). The waves of immigration for the first hundred years across the Atlantic and then later across the Pacific have less to do with water than with peaks and troughs as immigration increased and decreased – sometimes dramatically. Let's have a brief look at four of these waves.

**Infobox**

**First wave** (cresting in the mid 19th century):

- from where: mostly from Western and Northern Europe (major countries of origin: Germany, Ireland, Britain)
- push factors: Irish potato famine, revolutions in Europe, political and religious persecution, overcrowding, unemployment
- pull factors: jobs, California Gold Rush

The American party was created in the mid 19th century as the first political party with the goal of creating laws to restrict immigration, especially of Catholics. Since members of the party were secretive, answering questions about the party with "I don't know," they gained the popular name "Know Nothings."

**Second wave** (from the late 19th to early 20th century with a very high peak just after the turn of the century):

- from where: mostly southern and eastern Europe (Italy, Hungary, Poland, Russia, Greece, Balkans and others), the first Chinese and Japanese immigrants
- push factors: poverty, religious and political persecution
- pull factors: effects of the Homestead Act (2), many jobs in industry and transportation (for example, the building of railroads especially using cheap Irish and Chinese laborers (2))

The Statue of Liberty was a gift from France to commemorate the French-American alliance during the War of Independence and arrived in New York in the late 1880s in time to welcome the millions of immigrants who began to arrive by ship in New York. On an island near the Statue of Liberty, a receiving station was opened up and Ellis Island became the first stop for millions on their way to a new life.

Laws and agreements drastically restricted immigration from Asia. Later at the end of the 1920s the Great Depression erased all America's economic pull factors, and government law began to restrict immigration from eastern and southern Europe by establishing quotas that favored the majority with western European heritage.

**Third wave** (from World War II to the 90s)

- from where: at first from Germany and Eastern Europe but increasingly from the Western Hemisphere (Canada, Mexico, Cuba and the West Indies), Asia (Philippines, Korea, India, China, Vietnam), and the Middle East
- push factors: war refugees (from hot wars like World War II, Korea, Vietnam, and from the Cold War), poverty, unemployment, political persecution
- pull factors: jobs, freedom and peaceful living conditions, family reunions

During World War II and especially after the attack on Pearl Harbor, Japanese-American citizens were subject to internment camps, which the US government officially apologized for – nearly half a century later.

Restrictive immigration policies were somewhat loosened and national quotas were gradually dropped, allowing a huge increase of immigrants from Latin America and Asia. Reunifying families became an important reason for the government to grant visas.

**Fourth wave** (still going on)

- from where: more than half of all immigrants come from Latin America (especially Mexico but also the Dominican Republic, Cuba, and El Salvador) and a quarter from Asia (especially the Philippines, China, India, Vietnam)
- push factors: poverty, desire to join relatives and family in the US
- pull factors: money and the chance of supporting their impoverished families just over the side of the border attracts growing numbers of Mexicans

This wave contains the biggest crest of any wave and the highest number of immigrants who ever came to the US in the 90s measured in absolute terms, but in the percentage of the total population the peak of the second wave in the late 19th century is still greater.

With the number of illegal immigrants growing, the government has given them the chance to seek legal status. The US now accepts more legal immigrants per year – on average roughly one million including those who are granted legal status while already in the US – more than any other country on earth. On the other hand in the wake of the 9/11 attacks some laws have been passed curtailing the rights of immigrants. And the building of controversial fences and walls along parts of the long border between the US and Mexico is an attempt to control illegal immigration.

After a glance at the great waves of immigration, let's have a more detailed look at a few minority groups. We'll begin with the one group who migrated a long, long time ago.

from Wounded Knee...

During a time when America was undergoing the same sort of cultural changes as Europe, when African Americans were demonstrating, and protests against the Vietnam War were filling the front pages of newspapers, a book entitled *Bury My Heart at Wounded Knee* appeared and became a bestseller that would change the way the relationship between the government and American Indians was portrayed. More than 35 years after the book's publication in 1970, an award-winning television film adaption appeared and reminded many viewers of the story of the massacre of the Lakota Sioux (pronounced su) tribe by the US Army near a small river called Wounded Knee.

... the Trail of Tears back to Wounded Knee

We've already encountered American Indians earlier and learned how they were moved – or more accurately – herded across the country by newer European immigrants hungry for land (2). We heard about what Manifest Destiny implied to the white Americans – the relentless move westwards all the way to the Pacific because it was the will of God (6). We could briefly summarize the fate of Native Americans in general as being a kind of westward movement like the movement that resulted in the United States eventually stretching from the east to west coast – with the very important difference that the Native Americans were driven further and further west by white settlers who needed more land. The Trail of Tears was started in 1835 by a president we've already heard of: Andrew Jackson, who believed that Indians were "savage hunters" (2). This forced movement west ended in 1890 at Wounded Knee in what was later to become the state of South Dakota with the massacre of the Sioux by the US Army. More than eighty years later armed supporters of what had become the American Indian Movement (AIM) seized the site Wounded Knee, demanding a US Senate investigation of Native American problems. Promises made by the US government were broken yet again. But in contrast to the 19$^{\text{th}}$ century, the 20$^{\text{th}}$ and 21$^{\text{st}}$ centuries have seen some progress in American Indians gaining some of the rights taken away from them.

Native American Indians?

Let's take a closer look at their status now and begin with the problem of naming. As is the case with many minority groups and, as we will see with African Americans and Hispanics in the US and with the Asians in the UK, naming can be a big issue. The term "Indian," as we learned in our first American history appetizer, can refer to the indigenous people who inhabited the American continents when the Europeans arrived or to those people living on the subcontinent India that some explorers were looking for when they stumbled upon a New World. One humorous way to distinguish the two is to add the phrase "with the feather" to designate American Indians or "with the dot" to designate Indians from India. The term "Native American" came into use in the 1960s in the US in an attempt to avoid one ambiguity but actually ended up by producing another ambiguity: all people born in the United States could be called Native Americans. And many people who might be called American Indians or Native Americans themselves prefer to be called by their tribal names, but which tribes should we choose out of the many hundreds present when the Europeans arrived? Alphabetically and geographically we could go from the Absentee-Shawnee Tribe, one group of Shawnees who lived by farming and hunting on the East coast, to the Zuni, one of the Pueblo peoples who lived as farmers in the deserts of the southwest. Perhaps better known are the nomadic Apaches and Navajos in the west, the Cheyenne in the Great Plains, the

Cherokees in the southeast. As you might have already noticed, we're using the name "American Indian" in this book since some surveys indicate that a majority of American Indians or Native Americans or Amerindians or Red Indians or Indigenous Peoples of the Americas prefer to be called "American Indians" although they also accept the term "Native Americans."

road to citizenship

Now that we've settled one fairly complicated issue, we can turn to the next rather complicated issue: the relationship between the American Indians and the federal government. One reason for the complicatedness is the degree of autonomy that the American Indians have had. The $14^{th}$ Amendment to the Constitution, which we've heard about in the context of the Reconstruction (2), had granted full citizenship to all people born or naturalized in the United States, but a Supreme Court ruling (Elk v. Wilkins) in the late $19^{th}$ century claimed that since the federal government made treaties with Indian reservations similar to treaties with foreign nations, the people born on these reservations couldn't be automatically granted American citizenship. The Indian Citizenship Act of 1924 finally granted full citizenship rights to all Indians.

current status

About 1% of all Americans claim to be at least partly American Indian with the majority of them living in western states like California, Arizona, and New Mexico. Some of the protests and reforms that began in the 70s have improved the life of American Indians nowadays although poverty and malnutrition are still big problems for American Indians living on reservations. But some tribes are able to make money from casinos or from tourism or from the management of the natural resources found on their land. The view of American Indians as savages, held not only by Andrew Jackson, is becoming more and more a relic of the past. While you might be able to find accurate portrayals of Indians in a few western films, perhaps it wasn't until Kevin Costner's very popular and award-winning film *Dancing with Wolves* in the 1990s that American Indians were presented as being neither the idealized noble savage nor the demonized brutal savage. But the film's story was set in Civil War times. It remains to be seen what the current and future role of the American Indian will be within the broader context of American identity.

from Negros to African Americans

We've begun our look at American immigrant minority groups with the American Indians, who in a sense didn't immigrate but were simply there first or at least there before others arrived. We'll continue now with the one group who didn't immigrate but were herded over on some of the very first ships that the Europeans sailed with to the New World. African Americans have been such a popular topic at German schools that you probably don't need much of a review here, so I'll try and provide you with some details that perhaps you weren't aware of. As with the American Indians, we'll begin with the problem of naming: Negros, Colored, Blacks, Afro-Americans, and African Americans. These are all names you'll find in sources, but only the terms African Americans and Blacks are commonly used nowadays. But before we look at the different names for African Americans, we need to look at the problems of the word "race."

race

The US Census Bureau has had a difficult struggle with using the word "race" in their statistics. In the past some thought that it was possible to use objectively definable characteristics such as skin color or facial features to be able to classify a human being as belonging to a particular race. A hundred and fifty years ago, the US government gave people the choice between three colors only: white, black, and mulatto. A few decades later with the increase of immigration from China and most probably the need to count American Indians the color palette was expanded to Chinese and Indian. Nowadays the Census Bureau gives people fifteen different choices for race with multiple choices possible, evidence of just how mixed Americans have become. The Census Bureau also admits that race categories include both racial and national-origin groups and are "sociopolitical constructs." It's sometimes difficult to believe that in just a half a century the issue of race has become a matter of personal choice and not a matter that could decide choice of school, which part of the bus, or which toilets people could use.

separate but equal?

We should perhaps do a quick review of history here. Although the Supreme Court decision Plessy v. Ferguson at the end of the $19^{th}$ century wouldn't contribute to another Civil War, the separate but equal doctrine contained in the decision was one reason why the equal rights promised to former slaves at the end of the Civil War would take another fifty years at least to be fulfilled. The Court's separate but equal decision confirmed the Jim Crow laws, which effectively set up a system of segregation in public buildings and public transport. Jim Crow was, by the way, a figure used in minstrel shows to ridicule former slaves. Jim Crow laws remained in effect until long after the end of the Gilded and the Jazz Ages (11).

separate can't be equal

The Supreme Court was to decide yet again on the separate but equal doctrine in the 1950s. Remember the story of Oliver Brown and his daughter, who wanted to attend a school near her home in Topeka, Kansas (2)? One of the oldest and most influential civil rights organizations in American history, the National Association for the Advancement of Colored People (NAACP, pronounced N-doubleA-C-P), encouraged Brown and other parents with the same complaint to sue, and four years later the Supreme Court ruled in the landmark decision Brown v. Board of Education that separate educational facilities were inherently unequal. This decision not only overturned the earlier Supreme Court decision Plessy v. Ferguson with its separate but equal doctrine but also paved the way for the desegregation of schools and further desegregation in general.

Deals for a Great Society

While we're on the topic of history, you may remember reading about the Square Deal (associated with Theodore Roosevelt, 2) and the New Deal (associated with another Roosevelt, FDR, 3). FDR's successor was Harry S. Truman, who attempted to have Congress pass some of the provisions of what he called a Fair Deal. Many of the programs in this Fair Deal were supposed to give the African Americans the full rights they should have gotten after the Civil War. But these programs weren't fully implemented until a generation after Truman with Lyndon B. Johnson's Great Society. (Johnson, by the way, was also known as LBJ – yet another example of the Americans' love of shortening the names of their presidents to three initials).

Speaking of names, we need now to return to the important issue of naming.

Colored, Negro, Afro-American

"Colored" as a name for African Americans was used as a polite euphemism until the middle of the 20th century and can still be found in organizations like the NAACP, founded at the beginning of the 20th century by a group of intellectuals including W. E. B. DuBois. The NAACP is still today a large and respected national organization with the goal of helping African Americans to achieve full equality (including helping in the Supreme Court case Brown v. Board of Education, as you might remember). "Negro," originally meaning merely "black," was commonly used until the middle of the 20th century and is still to be found in some organizations like the United Negro College Fund (UNCF), an organization founded in the 1940s to raise money for colleges and universities serving African Americans and scholarships for African American students. Nowadays Negro isn't used anymore as a name for African Americans and can be considered offensive. But during the Civil Rights Movement both the terms Negro and Black were used. Martin Luther King used both terms in his famous "I Have a Dream" speech in 1963. Gradually though "Negro" became replaced by "black" (either beginning with a small or with a capital letter), which became used in the expressions "black pride," "black power" and "black is beautiful." Another popular name associated with the late 60s and 70s is "Afro-American"; the word "afro" also referred to the large hairstyle associated with musicians like Jimi Hendrix and much more recently Lauryn Hill.

black, African American

"Black" as a name for African Americans has some disadvantages: as a description of skin color and racial characteristics it doesn't apply to all African Americans, and using the word "black" can also include immigrants from the Caribbean and South America who don't share the same heritage as the descendants of former slaves. While "African American" has also been criticized for its over emphasis on an African heritage which many African Americans may not identify with, the name has become along with "black" the most commonly accepted name for those Americans whose ancestors originally were forced to emigrate from Africa as slaves. President Barack Obama describes himself as black although his mother was white and his father was a student from Kenya who never became an American citizen and after Obama's birth returned to Africa. African American has become the most commonly used name partly perhaps because it makes an explicit comparison with other ethnic groups like German Americans or Asian Americans. Now that we've looked at names for African Americans in general, let's look at a few names of individual African Americans whom you may not know: W. E. B. Du Bois, Shirley Chisholm, Cicely Tyson.

W. E. B. Du Bois

If the name W. E. B. Du Bois rings a bell, then you were paying very close attention. He was one of the founders of the NAACP. Maybe you noticed his very French-looking name. His father was of French Huguenot ancestry. Du Bois attended the University of

Fig. 7.1 | *Du Bois postage stamp*

Berlin as a student in the late 19th century and became the first black ever to gain a PhD from Harvard. He became a leading sociologist in this new discipline, doing research into the situation of blacks in America. In contrast to another highly respected black scholar, Booker T. Washington (whom we could've chosen instead), Du Bois didn't believe in full integration and instead believed that agitation and protest were sometimes necessary. He wasn't only a political activist with the goal of equality for African Americans, he was also a peace activist and interested in Marxism, who visited the Soviet Union and China in the late 1950s. Always interested in Africa and embittered by US government treatment, he became a citizen of the African country of Ghana just before he died in his mid-nineties. In spite of his very critical attitude towards America the US Postal Service honored Du Bois with a special stamp in 1992.

Shirley Chisholm

Maybe you thought Hillary Clinton was the first woman to run for the presidency? While Clinton was the first serious contender to become the nominee of a major political party, the first black woman elected to Congress, Shirley Chisholm, was also the first African American to run for the nomination of one of the two major parties. Chisholm was born in New York, spent her childhood on Barbados, one of the islands of the West Indies, an area of the world with immigrants connected more with the UK, which we'll be hearing more about later. Chisholm's autobiography *Unbought and Unbossed* summarizes her determination to change the status quo of white male dominance in American politics.

Cicely Tyson

At first working as a model and later as an actress, Cicely Tyson has played strong African American women in films, among others Harriet Tubman, whom you might remember from history (🔔 2) as *A Woman Called Moses* (the title of the TV movie too), and Sojourner Truth, another abolitionist whom we didn't have room to mention in our look at the American Civil War. Tyson has also played much more recent important African Americans like Coretta Scott King, the wife of Martin Luther King , and Rosa Parks, the woman who refused to give up her seat to a white passenger in the mid-50s and who is now sometimes called the Mother of the Civil Rights Movement.

affirmative action

Before we turn to our next minority group, let's look at one government policy that has attempted to right historic wrongs not only for African Americans but for other minority groups as well. One of the important policy decisions of LBJ's Great Society program of the mid 60s, which we've mentioned briefly above, was the effort to improve opportunities in education and in employment for minorities and for women. Affirmative action was designed to give those who had suffered most from a history of discrimination preference in being accepted at universities and getting jobs in businesses that received federal funding. By the late 70s some began to criticize affirmative action as a kind of "reverse discrimination" that led to white students and job seekers not being given a chance to compete. By the end of the 90s many laws were being changed to prohibit government agencies from giving preference to individuals based solely on race or sex. One of the African American Democratic presidential nominee Obama's views in 2008 was that affirmative action should be applied by class and not race, a sign that overt discrimination based on race had to some degree changed.

One definite change in matters pertaining to immigrant minority groups is the rise of the Hispanics as the US's fastest-growing and now second-largest group. We'll begin our look at Hispanics with a familiar issue.

Hispanic, Latino, ...

As with the name American Indians or Native Americans, we have here a problem with naming too. The word "Hispanic" is currently commonly used to refer to people whose country of origin is one of the Spanish-speaking countries of the Western Hemisphere. The US Census Bureau designated four groups in the 2000 census: Mexican, Puerto Rican, Cuban, or "other Spanish, Hispanic, or Latino." As we will see with the word "Asian" in the UK, the term "Hispanic" isn't as popular with those identified by such a name as with those non-Hispanics who need a convenient category to classify other people. The Census Bureau had many subcategories for the Hispanics or Latinos in the 2000 census: Mexican, Puerto Rican, Cuban, Dominican Republic; Central American: Costa Rican, Guatemalan, Honduran, Nicaraguan, Panamanian, Salvadoran, Other Central American; South American: Argentinian, Bolivian, Chilean, Colombian, Ecuadorian, Paraguayan, Peruvian, Uruguayan, Venezuelan, Other South American; Other Hispanic or Latino: Spaniard, Spanish, Spanish American; All other Hispanic or Latino. What do almost all of these terms have in common? Right, they refer to a country of origin (except for the strange Spaniard and Spanish: can a Spaniard not be Spanish?), one common way to define minority groups who come from another country. Regardless of their country of origin, Hispanics are proud of their Spanish-speaking heritage, and they are currently the fastest-growing minority group in the US and recently overtook African Americans to become the largest minority group. While their language and their Roman Catholic religion are important characteristics that all Hispanics share, Hispanics themselves often prefer to be called by their country of origin. And the three largest groups, the Mexican Americans, the Puerto Ricans, and the Cubans, also differ from one another in many important ways.

Mexican roots

Let's start with the largest group (more than half of all Hispanics have roots in Mexico) who've also been in America the longest (more than 150 years): the Mexican Americans. The Mexicans, who won independence from Spain in 1821, had a large piece of land between the Rio Grande and the border of the Louisiana Purchase (2) but not many settlers, so they offered Americans moving west the chance to become Mexicans and gain land. We can thus see that in the early 19th century we have the unusual case of Americans becoming Mexicans. Conflicts led to the founding of the Republic of Texas. The call "Remember the Alamo!" originates from this time and refers to the Mexican execution of Texan forces in the Alamo mission. This defeat encouraged more resistance and eventually the victory of the Texans against the Mexicans. Texas becoming part of the US led to the Mexican-American War, which resulted not only in the first use of the phrase Manifest Destiny (6) but also in the ceding of a huge portion of land from Mexico to the US that would later become the states of California, Nevada, Utah, and parts of Colorado, Arizona, New Mexico, and Wyoming.

Mexican Americans or Chicanos or ...

Mexican Americans are the group with the most names, either the official one like Mexican American, or unofficial but accepted ones like Chicano or La Raza (which simply means "race" in Spanish and is also the name of a small political party and a local community newspaper for Mexican Americans in Chicago). In addition to their size and the long history of their heritage within America, Mexican Americans also share a common border with the country that gives them their name, a border that's more than 3,000 kilometers long and said to be the most frequently legally crossed border in the world. This border has posed political, social, and economic challenges on both sides; the American government has been debating building a wall or fence or other barrier to prevent illegal crossings. A huge march of legal and illegal immigrants on 1 May 2006 made worldwide news headlines and at least for a day put the needs of Mexican Americans on the front page. Mexican Americans have a history as poor farm workers and as a group are still economically disadvantaged. One of the heroes of the Chicano movement, a civil rights movement that began in the 1960s, is Cesar Chavez, a Mexican labor leader, who fought for the rights of the migrant workers.

Fig. 7.2
*Chavez postage stamp*

Another famous Mexican American is the musician Carlos Santana.

Puerto Ricans

We've already encountered Puerto Rico as a possible 51st state in one of our geography appetizers and in the last chapter too. Puerto Ricans form the second-largest group of Hispanics and began emigrating from their island in the Caribbean to New York City more than fifty years ago. (The United States had invaded and occupied Puerto Rico at the end of the Spanish-American War more than one hundred years ago.) Nowadays Puerto Ricans have spread both west to California and south to Florida and many places in between too, like Chicago. Poverty and low educational achievement have been persistent characteristics of Puerto Ricans in spite of the fact that they form the only Hispanic group to arrive in the US with US citizenship. But Puerto Ricans have also become very successful. The vast majority of Americans were in favor of Obama's nomination of Sonia Sotomayor to the Supreme Court, the first Hispanic and third woman to serve in the history of the Supreme Court. The number of Puerto Ricans living in the US is now almost 4 million and thus roughly equal to those living in Puerto Rico, an astonishing fact if we try to understand minority groups based on their country of origin. How will the Puerto Ricans define themselves when the majority of them won't have been born on the island that gives them their name but instead "stateside"?

Westside Story

All of you have no doubt heard of Ricky Martin, born in Puerto Rico, and Jennifer Lopez, born to Puerto Rican parents in New York, stars who are also popular in Germany. What you may not have seen is *Westside Story*, a popular Broadway musical and Oscar-winning film from the early 1960s with music composed by Leonard Bernstein and lyrics by Stephen Sondheim. Neither

Bernstein nor Sondheim had Puerto Rican roots, but *Westside Story*, a modern Romeo and Juliet, was written at the time when Puerto Ricans were immigrating in large numbers to New York City. You've probably at least heard the melody of songs like "Maria," "Tomorrow," or "America," in which Puerto Rico and Manhattan are compared rhythmically and humorously.

Some of you have perhaps seen episodes of the popular American 50s *I Love Lucy*. Lucy's husband both on and off screen was the Cuban American Desi Arnaz, who played a Cuban bandleader Ricky Ricardo in the series and who gave millions of Americans their first positive image of Hispanics. Arnaz wasn't only Lucy's husband but also a shrewd businessman and the producer of many popular television series. Cubans began to arrive in larger numbers towards the end of the run of *I Love Lucy* when Fidel Castro assumed power. The mostly middle-class and highly educated Cuban Americans were welcomed as political refugees by the American government. With their more privileged background, Cuban Americans are the wealthiest and most successful Hispanic group, and in spite of the American embargo they still have strong ties to their homeland and a strong sense of identity. The songs of the popular singer Gloria Esteban testify to the passion Cuban Americans feel towards their roots in Cuba. Partly due to the failure of the Bay of Pigs invasion, which America had supported in the early 60s in a failed attempt to depose Fidel Castro, Cuban Americans are mostly conservative Republicans politically. Cuban Americans are the third- largest group of Hispanics with more than one million mostly living in southern Florida, and they exercise considerable clout at the local, state, and federal level as Cuban American mayors and former mayors of Miami, senators and representatives from Florida and New Jersey, US ambassadors, and members of the cabinet.

Hispanic future

The future of America is Hispanic? When the US Census Bureau announced that the population had passed the 300,000,000 mark, many people wondered who exactly was the 300,000,000th baby. In one of the country's most ethnically diverse area, the borough of Queens in New York City, the local hospital proclaimed the baby of two immigrants from Mexico as the special one. Of course this was a publicity gimmick and there are others who claim to be number 300,000,000 including an Asian American baby and one with Jamaican and Puerto Rican roots.

Demographers can tell us with more certainty that 25% of all Americans under five years old belong to the Hispanic group and that the Hispanics are likely to make up a quarter of the entire population by the middle of the 21st century. We can also see the growth of Hispanics in the ranking of surnames: Garcia and Rodriguez have now made it to the top 10 of the most common American family names.

melting pot or pizza?

When you put together the American Indians with all their various tribes, the African Americans with their unique history as non-voluntary immigrants, German-Americans with their high degree of assimilation, and Hispanics with their strong pride in their own heritage and their reluctance to give up their identity, what do you get? A melting pot? A salad? A mosaic? A pizza? A mess?

The phrase "melting pot" became a widely known and used metaphor to describe American society more than a hundred years ago in a play entitled *The Melting Pot* by the English playwright Israel Zangwill, whose Russian Jewish parents had immigrated to London. Like the far more popular musical *Westside Story* fifty years later, *The Melting Pot* was also an adaptation of Shakespeare's *Romeo and Juliet*. In Zangwill's play, the two young lovers are Russian immigrants (typical, as we've seen, of immigration to America at the turn of the 20th century) and in contrast to Shakespeare and to *Westside Story*, *The Melting Pot* has a happy ending. The image of the melting pot is used positively as a promise of new identity (although would anyone every really want to be thrown into a melting pot?) in a scene with sunset and the Statue of Liberty in the background. Since then other metaphors have been created in an attempt to describe American society with a more complicated sense of American identity. The differences can be tasted as with "salad bowl" or "pizza" or heard as in "symphony" or seen as in "mosaic." Not many people would be surprised at images of America as a melting pot or salad bowl or mosaic. Minority groups and the American dream are simply too well known a part of what America seems to be – even if the metaphors don't always fit so nicely. Just as the past of America was defined by its immigrants, the future of the country will also be dependent on immigrant groups. And one possible explanation for Americans' enthusiasm for researching their family trees and finding out more about their roots stems from this need to know where they came from, one of the questions that we began this chapter with.

UK immigration: where to begin?

As we did with our survey of American immigration and minorities, let's begin here too with a brief look at immigration to the UK and the challenge of defining Britishness in the context of a multicultural country. We can apply what we've learned about the push and pull factors for American immigrant to immigrant groups in Britain too. We also begin with the same question as with American immigration: When do we begin? Based on what we've already covered in British history, we could begin as early as ... (have a look at the history chapter again to come up with a date). Should we look at the Romans as the first immigrants? We could also consider the Anglo-Saxon invaders, the Vikings, or the Normans as immigrants. But the Anglo-Saxons can no longer be identified as a group in Britain having merged with the descendants of the Normans almost a thousand years ago; and while the Vikings came to visit and plunder, they didn't stay. Another possible starting point for immigration to Britain could be the 16th and 17th centuries with Dutch Protestants and French Protestants (Huguenots) fleeing their homes because of religious persecution.

emigration vs. immigration

A glance at British history as a whole could indicate that in the last thousand years or so, more people left the island – as sailors or adventurers or colonists – than arrived there. And one current worry among some in the UK is that this trend has now returned with an increasing number of people leaving Britain. Britain already has a higher number of expatriots (citizens of one country living in another) than any other country except Mexico. We can also see the history of modern British immigration as having become increasingly restrictive. The first codified law was a truly imperial policy of granting the status of British subject (in a monarchy the equivalent of citizen) to all born in His Majesty's dominions: "His" Majesty since this Act was passed during the reign of George V at the beginning of World War I and "dominions" referring to much of what was the British Empire in the early 20th century (6). This first law had a long name: The British Nationality and Status of Aliens Act. In spite of the name "alien," which means both a person from a foreign country and a person from another planet, the policy itself was generous, providing the status of British subject to almost everyone born in practically all of the Empire. This generous policy was maintained with the British Nationality Act (shorter name at least), passed shortly after World War II, and recognizing that each member country of the Commonwealth was able to grant its own people national citizenship while allowing all 800 million inhabitants of the Commonwealth to maintain the status of British subjects with the right to live and work in the UK. This astonishing policy was possible because no one at the time thought many Commonwealth inhabitants would be coming to Britain.

Old and New Commonwealth

As, however, more and more people began to arrive in Britain to live and work in the 1950s and 60s and as former British colonies became independent, restrictions on immigration and the right to live and work in Britain increased. Finally the right of citizens of Commonwealth countries to automatically be entitled to live and work in Britain was abolished in the 80s. While we've already heard briefly about the changes from Empire to Commonwealth in other contexts, here we need to distinguish between the Old Commonwealth – countries with large white populations like Canada, Australia, and New Zealand – and the New Commonwealth (2, 6). New Commonwealth countries with large non-white populations include islands of the West Indies like Jamaica (with the largest group), Barbados, or Trinidad and Tobago. Other important national origins of immigrants to Britain include Asian nations like India, Pakistan, Bangladesh, and China; and African nations like Nigeria, Ghana, or Zimbabwe. While it would be a nice easy way to distinguish minority groups in Britain according to their country of origin, and it's the way we'll categorize our groups a little later, both historical developments and one African dictator have made the situation a bit more difficult to understand. But let's start with a simple fact and what came to be known as a very symbolic journey. After all, we still haven't decided about where to begin our story of immigration to Britain.

Windrush

A ship that had been used for Nazis to take vacation cruises as part of the "Kraft durch Freude" program and was later taken over by the British government and renamed the Empire Windrush sailed into the port of Tilbury in southeast England in June 1948 with around five hundred young immigrants mostly from Jamaica and Trinidad. With this voyage the modern era of immigration to Britain begins and the answers to what is really British become more varied. Before we look at those groups who look different, let's begin with a group that may surprise you.

the Irish?

Probably most people who hear the words "immigration, minorities, Britain" wouldn't immediately think of the Irish, but if we look at the number of British people who say that their ancestors come from another country, the Irish are by far the biggest group. People with British passports can easily acquire Irish citizenship if they have an Irish grandfather or grandmother. And if we consider that Northern Ireland is a part of the United Kingdom of Great Britain and Northern Ireland, then we automatically have a large minority group. Some surveys claim that up to 25% of all people living in Britain have some Irish ancestry. The 2001 census was the first to give all people the choice to tick Irish as the group they thought they belonged to. Numbers were far lower than expected perhaps because people confused Irish ethnicity with place of birth. The numbers will be very interesting in the next census in 2011 when for the first time ever respondents will be able to check English, Welsh, Scottish, British, and others as possible answers to national identity and ethnicity and thus give us a more accurate and probably more complicated picture of the British mosaic. The Irish as a minority group have one special characteristic that they share with the Puerto Ricans (other than their island status): there are more Irish abroad than live in Ireland itself. We've already learned about reasons why there are so many Irish abroad. One of the strongest push factors to drive people away from their homes is also one of the most basic human needs: hunger, and the Great Famine is one important event in Irish history (2).

what's in a name?

The Irish have at least a clear name for themselves (if you ignore some of the rarely used or clumsy names like British Irish or Irish Briton or Irish in England). You could ask along with Shakespeare's Juliet, "What's in a name?" but perhaps should remember that what happened to Juliet and Romeo because of their names wasn't very nice. Names are important as we've already heard again and again in our look at immigrant groups in the US – especially the names immigrant groups give themselves in comparison with the names they are given. We can start with a name that can be confusing depending on which variety of English you're familiar with and how much you know about world history. The largest immigrant group in Britain is often referred to in British English as Asian. What do you think of when you hear the word "Asian" or the German translation of the word? Probably not exactly the same thing that many Brits would think of and certainly not the same thing that's meant in British newspaper articles.

Asian: different names for different peoples

The term "Asian" in British English usually refers to immigrants from Bangladesh, India, Nepal, Pakistan, and Sri Lanka and excludes immigrants from East Asian countries like China or Korea, who are often referred to only by the country of origin. Some people resent being grouped together under one name that doesn't take into account some of the important differences between people born in India or Pakistan (or even people born in different parts of India or Pakistan). At least one of the original reasons for using Asian as a term for so many different groups of people had a good intention. If the Muslim from Pakistan could acquire an identity as Asian upon arrival in Britain, then maybe some of the violent disagreements between Muslim Pakistanis and Hindu Indians could be avoided.

African Caribbean and East African Asian

Another naming confusion points to groups that went through two major immigration journeys: the African Caribbeans as their name implies can trace some of their roots back to Africa in the 17$^{th}$ and 18$^{th}$ centuries when they were brought as slaves to islands like Barbados or Jamaica, then part of the British Empire. Large-scale immigration to Britain began as we saw after World War II – symbolically with ... (remember the name of the ship?). East African Asians first emigrated from India to other British colonies in East Africa like Uganda and Kenya. While they represent a group due to their place of origin immediately before coming to Britain, their ethnic grouping is varied. Most of them were professionals, and all of them had to leave their second homes in Uganda and Kenya after these colonies became independent countries. The Ugandan dictator Idi Amin expelled them in the late 60s and early 70s; some also left Kenya under the pressure of increasing African nationalization.

As you can see, some immigrants to Britain travel through various cultures and countries and continents before arriving. Even though immigrant groups are becoming more mixed, for the sake of simplicity we'll look at the groups separately. Keep in mind that all of the following groups made up large parts of immigration to Britain from the late 40s to the 60s. Legal restric-

**Infobox**

Names for this group: **Indian, British Indian, Indian British**

- When did they arrive?
  While most arrived in the 1950s, Britain had been active in India from the 17th century up until India gained its independence in 1947. Large parts of India were under the direct rule of the Crown for about a hundred years, and India has been a member of the Commonwealth since independence. Some Indians arrived after independence because of the violence that came with the partition of former British India into India and Pakistan. Other Indians who had gone to other British colonies in Africa like Uganda and Kenya were forcibly expelled when these former colonies became independent in the 60s and 70s.
- Where do they live in Britain?
  While British Indians can be found throughout England with fewer in Scotland and Wales, most live in London and the Midlands, where, for example, they make up almost a quarter of the population of Leicester.
- How many live in Britain today?
  According to 2006 government estimates more than 1.2 million live in England, thus forming the largest ethnic minority group in the UK.
- What are typical occupations?
  Indians work in a wide variety of jobs ranging from running their own corner shops to working in the medical profession (some first-generation immigrants from India were trained for the NHS, nowadays there are more than ten times more Indians working in medical professions than white Britons) and they are more likely to have managerial or professional occupations and to own their own homes than other immigrant ethnic groups. Some of Britain's most successful business people are of Indian origin, and the richest person in the UK is Lakshmi Mittal, a billionaire industrialist.
- What are some typical characteristics, specialties?
  The Indian community in Britain uses digital communication more frequently than the population as a whole. Their influence on British culture ranges from food (although many Indian restaurants are actually run by British of Pakistani and Bangladeshi origin) to popular films like *Bend It Like Beckham* (the film's director Gurinder Chadha was born in Kenya, → 8).

  And Bollywood – the nickname for the Indian film industry, a word play on Hollywood and Bombay (now called Mumbai, the largest city in India) – has its largest audience outside India now in Britain. By the way, the "dot" that we used humorously to distinguish American Indians from India Indians earlier in this chapter is called a bindi and is a forehead decoration worn by many women from India.
- And a couple of famous people...
  One you might not expect is Freddie Mercury, the lead singer of the band Queen, not only for his non-Indian sounding name but also because he kept his heritage a secret. Mercury spent much of his childhood in India. Those who know the actor Ben Kingsley from his role as Gandhi may not be surprised about his Indian origins. The prize-winning author Salman Rushdie has made his Indian heritage a central topic in many of his books (→ 8).

tions effectively stopped the flow in the late 60s, but immigrants from India, Pakistan, Bangladesh, the Caribbean, Black Africa, and China have changed the face of Britain forever.

future of immigrant minorities in the UK

To predict the future let's take a look at the past, choosing two violent events from the past and see what positive changes they brought about. We'll begin with one of the examples of minority culture that we've just covered: the Notting Hill Carnival, which most people would consider positive: music, parades, costumes, dancing, food. The reason for the celebration wasn't positive at all. In the late 1950s a series of riots took place in the Notting Hill area of London. Young poor white working-class men, provoked by politicians with slogans like "Keep Britain White," started to destroy Caribbean cafes and began to chase, attack, and seriously injure black Caribbean immigrants during a week in late summer. One result of the highly publicized riots and violence was the Notting Hill Carnival, which was supposed to demonstrate the positive influences of the Afro-Caribbean population living in this area of London. While some violence and disturbances still occur during the Carnival – with more than a million visitors the biggest in Europe – the news from Notting Hill has dramatically improved since the riots of the late 50s.

Stephen Lawrence

One April evening in 1993 two young black men were waiting at a bus stop in south London when a group of five young white men approached and stabbed the teenager Stephen Lawrence to death. Although all five suspects were tried, all five were freed because of "insufficient evidence." The outrage expressed by the public, by the press, and the campaign organized by Lawrence's family, who had emigrated from Jamaica, and their supporters resulted in a formal investigation and a report which revealed institutional racism in the London police force and proposed reforms. While the murderers still haven't been convicted, the Stephen Lawrence case was instrumental in changing law in England and Wales, allowing defendants to be retried for the same crime after being acquitted once. And the publicity surrounding the case put racism on the front pages of national newspapers. An annual architectural prize (Lawrence had planned to study architecture) as well as scholarships from the Stephen Lawrence Charitable Trust are awarded in his memory.

restrict immigration and restrict racism

We can see the past change in attitudes among some whites as a weakening of working-class solidarity and an increase in

**Infobox**

Names for this group: **British Pakistani**

- When did they arrive?
  If we take the name Pakistani literally as referring to Pakistan as the country of origin, then the earliest any could have arrived would have been in 1947 when Pakistan was created as a nation. Of course Muslims from British India had emigrated to Britain much earlier, but in much smaller numbers. British Pakistanis came to the UK for some of the same reasons that British Indians had: violence due to religious persecution and the wars between India (mainly Hindu) and Pakistan (mainly Muslim) after independence, and the economic needs of postwar Britain.
- Where do they live in Britain?
  Roughly an equal number of Pakistanis live in London, the West Midlands, Yorkshire, and the North West, making them a much more widely dispersed group than the Bangladeshis, Black Africans, and Black Caribbeans.
- How many live in Britain today?
  According to 2006 government estimates more than 800 thousand live in England, making British Pakistanis the second biggest immigrant ethnic group.
- What are typical occupations?
  Transport and communication industries, self-employed, taxi drivers.
- What are some typical characteristics, specialties?
  While British Pakistanis came from very different backgrounds in Pakistan, the overwhelming majority are Muslim.
- Just a few famous people...
  Mohammad Sarwar and Shahid Malik are Members of Parliament, Amir Khan is a well-known boxing champion, Sarfraz Manzoor a respected journalist. James Caan may share the same name as the American actor, but the businessman originally called Nazim Khan is one of Britain's most successful entrepreneurs. Hanif Kureishi is a famous writer whose work, like the screenplay to the film *My Beautiful Launderette* or the novel *The Buddha in Suburbia*, focuses on Pakistani or Indian life in a British context.

white racism, best summarized in the politician Enoch Powell's infamous "Rivers of Blood" speech in the late 60s, in which he warned against the results of too much immigration and advocated returning black immigrants to their country of origin. While there's evidence that the violence and xenophobia that began in the 50s in Britain is still present today, there's also evidence that a discussion of what it means to be British may be providing a more peaceful way to learn how to live together. While government law has dramatically restricted immigration from what had been an integral part of the old British Empire, government law has also attempted to ban racism and to encourage if not enforce integration. It's important to know that at the turn of the

20th century less than 1% of the population was foreign born, at the beginning of the 1970s the percentage had increased to more than 5% and less than forty years later almost one in ten of all inhabitants of the United Kingdom were born abroad, with a shift in the last few years from New Commonwealth to New European Union immigrants (whom we've not mentioned at all) as well as from the US (of all places!), Australia, and South Africa – thus reversing a trend started hundreds of years ago. And asylum seekers from war-torn countries in Africa and Asia are coming too.

How to become a Brit?

The test that the government devised in 2005 was supposed to ensure that all those who passed possessed "knowledge of life in the United Kingdom" and has become a requirement for all who wish to remain indefinitely in the UK. Maybe you noticed

**Infobox**

Names for this group: **Chinese, British Chinese, British-born Chinese**

- When did they arrive?
  The first recorded Chinese visitor was back in the court of James II (for those who don't want to check the history chapter when that was: in the late 17th century), but most Chinese arrived as the "takeaway generation" in the 60s from Hong Kong, making chow mein a popular dish. Many Chinese arrive from other countries, making multistep immigration journeys like the East African Asians.
- Where do they live in Britain?
  The British Chinese live throughout urban areas with Chinatowns in London, Manchester, Birmingham; the oldest Chinatown is in Liverpool.
- How many live in Britain today?
  According to 2006 government estimates almost 400 thousand live in England. British Chinese are currently the fastest-growing ethnic minority, most of which is due to net migration in the last five years.
- What are typical occupations?
  About half of all Chinese men work in hotels and restaurants. Many of the first Chinese immigrants in the early 20th century set up laundries, which they later converted to restaurants. British Chinese have the highest proportion managerial and professional occupations of any ethnic group.
- What are some typical characteristics, specialities?
  Chinese girls are the most likely to achieve the highest grades at school, and the Chinese are the group most likely to achieve university degrees, Chinese men and women have the lowest rates of disability.
- Just a few famous people...
  Ching He Huang is a TV chef, Baroness Dunn is the first person of Chinese descent to sit in the House of Lords as a life peer, Alex Yoong is a race car driver.

**Infobox**

Names for this group: **British Bangladeshi**

- When did they arrive?
  Bangladesh (former East Pakistan) came into existence after winning a war against the former West Pakistan in the early 1970s.
- Where do they live in Britain?
  The majority of Bangladeshis live in London.
- How many live in Britain today?
  According to 2006 government estimates more than 300 thousand live in England.
- What are typical occupations?
  Many Bangladeshis work in hotels and restaurants as chefs, cooks, and waiters. They are among the poorest of the immigrant ethnic groups and also have the highest unemployment rate.
- What are some typical characteristics, specialities?
  An area of East London now known as Banglatown because of its overwhelming Bangladeshi population has become popular for its many restaurants and lively market – evidence that it has become a positively different place than it was in the 70s where it was known for the scene of attacks by white racists. The overwhelming majority of Bangladeshis are Muslim.
- Just a few famous people...
  Pola Uddin is the first Muslim woman to gain a seat in the House of Lords. Well-known news reporters and television personalities include Lisa Aziz and Nina Hossain.

**Infobox**

Names for this group: **Afro-Caribbean, African Caribbean, Black Caribbean, the British Afro-Caribbean community**

- When did they arrive?
  Although some African Caribbeans have been in Britain for hundreds of years, the date of large-scale immigration is given with the arrival of the Empire Windrush as we saw a bit earlier.
- Where do they live in Britain?
  The overwhelming majority of Black Caribbeans live in London, larger groups also live in the large industrial cities like Birmingham and Manchester.
- How many live in Britain today?
  According to 2006 government estimates almost 600 thousand in England, thus forming the fourth-largest ethnic minority group in the UK.
- What are typical occupations?
  Public transportation, restaurants.
- What are some typical characteristics, specialities?
  Reggae music, the Notting Hill Carnival (details below).
- Just a few famous people...
  Television and radio personality, actor, comedian and writer Lenny Henry; model Naomi Campbell; journalist Trevor McDonald.

**Infobox**

Names for this group: **African British, Black British** (somewhat ambiguous since Black British can also refer to the Black Caribbean community)

- When did they arrive?
  While Black Africans have been part of British life to a small degree for a long time, many Black Africans began arriving in the 80s from Nigeria, Ghana, Kenya, and Zimbabwe.
- Where do they live in Britain?
  Almost 80 % of Black Africans live in London, according to the 2001 census, with Ghanaian communities in Tottenham, Peckham, and East London; but there's a small Somali community in Cardiff and Sudanese in Birmingham, showing the diversity of country of origin as well as geographical distribution in the UK.
- How many live in Britain today?
  According to 2006 government estimates almost 700 thousand live in England, thus forming the third-largest ethnic minority group in the UK, having recently overtaken the Black Caribbean community. Black African British are the second-fastest-growing group. Asylum seekers from Zimbabwe and Somalia have made a particular contribution to the growth in this ethnic group. The Nigerian British form the largest group from a single country of origin.
- What are typical occupations?
  Black Africans are the least likely of all groups to be self-employed.
- What are some typical characteristics, specialties?
  The growing number of second and third generation Black African British are making their mark on fashion, art, music, and food.
- Just a few famous people...
  Award-winning and controversial painter Chris Ofili; the first black Archbishop of York, John Sentamu, was born in Uganda (and thus is not one of the East African Asians mentioned above) and fled during the dictatorship of Idi Amin's (who had expelled the East African Asians) in the early 70s; television presenter June Sarpong.

the title of the guide at the beginning of this chapter: "Life in the United Kingdom – A Journey to Citizenship." I'm sure you would have noticed that the government guidebook, which was supposed to prepare people for the test, contained some embarrassing factual mistakes. But the government has come out with a revised handbook, and the BBC and British press has done its duty in ridiculing the whole matter while recognizing that the underlying intention is good. The end of the journeys that have brought millions of new people to the United Kingdom in the last half century should be citizenship. And the end of the journey should help to ensure that people of different cultural and ethnic backgrounds can live together on an island without killing one another and maybe even learn how to understand and appreciate one another's different roots. After all, the Irish, the Welsh, the English, and the Scots eventually learned to stop killing each other after centuries of doing so on the islands of Great Britain. In Ireland at least the carnage has been reduced. Maybe it won't take as long to stop the violence against the new British from the New Commonwealth.

**Fig. 7.3** *One delicious result of the integration of immigrants in London*

One factor of identity that has posed some problems in integration for many of the groups we've read about in this chapter is religion, which we've not described in detail yet. But religion is important enough to deserve a chapter of its own.

## Exercises

1. Look for an illustration of a street name in another part of the book (hint: think geography) and guess what relevance this street might have for the topic minorities UK.
2. How are American immigrant groups presented differently from groups in Britain in the chapter? (the easy part) Why? (tricky part)
3. Which group is missing from the US part of the chapter that, considering the intended audience of this book, you could've certainly expected to read about? (easy part) Why? (very tricky part)

Challenging interesting projects:

Keep a diary on your next trip to the UK and record all the evidence you can find about the influence of immigrants on everyday life in Britain. If you go to London, try and find evidence for (and maybe even a little evidence against) the claim that London is the most diverse city in the world.

Ask as many Americans as you have time to talk to about their ancestors (Americans love to do research on and to talk about their roots) and be prepared to note down lots and lots of foreign countries.

And finally the oh-my-god-if-you-can-do-this-you-could-get-a-statue-dedicated-to-you-on-Ellis-Island-or-get-to-lead-the-Nottinghill-Carnival-Parade tasks:

Come up with a definition of British and of American that both includes all inhabitants and gives all inhabitants a sense of where they came from, how they're different from other British and American people but also what they have in common. Maybe a definition of identity using civic and cultural characteristics rather than racial and ethnic ones will help. The creation of this identity should then help each person answer the opening questions of this chapter in a way that gives him or her not only a sense of identity but also the ability to live together peacefully.

And further topics not dealt with in this chapter… for those with time and passion for all things multicultural and the desire to discover even more roots and maybe even answer the three philosophically challenging questions at the very beginning of this chapter:

Asian Americans; Chinatowns; treatment of the Japanese during World War II; Little Italy; theories of assimilation and multiculturalism to explain immigration to the US and the UK; newer immigrants to the UK from Eastern Europe; influence of the caste system on British Indians; the combination of immigration laws and race relations policy as attempts at integration in Britain; …

# 8 | Weddings, Baptisms, and Funerals in The City on the Hill (religion)

"For we must consider that we shall be as a city upon a hill. The eyes of all people are upon us..." John Winthrop, "A Model of Christian Charity" 1640

Welcome to the Church of England [...] Life events: Planning a wedding? Arranging a baptism or confirmation? Organising a funeral? taken from the Church of England's website

If you've traveled in the US, you might have wondered about the vast number of churches in an astonishing variety of buildings that looked more like clothing stores, gas stations, or private homes (and often were gas stations or clothing stores before they were turned into churches). You might have wondered too about the variety of names on the buildings and the presence of advertising. You might have seen bumper stickers on cars or T-shirts with obviously religious messages. America seems to be a very religious country, and American politicians use religious phrases in a way unthinkable here or in Britain.

If you've traveled in Britain, you've probably either visited many beautiful cathedrals or tried to avoid the ABCs (another bloody church) included in most sightseeing tours. Religion is as important for British architecture as castles and palaces. Yet if you happened to attend the services in an English cathedral, say in the beautiful cathedral in Gloucester, for example, as I did, you might have been surprised at how much room there was inside and about how few people were there for Holy Communion or even for the Sung Eucharist. The local Marks and Spencer would easily win a popularity contest with the soaring space of the Cathedral.

In this chapter you'll be finding out more about the presence of religion in the US and in Britain. To understand what role religions play in modern American and British life, we'll need to use some of the information provided in the chapters on history, political life, education, minorities and immigration, and the arts.

When you finish the chapter, you should be able to say something about

- the importance of religion and of the Puritan heritage for Americans
- the paradox that religion in America is both diverse and similar
- concrete examples of a range of American religions and denominations
- the interaction of religion with other areas of American life
- the importance of the separation of church and state and the concept of Civil Religion
- some consequences of the fact that the Church of England is an established church
- current controversies in the Church of England
- the role religion plays in identity of adherents of non-Christian religions in Britain
- future challenges that religion in general will face in both the US and the UK.

Puritan heritage

John Winthrop, a Puritan from England who became a colonial administrator in the New World and was elected governor in what was to become the Massachusetts Bay Colony, gave a sermon either before leaving England for the New World or on the ship just before landing. His words have been quoted through the centuries to express a view Americans have of themselves and a view that others have repeatedly used to describe America. As early as 1630, long before the settlements on the east coast of North America were to form a new nation, the first settlers were thinking of themselves as true pioneers in a very religious context. Winthrop was one of many English settlers who left their homeland because they were dissatisfied with the established church there, the Anglican Church founded by a king who was – the irony is almost unbelievable – especially honored for his loyalty to the Roman Catholic Church and for his resistance to the Reformation.

American exceptionalism

Winthrop was one of many Puritans and Pilgrims to sail to the New World in the 17$^{th}$ and 18$^{th}$ centuries; their beliefs have influenced many mainstream American Protestant denominations. The Puritan tradition is one of the main factors that sociologists have used to try to describe American society: Americans have a special role in the world ("exceptionalism"), democratic decisions are preferable to hierarchical structures, hard work and wealth are positive virtues, pleasure for its own sake is bad, intolerance towards other faiths justified. Although the Puritans fled England because of religious persecution there, they themselves were intolerant of other beliefs. This intolerance antagonized other settlers and resulted in another key characteristic of American religious experience: the importance of religious freedom.

Roger Williams, religious freedom, Baptists

Roger Williams, another Puritan emigrant from England, believed strongly in religious freedom, in a "wall of separation" between religion and the state. He was probably bothered by Winthrop's assertion that the Puritans were building their own city on the hill without taking into account that the hill belonged not to the settlers but to the American Indians: Williams was an early champion of the rights of the Native Americans. He soon left what later was to become the state of Massachusetts and settled another area on the east coast which was later to become the state of Rhode Island. Williams not only founded the colony of Rhode Island but by baptizing fellow settlers he also came to be considered the founder of the first Baptist Church in the New World. The Baptists are currently the largest Protestant denominational family in the US; the conservative Southern Baptist Convention is the largest single Protestant group in the US; common to all Baptist denominations is adult baptism.

wall of separation

What so many of the early English settlers shared was their religious motivation. This historical fact can help us to understand the importance of religion in everyday American life. The Founding Fathers – those men who were instrumental in the founding of the new nation and who wrote and signed the Declaration of Independence and the Constitution – were almost exclusively Christian but from at least half a dozen different separate denominations. Their differences and their common experience of the suffering that an established state church could inflict no doubt helped to lead the writers of the Bill of Rights to use William's "wall of separation" in the very first words of the very 1st Amendment to the Constitution: "Congress shall make no law respecting an establishment of religion, or prohibiting the free exercise thereof." What seems to be a clear separation, a high wall between matters of the churches and matters of the state, can actually seem to be full of contradictions. Before we look at some of these contradictions, however, we should have a look at another possibly contradictory feature of religion in America.

While America is often described as having an incredibly diverse religious culture, we could with as much evidence say that American religious experience is astonishingly uniform. What perhaps is also astonishing is the lack of conflict among the groups – especially if we compare the long and bloody history of religious conflict in the UK, a history which has continued to the present in Northern Ireland. One possible explanation for this lack of violent controversy might be the tendency for American Protestant denominations to simply split or unite with other churches when disagreements surface. Another explanation might be the general underlying sense of sharing other common characteristics that transcend the differences among the various denominations. In addition to the unifying factors of the Puritan heritage, the common sense of most Americans being able to call themselves WASPs (White Anglo-Saxon Protestants) provided a sense of identity. While the WASPs are now heading towards minority status, common characteristics of what has become known as civil religion, which we'll turn to again later in this chapter, might still be enough to continue the sense of uniformity in matters of religion. diversity

Evidence that shows the uniformity of religious attitudes in the US can be seen in the results of surveys: more than 80 % of all Americans believe in heaven and 70 % believe in hell compared to 38 % of all Germans who believe in life after death. Only 15 % of all Americans feel that religion is not very important in their lives. So even with the large number of different denominations having split and united in the past two hundred years, many Americans still share some basic attitudes towards the importance of religion in general. uniformity

Want an example of splitting and uniting? Methodism, for example, started with the "methods" taught by John Wesley, an English theologian who left England as an Anglican missionary and visited my home town of Savannah, Georgia, during colonial times (The Wesley Monumental United Methodist Church is still there). Methodists then and now

He met some German Moravians there and even translated some of their songs into English. Later he became convinced that salvation was possible through individual faith in Jesus Christ and thus founded Methodism as an alternative to the formal hierarchy of the Church of England especially for the working

Fig. 8.1 | *John Wesley*

denominations and enumerations

classes. One Methodist Church soon divided into many different churches: the African Methodist Episcopal Church and the African Methodist Zion Church for blacks, many of them freed slaves; the Methodist Episcopal Church South was founded by slave owners; the Free Methodist Church developed, as did the Christian Methodist Episcopal Church. Holiness Churches and the Church of the Nazarene were also branches of Methodism, as were small German ethnic denominations. Later, starting in the 20th century, some of these smaller denominations began to unite to form the United Methodist Church, the second largest Protestant denomination, but there are up to 40 other denominations that also call themselves Methodists or share some of the same characteristics.

The splitting and uniting of religious groups, which has perhaps helped to maintain a general atmosphere of tolerance in the US, results in a dizzying number of names of groups with dizzying estimates about numbers. If you were interested in finding out just how many Catholics or Protestants are living in Germany, you probably wouldn't have a hard time (as long as you consider belonging to a church to be more or less equivalent to paying church tax) since the German government is involved in taking in church tax. As we'll later see in Britain, although church membership isn't documented in any official way as it is in Germany, the numbers of people who feel part of which religion are relatively easy to come by. In the US the situation is entirely different. Although a national census has existed since 1790, there are no questions about church membership due to the constitutional separation of church and state. This lack of governmental statistics is offset, however, by numerous surveys and scholarly research projects. One piece of evidence for the diversity of American religious groups is the sheer number of separate churches. The main Christian denominations are probably familiar to most of us in Germany: Catholics, Baptists, Methodists, Lutherans, Presbyterians. But even these few familiar names can be misleading since there are often big differences within some of the same denominational families. The Southern Baptist Convention, for example, is far more conservative than the Cooperative Baptist Fellowship, which ordains women; but both could be considered part of the Baptist denominational family. And what words should we use to capture this diversity: religion, branch, denominational family, denomination, religious body, congregation, church, sect, or cult? Should we use names like Western Liturgical, Pentecostal Family, Adventist Family, Communal Family to categorize American religions? Or just leave the whole thorny issue to philosophers?

denominations to choose from

Assuming that we've all agreed to let philosophers deal with the categorizing, let's turn to just two specific examples. Of the many different denominations or churches or religious groups to choose from, I'd like for us to look at two in somewhat more detail, not because they're the largest – Roman Catholics, Baptists, and Methodists are larger – or because they're the oldest – many current Protestant denominations like the Methodists, Lutherans, Presbyterians, and Episcopalians, and Church of Christ can trace their history in some form back to the colonial period. Many of us – even those who haven't been to the US – might have had some sort of personal contact with one of my examples. The other example – one of the popular choices of student-teachers in my Anglo-American Studies courses – is connected to a language that would sound strangely familiar to many of us.

Mormons

A young boy with the common American name Joseph Smith receives a vision in a grove of trees in a small town in upstate New York around the year 1820. Someone whom the Mormons would later call a "prophet" but who often resembles an angel on the Mormon temples with the very uncommon name Moroni tells young Joseph where he can find gold plates, which an ancient American prophet Mormon used to record the story of his people in an ancient language that Joseph has to translate. Ten years later the first printed versions of the Book of Mormon are available – not on gold plates of course – and a great American success story begins. For some reason – maybe envy because of the rapid increase in the number of converts, maybe because Smith was said to have behaved like a monarch and to also have practiced polygamy – the early Mormons made enemies and were driven westwards: to Missouri, Ohio, Illinois. A mob murdered both Joseph Smith and his brother in their prison cell in Illinois where they were awaiting trial for inciting violence. The loss of their leader didn't stop the believers, who called themselves "latter day saints": "saints" in the meaning "set apart" and "latter day" since they believed that the original church that Jesus Christ founded had to be restored much later. As they moved further west, they – typical of so many American denominations – split into several groups, some of which have remained separate until today. The majority moved across the Rockies to what is now Utah and settled around what was to become Salt Lake City. Brigham Young became the leader of the Latter-Day Saints, had many wives and even more children. The issue of polygamy caused the American government to send troops into the Utah territory and an outright military conflict was narrowly avoided. Official church doctrine later condemned polygamy.

education and missionary work

Brigham Young University was named after the second leader of the Mormons, has an abundance of foreign language courses, runs a large study-abroad program, and seems not to have the problems with drugs or binge drinking that other American universities are faced with. The honor code which BYU students and faculty have to adhere to includes regulations about clothing, about facial hair for men, and about sexual activity. The issue of academic freedom at a religious university has been the subject of public debate in the US. In German cities you've probably seen Mormons; their clean-cut appearance with their white shirts and ties usually sets them apart, as does their friendly approach and their thick American accent combined with a surprising command of German. Missionary work is considered an important task for Mormons; the official website of the Church of Jesus Christ of Latter Day Saints is attractively designed and available in more than twenty languages.

the Puritan tradition and the search for one's roots

The Mormons in America and abroad display some of what could be considered Puritan traditions: no alcohol, no tobacco, not even coffee is allowed; premarital sex is condemned too. On the other hand although divorce isn't encouraged, it's not prohibited. The Mormons could also be considered a typical American phenomenon for other reasons: the movement west to a newer and better life, the belief in economic progress, the belief in individual responsibility and the obligation for individuals to participate actively in the church. The Mormons have also made the search for one's roots – genealogy – much easier by creating a huge online databank of information. And America as a country of immigrants is also a country in search of where it came from. In contrast to most of the other religions and denominations in the US, the Mormons are a "home-grown" religion having been founded in America and still having the majority of their believers there – although their missionary work has caused the church to grow in other countries too.

critical views

Aspects that have been criticized about the Mormons are the authoritarian structure of the church, the treatment of minority groups and of women. Blacks were excluded from becoming ordained until the 1970s, women are excluded from all positions of leadership. The tensions between the government and the Mormons, which began with the banning of polygamy at the end of the 19th century, have continued into the 21st century. The deep-seated American belief in the separation of church and states seems at odds with the theocratic structures of the Church of Jesus Christ of Latter Day Saints. You can experience one critical but also moving view of the Mormons in the acclaimed Pulitzer Prize-winning two-part play *Angels in America*, written by Tony Kushner and first performed in 1990 and in 1992, which won Tony Awards as Best Play two years in a row. The play was later made into a multi-award-winning television miniseries starring Meryl Streep, Al Pacino, Emma Thompson and directed by Mike Nicols.

Not only in Utah has the height of the wall separating church and state been tested; on the other side of the US, in what would seem to be another world, issues of church and state have also played a significant role.

Amish

*Ordnung, hochmut, demut, gelassenheit, herumspringa*: these words probably won't appear very foreign to you (except maybe the last one) … or to around 150,000 people in parts of Pennsylvania, Ohio, and Indiana, who probably dress and look very different from most of the readers of this book. The Amish are a very unusual group of devout farmers, who have managed to resist most of what we all take for granted in modern civilization. This time the story starts not with a young boy but with an old man, Jakob Amman, a Swiss Anabaptist (one early branch of what later developed into quite a few Protestant denominations, among others the Baptists). He believed in the principle of *meidung*, of excommunicating believers who didn't follow strict rules. Because the followers of Amman were persecuted in Europe, they fled to the New World, like other religious groups, and began to call themselves the Amish after the old Swiss man. The Amish arrived in an area called Pennsylvania and still look and act much as they did almost 300 years earlier. Pennsylvania, literally Penn's Woods, was named after William Penn, a member of the Quakers, another small but interesting religious group that still exists today. Penn was, like Roger Williams and other American colonists, a fervent believer in religious freedom. Perhaps you've seen or even eaten the famous Quaker Oats cereal with William Penn's picture on the package?

Amish as tourist attraction?

But now back to the Amish. Their appearance and customs are what sets the Amish apart and makes them so interesting – certainly for tourists of the Pennsylvania Dutch area (called Dutch not after the people in Holland but after what non-German-speaking Americans understood as *Deutsch*). The Amish mostly avoid the use of electricity and telephones and cars, use buggies for transportation and horse-drawn ploughs for farming; the men wear broad-brimmed hats and the women bonnets, and men and women use hooks instead of buttons on their clothing. While tourists have helped the economy of the Amish by buying bread or beautiful quilts, tourists have also caused problems by photographing them – *ablichten* is the word the Amish use. The Amish regard photography as breaking the Second Commandment and as a sign of vanity. Some even see photographs as a kind of theft of their souls. Ironically, the Amish are sometimes regarded as the most photographed ethnic group in the world.

Amish characteristics

While the *ordnung* determines the concrete regulations for the use of modern technology and dress for each community, in general the Amish are forbidden to marry outside the community, they are supposed to avoid *hochmut* and strive for *demut*, to show *gelassenheit* even when confronted with outsiders who aren't tolerant of their special way of life. After a period of teenage *herumspringa*, young adults are baptized and accepted as members of the church and community. The long Sunday services are conducted in individual homes and are followed by the entire community eating together. While many Amish are still farmers, some work in non-agricultural areas. The Amish are growing quickly with no contraception allowed and large families encouraged. Perhaps it's difficult to understand for most non-Amish, but the number of young people who decide to leave these isolated communities is low. One movie popular in Germany that made aspects of Amish life visible including the tradition of barn raising was Australian director Peter Weir's 1985 film *Witness* starring Harrison Ford.

wall of separation, again...

The Amish have tested the height of the famous wall of separation between church and state in several court cases. The Amish are not forced to pay into the Social Security system as almost all other Americans do since the Amish believe their community is responsible for the welfare of all its members. The Amish were also granted an exemption from military service even in wartime because of their belief in non-violence but were required to do their obligatory military service in civilian jobs during World War II. The belief that regular school attendance was unnecessary for a life within the community resulted in a famous Supreme Court case that gave the Amish the right to be exempt from obligatory education requirements after eighth grade. Amish children attend the first eight grades of school in one-room classrooms at private religious schools. The tragic Amish school shootings in 2006, in which a gunman killed five young Amish girls and then himself, catapulted the gentle pacifist Amish into unwanted world attention. The Amish response – asking for forgiveness for the murderer instead of retribution – was very moving testimony to the importance of non-violence and charity in this unique community (🔔 4).

"In God We Trust"

As we have seen, the strict separation of church and state as stated in the First Amendment to the Constitution leads to interesting issues with concrete religious groups such as the Mormons and the Amish. We can easily find more well-known examples for what seems to be a contradiction in American public life: in spite of the First Amendment religion seems to play a central role in American life in ways that would seem foreign to the English or to the Germans. Take a look at any American coin – say the penny or the nickel or the dime or the quarter – and you can find not only the presidents Lincoln, Jefferson, Roosevelt, and Washington on the front but also the words "In God We Trust." The word "God" thus appears each and every day in millions of American transactions. The words "In God We Trust" appear not only on all regular coins in circulation but also on beautiful new $50 dollar gold coins. The phrase was first used shortly after the Civil War but didn't become common on all coins until the beginning of the 20th century and not on paper money until the late 1950s when it was also officially adopted by Congress as the national motto. Although the use of this motto has been debated heatedly in the context of the separation of church and state, it

Fig. 8.2
*American Eagle gold bullion*

has been adopted on other official American signs like the new state flag of Georgia.

"God Bless America"

At the beginning of each school day millions of American students stand in front of the American flag to say the Pledge of Allegiance including the words "one nation under God." Congress opens with a prayer, presidents swear on the Bible during their inauguration, "God Bless America" isn't the national anthem but is much easier to sing and no doubt sung more often than the official "Star-Spangled Banner." Political speeches often seem to be religious in a way that would be impossible in Germany and sound strange in Britain. On the other hand, there are no official religious holidays like in both Germany and in Britain, and school prayer in all forms has been declared unconstitutional in all public schools since the early 1960s.

contradictions?

Some issues involving religion in America cause heated controversies at a level that's difficult for Germans to understand. The debates about allowing school prayer in public schools, for example, have continued ever since the Supreme Court ruled in the early 1960s that according to the First Amendment to the Constitution school prayer in public schools was unconstitutional. What had been accepted in the hundred years or so of American education as something normal – Christian prayer being a part of each school day – has become a matter of great public debate and has even led to attempts to create a new amendment to the Constitution specifically allowing school prayer. Even though probably a majority of Americans would support some sort of voluntary school prayer, the attempt to pass an Amendment hasn't been successful, partly due to how difficult the procedure to amend the Constitution is (5). You can read regularly of court cases in which manger scenes or the Ten Commandments have to be removed from public buildings – often in spite of protests by local residents from communities which are relatively homogeneous in regard to religion. Thus even with the clear separation of church and state in the 1st Amendment, the issue of how much separation is possible and necessary before freedom becomes impaired is an issue that remains debatable, even more than 200 years after the 1st Amendment to the American Constitution was ratified as part of the Bill of Rights.

American-German differences

The strict separation of church and state has resulted in issues that not only lead to controversies within the US like school prayer in public schools or religious symbols in public spaces, the separation of church and state can also lead to public misunderstandings between the German and American government. The US Department of State, for example, has criticized Germany for not respecting the religious freedom of minority religious groups like Scientologists or Jehovah's Witnesses. I remember being surprised by the very strong emotions on both sides when a few prominent American politicians and celebrities openly criticized what they saw as the German government policy of prohibiting practicing Scientologists from entering the country. While Scientology manages to evoke strong emotions and has been severely criticized in the US, at least some prominent American critics of German policy mentioned the importance of the freedom of religion as central to American criticism. While Scientology is certainly controversial in the US, perhaps one sign of the diversity of American religious belief is the tolerance and acceptance of a wide range of groups as serious religious denominations, groups that in Germany would be called *Sekte* with all the negative connotations of the word.

religion and sexuality: gays

Other areas of life where religion plays a role to an extent in America that seems extreme in most Western secularized countries are sexuality, the media, and politics. One example that has also made the news in Germany is Exodus International, an interdenominational organization with the goal of "freedom from homosexuality through the power of Jesus Christ." While I personally as a gay man would resent the influence of such an organization, the underlying principles are typical of American religious experience and perhaps in some ways of the American way of life in general: there are clear-cut boundaries between "good" and "evil" and redemption is possible through hard work. Other religions in America have far different attitudes towards sexuality. While the Puritan influence (no sex outside marriage, homosexuality as an abomination, no birth control) is visible in many Protestant denominations in the US, we should also note that the first openly gay Episcopal bishop was ordained in America and that same-sex unions are blessed in some denominations and that even some traditionally Protestant denominations have allowed same-sex marriage ceremonies. (The Episcopal Church is, by the way, the American branch of the Anglican Communion, which we'll be dealing with in the British part of this chapter.)

American Catholic bishops take a more liberal stance on issues of birth control than some bishops in Germany, and the Metropolitan Community Church, founded in the late 60s in Los Angeles, was the first organized Christian religion explicitly embracing gays and lesbians.

religion and the media: televangelism

The longing for answers and guidance combined with the belief that self-improvement if in the guise of redemption is possible also explains the popularity of televangelism, at first a uniquely American combination of television and evangelism that has since spread to Britain and to other parts of the world. It might seem easy to ridicule the entertainment factor of televangelists and parody their hypocrisy – famously done, for example, by the pop band Genesis (strangely enough, a band named after the first book of the Bible). Televangelism isn't anything new in American religious experience but can be traced back to revivals, the "Awakenings," which contributed to the success of the Mormons, for example, have happened again and again in American history. While the revivals in the 18$^{th}$ and 19$^{th}$ centuries could last for days, the radio broadcasts by such famous evangelists as Billy Graham in the 1950s, and later television broadcasts by Rex Humbard, Robert Schuller, Oral Roberts, and Jimmy Swaggart were just a few hours long but at times managed to combine professional showmanship in addition to a sign of sincere faith. The format of televangelist broadcasts today can range from filmed church services with preaching and singing to talk shows with guests. Televangelism has been seriously criticized for its isolationist tendencies that encourage believers to stay in the comfort of their home instead of joining a community or for its simplistic promises made in return for donations, for its overt sales pitches, or for its proven cases of fraud. Televangelists were involved in well-publicized sex and money scandals in the 1980s just as they had reached the height of their political power. The future of televangelism is most probably tied with the future of media in general; in a post-television society the revivals from early America will no doubt adopt new forms.

religion and politics: power

The political power of Christian fundamentalists in the 1980s helped to elect Ronald Reagan as president. Jerry Falwell, a televangelist and founder of Liberty University (with Brigham Young University, which you may remember reading about earlier, as a model), organized the so-called Moral Majority, a political lobby that reflected fundamentalist Christian values: against abortion, for traditional families, against homosexuality, for increased military spending, against expansion of social welfare programs, for media censorship. While the Moral Majority as an organization was disbanded in the 1980s, one of its successors, the Christian Coalition, founded by the famous televangelist Pat Robertson, continues to exist and claims to be the largest and most active conservative grassroots political organization in America and contributed to the reelection of George W. Bush in 2004. In spite of the success of fundamentalist Christian churches and organizations, the views of Christian fundamentalists certainly can't be taken as common to all Americans. One best-selling reply to the fundamentalist surge has been written by former president Jimmy Carter, a professed devout Christian himself, who argues for a separation of church and state, a separation that Christian fundamentalist organizations have been trying to narrow. Whether Carter's view is a sign that the pendulum is now swaying back towards a higher wall between things religious and things political remains to be seen. The ongoing discussion of the separation of church and state is certainly one aspect of the kind of religious glue uniting the divergent strands of American religious experience.

civil religion

Another kind of social glue that has prevented religious revolution and violence of the kind all too common in so many societies is something that has been named civic or civil religion. This phenomenon is based on among other things a common tradition. All the religions we've mentioned so far would fit into what is often called the "Judaeo-Christian tradition"; although the individual denominations may vary widely – as we've seen by comparing the Mormons with the Amish – a common Christian heritage is evident. When we add the Jews, who make up only around 2 % of the population but who have greatly influenced many aspects of American life (the arts, business, education), we can create a background that probably most Americans would identify with. This shared sense of identity may indeed change with the increase in immigrants from parts of the world that don't share a Judaeo-Christian heritage (Asia for example). Already the common strand of identity called WASP (white Anglo-Saxon Protestant) has been changed by the influence of the Hispanics, who are overwhelmingly Catholic and are proud of their language and their culture (7). The challenge of maintaining a cultural identity that everyone can accept will be one of the major challenges for Americans in the 21st century (12).

Civil religion has been a common "faith" of very many Americans. The fervor with which some Americans sing the national anthem or speak about the Constitution or affirm their belief that Americans are a chosen people could seem on par with religious feelings in other cultures. Symbols and rituals such as the saying the Pledge of Allegiance, celebrating the Fourth of July or Presidents Day with a reverence for the presidents that seems to put them on par with saints, the use of "God Bless America" as a tag line in many speeches, putting the American flag on the altar in churches: all these examples are evidence of a shared sense of what's important or sacred.

**Fig. 8.3**
*An unusual combination of church and rocket found only in America (Church in Maryland).*

American holidays, not holy days

Presidents Day, celebrated on the third Monday in February, used to be called just Washington's Birthday and used to be celebrated really on Washington's birthday (Washington can be seen on the old quarter and on the new gold dollar coin). Monday holidays have become popular to ensure that federal and most state workers have a long weekend and also to encourage business and shopping (6). The Monday holiday Presidents Day also honors Lincoln (who can be seen on the penny and the new silver dollar coin) and in some states other presidents too.

**Fig. 8.4**
*Washington Presidential Dollar coin*

Another aspect of America's civil religion is manifested in the Greco-Roman "wedding cake architecture" you can find all over the country. The question remains to what extent Americans from other cultures can identify with the Greco-Roman tradition embodied in the monuments of Washington, D.C. for example, and to what extent they can accept aspects of the American dream such as self-reliance, hard work, individual material success as a sign of being blessed, balanced by volunteerism and a sense of work for a larger community. John Winthrop's proclamation of founding a "city upon the hill" for all the world to look upon is still common currency in American life. To come up with a more precise description of what this "city upon a hill" should look like with its new immigrants and new non-Judaeo-Christian religions will remain an ongoing task for Americans in the future.

|Fig. 8.5
*Lincoln Silver Dollar coin*

|Fig. 8.6
*Not a temple but the Capitol of the United States in Washington, D.C.*

|Fig. 8.7
*Not a temple but the Jefferson Memorial in Washington, D.C.*

Church of England

In Britain there seems to have been no need for a civil religion, perhaps because the Church of England (often abbreviated to CoE) serves the purpose of granting a sense of identity – at least for the English – at a relatively low cost: there are no church taxes as in Germany, the variety of doctrine and belief and even of church services is astoundingly great for one religion. Some parishes with "high churches" are closer in their use of ritual and celebration of hierarchy to the Catholic Church; the "low churches" have less formalized services.

monarch as head of church

Unlike many other religions, the origins of the Church of England can be dated precisely to several documents. Henry VIII didn't intend to start a fully new religion – he was after all opposed to the Reformation and to Martin Luther at first and

**Fig. 8.8** *Gold coin with Edward VIII*

**Fig. 8.9** *Gold Britannia coin*

had even been granted the title of fidei defensor, "Defender of the Faith," by the Pope. He did, however, very much want a divorce from his first wife, Catherine of Aragon, because she hadn't been able to provide him with the son he wanted. And of course once Henry rebelled against Rome, he was able to distribute the spoils gained by taking over the rich lands and monasteries owned previously by the Catholic Church. His daughter Elizabeth I did much to solidify the break with Rome and established traditions that have continued to this very day (2). The Church of England is one of the very few established church religions in the world. The title fidei defensor abbreviated as F D or Fid Def has appeared on all coins for hundreds of years, even on coins that were never released such as the one with Edward VIII, who as we'll shortly see abdicated before he was crowned.

Not quite as rare but also not in common circulation is the gold Britannia coin, which also displays the title fidei defensor in the abbreviation FID DEF.

Defender of (the?) Faith

Although future monarchs will most probably assume the title Supreme Governor of the Church of England, Charles has publicly expressed discontent with the use of the title fidei defensor; the Prince would rather be known as "Defender of Faith," not of "The Faith" because of the other faiths that have since become part of religious life of Britain and which we'll be turning to shortly. The connections between the established Church of England and the British government probably appear very odd to us in a largely secularized Germany. Some of them seem to be of ceremonial nature: the Lords Spiritual, who sit in the House of Lords, have little power to make changes that would dramatically affect the life of the most people in Britain, the monarch has the power to name the Archbishops of Canterbury and York but practically does so only on the advice of the Prime Minister (5). Of course we could go more into detail here about the structures of the Established Church – the dioceses, the General Synod, the role of the CoE in the Anglican Communion (a much broader community of churches around the world), the Lambeth Conference, the personalities and powers of the Archbishops of Canterbury and of York, ... But – except for those of us perhaps wanting to become an Archbishop – we can also approach the importance of the Church of England for people living in

Britain and abroad from another angle: Romance with a capital "R".

religion and romance

Even though weekly church attendance in the UK has been on the decline now for many years, formal aspects connected with the Church of England still play an astoundingly important role – at least for the Royals and thus also for the readers of newspapers, magazines, and blogs around the world. Most people, including those who aren't really interested in such things, couldn't escape the media presence of Lady Diana, from the fairy-tale wedding with Prince Charles to her death in an automobile accident, followed by probably the most televised funeral in the history of the world. One of the most televised weddings had taken place seventeen years earlier in the one Anglican cathedral that probably no tourist can escape: St. Paul's Cathedral in London. It's probably not so unusual that a couple marries in a church or is married by a bishop or even an Archbishop. But Charles' great uncle, Edward VIII (whose portrait was on the gold coin above), would have no doubt very much longed to have been married there, and if a marriage had been possible, then maybe we'd have a very different monarch on the British throne today.

crown for true love

This story is too long for us to start at the very beginning, so let's jump right to the heart of the matter. The last – at least up to now – of many kings with the name Edward was Edward VIII, the son of one of the many Georges (George V to be exact). After George V died, his eldest son became king. In addition to the many economic and political problems facing Britain in 1936, Edward, who became supreme governor of the Church of England at the same time as becoming king, had the problem of not being able to marry the woman he loved, the American socialite Wallis Simpson, because she had already been married twice and both husbands were still alive. The prime minister at the time, Stanley Baldwin, was much opposed to the planned wedding. Edward then decided to give up the throne to marry the woman he loved. (How ironic when you think of the fact that the Church of England was founded to allow a king to divorce his wife.) Unexpectedly his younger brother, yet another George (the VI), became king, and upon the unexpectedly early death of George, his daughter Elizabeth became queen and simultaneously the supreme governor of the Church of England. While she hasn't had marriage or divorce problems herself and thus no difficulties being an important part of the Church of England and simultaneously queen, her children have had all sorts of problems of this sort.

a more recent romance

But the Church of England has changed with the times, and even the marriage of the widower Charles to the divorcee Camilla Parker Bowles has become possible – although they weren't married in such a grand setting as St. Paul's but only in a small civil ceremony in the Guildhall in Windsor, a town hall where marriage ceremonies are performed, a hall which was at least finished by the famous architect of St. Paul's Cathedral, Christopher Wren. The Queen as supreme governor of the Church of England didn't attend the ceremony (putting the Church before Charles) but did attend the prayer service afterwards, during which both Charles and Camilla were blessed by the Archbishop of Canterbury. The CoE has not only had concerns with royally romantic entanglements; there have also been some concrete potentially explosive (in the sense of exploding the Anglican Communion by causing a schism between the various branches) issues in the last few years involving two "minority" groups: women and homosexuals.

ordination of women

Although a woman, albeit a very special woman, Queen Elizabeth I, was responsible for the real founding of the Church of England, women had little influence in the CoE until the 1990s – except of course for the roles of the Queens Anne, Victoria, and Elizabeth as Supreme Governors. The Episcopal Church in the US, a member of the Anglican Communion, was the first to ordain women as priests and later as bishops in the 1980s. After much debate and the threat of a schism within the Anglican Communion, general acceptance of women as priests has grown. In 1994 the first women priests were ordained in Bristol Cathedral. The first female bishops are due to be ordained within the Church of England in 2012 at the latest. As a result of the ordination of women in the CoE some members of the clergy and of congregations converted to Roman Catholicism.

ordination of homosexuals

The Archbishop of Canterbury Rowan Williams was open in his criticism of the Church of England's ban on ordaining practicing homosexuals when he was appointed archbishop in 2003. As with the previous process involving the ordination of women, the danger that the Anglican Communion could break apart over the issue of ordaining gay priests is present. As with the ordination of women, the American Episcopal Church has played the maverick by appointing an openly gay bishop in 2003. Other members of the Anglican Communion, especially those in Africa, have threatened to withdraw if gay clergy members are permitted, thus perhaps bringing about a schism that would shatter the Anglican Communion, of which the Church of England has been the center for hundreds of years. The special established status of the Church of England could play a role in the ordination of women and of homosexuals: Parliament has the right to veto church decisions although conflict between the Church of England and Parliament has mostly been avoided in the last few hundred years. How the Church of England and the Anglican Communion in general will deal with the issue of the ordination of practicing homosexuals could determine the future of both the Church of England and the Anglican Communion in unexpected ways.

Roman Catholics

English history – and to a certain extent British history as well – could be described as a series of conflicts first between church and state and then between the Roman Catholic Church and the Church of England. Even after Henry's break with Rome, Roman Catholics remained in Britain and were given back some of the rights they lost as early (or as late) as 1829 with the Catholic Emancipation Act. Nowadays Catholics have all the rights anyone else has in the United Kingdom, except of course that a Catholic can't become king or queen or marry one either. But with all the public problems the Royal Family has endured in the last few decades, probably few Catholics feel this restriction to be very important. Catholics make up around a fifth of the population and their attendance at Mass is higher than the very low attendance of Anglicans – if we can believe the statistics. The number of Catholics has increased with Irish immigration to Britain as well as to some degree immigration from other countries in Asia and Africa. There are of course some beautiful cathedrals in Britain; the mother church is in London, Westminster Cathedral. While the question of personal religious affiliation seems to be declining in importance, the question of Tony Blair's possible conversion to Catholicism was still deemed interesting enough to make headline news before he resigned as prime minister in 2007. If he had converted before resigning, he would have become the first Catholic prime minister, a fact no doubt deserving the same publicity as John F. Kennedy becoming the first and at least until now the only Catholic US president.

Northern Ireland

Religion seems not to play an important role in the life of many people in Britain: the vast majority only go to church for baptisms, weddings, and funerals and according to one very surprising survey conducted by a Christian charity only slightly more than half of the population even profess to be Christian. Religion, however, has been a matter of life and death in Northern Ireland for the last five hundred years at least, where more than three-quarters of the population are Christian. While officially there is no established church like in England since the Church of Ireland was disestablished in the latter part of the 19th century, most Unionists, who support a continuation of Northern Ireland's place in the United Kingdom, are either members of the Anglican Church of Ireland or of the Protestant Presbyterian Church. Nationalists, who support the dissolution of Northern Ireland from the United Kingdom and a union with the Republic of Ireland, are Roman Catholic. Trying to find a solution to the Irish Troubles will no doubt also involve untangling the ancient religious political knot that has threatened to strangle the Irish in both parts of the Emerald Isle for so many centuries.

non-Christian religions

Whereas the conflicts between the Roman Catholics and the Anglicans are mostly historical – except for the current situation in Northern Ireland of course – religious conflicts of another sort have become widely publicized. At least ever since the first immigrants from the colonies and former colonies of the British Empire arrived in the UK, non-Christian religions have made their appearance in Britain, an appearance which has become conspicuous in a beautiful sense with the building of temples and mosques but also conspicuous in an ugly sense with demonstrations, the burning of effigies, and bombs. Believers in non-Christian religions make up less than one-tenth of the population of Britain. The main religions: Islam, Hinduism, Sikhism, and Buddhism are the faiths of the ethnic minorities who began to come in large numbers to the UK after World War II and who have since changed the face of Britain. Religion and ethnicity are as closely tied together for most non-Christians in Britain as religion and the political parties are linked for the Catholics and Protestants in Northern Ireland. Only the Buddhists, the smallest major non-Christian group, have believers across the ethnic spectrum.

Hindus

Hinduism is one of the oldest of the world's major religions and one of the most diverse with various doctrines and many gods and divinities and holy days and festivals. The belief that the soul wanders through many forms (reincarnation) is one of the central tenets of Hinduism. Around 1% of the British population, and thus far more than the 150,000 Buddhists, identify themselves as being Hindu. What seems to be a very small percentage throughout the country as a whole is very unevenly distributed. About half of all Hindus in the United Kingdom are concentrated in London; Hindus also account for 15% of the population of Leicester. Hindus first began arriving in larger numbers in the UK after the independence of India from Britain and with the partition of India and Pakistan. Other Hindus were expelled from former British colonies in East Africa in the 1970s (7). In the 2001 census Hindus were the least likely of the non-Christians to have been born in the UK: 30% were born in India and 20% in Africa. What some people may see as an Indian influence on British culture, the Indian restaurant, is often run by Muslim Pakistanis or Bangladeshis. Speaking of food, most Hindus are vegetarians.

stable but integrated?

A study funded by the British government and the Hindu Forum of Britain came to the conclusion that in 2006 Hindu families were stable and that Hindus were successful economically but that the traits of being self-sufficient had hindered Hindus from becoming more politically and socially active within wider British society. Hindus have formed many organizations, among them the somewhat controversial Hindu Forum, but Hindus are underrepresented in Parliament with just two MP in the House of Commons; at least the first Asian woman to sit in the House of Lords is of Hindu background. The first Hindu state-funded faith school is due to open in London in 2010. There are already hundreds of Hindu temples in Britain; the first traditional Hindu temple and one of the largest outside India was opened in London in 1995. Diwali, the Hindu festival of lights and a sort of Hindu New Year, has become a well-known celebration in Britain, especially in the city of Leicester.

Sikhs

Sikhism was founded in the 15th century in India and is thus the youngest of the three large non-Christian religions in the UK.

Sikhs believe in one God just as Christians and Muslims do and place emphasis on living honestly, working hard, and treating everyone equally. While many of the first generation of Sikh immigrants from India adapted to their home country by removing their turbans and cutting their beards, later immigrants from East Africa kept up their minority status by openly displaying the symbols of their faith and fought to be allowed to do so. The typical turbans worn to cover their long hair have caused some Sikh men problems with American and Irish security regulations but have now become part of English life – especially in the areas with high numbers of Sikhs. Slightly more than 0.5% of all British people are Sikhs, but while there are very few Sikhs in Wales or Scotland, more than 8% of the population in the West Midlands area is Sikh. More than 90% of all Sikhs are from an Indian ethnic background.

stable and integrated?

The majority of Sikhs were born in the UK and – if we take the fact that 82% of all Sikhs own their own homes as a sign of integration – have assimilated themselves well. There are Sikh members in the House of Commons and one in the House of Lords, the President of the Royal Institute of British Architects is a Sikh, and there have been Sikh mayors in Coventry, Leicester, and Gloucester, and a cult Sikh cricket player, Monty Panesar. The Gurdwara is the place where Sikhs congregate for worship. There are about 200 Gurdwaras in Britain; while Sikhs don't have a special holy day like Sunday for Christians, Saturday for Jews, or Friday for Muslims, most Sikhs go to a Gurdwara on Sundays. The largest Gurdwara outside India is in London and was opened in 2003. *Bend It Like Beckham* (the German title was *Kick It Like Beckham*), a movie released in 2002 and directed by Kenyan-born Gurinder Chadha, offers one view of Sikh family life in Britain with a traditional mother, an understanding father, and a daughter who loves to play soccer (7). The movie also has a German connection.

Muslims

Islam is the youngest of the world's major religions and was founded by the prophet Mohammed in what is now Saudi Arabia in the 7th century. The monotheistic religion spread rapidly throughout the Middle East, North Africa, and into Europe during the following centuries and is now the second-largest religion in the world. The relations between the Islamic and the Western world have ranged from peaceful and fruitful coexistence to the violence of the medieval crusades and terrorism of the 21st century. Muslims make up more than half of all non-Christian religion adherents, are the fastest-growing religious group in Britain with more than one-third of all Muslims under the age of 16, and make up more than 3% of the total population (7). While contact between Britain and Muslims can be traced back hundreds of years, the majority of Muslims in Britain today came as immigrants from Pakistan and Bangladesh starting in the late 1940s. Muslims have the highest unemployment rates of any religious group and the lowest rate of educational qualification (two factors that tend to go hand-in-hand in industrialized societies). While most Muslims have an Asian ethnic background, large minorities have a white or black ethnic background, contributing to a great diversity of ethnicity. As with the Hindus and the Sikhs, the majority of Muslims live in London and urban areas of the West Midlands or in areas of Yorkshire.

Members of the House of Lords include the first non-converted Muslim life peer, Baron Ahmed; the youngest and first openly gay life peer, Lord Waheed Alli; as well as the first female life peer Muslim, Baroness Uddin. The first British-born Muslims were elected to the House of Commons fifty years after Muslim immigrants began arriving in large numbers in Britain. Some of the many mosques in Britain date back a century; large mosques can be found in London, Glasgow, Birmingham, Manchester, and Liverpool. The first recorded mosque was supposedly built in the Welsh capital of Cardiff in the mid 19th century.

Satanic Verses and London bombings

One major sign of the deep-seated differences between Muslim belief and British values became obvious during the public protests about the novel *The Satanic Verses*, written by the award-winning British-Indian writer Salman Rushdie and published in 1988, which many Muslims regarded as being blasphemous. Bookstores that sold the book in the UK and abroad were bombed, copies of the book were burned during demonstrations, and the Iranian leader Khomeini called for the death of Rushdie and his publishers, resulting in a rupture in diplomatic relations between Britain and Iran. Controversy over the author continued when Rushdie was knighted by Queen Elizabeth ten years after the controversy. Another incident which has caused increased tensions within the British Muslim community and between

Muslims and non-Muslims was the London bombings in 2005 resulting in more than 50 deaths. The suicide bombers were all Muslim and their religious beliefs seemed to have played a major role in the attacks. The Muslim community in the UK reacted with shock and condemnation but also with some understanding of what they saw as reasons behind the terror: discrimination, British foreign policy hostile to Muslim interests, immorality on the part of British society as a whole. How British society and British Muslims come to terms with different attitudes towards religious freedom, towards blasphemy and censorship, towards individual rights and community responsibility along with obvious economic differences will determine if violence remains associated with Muslim life in Britain.

assimilation and integration

Assimilation and integration problems with questions of Muslim/Asian identity have been dealt with to varying degrees in films like *My Beautiful Launderette* or *East is East* or the lesser-known *My Son the Fanatic* – the last one with a German connection. The well-known English pop singer of Greek ethnic background Cat Stevens converted to Islam in 1977 and changed his name to Yusuf Islam and was one of the founders of the Islamia Primary School in London, the first state-funded Muslim school.

**Fig. 8.10** | *Islamia Primary School*

As we saw in the chapter on minorities and immigration in the UK, problems of race as opposed to problems of religion in Britain were paramount in the past; the religion of Stephen Lawrence played no role in his murder or in the publicity that followed. Britain has certainly been no stranger to religiously motivated violence with a history of conflicts between state and one church and then between Catholics and Protestants and later between Protestants and Protestants. Except for Northern Ireland, though, (and even there the conflict is at least as much British versus Irish as Catholic vs. Protestant) the role of religion has declined in importance for many Britons and religion had thus lost its power to motivate extreme violent action. Britain has even been looked upon as a model of multicultural tolerance and as providing an environment that allows people to live together peacefully, people who in other parts of

future of religion in Britain

the world like India, Pakistan, and the former Yugoslavia resort to violence over religious differences.

Perhaps this multicultural model can be implemented more easily in Britain than elsewhere because the situation in Britain is of course in many ways different from the situation in Germany – Muslims and Hindus and Sikhs are minority groups that come from the Commonwealth, from countries that shared at least parts of a common culture with the motherland; Muslims in Germany are now in the third and fourth generation but still are regarded as foreign and seem to feel themselves as a foreign element. Integration will and must come; the economic factor is simply too important. With a broader interpretation of what it means to be British – as opposed to being English, Welsh, Scottish – Muslims can identify themselves in the UK as full citizens. Practically all UK-born Christians and Jews as well as around 90% of all Muslims, Hindus, Sikhs, and Buddhists who were born in the UK identify themselves as British according to the 2001 census, the first time that the government asked its citizens about religious affiliation and identity. The census report also found that more than 50% of Jewish, Muslim, Sikh and Hindu adults living in England and Wales said that their religion was important to their identity. Other surveys have pointed out higher numbers of Hindus, Sikhs, and Muslims who do not feel British. The fact remains that while violence has erupted in connection with Islamic terrorism, violence hasn't taken place between the various religious groups.

Some Hindus and Sikhs have begun to become dissatisfied with the term "Asian" – partly to separate themselves from Muslims and partly to show their identity as British citizens (7). It will remain the task of British society to find ways to integrate and include all faiths now found in Britain. The test will be if the monarch can change from being the defender of the faith to a defender of faiths and if British society can find room for the sound of the muezzin and the presence of veils, turbans, saris, and bindis as valid demonstrations of religious belief in a secular society where for most people religion has a major role only in issues of "hatch, match, and dispatch" – baptisms, weddings, and funerals.

## Exercises

1. Compare the following two pie charts:

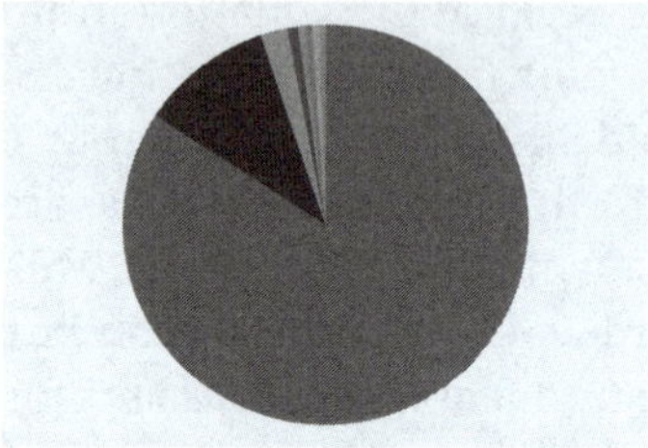

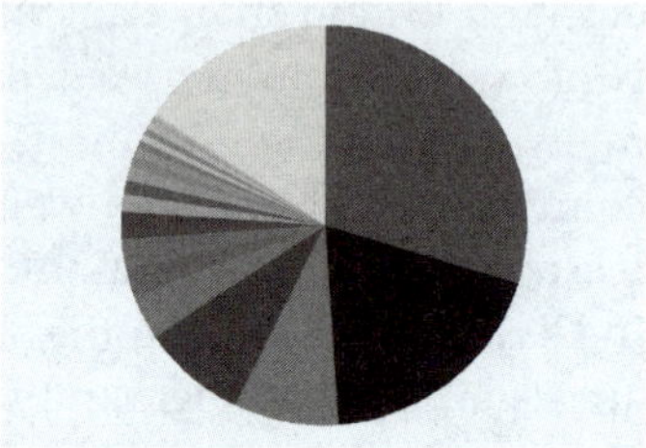

   Although they look quite different, they both represent the uniformity and diversity of American religion. Try and guess what the various slices could mean.
2. Where does the phrase "city on the hill" originate from?
3. Distinguish Westminster Cathedral from Westminster Abbey.
4. Name three different religions that you can find in the US.
5. Give two examples of how church and state are (not) separated in the US.
6. Who established the Church of England and why?
7. What role did romance play in religion in the last century and what role could it play in this century?
8. Name two non-Christian religions in the UK and describe the ethnic background of the adherents.

Challenging questions and interesting projects:

On your next trip to Britain, look for an Anglican Cathedral and note the activities advertised there. If possible, attend a service and describe your reactions and try to identify components from Roman Catholic churches and components from Protestant churches.

Look for the transcript of the speech of any American politician and list the number of phrases that seem to have a religious ring to them.

And finally the oh-my-god-if-you-can-do-this-you'll-maybe-become-a-saint tasks:

Try and come up with a solution that would please both those Americans who believe that a voluntary prayer in public schools is necessary and those Americans who believe that the Constitution forbids such actions.

Devise a plan that would integrate British Muslims into British life fully, giving the Muslims a sense of belonging that the non-Muslim British population could also feel comfortable with.

And finally, further topics not dealt with in this chapter... for those with time and passion in this life or if not in the next:

Roman Catholic belief in the US; the megachurches; the Left Behind series; finding names for religions and for American religious experience; Black Muslims; tests used by the Supreme Court to judge the constitutionality of public prayer, creationism and evolution in schools; characteristics of the Church of England: English, reformed, established, comprehensive; important differences between the UK and the US regarding the role of religion in public life; Judaism in the US and the UK; free churches in the UK; the Church of Scotland; religion in Wales; religion in education in the UK, especially Christian-run and state-maintained schools and the growing number of Muslim-run schools; interesting, typically eccentric English religions like those of the Pagans, Druids...

# 9 | From National Parks to National Disasters (environmental concerns)

O beautiful, for spacious skies,
For amber waves of grain,
For purple mountain majesties
Above the fruited plain!
America! America! God shed His grace on thee,
And crown thy good with brotherhood, from sea to shining sea.
first stanza of the patriotic song "America the Beautiful"

We also look after forests, woods, fens, beaches, farmland, downs, moorland, islands, archaeological remains, castles, nature reserves, villages – for ever, for everyone.
from the website of the National Trust (in England, Wales, and Northern Ireland)

What comes to your mind when you think of "Britain" and "landscape"? Rolling green hills and hedgerows in the heart of England? Romantic or dramatic moorland in places with names like Dartmoor in southwest England? The soft hills of Wales, the peaks of the Scottish Highlands, or the white cliffs of Dover? "America" and "landscape" would probably trigger some of the tourist attractions mentioned in the geography appetizers (🔔 1). In this chapter you'll be finding out more about some of the natural wonders in America and in Britain, as well as about some of the natural disasters caused by nature and by humankind.

When you finish the chapter, you should be able to say something about

- some typical landscapes and animals in the US and the UK
- some American and British national parks
- the role of the government in protecting and exploiting the environment
- some of the major disasters to have hit the US and the UK
- some examples of environmental awareness in the US and the UK.

a national landscape?

The attempt to link the identity of a people with a particular kind of landscape is nothing new although it's become a popular topic again in cultural studies, which we'll be turning to soon in Part II of this book. Think for a minute about what sources are responsible for what you see in your mind when you think of typical American or British landscapes. Even though I grew up in the flat wooded southeast, the first images of American landscape that come to my mind are the vast open Great Plains and the Rocky Mountains. And English landscape is for me the gently green rolling hills with sheep dotted picturesquely here and there that I've seen in paintings and in movies like *Barry Lyndon*. When I traveled to the heart of England, the Cotswolds area, for the first time, it all seemed very familiar. Scottish landscape is for me and probably for many of you the Highlands with their craggy peaks – and not the areas of southeastern Scotland that I've actually experienced. And British landscape just results in a blank in my mind since I'm not sure what that could be – maybe Stonehenge since it can't be classified as English, Welsh, or Scottish if you're willing to see it as an example of landscape?

problems with a national landscape?

Of course there are problems with assigning landscape to national identity. While a river like the Rio Grande can be taken as a clear way of distinguishing the border of two countries, the US and Mexico, what aspects of landscape change when you travel in the border country area of north England and south Scotland or of western England and eastern Wales? History buffs (2) might want to point to Hadrian's Wall as a way of distinguishing the English from the Scottish side of the border except that Hadrian's Wall is now to be found completely within England. And while a couple of rivers form part of the border between England and Wales, the area of the Black Mountains looks the same on both sides of the border. Do the American Rockies look a lot different than the Swiss Alps? Where do we get our images of national landscape from? For many of us no doubt from tourist brochures or movies, paintings, the mass media, or from the lyrics of patriotic songs like "America the Beautiful," which opened this chapter. We could've also chosen a few lines from Woody Guthrie's famous folk song "This Land is Your Land": "From California to the New York Island/From the Redwood Forest to the Gulf Stream waters." Since neither tourism nor painting nor movies nor media are our topics yet, we can leave the theoretical problem of linking national identity with a specific landscape and turn to concrete positive examples of government stewardship of the environment. But first let's take a brief look at some animals and plants.

an American bird?

If it's difficult to connect landscape with national identity, what about fauna and flora, animals and plants? Are there uniquely American animals or English plants? Does it make sense to discuss animals from a national cultural point of view? Animals most probably don't feel English, Scottish, Welsh or Pakistani or Black Caribbean, but they can get UK passports – as part of EU regulations on the movement of pet animals. The American bald eagle certainly doesn't need a passport to show that it's been a symbol of America since the American Revolution (2) and can still be found in the Great Seal of the United States and on coins (8) and dollar bills.

Fig. 9.1 *Great Seal of the United States*

Why the bald eagle – the word "bald" here refers to the bird's white feathers – as the national bird? Eagles are seen as symbols of strength and courage, and the bald eagle is indigenous only to North America. One of the founding fathers, Benjamin Franklin (2), was in favor of the turkey as the national bird. But most Americans point with pride to the bald eagle as a national symbol. President John F. Kennedy praised the bald eagle's "fierce beauty and proud independence" in a letter to the National Audubon Society as fitting symbols but also warned of the dangers the bald eagle was facing. At the beginning of the 1960s Americans were becoming aware of the effects of pollution. The biologist and writer Rachel Carson published the bestseller *Silent Spring* and made the general public aware of the dangers of pesticides, especially DDT, for birds. Without the environmental activism that began at this time and grew strongly during the 1970s, the American bald eagle might well have become extinct and was for many years on the government's official Endangered Species List. Even though the population of bald eagles nationwide has now stabilized, it is still strictly against US law to disturb them in any way.

a British squirrel?

You may have noticed the word "indigenous" to describe the bald eagle above. This word can refer to any animals (including humans) that are native to a certain region of the world. Animals that aren't indigenous must have come from somewhere else, and one small animal that scurries across parks and fields in search of food and that comes in various colors is a good example of the connection that some people can make between nationality and animals. The gray squirrel is one of the most common animals in American city parks and can be seen throughout suburbs in much of the country. More than a century ago gray squirrels from North America found their way over to Britain and perhaps due to their size and strength were able to compete successfully with the native red squirrels, whose numbers have now plummeted to a degree that they are in danger of becoming extinct in the UK. Prince Charles, patron of the Red Squirrel Survival Trust, called the gray squirrel an "alien species" in competition with "one of the most utterly charming British native mammals." Some British media reports were ecstatic about a new breed of black squirrel that seemed to be as dangerous for the immigrant gray squirrels as the gray ones are for the "native" red ones, which by the way aren't called British or English or Welsh red squirrels (in spite of an effort to populate the Welsh island of Anglesey with only red squirrels). The official name for this "charming British native mammal" is the European or Eurasian red squirrel to distinguish it from the American red squirrel. Incidentally, red squirrels can have gray-colored fur just as gray squirrels can be reddish, complicating the matter of discrimination according to color.

red robins and foxes

Red is also the color of the unofficial national bird of Britain, which in spite of its official name "European robin" received the most votes for the British national bird in a newspaper survey a half century ago. (A move to officially name the golden eagle as Scotland's national bird hasn't yet been passed.) Even if Britain doesn't have an official national bird, it does have Europe's largest conservation charity, the Royal Society for the Protection of Birds (RSPB for short), founded more than a hundred years ago and still very popular. The RSPB makes use of the British love of nature by encouraging people to count not only birds but recently also other kinds of wildlife in their own gardens. Another large organization with a long name is the Royal Society for the Prevention of Cruelty to Animals (RSPCA), which has come out in support of one red-colored animal that isn't found as often in gardens as it has been in national headlines over the last decade. This animal would no doubt want to obtain a passport to be able to emigrate out of the rural areas where fox hunting is still practiced even if it's now against the law.

The debate over allowing or banning fox hunting was accompanied by huge demonstrations even though foxes have never been hunted by more than a small percentage of the British population, many of them from the upper classes. Even though fox hunting has been illegal in all parts of the UK except for Northern Ireland for the past few years, ceremonies connected with fox hunting and sometimes the hunting itself illegally continues. Supporters of fox hunting claim that the debate leading up to the ban has actually increased people's awareness of a great tradition associated with rural life and that fox hunting performs a service in controlling the numbers of foxes. It remains to be seen if the hunters' bright red jackets and their barking hounds will continue to help define one kind of rural British identity.

One identifying aspect of rural Britain has remained visible to varying degrees in the last thousand years. Take a look at what you might consider to be a typical photo of the English countryside.

Fig. 9.2 | *Hedgerows in the country-side near Exeter*

hedgerows

The lines that divide up the green rolling hills are hedgerows, a typically English feature of the landscape, made of shrubs and bushes from the rose and hawthorn families as well as trees like the elm, oak, and ash, which have been pruned sometimes over many hundreds of years to establish a natural border between fields (sometimes going back to Roman times) or to separate roads from fields. (The word *hedge*, by the way, is etymologically related to the German word *Hecke*.) While modern farming methods with the use of large machinery have resulted in the loss of hedges, national societies dedicated to their preservation are helping to slow their destruction. Even though hedges are a more common feature of the English countryside, the world's largest hedgerow, made up of a living wall of beech trees, is said to be found in Scotland.

*a capable gardener and the English garden*

Of course you can find hedges in gardens too although more often in formal French gardens than in the type that came to be called English and spread throughout Europe and the rest of the world in the 18th and 19th centuries. In the middle of the 18th century a gardener with the romantic first name Lancelot and the very common family name Brown came to be called "Capability" because of his talents in transforming land around some of the grand private homes into parks that displayed none of the previously popular formality. Through the understated placement of trees and small lakes the landscape seemed natural but the effect of space and vistas was in fact carefully planned. Some claim that the new kind of landscape gardening that Brown introduced to England and then to the rest of the world is one of the most significant English contributions to European culture (the other one being the perpendicular style of architecture 11). You can still visit some of Brown's many parks and gardens scattered all over southern England.

*government and the world's first national park*

About a century after Capability Brown had left his mark on English landscape gardening, people on the other side of the world were beginning to agree that the government had the responsibility to set aside land for public use, recreation, and for preservation. Although Americans get a very bad press (often justifiably so) on environmental issues, sometimes people forget the leading role some Americans played in environmental awareness long before the color green became political. Even before the western part of the United States had been mostly settled by the end of the 19th century (the closing of the frontier 2), many ideas about environmental protection were first being put into practice. The United States had acquired a lot of land as Americans moved from east to west, land with some breathtakingly beautiful scenery. At the end of the 19th century the world's first national park was planned in what would later become the states of Wyoming, Montana, and Idaho and named after the river that originates within it: Yellowstone. Although Yellowstone was officially founded in 1872 by President Ulysses S. Grant, it would take years before the government could be convinced that setting aside areas of land for preservation and recreation was worth investing money in. One conservationist we met briefly earlier in the book as the husband of the woman credited with establishing kindergartens in the US, Carl Schurz (4), used his position as Secretary of the Interior to encourage setting aside land for national forests. One of the presidents we've met several times in previous chapters (as you might remember from a history appetizer 2) became a champion of the movement that would lead to many more national parks being founded. One of the lesser-known national parks was named after him: Theodore Roosevelt National Park in North Dakota. Roosevelt was a conservationist. A famous preservationist – someone who believes that the land should be preserved for its own sake and not just for human use – was John Muir, founder of the Sierra Club.

from Acadia to Zion

In the next century more than fifty national parks were to follow. The largest of them, Wrangell St. Elias, founded just a couple of decades ago in the largest US state in area, Alaska (1), occupies more land than the entire German federal state of Lower Saxony. The majority of national parks are in the western states with landscape varying greatly from the most famous geyser in America, Old Faithful, in Yellowstone, to the swamps of Everglades National Park in Florida to the caves of Carlsbad Caverns National Park in New Mexico to the volcanoes in the park appropriately named Hawaii Volcanoes National Park in the newest American state (1). The national parks with the most visitors include the Great Smoky Mountains National Park in the Appalachians (1), which may surprise you; Grand Canyon National Park, which you no doubt expected; Acadia National Park in Maine at the top; Zion National Park in Utah at the bottom of the alphabetical list but among the most popular top ten with more than two million visitors a year; and Cuyahoga Valley National Park, the only one in the state of Ohio and one of the newest parks, founded just a decade ago.

from Wordsworth to South Downs

Remember the item in our first chapter about "interesting and unusual physical features" in the UK? Maybe some of you who are fans of Romantic poetry or know something about tourism in Britain were surprised not to find one truly beautiful area in north England not far from the Scottish border, an area that would become one of Britain's first national parks. At the same time as Americans were becoming aware of the need to protect some of the vast land they were taking over, famous 19th century Romantic poets like William Wordsworth were writing poetry about the beautiful landscape of the Lake District in northwest England. The first national parks weren't founded in Britain until the 1950s after conflicts about the right to roam and the right of access to the countryside were settled. Within a decade, ten of the current fifteen parks were founded. The map shows that the parks are spread around the entire island of Great Britain, with large areas of Wales as part of national parks. National parks in Britain aren't as remote from cities and towns as most of the American parks are. Large areas of British national parks are pri-

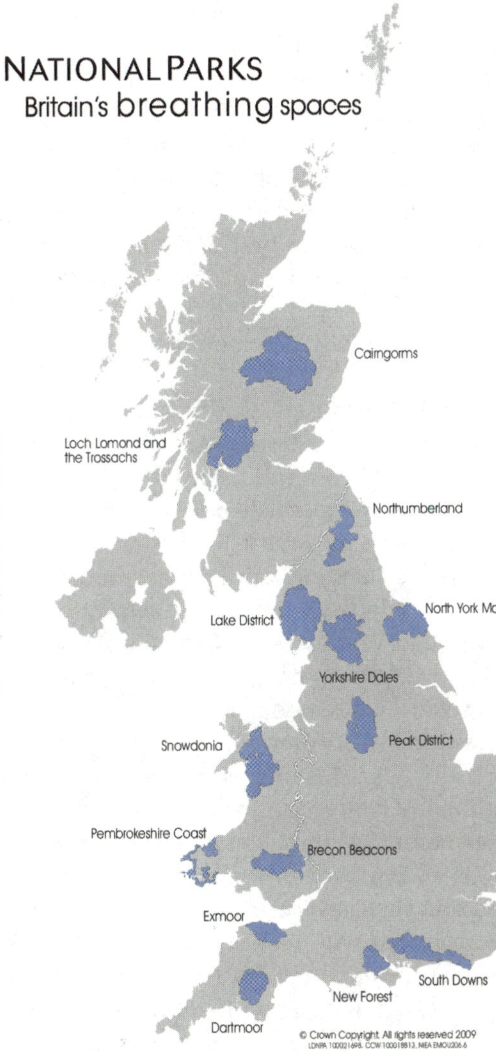


**Fig. 9.3**
*National Parks in the UK. Crown Copyright. All rights reserved 2009.*

vately owned and still used – you can find farms, villages, and towns within the boundaries – unthinkable in the US. Population figures vary from a few thousand to more than one hundred thousand in the newest of the national parks, South Downs. And there aren't only national parks but also national forests in Britain. The area fittingly called the National Forest, located in the very heart of England in the center of the Midlands and nicknamed "a forest in the making," is just one example of how Britain is now attempting to save its forests. In general trees can't be cut down without permission, and trees in government care that die are replaced. While there most probably won't be a return to the thickly forested island that humans inhabited thousands of years ago, since the 1940s forested land has doubled in size, so there are signs that future Robin Hoods will have a place to live. While the British national parks don't have the same extraordinary variety of landscape as in the US, they still draw millions of visitors each year. It's the balance between use of the land, encouraging tourism, and protecting the environment that is often difficult to achieve and will no doubt continue to be a challenge in future.

The balance between preservation and recreation will remain challenging for both the British Association of National Parks Authorities and the American National Parks Service. Other American attempts to replenish or subdue nature also show both positive and negative effects.

from TVA to the Hoover Dam

Until the 1930s flooding was a typical problem in the Tennessee Valley, an area in the southeast United States stretching from Kentucky through Tennessee to North Carolina and Virginia. As part of FDR's New Deal and yet another example of the alphabet agencies you may remember from a history appetizer (2), the Tennessee Valley Authority (TVA) improved the lives of the poor farmers living in this impoverished area, generated electricity through many new dams, provided lakes for recreation, and was used as proof that the federal government could positively affect people's lives through huge engineering projects in spite of criticism that such government action was a sign of socialism. But planned projects with nuclear power in the Tennessee Valley were cancelled in the 1980s because of problems with quality, and a major pollution catastrophe occurred at the end of 2008, tarnishing the success of more than seven decades of the TVA.

Another massive engineering project from the same time period which you may remember from our geography appetizers (🔔 1) was at first called Boulder Canyon Project and later named after President Herbert Hoover. Hoover Dam, like the TVA, was supposed to control flooding and generate electricity and was considered successful in taming the Colorado River, which the dam holds back at the Nevada-Arizona border (which also separates the Mountain Time from the Pacific Time Zone). While positive results of the Hoover Dam include flood control, the production of hydroelectricity, and irrigation – in effect transforming the southwestern area of the US – the dam also choked off the mighty Colorado, which now no longer regularly flows into the Gulf of California but often dries up in the desert. A former president of the Sierra Club, the oldest and largest American environmental organization, has suggested draining mighty Lake Powell, formed by another dam on the Colorado, the Glen Canyon Dam, and returning the Colorado to its previous condition as a wild flowing river.

The belief in the wonders of technology that led to the building of the Hoover Dam in the 1930s was shaken by two events in the 70s, which largely contributed to the growth of environmental awareness in America.

from Love Canal to Three Mile Island

A neighborhood of the city of Niagara Falls (named for the famous landmark found there) in New York State with the romantic name Love Canal became the focus of national and international attention in the late 70s when huge amounts of highly poisonous chemical waste began to rise above the surface of the ground where homes and a school had been built decades earlier. For the first time in American history, emergency government funds were spent on clearing the aftermath not of a "natural" but of a manmade disaster, a chemical dumpsite turned into a residential neighborhood. Just a few years later another environmental scandal was exposed in another neighborhood, Times Beach in the state of Missouri, with the same results: evacuation of families, serious health effects for those who had lived in areas that were full of toxic waste, a change of attitude about the role of the government in protecting the environment. The Environmental Protection Agency (EPA), a federal government agency established at the beginning of the 70s, became authorized to use money (called the Superfund) to compensate those harmed and to clean up the mess left behind at Love Canal and other sites across the country. Only a couple hundred kilometers from Love Canal near Harrisburg, the state capital of Pennsylvania (1), and not far from an area with a substantial Amish population (8) lies an island in the Susquehanna River where two nuclear power plants were built in the 70s, three miles from the town of Middletown. The Three Mile Island nuclear accident caused by equipment malfunctions and worker errors didn't result in the death and destruction caused by Chernobyl seven years later but did result in a dramatic change in attitude towards nuclear power. The Nuclear Regulatory Commission, a government agency established a few years earlier, tightened regulations on new nuclear power plants in the wake of Three Mile Island. No more nuclear power plants were to be built for the next forty years.

green-collar jobs in a Green New Deal?

With the election of President Barack Obama the environmental movement, which had its heyday in the 1970s, is back on the agenda after being put on the back burner during the Bush administration. The degree to which the government is now involved in the economy has reminded many of FDR's New Deal of the 30s (1, 3), and the current investment of billions of dollars in renewable energy and increasing energy efficiency is sometimes described as a Green New Deal. The government is funding the training of green-collar workers in environmentally related fields. (The new term "green-collar" is used in analogy to traditional blue-collar workers in manufacturing and industry and white-collar workers in administration and finance). In order to judge more comprehensively American attitudes towards the environment and towards energy, we need to take into account some characteristics of the country as a whole and of Americans themselves.

moving across a land not fit for human habitation?

One result of engineering feats like the Hoover Dam and the Glen Canyon Dam (1) was the growth of Las Vegas, which could be taken for a fata morgana in the middle of arid wasteland if it didn't take so much real energy and water to maintain the city. Las Vegas can't exist without the water diverted from the Colorado River; some people wonder if it's necessary to build cities in areas that aren't fit for comfortable human habitation. We also need to keep in mind that for all its enormous size, most of the United States isn't fit for comfortable human habitation without central heating (for most of the Central Plains and the entire northern half of the country) or air-conditioning (for the swelteringly humid summers of the entire southern part and most of the East coast) or sophisticated weather services to warn people of impending hurricanes, tornados, blizzards, and floods (for most areas of the entire country). Of course there are areas where you can live comfortably without powerful heating or air conditioning: some areas of California are climatically very comfortable ... until the next earthquake. Perhaps one of the most mysterious and strangely attractive characteristics of Americans is their willingness to live in areas that require enormous expenditures of energy to be made habitable. Perhaps we can find an explanation in American history, the drive to move on to bigger and better places, to harness the land, to find the gold at the end of the rainbow. This restlessness has continued to the present with freedom of movement being a key to understanding the American spirit. Remember how we tried to imagine the vastness of the US by driving across country (1)?

on autobahns to urban sprawl

And two typical characteristics of American cities also pose challenges for energy efficiency and for environmental protection. At first glance they seem contradictory: vertical expansion with skyscrapers and horizontal expansion – suburbs and beyond – spurred by economic factors like cheaper automobiles, improved roads, and the American dream of owning a house and yard. After World War II new houses were built in the suburbs around the cities with people moving from the city to larger houses in the suburbs. The resulting rise in car ownership was due to increased travel from home in the suburbs to work in the cities. The increased road traffic led to the building of networks of highways like the mammoth US Interstate Highway System, proposed by President Eisenhower and based on his experience of the German autobahn system during his duty in Germany in World War II. This system, the largest highway system in the world, was originally planned for military movement, which has frequently proved useful in evacuations in the wake of hurricanes.

Urban sprawl, the ugly spreading out of cities, isn't limited to America but certainly is a typical characteristic of American urban areas and the result of the dramatic increase in the use of the automobile, which has remained the mode of transportation for the vast majority of Americans. Even the first "transcontinental railroad" that we heard about in American history wasn't really transcontinental ( 1), and it actually wasn't until the 1990s that the first real passenger transcontinental railroad connected Los Angeles at the Pacific with Miami at the Atlantic, but even this line was discontinued. Now, however, with increased gasoline prices, Americans have started to ride the bus and train much more frequently, but the infrastructure isn't always able to adjust in time to the increased demand. Will the birthplace of mass-produced automobiles become the land of mass transport in the future? While seemingly unlikely now, it wouldn't be the first American contradiction in the context of the environment.

American contradictions

While Americans were killing the buffalo, eroding the soil of the Dust Bowl, and drying up the Colorado River, they were also as we've seen in this chapter creating the world's first national parks, establishing the world's first environmental organizations, and founding universities that would turn out scientists and economists, and politicians as leaders for a new way of looking at the planet – including the vast expanse of the United States – as something to be preserved or left alone in spite of all other factors. These contradictions could help us understand some of the environmental and energy problems and challenges the country will continue to face. Leaving the Americans with their inherently contradictory attitudes towards preservation and consumption, we now must return to Britain, not to visit another national park but to look at a national disaster.

from Windscale to Sellafield

Which name do you need to complete the following analogy: Three Mile Island is to the Americans as … is to the British? Well, you could actually pick Sellafield or Windscale, both names for a nuclear processing area on the northwest English coast not far from the Lake District. The Windscale reactors were originally used for developing nuclear weapons in the 40s and 50s. Queen Elizabeth II pulled the lever to start the UK's first civilian nuclear power station called Calder Hall, not far from Windscale, in 1956. Her optimism about the uses of nuclear power echoed the optimism in much of the industrialized world at the time: "This new power, which has proved itself to be such a terrifying weapon of destruction, is harnessed for the first time for the common good of our community." Just a year later the Windscale fire, the first fire in any nuclear reactor, released radiation but was largely contained although reports of health problems among local residents have continued until the present day. What has been called "Britain's Biggest Nuclear Disaster" in a recent BBC documentary is sometimes compared with the Three Mile Island accident. In an attempt to improve its public image, Windscale's name was changed to Sellafield. But a later series of accidents and leaks has kept Sellafield, too, in the headlines and created tension between the Irish and British government, Sellafield being just across the narrow Irish Sea from Ireland. Sellafield hasn't only been used to generate electricity but also to reprocess nuclear fuel from other nuclear reactors – including reactors in Germany. And thus it has become a focus of criticism by many environmental organizations like Greenpeace. The use of nuclear power has remained controversial in spite of recent Labour government plans to keep atomic energy on the agenda because of carbon dioxide limits and because of the increasing costs of oil and coal. It remains to be seen if the work of the Nuclear Decommissioning Authority (NDA), a government body with the task of shutting down and cleaning up Britain's nuclear reactors, will increase or decrease in the future.

from the Tube to the Congestion Charge

While possible problems with nuclear energy remain on the agenda for political and environmental action, at least one problem is being dealt with on a smaller scale: traffic in central London. London can boast of having the world's first – and also oldest – underground public transportation system, the famous London Tube. But both traffic in the London Underground, the official name of the Tube, and aboveground is extremely congested. In 2003 when traffic in central London had slowed to the pace of a (tired) horse and buggy, Mayor Ken Livingstone introduced a congestion charge requiring motorists to pay a fee to enter parts of London during the week with closed circuit television (CCTV) used to ensure compliance. While the charge worked better than some expected, it isn't clear how much the fee has really reduced pollution.

Due certainly in part to the worldwide recession, Britain like the US has also experienced unprecedented demand for rail travel. While environmentalists see these increases and changes in attitude positively, the public transport infrastructure in the UK, just like in the US as we saw above, isn't always able to adjust to dramatically increased demand.

weather and the Weather Channel

One basic environmental difference between the UK and the US is the occurrence of natural disasters. Blizzards, droughts, hurricanes, tornadoes, fires, floods, earthquakes, even volcanic eruptions are part of the reason why the Weather Channel is a popular network (10) in the US. And even though the weather is supposed to be a popular topic for small talk in Britain, the dramatic natural disasters that the US Weather Channel reports on round the clock and throughout the year just don't happen in Britain. The British version of the Weather Channel was discontinued after just a few years of operation due to a low number of viewers. But Britain also has its share of natural catastrophes: the 2007 floods were among the worst of the previous hundred years. The long-term effects of the rise in sea levels could result in parts of the island of Great Britain disappearing into the waves.

Prince Charles and Poundbury

Of course it wouldn't be very nice ending this chapter with the catastrophic image of parts of Britain disappearing into the sea, so let's return briefly to Prince Charles. We heard earlier in this chapter about Prince Charles' attitude towards the "alien" gray squirrel. The Prince has championed other environmental causes including his own brand of organic foods with the profits being donated to his charities and foundations. He's also a supporter of the new environmentally friendly village of Poundbury, developed on land managed by the Duke of Cornwall, one of Prince Charles' titles.

the nation and the National Trust

We began this chapter by looking at some of the ways in which landscape and national identity can be combined, and we're concluding the chapter with a look at a British institution with "nation" in its name (a British institution if you include the Scots, who have their own National Trust for Scotland, but with roughly the same goals). The National Trust, founded more than a hundred years ago and now the largest conservation charity in Europe, combines both a British love of countryside and a love of the past by preserving places of "historic interest" or "natural beauty" like Wakehurst Place Garden in southern England or the Conwy Suspension Bridge in northern Wales or the Macquarie Mausoleum on the west coast Scottish island of Mull or the UNESCO World Heritage Site Giant's Causeway in Northern Ireland (1). The National Trust owns more land than almost anyone else in the UK (except for the Crown) and has the motto "for ever, for everyone," a motto that seems to erase the boundaries of the nation while the National Trust at the same time preserves evidence both natural and manmade of a specific national culture. Natural like Fair Isle between the Shetland and the Orkney Islands in northeastern Scotland (🔔 1) or one of the world's largest natural harbors at St. Anthony Head in southwestern Cornwall or Rhossili Bay in Wales. Manmade like the Chedworth Roman Villa in southern England or Crathes Castle in northeastern Scotland or the Dolaucothi Gold Mines in southern Wales. We'll continue our look at how borders can be transcended both physically and virtually in our next chapter.

## Exercises

1. Which national parks were mentioned in the chapter? How could you categorize them?
2. Look again at the geography appetizers and see if you can locate the following picture.

Fig. 9.4

And on a totally different topic: Look again at Chapter 1 and see if you can find a photo that could help you guess which station was on the world's first underground railway.

3. How could you categorize some of the organizations mentioned in this chapter?
4. Which organization of the ones you've come up with in the answer to question 3 do you think could refer to itself as the "extended shadow of Rachel Carson"?

5. What do you notice about the title of this chapter in comparison with the content (the easy part)? What could you criticize about the use of this title (tricky part)?

Interesting projects:

If you've been to national parks in the US or the UK, list your impressions and rank the parks you've visited according to preference. If you haven't yet been there and don't know anyone who has, use the parks' web presence to create a table with the main attractions.

Ask American and British people to describe the role weather plays in their lives and note the words they use. Compare what they say with the information given in the geography appetizer chapter and in this chapter.

And the if-you-can-do-this-maybe-you'll-get-a-national-park-or-at-least-a-world-famous-dam-named-after-you:

Devise a plan that will maintain the highest degree of preservation possible for parts of the natural environment while at the same time justifying the use of taxpayers' funding for creating land that the taxpayers won't be able to experience as they might like because the land is supposed to be protected.

And finally, further topics not dealt with in this chapter … for those who have time to travel further than just the main tourist attractions:

effects of global warming on the climate of the UK and the US; details of the debate between preservationists like John Muir and the Sierra Club and conservationists like Theodore Roosevelt; other dams and manmade attempts to harness nature; importance of solar, wind, and tidal power; other animals and plants indigenous to the US and UK; air and water pollution; recycling; use of the catalytic converter as an example of California as a forerunner in all things environmentally friendly; Exxon Valdez as an example of how much damage can be done to the environment by one drunk ship captain; ecowarriors as a special British contribution to environmentalism; the anti-roads movement in the UK; the American and British Green parties; tree sitting …

# Bread and Circuses (the arts, leisure time activities and sports, food) | 11

"A land without music? Parry, Holst and Elgar to you, Schmitz" Title of an article by Boris Johnson (not yet Mayor of London) in the online version of the British newspaper The Telegraph

"You see, this is my life! It always will be! Nothing else! Just us, the cameras, and those wonderful people out there in the dark!... All right, Mr. DeMille, I'm ready for my close-up." Norma Desmond's last lines in Billy Wilder's iconic film *Sunset Boulevard*

"Football is a simple game; 22 men chase a ball for 90 minutes and at the end, the Germans win." Gary Lineker, former football player and sports broadcaster, quoted after England lost to Germany in the semifinals of the World Cup 1990

"If you're going to America, bring your own food." American writer and humorist Fran Lebowitz in *Social Studies*

If you asked any serious scholar of the past (up until around the late 1950s) about the importance of food in fashioning national identity or the importance of fashion in looking at the arts, he (female scholars being not serious by definition back then) would've laughed. Even though just a glance at some insulting terms in English for other nationalities shows us the linguistic links between food and (other) people: frogs (for the French) and krauts (for the Germans). And not just wearing certain clothes, even wearing certain colors (like royal purple reserved for royalty) used to be an age-old way of distinguishing who was who.

While some things have changed, others haven't. People still spend a good portion of their lifetimes shopping for, preparing, and eating food – in spite of the fast food convenience food developments that started in the land of the hamburger and hotdog. Not only what we eat, but how we eat, and when we eat can help define who we are. And what better way to spend our time after dinner than going to the movies or the theatre or the opera? Or going to a ballgame or watching our favorite sports team on TV? And those who would rather stay home than go to an art museum or to an arena can still listen to music that we might identify as American or English just by hearing the first few notes.

When you finish the chapter, you should be able to say something about

- the broad range of arts
- examples of typical English and American architecture as well as of architectural "follies"
- some famous American and British directors and actors
- typical movie genres with examples
- English classical music from Purcell to Britten
- British and American popular music and festivals
- the shock value of BritArt and the presence of American pop art in Germany
- some leisure time activities in both countries
- a few typical American and British sports
- different kinds of British and American food.

Let's begin this diverse chapter with the arts topic and start by looking at the word "arts" with its manifold varieties. We have the visual arts, which can include architecture and painting; the performing arts, which could include music and movies; the fine arts which could include all of the above; the liberal arts, which you've encountered before in a different, educational context. The word "arts" in the Bachelor of Arts degree is used in its widest sense and could include any of the topics dealt with in this chapter (🔔 4). We could also include design and fashion as art, and if we take the origin of the English word back to its Latin root, *ars*, we'd come across meanings that include "cunning" as opposed to "natural," "cunning" being related to *Kunst*, which as Karl Valentin tells us can be nice and pretty but involves a lot of work.

Which art to begin with? We could start alphabetically and historically at the very beginning with "a" for "architecture."

## 11.1 | A for architecture

Is there such a thing as American or British architecture? What comes to your mind when you hear this combination of nationality and buildings? Let's take a look at temples of God and temples of mammon in both countries and then glance at what is usually considered a uniquely British – or mostly English – kind of architecture.

temples of God

While it might be difficult to assign many European cathedrals to a particular nation, one particularly English contribution to European architecture has the word "English" in its name and is often referred to as English Gothic. English Gothic is usually divided into three periods: Early, Decorated, and Perpendicular. A good example of Early English Gothic architecture is Salisbury Cathedral in southern England, which isn't as decorative as Exeter Cathedral, an example of the Decorated style.

**Fig. 11.1**
*Interior of Exeter Cathedral with a view of the longest continuous piece of Gothic vaulted ceiling (almost 100 meters) in the world, described as an avenue of palms. The stained glass is modern, most of the original stained glass lost during World War II bombing.*

Perpendicular lines are characteristic of Gothic cathedrals in general, and the Perpendicular style in England is characterized by soaring walls, huge stained glass windows, and ceilings with fan vaulting, a particularly English design. You can find wonderful examples of ceilings with fan vaulting in the cathedrals in Gloucester (🔔 8) and Canterbury and also in King's College, part of Cambridge University (🔔 4), which has the largest fan vault ceiling in the word While Gothic architecture was replaced by other styles from the 16th century onwards, many elements of Gothic architecture became popular again from the 19th century onwards. You could say Gothic was "revived." Examples of Gothic Revival or neo-Gothic design include one of the most popular American buildings, the National Cathedral in Washington DC. A cathedral that looks so similar to so many others in Europe doesn't convey the same sense of American identity as small churches in New England villages do with their simple architecture and just their high steeples to distinguish them from the surrounding neighborhood.

**from temples of power to temples of mammon**

You won't only find examples of neo-Gothic in religious buildings like cathedrals: the Palace of Westminster (also known as the Houses of Parliament) (🔔 5) is also a famous example of Gothic Revival. We've now shifted from cathedrals to government, but we'd almost have to shift back if we considered any of the great monuments in Washington DC, the "wedding cake architecture," which often look like Greek temples (the Jefferson (🔔 5) and Lincoln Memorials, for example). As we've seen, civil religion in America makes a connection between government and religion and between temples of God and temples of political power (🔔 5). You'd probably automatically think of skyscrapers in connection with "architecture" and "America"; and these temples of mammon, as they could be critically described in our economic world, are perhaps the most visible aspect of American architecture even if most skyscrapers and all the highest ones are now to be found in Asia or in the Middle East. No longer among the Top Ten highest in the world but still the most popular American building according to one survey is the Empire State Building in Manhattan, built in the Great Depression of the 1930s. Until the completion of the World Trade Center in the 1970s, the Empire State was the highest building in New York City. After the destruction of the Twin Towers in the 9/11 attacks, it regained its status as the highest in New York and the second highest in the US. Incidentally, the invention of the electric elevator by the German inventor Werner von Siemens in the late 19th century helped to make skyscrapers possible. The verticality that was a unique characteristic of American cities like New York and Chicago in the last century is now a characteristic of urban areas around the world.

**follies: just for fun?**

One particular architectural form can be found in other places in the world but is most often found in Britain: buildings not to glorify God or to demonstrate the power of the state but "just for fun" and often called "follies." A few, like the Triangular Lodge in the English Midlands, were built for more serious reasons. The builder wanted to express his Catholic faith more or less secretly in Protestant Elizabethan England (🔔 2) by using architectural elements in threes (three walls, three floors among many others) – three designating the Trinity. Other follies were either built to look like ruins or in effect became ruins because they were never finished, like the National Monument in Edinburgh, which was supposed to eventually resemble the Parthenon and thus justify Edinburgh's claim to be the Athens of the North but for unclear reasons was never finished. Today you can find most follies in amusement parks, which we'll be visiting later in the chapter.

an American castle

Before we leave architecture, let's return briefly to our opening question of nationality and architecture. While you perhaps identified Britain with words like "cathedrals" or "castles" and America with "skyscrapers" or "monuments," you most probably didn't connect America with "castle" (unless you were thinking of an amusement park like Disneyland). But there is one castle on the California coast between Los Angeles and San Francisco built by a woman (Julia Morgan) for a man you may remember having read about and will be meeting again later in the chapter (William Randolph Hearst). The wild mixture of architectural styles and the overall gaudiness of the estate may not be to everyone's taste (although it attracts many visitors), but Hearst Castle, which Hearst originally called La Cuesta Encantada (the enchanted hill), is a state historical monument and certainly something you'd find only in America.

## F for fashion

| 11.2

And what about fashion? Is fashion an art? It certainly can play a role in national identity. Just think of a bowler hat and an umbrella as the way the typical Englishman was presented in German school books, think of the Queen's robes and her crowns, of Scottish tartan and kilts. What about headscarves and bangles? There have been court cases in Britain about the rights of students to wear jewelry or clothing that expresses their religious identity. Here we see clearly the importance of fashion as a statement about personal identity that can lead to suits (lawsuits here, not business suits, which are themselves an interesting sign of identity and power) and front page news. And of course there are school uniforms (🔔 4) both in Britain and in private schools in the US too. Clothes and America? Jeans of course. One of the very many Germans who immigrated to America in the middle of the $19^{th}$ century (🔔 7) was someone born with the name Löb Strauß, which became Levi Strauss. And the rest is blue jeans history.

Eileen Gray

When we shift from fashion to furniture design, we have a nice example from Ireland. Since Ireland was part of the United Kingdom until the 1920s as we learned in a history appetizer (2), we could still keep to the restrictions of the title Anglo-American Studies and mention one famous designer – and architect – who was born in Ireland when it was still part of the UK. You might have seen imitations of one of her most famous pieces of furniture although you might not have known that Eileen Gray was the designer of the Adjustable Side Table of steel tubing and glass that can be found in lots of German furniture stores.

Fig. 11.2 | *Eileen Gray Table*

## 11.3 | F for film

We could've called this section in British English "C for cinema" or in American English "M for movies" and thus have distinguished the two more or less easily. But the questions "Who's American?" and "Who's British?" aren't as easy to answer. What about the director Stanley Kubrick, who directed world famous movies like *2001: A Space Odyssey*, *A Clockwork Orange*, *Full Metal Jacket*, and *Eyes Wide Shut* and who spent most of his adult life in England? An American citizen, but an American director? Movie star Elizabeth Taylor was born in England (and thus a British subject) to American parents (and thus an American citizen). The director Alfred Hitchcock was also born in England (with personal experience of German cinema in the early 20th century), directed the first British film with sound ("talkie"), was influential in early English cinema, but later emigrated to America and became an American citizen.

Hollywood, of course

Probably the first word that comes to mind in connection with American movies is Hollywood, which was originally founded as a small town near what was a small but very fast-growing city called Los Angeles at the turn of the 20th century. Some of the producers of the growing new film industry moved from the east to California because of the good weather and the wide range of landscapes (mountains with snow, desert, and ocean) available within a short distance. D. W. Griffith, who made the first movie set in Hollywood, is considered the pioneer motion picture director and is sometimes called the Father of the Motion Picture. Griffith made movies on a grand scale by using monumental sets and many actors and refining many of the then current techniques in editing and cinematography. Griffith's *The Birth of a Nation* about the period of Reconstruction (2) was released in 1915 and is considered one of the most important films of all time although the racist content of the film, which portrayed the Ku Klux Klan as heroes restoring order to the south, provoked riots in some cities and was banned or censored in some states. Shocked by the critical response, Griffith directed the film *Intolerance* as an answer to those who had accused him of racism. While *Intolerance* was financially a failure in contrast to the huge profits *The Birth of a Nation* made, the later film has come to be seen as vastly influential on the development of cinema as an art form.

By the 1930s "talkies," films with synchronized sound, were becoming enormously popular. With the advent of sound, two especially American film genres became popular: gangster films based partly on the violence caused by Prohibition (2), and musicals. The first feature length film with dialogue and songs and thus the first musical was *The Jazz Singer*. By the time of the Great Depression in the 1930s, the large production companies in Hollywood were turning out hundreds of films each year. Hollywood has continued to represent mainstream American cinema to the present. And Sunset Boulevard, more than 30 kilometers long from downtown Los Angeles through Hollywood to the Pacific Ocean, is often associated with the glamour and the corruption of Hollywood. In addition to Griffith, perhaps the most important American film director of the silent era, another famous director, Cecille B. DeMille, mentioned in the last lines of the silent movie star in *Sunset Boulevard* quoted at the opening of this chapter, had a career spanning more than forty years from silent western movies to epic films like *The Greatest Show on Earth* and the *Ten Commandments*.

American film genres

In addition to using Hollywood as a category for American movies, you could also categorize them according to famous directors and actors (both male and female of course), to studios, and to film genres. We've already heard of one famous early American director, D. W. Griffith and two film genres, the gangster film and the musical. What some claim is the most successful movie of all time, *Gone with the Wind*, was released during Hollywood's Golden Era in the 1930s and produced by David Selznick, who worked with three of the largest production companies of the time, RKO, Paramount, and MGM. *Gone with the Wind* is a prime example of the epic genre, which also includes films made much later like William Wyler's *Ben Hur* or Stephen Spielberg's *Schindler's List*. The genre western includes a variety of films like the 50s classic *The Searchers*, directed by John Ford and starring John Wayne, the very popular *Butch Cassidy and the Sundance Kid* with Paul Newman and Robert Redford made in the late 60s, or *Unforgiven*, directed by and starring Clint Eastwood in the 90s. Sports films include *Raging Bull*, directed by Martin Scorcese and starring Robert DeNiro, and *Rocky* with Sylvester Stallone, both about boxing, as well as *National Velvet*, a film about horse racing, with a very young Elizabeth Taylor. Walt Disney is famously connected to animated films, another genre that was very popular in Hollywood's Golden Age with *Snow White* and *Pinocchio*. The animated film has now experienced a renaissance with very varied films like *The Lion King*, *Finding Nemo*, and *Shrek*, produced by the film studio DreamWorks. Romantic film comedies span the time from the beginnings of Hollywood with Charlie Chaplin's silent film *City Lights* through *The Philadelphia Story* from the 40s directed by George Cukor and starring Cary Grant, Katharine Hepburn, and James Stewart, including Woody Allen's *Annie Hall* from the 70s and writer and director Nora Ephron's *Sleepless in Seattle* with Tom Hanks and Meg Ryan from the 90s. The film classic from the 30s *The Wizard of Oz* belongs to the fantasy genre along with another 30s classic *King Kong*. Other examples of the fantasy genre include director Francis Capra's *It's a Wonderful Life* (showing often at Christmas) and *Groundhog Day* with Bill Murray. Science fiction films include Stanley Kubrick's *2001*, George Lucas's *Star Wars* series, Steven Spielberg's *ET*, and Roland Emmerich's *Independence Day*.

Orson Welles

One director not mentioned above but in the context of American radio (🔔 10) is often regarded as having directed the greatest film of all time, *Citizen Kane*, a 40s drama about a newspaper magnate and supposedly based on the life of the publisher William Randolph Hearst, whose castle you might remember as being an example of American architecture.

from *Look Back in Anger* to *The Reader*

There would be a lot to say about British film, which began at around the same time as American film did but soon exported many of its directors and actors across the ocean. Films described as British social realism began in the late 50s and early 60s with directors like Tony Richardson, Jack Clayton, Karel Reisz, and John Schlesinger and with films like *Look Back in Anger* (based on the play by John Osborn), *Room at the Top*, *Saturday Night and Sunday Morning*, *A Kind of Loving*, and *Billy Liar*. A renaissance of British cinema began in the 80s with films like *Local Hero*, *Chariots of Fire*, and *Gandhi*. Currently important British directors include older men like Ken Loach, Mike Leigh, and Stephen Frears, director of *My Beautiful Lauderette* (7) and *The Queen*, as well as younger directors like Stephen Daldry, director of *Billy Eliot* and *The Reader*, based on the German novel by Bernhard Schlink.

Although we need now to turn our attention to another kind of art, music, where we'll have the chance to mention some British contributions at the very beginning, we can at least end this part of the chapter at a tourist attraction whose name shows how the originally American word "movie" has now also been adopted by the British to refer to film. The Movieum, near the London Eye (1) calls itself a "celebration of the British film industry."

Fig. 11.3
*Movieum London*

## M for music

11.4

P for Purcell

In order to understand the title of the article quoted at the beginning of this chapter, we'll have to do a quick survey of the history of important English composers in a few key names. We can begin with Henry Purcell, born 350 years ago in a part of London that we've now heard about again and again, namely Westminster. Purcell was a real wunderkind, composing his first works as a boy. His work *Dido and Aeneas* is considered to be the first English opera and is very short at around an hour. The subject matter is from the classical Roman poet Virgil's epic poem the *Aeneid*. Purcell also composed works like *The Fairy-Queen*, and *King Arthur*, which as the name indicates deals with a story closely connected to England, the King Arthur legend (2). Both these works are sometimes called semi-operas since they contain spoken language and dances.

Händel? Handel!

And after Purcell? Well, the name of the next very famous English composer doesn't sound very English. George Frideric Handel, who anglicized his first two names and gave up his umlaut when he emigrated to England, composed extraordinarily popular music like the *Water Music*, requested for a concert on the Thames by George I, who as you may remember was also German (2). Handel's *Music for the Royal Fireworks* was composed for another German King George of England, George II. At least Handel could speak better English than the kings. He also composed the *Messiah*, based on excerpts taken from the King James Bible. The movement often performed last (though not last in the work itself) is the very famous *Hallelujah Chorus*, at the beginning of which the audience traditionally stands up.

Delius, Parry, Holst, and Elgar

Another important English composer with a similar first name didn't change the spelling of his last name. Frederick Delius was also of German descent and although his music is said to celebrate his love of the English countryside, he spent most of his life in the US and later in France. An early piece inspired by Delius's stay near Jacksonville, Florida, is called the *Florida Suite*. And what about Parry, Holst, and Elgar, the composers quoted at the beginning of this chapter as evidence that Britain was not a land without music, as the German critic with the very German name Oscar Adolf Hermann Schmitz claimed in pre-World War I Europe, a time when Anglo-German relations weren't the best? Sir Hubert Parry is an English composer from the late $19^{th}$ century known for the anthem "I Was Glad," used during the coronation of all monarchs since Edward VII. Gustav Holst was born in England, but his name points to his Swedish ancestors. While you might not know his orchestral suite called *The Planets* by name, you've probably heard parts of it on television commercials, movie scenes, or quoted in many popular music pieces.

If you've experienced a typical American graduation ceremony, then you've certainly heard one of the *Pomp and Circumstance Military Marches*, one of the most famous pieces by Sir Edward Elgar. And if you've experienced any of the annual summer concerts in London known as the Proms, especially the Last Night at the Proms, then you've no doubt heard this tune sung to the words of "Land of Hope of Glory" with much flag-waving and singing, behavior that is one example of a lack of a division between "serious" and "popular" music, such as is often made in Germany.

Britten

What would be more appropriate to round off our brief look at British classical music than to end with a British composer named Britten? And Benjamin Britten is indeed considered to be one of the most important composers of the 20th century with operas like *Billy Bud*, *The Turn of the Screw*, and *Death in Venice* (based on short stories by the American and German writers Herman Melville, Henry James, and Thomas Mann). His many works include the *War Requiem*, written for the completion of a new cathedral in Coventry next to the one destroyed by German bombs in World War II. One of Britten's most popular pieces is called *The Young Person's Guide to the Orchestra* and is just that – a musical guide to various instruments. Britten uses a theme from Purcell and thus provides us with a second nice example of how serious and popular music aren't differentiated in English music as they are often in Germany. By the way, Purcell also had an influence on British rock music, but that's another story…

Britpop

While Britain may have had the reputation of being a land without music earlier, the "British invasion" of the US in the 1960s with the overwhelming success of the Beatles and the Rolling Stones – among other bands – granted the UK a leading status in pop music. (The British invasion of American arts in general from the 60s and 70s also included Britcoms and television series like *Civilisation* 10.) You've probably all heard of the Beatles as well as some of their music although you might not know it was composed by John Lennon or Paul McCartney, two of the four musicians and composers who along with George Harrison and Ringo Starr made up the most successful popular music group in western history. A generation after the breakup of the Fab Four, the words Britain and pop were fused into Britpop, partly a response to an American invasion of popular music in the 90s. Bands like Oasis and Blur explicitly indicated their admiration of the Beatles and of their roots in the north of England. Other world-famous musicians with British roots are Phil Collins, Elton John, David Bowie, Sting, and Robbie Williams – and to name just one woman: Amy Winehouse.

from Elvis to Woodstock

We started this section with the first big name in music from Britain from the distant past, Purcell; we'll end it with two anniversaries of important events in American music. The 30th anniversary of Elvis Presley's death made the news in 2007 to remind those too young to have experienced him live of his enormous impact on popular music with a style that combined elements of African American music with country music and American pop music. A list of musicians influenced by Presley's music could function as a summary of modern Anglo-American popular music and culture. A summary of important Anglo-American music of the 70s can be found by looking at those who performed at the legendary Woodstock festival, which celebrated its fortieth anniversary in 2009. The festival, held in the open air at a rural dairy north of New York City included a variety of musical styles representative of American and British music of the time. Folk singers like Joan Baez and Arlo Guthrie; rock singers like Joe Cocker, Jimi Hendrix, Janis Joplin; bands like Blood, Sweat, and Tears; Creedence Clearwater Revival; Crosby, Stills, Nash and Young; the Grateful Dead; Jefferson Airplane; Santana; Sly and the Family Stone; and The Who. The organizers had planned to sell tickets; most of the crowd was let in for free when far more arrived than expected. People experimented openly with drugs and sex and seemed to enjoy the rain that started during the festival and turned the farm into a sea of mud. In spite of the huge and unexpected crowds, there was no violence. The documentary film *Woodstock* was released the following year and proved enormously popular. The "three days of peace and music" became a symbol of the counterculture movement and both shocked and fascinated Americans.

## 11.5 | V for visual arts

S for Sensation

Visual arts can shock and fascinate people just as much as music and festivals can, so we'll start our look at British visual arts with a contemporary group of British artists often labeled with a name modeled after Britpop: BritArt. While the kind of art created by those who came to be called the Young British Artists or YBA has varied widely, its ability to shock people is one common aspect. The first and now famous art exhibit of artists like Damien Hirst, Tracey Emin, Marcus Harvey, and Chris Ofili was appropriately enough called "Sensation: Young British Artists from the Saatchi Collection," and it caused a sensation at the Royal Academy of Arts in London, where it opened in 1997, before moving to Berlin and then closing at the Brooklyn Museum of Art in New York. Marcus Harvey's painting "Myra" might look ordinary enough to most people outside of Britain, but it's based on one of the most widely known images in Britain, a photograph made by police upon the arrest of Myra Hindley, a serial killer of young children, convicted in the mid 1960s. What was especially controversial was Harvey's use of small children's handprints to create the picture. While "Myra" was the most controversial item in the exhibit in London, what was most controversial in New York was a picture by Chris Ofili, a British artist of Nigerian ancestry. Ofili used elephant dung and small pieces of pornographic magazines to portray a black Virgin Mary, a mixture of African and Western art that Americans found obscene and blasphemous. The publicity – both negative and positive – contributed to making the exhibit "Sensation" a sensational success, also for the sponsor and advertising mogul Charles Saatchi, who later sold the works he'd bought for large profits.

Damien Hirst was also represented in "Sensation" and originally belonged to the YBAs, and has since become one of the most famous and richest artists in the western world. Nowadays Hirst is associated with a replica of a human skull decorated with thousands of diamonds or with glass boxes containing preserved dead animals. The installation of a shark with the long title "The Physical Impossibility of Death in the Mind of Someone Living" has become the most famous example of BritArt. Hirst won the Turner Prize for another one of his dead animal installations in the mid 1990s. But what's the Turner Prize?

the Turner Prize and Turner

First presented in 1984 and organized by the Tate, an institution composed of several museums with the goal of increasing public appreciation of British art from the 16th century to the present, the Turner Prize creates a connection between perhaps the most famous English painter of all times, John Mallord William Turner, and contemporary artists, some of whom have made a lot of money through shocking exhibitions. Turner, who painted landscapes in the first half of the 19th century and whose later work became especially influential, was himself controversial in his own time although none of his works would cause any protests now. The Turner Prize has become the most publicized art award in Britain and is awarded annually to British artists younger than 50 for an outstanding exhibition or presentation of their work. "British" no longer means born in Britain. Since the requirement was changed to include not only British-born artists but also foreigners who live and work in the UK, two German-born artists have won: In 2000 Wolfgang Tillmans was the first photographer and the first person not born in Britain to receive the Turner Prize, followed six years later by the German-born painter Tomma Abts.

American pop art... on German postage stamps

Fig. 11.4

Fig. 11.5

If you're interested in American painting, you can easily see masterpieces by famous pop artists like Roy Lichtenstein, Robert Rauschenberg, Jasper Johns, and of course Andy Warhol in art museums in Cologne and Frankfurt. One of the first and best-known pieces of pop art (created not by an American artist but by the English painter Richard Hamilton) is a collage with the long title "Just What Is It that Makes Today's Homes So Different, So Appealing?" and can be found in Tübingen. The contemporary American pop artist James Rizzi was the first living artist ever to be given a commission to design German postage stamps in 2008 thus turning thousands of letters posted in Germany into little works of American pop art.

We could now include some of the arts not mentioned earlier like dancing, for example. While distinguishing between ballet and square dancing would be a great topic to show differences in class and national/regional identity, I've chosen instead to present some of the ways the British and Americans spend their leisure time.

## 11.6 Leisure Time Activities

Disneyland

Remember how much vacation Americans have (6)? The question could be asked – do Americans have any time at all for leisure activities? Maybe because of the pioneer spirit or American restlessness or just because the idea of a vacation as "having nothing to do and all day to do it in," as the American magician

Robert Orben claimed, isn't attractive to Americans... In any case many Americans even fill up their vacations with activities. And one very popular attraction was built in Anaheim (a city founded by Germans, by the way), California, in the mid 1950s by someone we've now met several times in this chapter: Walt Disney. His Disneyland Theme Park was followed by a similar but even larger resort on the other side of the country in Orlando, Florida, twenty years later. We mentioned follies as an example of typical British eccentricity earlier in the chapter. The most famous follies are probably those in Disneyland, buildings that look like castles or old mansions or swans but function as shops or settings for rides or hotels or restaurants (in contrast to Hearst's Castle or Michael Jackson's Neverland Ranch, which functioned as homes).

piers and birds and hunting

Disney has been exported to Tokyo, Hong Kong, and – at first less successfully – to Paris, but not at all to Britain, where amusement parks like Pleasure Beach in Blackpool in the north of England and Alton Towers in the Midlands can be found. There are also older seaside attractions with piers at places like Brighton (1) although the traditional seaside resorts have suffered economically from the mass tourism that began in the 60s with inexpensive package holidays in Spain or France. But the British don't need to leave the country to enjoy one of the most popular leisure activities in Britain: bird watching – or at least becoming a member of the RSPB (9). And as we've also heard, fox hunting although controversial is still practiced (9). Hunting isn't nearly as controversial in the US, where it's a very popular leisure activity. Americans may allow laws to prevent drinking (2) or smoking but laws to prevent hunting or to restrict the right to own guns can provoke strong protest (3). Americans believe they have a constitutional right to hunt and fish, and in the state of Oklahoma it really is anchored in the state constitution.

scandals and politics: it's all a game

A game that most of you have probably watched on German TV was originally a British television game show. "*Who Wants to Be a Millionaire?*" has been exported to many countries. One famous American forerunner of this popular TV game show was the *$64,000 Question*. As you might guess by the low sum of money, this game show was popular a long a time ago – in the 1950s. In a famous quiz show scandal in the 50s involving a similar show called *Twenty One* producers tried to increase ratings

(10) by giving popular contestants the answers to the questions. Robert Redford later directed the award-winning movie *Quiz Show* based on this scandal. For another kind of game: Look in some of the other chapters of this book and find some of the programs of American presidents that were related to card games, yet another popular American and British leisure activity. And the answer is… Teddy Roosevelt's Square Deal, Franklin Delano Roosevelt's New Deal, Harry S. Truman's Fair Deal and also his saying "the buck stops here" used in the card game Poker.

circuses

Card games may seem a little old-fashioned in our modern age of media – although there are some electronic versions of old-fashioned card games like Solitaire or Poker or Bridge. Another somewhat old-fashioned leisure time activity can be traced back to Roman times and places like the Circus Maximus, literally the "greatest circle," where chariot races took place. (The movie buffs may have seen a film mentioned earlier in this chapter, *Ben Hur*, with its famous chariot race.) The first modern circus was in $18^{th}$ century London, the first American circus was started a few years later in Philadelphia. In addition to horses like in ancient Rome, wild animals, acrobatic acts, and clowns entertained the audience. Barnum and Bailey became famous names in late $19^{th}$ century America with their three-ring circus promising the "Greatest Show on Earth," which might remind you of yet another movie title mentioned earlier in the chapter. Ringling Brothers later joined with Barnum and Bailey and still tour America today. Modern-day circuses include the TheatroZinZanni on the American West coast with its combination of circus and dinner theatre and the Nofitstate circus in Wales with its emphasis on regional identity. Why mention circuses in this chapter? Because of the title and the final words of this chapter… but we're not quite there yet.

We could have had a look at one popular American and British activity: tourism. And tourist guides can provide an especially interesting look at a people's and a nation's identity, but let's turn now instead to another activity that has occupied human beings since they were able to spend time on other things than farming and hunting, an activity that plays an important role in many people's lives and not only in Britain and America: *sport* in British English or *sports* in American English.

## Sport(s)

| 11.7

from Anglo rugby to American football

Let's begin this section with a look at sports from an Anglo-American perspective although kicking balls around has been a human pastime since humans and balls existed. Legend has it that in the early 19th century at an English public school (🔔 4) appropriately enough named Rugby one student started to carry a ball that players had only been allowed to kick, and the sport rugby was born. Rugby became popular in the United States too and became known as American football (which is called "American football" only outside the US to distinguish this ball game from what is called soccer in the US). Even if you don't understand American football and aren't interested in the issues of identity, costume, and aggression connected with this sport, you still might be interested in one expression that was used continually during the presidential election of 2008 – a Hail Mary pass, which can now mean any action that only has a small chance of success. But to return to Britain: Those who kept to the old rules of football that banned any use of hands continued to play a game called association football, which came to be known informally as soccer and is still known as soccer in the US and as football in the rest of the world.

typical American sports

German immigrants brought with them their turnverein, which became translated into gymnastics clubs, in the mid 19th century about the same time as the combination of Christianity and physical fitness led to the founding of the Young Men's Christian Association, better known as the YMCA. Physical education became a subject at school and university. One president we've heard about in several different contexts (🔔 1, 9), Theodore Roosevelt, believed in doing sports as a way of overcoming sickness. The importance of sports has also contributed to the image that Americans demand of their presidents in general. But the only kind of sport of specifically American origin is basketball, invented within the YMCA organization more than a hundred years ago. And maybe you thought baseball, another very popular sport in the US, was originally American? While it's been played more than half a century longer than basketball, its origins are now thought to go back to an English game called rounders. And the rules of baseball are no doubt as mysterious and difficult to understand to non-fans as the rules of cricket in Britain. Weightlifting, bodybuilding, and gymnastics, although originating in the early 20th century, have become much more popular in the US since bodybuilders Arnold Schwarzenegger and Sylvester Stallone became movie stars or with the success of actor and activist Jane Fonda's gymnastics videos.

American values and American ethnicities

Americans like to see their values such as competition, self-improvement, and fair play as part of the reason for the popularity of sports in American life, even if some Americans sometimes criticize the abuse of intercollegiate sports in colleges and universities (4) as well as the enormous profits to be made in professional sports like basketball, baseball, and football. While sports, like so many other areas of American life, was originally segregated, the success of African American athletes goes back as far as the 1936 Olympics in Berlin when Jesse Owens annoyed Hitler by beating white "Aryan" German athletes in running and the long jump. Famous African American sportsmen include Carl Lewis (track and field), Tommie Smith and John Carlos (both track and field and football), baseball player Hank Aaron, tennis player Arthur Ashe, and of course world-famous boxers like Muhammad Ali and George Foreman. Smith and Carlos became internationally known after they used the Black Power Salute during the 1968 Olympics in Mexico City to protest American racism. Muhammad Ali was an outspoken critic of the Vietnam War. One of the most popular athletes today is golf star Tiger Woods, whose mixed ethnicity is sometimes called Cablinasian from Caucasian (white), black, Indian, and Asian.

Manchester United and English pop culture

Let's now make an abrupt transition in time and place. Remember Manchester from one of our history appetizers (2)? The historical connection was a Roman one, -chester being a suffix derived from Latin castrum meaning "camp" or "fortification." Our topic isn't Roman, but camp still plays a role as in football camps for young athletes, and Manchester United as one of the most famous football (what Americans would call soccer) teams in the world. The most famous of the many well-known players is ex-player David Beckham (now a player for an American soccer club), who joined the team at the age of 17, and who has since become one of the most recognizable people on earth. His fame is based not only on his athletic prowess but also on his marriage to Victoria Adams, one of the Spice Girls, themselves an iconic English girl group of the 1990s, as well as on his presence in the worlds of fashion and popular culture.

national identity and inter/national sports

While the national aspects of international football are obvious as in the English football player and broadcaster Gary Lineker's grudging praise of German talents mentioned at the very beginning of this chapter, let's remind ourselves here that the United Kingdom is made up of four nations. While Great Britain participates in the Olympics as one country, England and Wales can compete together against Scotland in cricket, a bat-and-ball sport (in some ways similar to American baseball) more popular in England than in Scotland or Northern Ireland. And England, Scotland, and Wales can compete against one another in rugby and in football. Through rituals and chanting, through wearing tattoos and dressing up or painting their faces in the colors of the English – or the Scottish or the Welsh – flag, even through arranging marriage ceremonies or having their ashes spread on the grounds of the stadium of their favorite team, fans express not only their connection to the sport but also their own identity as part of a group. The controversial Conservative politician Norman Tebbit used his "cricket test," which later became known as the "Tebbit test," to demonstrate that those immigrants to Britain who supported the teams of their country of birth hadn't yet learned to love their new country enough and lacked the necessary patriotism needed to become true English people. (Fans of Scottish cricket teams could be criticized in the same way for being loyal to their home country instead of to England.) Tebbit was aware of course of the tradition of cricket and the high quality of players in countries like India, Pakistan, Sri Lanka, and the West Indies.

That group identity can sometimes involve violence and hooliganism – a behavior especially connected with English football fans – is an aspect of sport much more prevalent in Britain than in America, a country which, strangely enough, experiences much more violence than Britain outside sports.

## Food? Food! | 11.8

food? food!

After all the work involved in art and the physical exertions in sport, we can now turn to one last leisure time activity that has most recently become popular (again) in television shows spanning the globe, a leisure-time activity that was once THE activity of human beings – or for that matter for any living species: eating.

from marmite to fish 'n chips to chicken tikka masala

Since we just mentioned the connection between sports and national identity, let's continue looking at identity but now from a culinary point of view. It's useful to remember that much of the English national diet has its origins more in the industrial revolution than in organic pastures. One of the most famous examples is a kind of yeast extract used as a spread on toast or as a flavoring, which many people (me too) find repulsive. Marmite, the brand name used for the product in Britain, is very popular in England – and in parts of the former Empire like Australia, New Zealand, South Africa – and has been produced since the beginning of the 20th century at first as a by-product of brewing beer. While Marmite has come to be considered as a typical English food, its name comes from the French word for a cooking pot and its existence is due at least in part to research done on meat extracts by a German scientist in the 19th century. Other examples of mass-produced food products popular in Britain are Twiglets – snacks that taste like Marmite – and KitKats, chocolate-covered wafers that have also become popular in the US and in Germany. Some say that such foods are the culinary equivalent of Britpop. In addition to these examples, which could be considered as mass produced junk food, another English food is also the product of the machine age: fish 'n chips (🔔 1). It was originally Jewish traders in London who fried fish to prevent it from spoiling quickly. And the hearty English breakfast that some tourists enjoy before the rigors of doing all the sights was originally intended as food for farm workers to get them through a long day of manual labor. The current most popular dish in Britain isn't fish 'n chips but a dish with no exact equivalent in India or Pakistan or Bangladesh and which has now become the national dish of Britain: chicken tikka masala, a combination of roast chicken chunks in a thick sauce. Some critics may argue that immigrant food has been so enthusiastically accepted because no one likes traditional food, not even the British. What's true in any case is that international flavors have made culinary life in Britain more varied, especially when the contrasts are right next door to one another as you might remember from an illustration in a previous chapter (🔔 7).

Even tea, something probably everyone would identify as a sign of Englishness if not Britishness, is made of tea leaves from China, India, or Sri Lanka and sweetened with sugar from other exotic places. The British were the ones, by the way, who brought the tradition of drinking tea to India, where it was little known in spite of the abundance of tea leaves. Of course with the increasing popularity of coffee, English tea maybe isn't as popular a pastime as in days gone by.

Fig. 11.6
*Starbucks*

Starbucks, the successful American coffee house chain that originated in Seattle, Washington, is now a part of many urban areas, and can be also found in the heart of London.

The Scottish people, who if we believed stereotypes would rather drink whiskey than tea or coffee, can be proud of some of their regional food officially recognized by the European Union: Scottish Farmed Salmon and Arbroath Smokies (a kind of haddock). More famous is of course haggis, a traditional Scottish dish that actually tastes a lot better than you might expect from its ingredients of seasoned sheep intestines. Other British products associated with regional identity in their names include Dorset blue cheese, Cornish clotted cream, Scotch beef and lamb, and Welsh lamb. And you may remember some other regional details from our geography appetizers (🔔 1) like Worcestershire. Or maybe you remember British aristocratic titles like earl (🔔 3)? The Earl of Sandwich's name is now known around the world, not so much for any noble accomplishments but for one of the most common kinds of food available in the Western world.

Jamie Oliver

More recently food and cooking in Britain has been making headlines not for its lack of nutrition or lack of tradition but for the modern awareness of the importance of healthy eating. Traffic light labeling for food with red, amber, and green circles to alert the consumer to possible health risks started in the UK and has now spread to Germany, too. Jamie Oliver has become well known not only in Britain for his television programs with catchy titles like *The Naked Chef* or *Jamie's Ministry of Food* along with his many cookbooks and public appearances making generations, especially school children, more aware of what they eat. Michael Caines is another example of an English chef changing the international reputation of British cuisine.

Julia Child

An American equivalent to Jamie Oliver is in some ways Julia Child, even though the American chef, cookbook writer, and television personality was most influential in the 60s and 70s of the last century. A film entitled *Julie and Julia* explores the relationship between Julia Child and Julie Powell. Meryl Streep plays the woman who some say did much to change the way Americans see food, and Amy Adams plays Julie Powell, an American blogger (10) who documents her cooking all 524 recipes in Child's bestseller *Mastering the Art of French Cooking*. Child's cookbook, published in the 1960s and 70s, is considered to be one of the most influential cookbooks in American history. Julia Child herself has been a figure in American popular culture from the 60s until today.

hamburgers and hotdogs... and gumbo

Probably most people wouldn't think of French cuisine when they imagine American food but instead of hamburgers and hotdogs. The hamburger and the hotdog can be as simple as meat or sausage on a bun or elaborate meals in themselves with exotic garnishes and seasonings. Being able to be fixed and eaten quickly without cutlery or plates helps account for the success of both kinds of food, developed from ground beef and sausages originally introduced by German immigrants in the early 19th century. While the name hamburger automatically reminds you of the German city, you'll also hear the German/Austrian connection for hotdogs when you hear the synonyms frankfurter or wiener. The growth of fast food chains now available all over the world provides evidence both for critics who point to the environmental waste and lack of nutrients in fast food as well as for those who claim that fast food can also carry connotations of progress and modernity. American food of course can also reflect the multiculturalism of American life. An example of delicious Creole cuisine in Louisiana is gumbo, a fish and vegetable soup or stew that combines French, American and African ingredients.

While Americans face problems of obesity from eating too much – at least partly to blame are the fast food restaurants with their extra large sizes and free refills of soft drinks – awareness of the dangers in eating too much is increasing. California will require all chain food restaurants to display calories and the amount of fat per item; restaurants in New York City already have menu-labeling regulations. Some public schools have begun to replace junk food and soda by fruits and vegetables in an effort to help Americans eat healthier.

At the very opening of this chapter I quoted the American humorist Fran Lebowitz (nomen est omen if you look at the last syllable of her last name). Even if she didn't mean her bon mot as a compliment for American cuisine, as we've seen here the immigrants who came and are still coming to America did bring their own food. While two common metaphors used to describe American society, pizza and salad, can't claim to be very original contributions to world cuisine (7), the huge variety of food that Americans eat reflects their origin as well as the limited variety of fast food restaurants. And Starbucks revitalized coffee, which had been considered as old-fashioned, first across the US and then across the world and in effect saved some of the European cafes that might have gone out of business had not coffee drinking become so popular again. The rest of the world will no doubt continue its love-hate relationship with American food and American eating habits.

We began the first part of our book with geography and history appetizers and are ending it with coffee and perhaps some German desserts since neither America nor Britain compares especially well with the German and Austrian selection of cakes and pies. You may have asked yourself what the title of this chapter referred to. We mentioned some American influences on the ancient leisure time activity of going to the circus. But the combination bread and circuses? I could give you the Latin expression *panem et circenses* and throw in some very fancy vocabulary like "hegemony" or "bricolage". But I think we all need a nice after dinner drink now followed by an afternoon nap before we tackle the rest of the book!

## Exercises

1. Name a characteristic of English Gothic architecture and give three good examples you could visit in the UK. Name two characteristics of follies and give one example in the UK and one in the US. Name one famous English architect mentioned in one of the history appetizers and again in the chapter on religion but not in this chapter, an architect who's best known for a cathedral in London that isn't Gothic.
2. What could you criticize about the parts of the chapter that deal with movies and with music?
3. What's the connection between one of the most famous English painters of the $19^{th}$ century and a German photographer who lives and works in London?
4. Name one example of German influence and two examples of British influence on American sports.
5. Name two connections between circuses and movies and one connection between food and movies.
6. Mention one example of German influence on American food, two examples of how food can be a sign of a multicultural society, and three chefs.

Challenging questions and interesting projects:

Ask American and British people what they would recommend to foreign visitors as the one most American or most British (or if it's easier: English or Welsh or Scottish) piece of art.

Ask the same people what they would cook if they wanted to give a foreign visitor the best taste of American or British food (or English or Welsh or Scottish if they respond with "there is no British food").

Have a look at all the German television programs you receive to count the number of American and British movies broadcast. Try to account for the choice. Which movies have you already seen? Which ones would you want to see?

Go to your nearest art museum and count the number of paintings you would consider American. Try and explain why there are so few British paintings there.

And finally the if-you-can-do-this-you-deserve-an-Oscar-and-a-Tony-and-an-Emmy-and-a-Grammy-and-maybe-even-the-Turner-Prize-but-certainly-a-meal-at-the-best-Michael-Caines-restaurant task:

Think of a way that the American and British governments can encourage and fund artists to criticize society while at the same time becoming popular enough to be heard from coast to coast and at the same time solve the increasing problem of obesity in both countries by convincing Americans and Brits that eating is a cultural activity that should prolong life, not cut it short.

And for those culture vultures who just can't get enough and who have the leisure time needed to pursue the arts, play and watch the sports, and enjoy all the cuisine Britain and America have to offer:

music as a sign of patriotism (other than the "Land of Hope and Glory" mentioned in this chapter); canonical works of art; tower block vs. front and back garden as reasons for the British not taking to living in high rise apartment buildings with the renovation of Keeling House as example of modern architecture; Council Housing in the UK compared with public housing in the US; American "classical" composers like Barber, Copland, and others like Bernstein, Gershwin; American folk art and quilts; Grandma Moses; German-British contemporary artists like the painter Peter Doig or the sculptor Tony Cragg; dances like the Charleston; the influence of pop music, of Madonna, and of MTV on world culture; connections between Bob Dylan's music and American films; connections between American jazz and rock music; the growth of American theatre out of minstrel and vaudeville; the influence of deconstruction on American architecture and architects like Frank Gehry; popular American photographers such as Spencer Tunick, Edward Weston, Robert Mapplethorpe, Connie Imboden, Ansel Adams, Man Ray, or Cindy Sherman; the issue of government support for the arts; "Washington Crossing the Delaware" as an iconic American painting by the German-American artist Emanuel Leutze; and finally to almost end this potpourri (or bricolage?) … many more details about food and fashion as elements of identity …

# Part II: Ways of Looking at Anglo-American Cultural Studies

Contents


12 Identity: Who's the Us, Who's the Them? ......... 229

13 Power: Those Who Got It and Those That Ain't .... 242

14 Gender: Wo-Men ................................ 256

15 New Media Was, Is, and Always Will Be the Message? ........................................ 270

16 Culture with a Big "C" and with a Little "c" in Anglo-American Cultural Studies ............... 283

We've now finished lunch, and hopefully you're still relishing the bread and circuses dessert. Maybe you've made notes of some of the strange tastes you may have experienced; you may have even bitten on a few things that you thought were really odd (but hopefully didn't spit out). In Part II we're going to be taking another look at some of the things in Part I but now from different perspectives in order to come to an understanding of some of the most popular buzzwords in academia, especially in the US and the UK but more and more around the world too. Perhaps you've noticed that "cultural studies" is part of the title of this book but wasn't mentioned in the title of Part I: "Specific Topics in Anglo-American Area Studies." What about the "cultural studies" part of Anglo-American Cultural Studies? Before we can answer this question, we'll have to come to grips with one small word in the dictionary, but one giant concept in academia and maybe even in life too: "culture."

Before we get to culture though, we'll continue with other ways of looking at some of the topics in Part I using the key words identity, power, gender, and media. Then we'll be able to turn finally to tackling "culture" and putting Anglo-American Studies in the context of other academic disciplines, some of which you've heard of, some of which may be new to you. And we'll end our after-dinner discussions with a final conclusion.

While the five chapters in this second part of our book follow the same pattern as most of the chapters in the first part, you'll notice one addition. Since individual academics, intellectuals, and scholars play such an important role in cultural studies, it's appropriate to do a bit of name-dropping. But name-dropping alone of course isn't enough, so you'll find some biographical details about each person in a new section called "biggies in boxes."

While we'll be adjusting our perspective in Part II, much of what we'll be looking at remains the same. To show the contrast, we're changing now from Part I to Part II; to indicate continuity we'll continue with Chapter 12 as the first chapter in Part II after Chapter 11 in Part I.

# Identity: Who's the Us, Who's the Them? 12

"...whence came all these people? They are a mixture of English, Scotch, Irish, French, Dutch, Germans, and Swedes... What, then, is the American, this new man? He is neither a European nor the descendant of a European; hence that strange mixture of blood, which you will find in no other country."
French-American writer J. Hector St. John de Crèvecœur
in *Letters from an American Farmer* in 1782

"Recently described as 'a place not a race; a vibe not a tribe', Britain is a more successful matrix for changing identities than almost any other European country. This makes it more, not less, difficult to understand what Britishness is all about; constantly renegotiated, it seems to be simply the state of play in an endless conversation."
from the back cover of a publication by the British Council:
*What is British?*
in celebration of its 70th anniversary in 2004.
The authors: Ziauddin Sardar, Piaras Mac Éinrí, Zrinka Bralo, and Csilla Hős.

Probably the first question human beings asked themselves when they became able to ask questions was: "Who am I?" In the past half century the concept of "identity" has become one of most popular concepts that academics have wrestled with. We could actually have used this chapter title for the entire book as the question of identity is perhaps the most central one in Anglo-American Area and Cultural Studies. We could also include class and gender here as aspects of identity, but let's reserve these topics for their own chapters.

When you finish this chapter, you should be able to say something about

- how national identity can be described
- the role of the nation as an "imagined community"
- characteristics of national identity using some aspects of identity that we've covered in previous chapters
- some reasons for the choice of facts in previous chapters combined with a critique of these choices and
- important scholars in the field of cultural studies.

If we look at the title of this book, then we're already in the middle of one view of identity. Can you imagine anyone answering the question: "Who are you" with "I'm an Anglo-American"? Answers like "I'm an American" or "I'm English" or "I'm Welsh" are much more common. Questions of identity often involve being members of nations and may seem at first glance wonderfully concrete. What's more concrete than a passport? Most people only have one. But the passport answer can be very problematic at second glance. Is "I'm a citizen of the United States" the same as "I'm an American"? I remember asking students to define what they thought being American was and one saying he could be American regardless of his nationality since being American was a state of mind. The following passport answer, in addition to being a bit clumsy, certainly wouldn't satisfy some English, Scottish, and Welsh people: "I'm a citizen of the United Kingdom of Great Britain and Northern Ireland." So you can see it isn't always easy to equate identity with nationality. And nationality itself isn't as simple as it may seem.

nations and states

The word "nation" is derived from a Latin word associated with "birth" and can refer to a group of people who all share the same place of birth. And all people born in the United States are automatically granted American citizenship (*jus soli*, a Latin expression for "the right of the soil"). Sometimes the word "nation" is used in contrast to the word "state" with "state" designating the political entity. So the United States is a state made up of 50 individual states (5). What is a nation? Does it make sense at all to talk about Britain or the United Kingdom as just one nation? Does knowing about political divisions in the US, like Congressional Districts for example, help us understand anything important about national identity? Perhaps we can at least agree that people tend to identify with places and call themselves after cities – Los Angelenos – or nations – Welsh – or regions – Geordie (the area of northeast England around Newcastle).

One person who spent some time thinking deeply about nations was born in China to an Irish father and an English mother. He grew up in California, attended Cambridge University, and later was thrown out of Indonesia after criticizing the government. Understandably enough considering his personal background, Benedict Anderson thought that nation, nationality, and nationalism were all very difficult to define and wrote a book whose title would become one of the most important concepts in the academic discussion of identity: *Imagined Communities.*

*the nation as imagined community*

Anderson understands a nation as a community that's imagined, limited, and independent. "Imagined" because the members of even the smallest nation would never get to know personally all the other members and thus can only imagine who these others are. "Limited" because the concept of nation includes other nations, no nation being large enough to include all people. "Independent" (or sovereign) because the concept of nation includes a sense of being able to control its own destiny in a state.

And here we have the distinction between "nation" and "state" which can explain the cause of many of the conflicts of the last half century. Some understood and still understand the Irish nation as deserving its own state: the entire island of Ireland. The United Kingdom has four nations, England, Scotland, Wales, and Northern Ireland, each of which would deserve its own state. We've seen how the process of devolution could help these four nations remain as a united kingdom in one state or perhaps lead to the breakup of United Kingdom into four nations in four separate states (5). One view of identity within the UK is that the Scottish and the Welsh have a binary sense of national identity like the "hyphenated Americans": Arab-American, Chinese-American, German-American. The Scottish and the Welsh thus see themselves as Scottish or Welsh and as British. The English, however, have a more difficult time distinguishing English from British identity and are also the ones with more identity problems.

*nations to kill and die for*

Although they can only be imagined, some nations are so important that people are willing to fight and to kill for and to die for them, too. You may remember a nice example of the belief in national destiny from our history appetizers: the concept of Manifest Destiny (2) was used to explain why – and how – the United States was able to move across the continent of North America taking over land owned by others. Of course people base such strong feelings of nationality on more than just an imagined idea of what their nation is; they also have symbols and actual objects made of marble or stone, which help people maintain their sense of national identity.

*monuments*

The Stone of Scone (which is also called the Stone of Destiny) is a symbol of Scottish identity, was used in the coronation ceremony of Scottish monarchs, later brought to Westminster Abbey hundreds of years ago and has been used ever since in the coronation ceremony of English and then British kings and queens. Just a decade ago, Queen Elizabeth decided to return the stone to Scotland (although it's to be sent back to London for future British coronations). The Stone is now in Edinburgh Castle (which is also called "Defender of the Nation"). But don't expect something truly grand – it really is just an old rock with two rusty rings on either side supposedly for transport, but the Scottish see it as part of their history and as evidence of their "rocky" relationship with the English. What do Germans see in the Loreley? I was almost as disappointed when I finally saw the Stone of Scone as I was when I finally saw the Loreley, which looked just another cliff to me. Monuments don't have to be visually impressive to carry special meaning for imagined communities.

A much more impressive monument for Scotland is the Scottish Parliament Building also in Edinburgh, which uses Scottish rock in a very modern attempt to symbolize the landscape of Scotland through the strikingly modern architecture of the building designed by the Catalan architect Enric Miralles. The Welsh Assembly designed by the British (not Welsh but at least not English) architect Richard Rogers (2) uses slate from Wales and Welsh Oak and was opened on St. David's Day, the day dedicated to the patron saint of Wales.

flags and ...

Speaking of saints, the English have St. George's Cross and the Scots St. Andrew's Cross. Instead of a saint's cross, the Welsh have a flag with a red dragon, which the Romans had brought to Britain (2).

**Fig. 12.1, 12.2, 12.3** | *Flags of England, Scotland, and Wales*

You may remember that the Union Jack represents a forced union (2). The American Stars and Stripes clearly symbolize fifty states with fifty stars (1) and thirteen original colonies with thirteen stripes (2). You can see both the Union Jack and the Stars and Stripes on the cover of our book. Flags can be interpreted in many ways. Black film historian and media critic Jim Pines sees the English St. George's Cross positively as a symbol of multicultural inclusiveness which can't help but also represent the generations of black English people who have grown up in England since Windrush (7); others might associate the English St. George's Cross negatively with the Crusades. And the Union Jack could be seen as a symbol of the British Empire. Paul Gilroy, who studied at Birmingham under Stuart Hall (a biggie whom we'll be meeting at the end of this chapter), wrote a famous book entitled *There Ain't No Black in the Union Jack*, which examined an imaginary national English white culture.

... colors and ...

Colors, too, not just on flags, can be a powerful representation of national identity as another tidbit from history reminds us. The color orange is connected with the Dutch dynasty that William belonged to before he was invited to become King of Great Britain in order to save the throne from the Catholics (2). In Irish history orange has the meaning of loyalty to the Protestant monarch of England and support of Protestant supremacy in Northern Ireland. Green stands for the green island of Ireland, for the green shamrock as a symbol of Ireland, and for Catholicism. When each year the parades to commemorate the defeat of the Catholics by the Protestant William of Orange take place, the colors orange and green can turn red from violence. The flag of the Republic of Ireland uses both green and orange but with a white center representing peace.

plants, animals, food

The Plantagenet kings in England used the symbol of plant as you remember from our history appetizer, and the Wars of the Roses used two roses for two opposing claims to the throne (2). The rose is also the symbol of the new Labour party or a symbol for the dead Princess Diana. Flowers can be also symbols that help members of imagined communities experience their sense of belonging and just like animals can become part of a sense of national identity as we've seen before (9). The old saying "you are what you eat" points to the meaning food has for (national) identity (11, 13).

national art?

To illustrate the complex issue of identity, let's have a brief look at one of the names from the chapter on arts. Remember the first photographer to win the Turner Prize? It was Wolfgang Tillmans (11). Why choose him when there are many other important artists in Britain whom I didn't mention? One reason is audience relevance: a German photographer for the German readers of this book. Another reason is the preoccupation of cultural studies with marginal groups (Tillmans is openly gay). And yet another reason is to raise the issue of national identity – Tillmans was the first artist not born in Britain to receive the Turner Prize.

Let's switch from British (?) photography to American (?) film. Note the films in the section American film genres (11). I didn't mention my criteria for choice of genre, by the way, but merely adopted the genres and top films provided by the American Film Institute. Does it make sense to call films like *Ben Hur*, set in Rome, or *Schindler's List*, about the Holocaust in Europe, American? I did mention that Alfred Hitchcock was actually born in England, but I sneaked through Charlie Chaplin's *City Lights* as an American film although Chaplin himself was English. You could reply by saying, "What does a person's nationality or place of birth have to do with a work of art?" You could perhaps point to Roland Emmerich and say that although he was born and educated in Germany, films like *Independence Day* and *The Patriot* are prime examples of Hollywood blockbusters with American settings and American themes. A very good cultural studies question that points out the complexity of identity: In what ways does it make sense to categorize films or for that matter any works or art as "American" or "English"?

And what about the role of legends and the choice of facts for a presentation of history in the identity of a nation? Apart from reminding ourselves about how many foreigners, some of whom couldn't even speak English (2), became English kings, let's wait just a bit for more details here about the US and the UK (16). For now, to illustrate the importance of the choice of perspective in establishing identity, let's look at our first biggie, who changed our ways of describing other cultures.

education's role in identity

While describing identity from the outside can be very difficult as Said claimed, even trying to decide on your own national identity may be very difficult. We heard about the subject of citizenship as a foundation course in the National Curriculum (4). What's not revealed on the official Curriculum's website is the ongoing debate about if or how these courses should be used to teach British identity and values. These issues aren't easy to understand, and maybe that's why teaching the courses is problematic in a good number of schools. What exactly is British and what are British values? We've already learned about the problem of the use of the term British in connection with geography (1). We'll be dealing with identity again and again and might be in an easier position to learn more about what it means to be British from the outside; just thinking about the ongoing debate about German *Leitkultur* can remind us of the difficulties of the subject from the "inside."

biggies in boxes

**Edward Said**, Jerusalem-born intellectual and founding father of postcolonial studies, late 20th century

Edward Said (his last name is pronounced in the Arabic way using two syllables: sigh-eed) was probably one of the best-known intellectuals in America in the 80s and 90s with many media appearances as the voice of the Palestinians. Said was born into an Arab Christian family in a Palestine still under British rule, went to an English school in Cairo, was later educated in America (his father had dual Palestinian-American citizenship) at the elite universities Princeton and Harvard. Certainly his personal life as an exile had an influence on his belief that essentialism, which we'll be looking at later, with its stereotyping was wrong and that all identity was hybrid. Said was a Christian Palestinian with an English first name in an anti-British country, Egypt, was in the US harshly criticized for his support of the Palestinians while he himself was critical of Arab governments that wanted no dialogue with America. While Said was a professor at the prestigious Columbia University for most of his life, he also taught at other highly reputable universities; his writings and interests ranged from literary criticism, theories of imperialism, anthropology, and political science to geography and music criticism. He himself was opposed to the strict separation of disciplines – one reason why he's become such an influential figure in cultural studies.

While Said's scholarly work covers a wide range, he's best known for the book published in the late 70s that has become the bible of postcolonial studies: *Orientalism*. Said criticized what he regarded as false assumptions that Western research had about Arab cultures, asking if objective representations of other cultures were possible at all. He investigated how one culture attempts to dominate and control another in the way it represents the other culture. Said claimed that the Western ways of looking at the Orient were limited by binary oppositions (much like the title of our chapter: "us versus them"): the West was seen as rational, democratic, dynamic, progressive; the East as irrational, despotic, static, backward. Even positive stereotyping – the East as exotic and romantic – was attributed to the Western desire to dominate the East. While some of Said's many critics have accused him of stereotyping the Westerner, other critics have recognized the enormous impact Said's work has had on the ways we can understand cultural identity.

As with so many of the biggies in cultural studies, Said would deserve a box in other chapters of this part of our book; his work on the relations between knowledge and power would justify a place in the next chapter just as much as his research into the nature of identity justifies his place here.

Fig. 12.4
*Edward Said*

And from the outside we can mention a couple more concrete aspects of British national identity: symbols on coins and the measurement system.

decimalization and metrification

Earlier in the chapter we mentioned some characteristics of national identity. If you skim through the book and note the illustrations, you'll no doubt notice one of the most common symbols of the nation: stamps and coins. The new designs for British coins show symbols that emphasize the importance of the four nations in one kingdom: the Royal Shield or Royal Coat of Arms with three lions for England, the rampant lion for Scotland, and the harp for Ireland. And what about Wales? Well, at least the designer Matthew Dent was born in Wales.

**Fig. 12.5** | *Royal Mint image*

For coin collectors and for older Brits who associate their complicated currency with the good old days, the pre-decimalized currency system was wonderful, with many different names and with a very special system of arithmetic: 2 farthings = 1 halfpenny (spelled sometimes "ha'penny" and pronounced "hayp-nee"); 4 farthings = 1 penny; 12 pence (the plural of "penny") = 1 shilling; 2 shillings = 1 florin; 2 shillings and 6 pence = half a crown; 5 shillings = 1 crown; 20 shillings = 1 pound (gold pound coins were called sovereigns); 21 shillings = 1 guinea. Just using these old names could provide us with some enlightening comparisons with European history. If you collect pre-euro European coins, then the names "shilling" and "florin" won't sound as foreign to you as they might to the young Brits today who have grown up with the very simple 100 pence = 1 pound system. The United Kingdom gave up its ancient currency system on D-Day or Decimal Day in 1971 with a changeover not unlike the introduction of the euro in Germany. While the changeover from shillings and crowns to pence and pounds was successful, the change from the Imperial Measurement System, based on measurements that have been in use since Roman, Celtic, and Anglo-Saxon times, to the metric system is still in progress. Not even the European Union has been able to quickly force the UK to change miles, pints, and acres into kilometers, liters, and hectares.

What do decimalization and metrification tell us about British identity? Decimalization tells us that the British are able to give up an unbelievably complicated monetary system and adopt an extraordinarily simple one. The metric system tells us that the British aren't yet fully able to give up an unbelievably complicated measuring system and adopt an extraordinarily simple one. Decimalization took place on one day in 1971; metrification is still an ongoing process and may never be fully finished.

problems with nationality: essentialism

An important aspect of the criticisms that Edward Said had of western views of the Orient can be summarized in one word: essentialism. (Some had criticized Said himself for using this same kind of generalizing, by the way.) The main question involves the possibility of defining something about being British or American that is present in every British or American person. Stereotypes are based on an essentialist view. If you skim through the chapter on minorities and immigration, you'll come across some of the problems involved with names like "African American" in the US or "Asian" in the UK (7). Those people with the same name always have at least one characteristic that distinguishes them from other groups with different names. The essentialist view sees these characteristics as permanent, as essential to the definition of the group. Examples of these permanent characteristics could be race, which is based on unique physical and genetic characteristics, which of course neither all Americans nor all British, all Welsh, all Scottish or all English share.

But there are other ways of looking at identity.

identity as action and performance

Those who've already done some linguistics courses may have come across the theory of speech acts. One kind of speech act, the performative, puts into effect exactly what it states. For example when you say "I promise that...," you do something – in this case make a promise – by saying it. Other examples are: "I pronounce you man and wife" or "The court sentences the convicted to ten years imprisonment." Many of those working in cultural studies prefer to describe identity not as something fixed or essential as described above, but as an action that the individual can perform. Identity – and gender too as we'll see later (14) – thus has to do with representation than with essential unchangeable characteristics. And people have more power over their own identity if they can represent it instead of being born with it.

... and choice

We've seen how the US Census Bureau deals with race and origin in American censuses (7). We'll know more about identity in Britain – at least which identity people choose themselves – with the results of the UK Census in 2011, which for the first time will have a question about national identity. The recommendation made in the Parekh Report (sponsored by the Runnymede Trust) at the turn of the millennium was that a multi-ethnic Britain needs to re-imagine itself. This recommendation has caused a lot of discussion about how the British should describe themselves and how political changes should reflect racial and ethnic changes. Most discussions nowadays of national identity and cultural identity involve the terms "multiculturalism"

**biggies in boxes**

**Fig. 12.6** | *Stuart Hall*

**Stuart Hall**, Jamaican-born founding father of cultural studies, 20th and 21st centuries

Stuart Hall came to Britain as a teenager as part of the Windrush (7) generation, studied at Oxford, worked on the important journal *New Left Review*, was one of the first people ever to teach the brand new discipline "media studies," co-wrote a book called *The Popular Arts* that led to his joining the Birmingham Centre for Contemporary Cultural Studies (CCCS) (16), where he later became director after Richard Hoggart (13) left. Hall has been called one of the academics who defined British cultural studies as a discipline and has made his mark as a Marxist scholar of mass media, ethnicity and gender and identity. Hall not only continued research on the popular arts that had begun with Hoggart and Raymond Williams (16), he also called into question the belief that those who watch television were mere consumers and thus easily manipulated by the producers of mass media (15). According to Hall, the consumers negotiate meaning through active response, which doesn't always agree with what the producers intended. As with other important British academics involved with establishing cultural studies as a discipline, Stuart Hall also became associated with adult education at the Open University (4), becoming a professor of sociology there after leaving the CCCS. And similar to other figures involved in cultural studies, Hall has been active in social movements and critical both of the Conservatives in power during Thatcher's government and New Labour under Tony Blair. Hall serves as patron of the Runnymede Trust (mentioned above), a charity dedicated to promoting a multi-ethnic Britain.

Maybe you think that putting Hall in this chapter makes sense regarding his origin and his later research into questions of identity. We could've just as justifiably put him in the next chapter in a context of power since Hall's work on explaining how Thatcher came to power is based on interpreting political power. We could've just as justifiably put him in the upcoming chapter on media since his research into the ways in which media users encode and decode meaning has been influential in understanding the way media works from a cultural studies perspective. But you'll hopefully agree that Hall certainly belongs in Part II of this book, the "cultural studies" part.

biggies in boxes

**Homi K. Bhabha**, Indian-born postcolonial theorist, 20th and 21st centuries

Even though Homi K. Bhabha (not to be confused with Homi J. Bhabha, an Indian nuclear scientist) has argued against identity being fully dependent on place of origin, his personal roots have no doubt played an important role in his work and are also a reason for including him as a biggie in this chapter. Bhabha was born in India just after independence from Britain (2) into a Parsi family. (Parsis are members of the ancient Zoroastrian religion who originally came from Persia and have lived in India for centuries. The Parsis have always been a small minority and have functioned as mediators between the Indians and the British during the centuries when India was part of the British Empire.) Bhabha studied in India and the UK, and has taught at highly reputable American universities like Princeton, the University of Chicago, and Harvard.

Bhabha has argued against a binary interpretation of identity present in writing about identity in a postcolonial world: he sees the colonizers and the colonized as interdependent. Describing identity needs a "third space," which could perhaps be easily understood as somewhere beyond the contrast of being authentically Muslim and authentically British (8). More difficult, abstract, and controversial is another meaning of "third space" involving the performance of culture, similar to a definition of gender as being not in a given role but its performance.

While Bhabha is certainly as important a name in postcolonial theory as Judith Butler (14) is for gender studies, both share one "prize" that helps explain why you won't find much of Bhabha's work in many cultural studies readers: winning the Bad Writing Contest run by the journal *Philosophy and Literature*. You could see the difficulty in understanding Bhabha's writings as being part of the difficulty in the subject matter. Identity, especially in its hybrid forms, isn't an easy thing to write about. And even though you won't find Bhabha's prose in many anthologies, you will come across his concept of the "third space" (or similar concepts such as "third place" or "third culture") in much writing about postcolonial and also about cultural studies.

**Fig. 12.7**
*Homi K. Bhabha*

and "hybridity" – both of which make our division of "us" and "them" more difficult to maintain.

Our last two biggies in this chapter, whom you'll now meet back-to-back, weren't born in the US or the UK but have had great influence in showing us how difficult it has become to define the "us" and the "them" both in the US and UK. And both have personal histories that place them firmly in the contents and complexities of this chapter.

You've already read in Part I about minority and ethnic groups in America and Britain, you've now heard about national identity, about the nation as an "imagined community," and you're aware of the pitfalls of essentialism. On the other hand you've also decided to study English and are certainly interested in Britain and America and probably know some English people or some Scots or some Americans. You've read things called American novels and watched things called American films, maybe you've drunk English tea or Scottish whiskey. And you've now read most of this book with chapters about two nation-states. Stuart Hall admits that the term "identity," no matter how much we may dislike it, remains a term that we can't avoid using. American identity has always been a mixture, and it's never been fully clear which elements are most important. American identity is perhaps as new as it was when the French-American (one of the many hyphenated Americans) writer Crèvecœur, whose words opened our chapter, first famously named the "new man" a couple of centuries ago (women weren't yet considered important enough to be mentioned then, but in just a few chapters, we'll be seeing how much things have changed since then). The British perhaps have a more difficult task with their identity, a combination of four different nations (at least) with more than a thousand years of history.

We've come to see how the term "national identity" is complicated and contradictory – in effect making the "us" and the "them" much more complicated and contradictory than we perhaps thought. But what if learning to live with a more complicated and contradictory view of the "us-es" and the "thems" might lead to a more peaceful world …

## Exercises

1. Can you explain the misuse of grammar in the title of this chapter and explain why the title mirrors the contents and answer the question the title poses?
2. Look back through Part I for visual examples of what was mentioned in Chapter 12 as one good example of American and British national identity. Why do you think these were chosen?
3. Look back through Part I and choose groups and events that could be used as examples of and explanations for national identity. Which one(s) would you consider most appropriate as examples considering what we've covered in this chapter?

Challenging questions and interesting projects:

On your next visit to Britain and/or to America, ask people you meet to describe their national identity. Then ask them to describe the national identity of their parents and their grandparents and note any differences. Ask them for details about what exactly they think has changed through the generations.

And finally the oh-my-god-if-you-can-do-this-you'll-maybe-become-known-as-the-biggest-and-brightest-new-hope-in-cultural-studies-task:

Come up with a new theory of national identity that takes into account both the sense of continuity that the nation once provided and the increasing mix of different peoples in one state. In other words, the new theory should solve the dilemma between imperialism (one fixed national identity that has a fixed value in comparison to all others) and relativism (in a multicultural society all identities are equally valuable, no objective evaluation is possible). This new theory should contribute to world peace and not to national confrontations.

And finally further topics not dealt with (or not dealt with in enough depth) in this chapter ... for those who just can't stop being fascinated by the complexities and challenges of "national identity":

other ways of looking at identity defined through ritual and family structure and food; the role of psychoanalysis in theories of identity; how the notion of hybridity has changed definitions of national identity; multiculturalism compared with essentialism; critical views of some of the metaphors used in Chapter 7 to describe American society (melting pot, salad bowl); the Runnymede Trust's role in current discussions on the future of a multi-ethnic Britain; the reception of the Parekh Report; the demise of national identity in a globalized world; the importance of regional affiliation versus old affiliation to out-of-date nation-states...

# 13 | Power: Those Who Got It and Those That Ain't

Clothes make the man. Naked people have little or no influence on society.
Mark Twain

"What makes power hold good, what makes it accepted, is simply the fact that it does not only weigh on us as a force that says no, but that it traverses and produces things, it induces pleasure, forms knowledge, produces discourse."
Michel Foucault
from "Truth and Power" in *Power/Knowledge*

When you finish the chapter, you should be able to say something about

- kinds of power and the special kind called hegemony
- some important scholars in cultural studies who analyzed power
- some classic research on resistance and creativity
- aspects of hegemony that we've covered and not covered in previous chapters
- signs of power that are difficult to overlook as well as those that aren't always obvious
- some of the complicated keywords used in the discourses on power.

kinds of power

One of the keywords you won't be able to avoid once you start reading anything about cultural studies is a fancy word with various pronunciations: hegemony (the stress is usually on the second syllable, the "g" can be pronounced like a "g" or a "j"). The word originally comes from ancient Greek meaning "lead," and the modern meaning of the word has to do with a special kind of leadership that involves another word that's much simpler to pronounce, and which is part of the title of this chapter: power. When you hear the word "power," you probably think of military and police power, that is mostly men with guns. You might also think of judges and the courts or of the kind of economic power that multinational corporations have. You could even think of the German education system with teachers having the power to decide on the school type children should attend, or think of professors with their power to make important decisions that affect the careers and lives of their students. You might also think of the power that American governments have – or claim they have – through the Constitution ("We the People") and through the election system or of the power British monarchs claimed in the past: supposedly given by God, the divine right of kings (and queens).

hegemony as a kind of power

Armies and police can force people to do things without their consent. The theory of hegemony analyses a kind of power that doesn't involve force of the same kind, namely, how voluntary agreements between the rulers and the ruled come about. We've already heard of Bhabha and Butler in the previous chapter and something they share with other academics both famous and poor – the fact that their writing is sometimes very difficult to understand (12). Maybe you could see this difficulty in understanding as something necessary for clarifying aspects of power (and of gender as we'll see in the next chapter) that otherwise might be taken for granted, aspects that some people aren't even aware of. The very strangeness of the word "hegemony" helps people realize what could otherwise seem to be the most natural thing in the world – like teachers having the power to assess students' work using simple numbers or letters and students accepting this power without question. Hegemony is a special kind of power, namely that of persuasion, persuasion by the ruling group of the sort that subordinate groups are open to because they think it's in their best interests. While the word "hegemony" is much older, it wasn't until the 1970s that the term began to be used frequently, especially in British cultural studies. And thanks go to one of the most influential scholars in British culture studies and in cultural studies around the world: our first biggie in this chapter.

civil society, political society, subaltern

Gramsci and others influenced by his work distinguish between civil society – comprising the family, the church, schools, trade unions, the mass media, youth culture, leisure time activities, etc. – and the state or political society – comprising the armed forces, the police, the government, the legal system and prison. Gramsci saw two possibilities for change: through a "war of maneuver" with a direct assault on state power through violent revolutions, for example, or through a "war of position" with

**biggies in boxes**

**Fig. 13.1** | *Antonio Gramsci*

**Antonio Gramsci**, Italian Communist party leader and Marxist political theorist and activist, early 20th century

You might be just a bit surprised by the name. Were you expecting someone with a more English-sounding name? (His name is pronounced "gram-she" by the way.) But maybe you're used to foreign-looking names after the last biggie in our previous chapter (12)? In any case Gramsci, born in Sardinia, never set foot in Britain, but still his writings strongly influenced those who became the founders of the new discipline of cultural studies in the UK. Almost any book on cultural studies that has a chapter on power includes him.

As a Communist party leader Gramsci was hated and feared by Mussolini's fascist regime. In spite of strict censorship, Gramsci managed to have thousands of pages of notes smuggled out of prison during the years he spent there, evidence that defied what the prosecutor famously had demanded of the judge in Gramsci's trial: "We must stop this brain from functioning for twenty years." Gramsci died soon after being released from prison at the age of 46, just a few years before the outbreak of World War II. What he wrote in prison wasn't published in English, however, until the 1970s as *Prison Notebooks*.

In his writings Gramsci attempted to understand how a ruling class maintains power over other groups in an ideological and cultural way. He wanted to know how the Italian fascists were able to gain the support of the working class when a fascist regime was obviously not in the working class's interest. Gramsci expanded the classical Marxist view of struggle as being primarily determined by an economic base to include a struggle among various groups not only over capital or production but also and especially over ideology and culture. The victorious group was the one who could convince the subordinate groups that they were acting in their own best interests through accepting the common sense world view of the ruling class.

You could see a crude kind of hegemony in politicians providing voters with presents or bribes, the practice in ancient Rome that was described by the phrase *panem et circenses*. If you remember the end of Part I and our talk about bread and circuses in ancient Rome, then you might not be too surprised to find an Italian here. And Gramsci won't be the only important non-English sounding name in this chapter...

a continual negotiation of power and influence between the rulers and the ruled. He believed that all ruling groups, no matter how authoritarian, must eventually use hegemony to maintain control, that they must eventually be able to convince people that the ideas and culture of the ruling classes were natural and in the best interests of all. In order for this persuasion to be successful, those in power sometimes have to make compromises and grant some of the wishes of the subordinate groups to create a common conception of the world that those in power want the others to believe in. Both groups – the rulers and the ruled – have to exist for there to be any power. Thus the rulers are in a way defined by those ruled; both are dependent on each another. A term that Gramsci used to describe those ruled, the subordinate groups who were usually not politically organized, was "subaltern." This term is now used in postcolonial studies (16) and also sometimes in cultural studies in general to indicate those groups who don't have power or don't even have any voice at all as the Indian philosopher and literary critic Gayatri Spivak claims in her famous essay "Can the Subaltern Speak?"

organic intellectuals

Gramsci uses the concept of the organic intellectual to describe someone who sees through the system and then is able to show the people that they are oppressed. Thus he mobilizes them to change their situation through a "war of position" and through negotiations that lead to changes in the culture and the common world view of the ruling class that they all are supposed to share. Organic intellectuals wouldn't come from the ruling class and would normally be educated to support the ruling class. If provided with a proper critical education, however, the organic intellectual could articulate the feelings that the subaltern felt but didn't know how to express. Establishing the kind of critical education that organic intellectuals needed to make reform possible wouldn't be easy. Gramsci's belief in people's innate ability to understand the world and to change it is central to the discipline that has come to be called cultural studies.

resistance and creativity

How exactly can people from subordinate groups change the world? They can negotiate with those in power as we saw above, and they can also take cultural practices or objects and use them for their own purpose. The creative ways in which young people in particular try to change power relationships were the topic of much of the research done at the University of Birmingham's famous Centre for Contemporary Cultural Studies (16) in the 1970s. This research looked at how smaller groups, sometimes called subcultures, defined themselves in relation to the dominant culture of the time. The teddy boys' use of upper class clothes from the Edwardian era (giving this group of working-class young men their name "teddy" as a short form of the name "Edward") in the 1950s was understood as their way of transforming how the dominant society had interpreted fashion. Since the punks, a subculture of the 60s and 70s didn't have the money to buy the sort of fashion that other British groups could use as markers of their identity, the punks often (ab)used their own bodies as a outward sign of their identity or used everyday objects like the safety pin, worn openly on clothing or even inserted through the skin, in a way that was offensive to the world outside of punk. Still other groups like motorbike boys or hippies defined themselves through the format and kind of music they listened to (singles or albums, rock and roll or progressive rock). Music associated with blacks like reggae was sometimes adopted by whites in northern England to express their own opposition to authority or their own liberation, perhaps similar to the American white rapper Eminem as a white boy playing in a black rap world. Studies were also made of how people used places in ways that the owners didn't intend, for example, how young Americans used shopping malls not to consume but as a place to congregate, to hang out. In the same way I can remember as a young man (ab)using restaurants by intentionally remaining with friends long after having finished eating although the restaurants didn't serve coffee or dessert because the guests were supposed to eat and leave and thus make room for other paying guests.

More recent studies of subcultures have criticized the ways in which earlier researchers had interpreted the use of fashion and music to define groups from an outsider perspective instead of using the group members' voices themselves. Initial ways of looking at subcultures as being the embodiment of resistance to a dominant culture have also changed now. But the connection between power and identity and fashion and music as an important focus of cultural studies has remained. After having looked at some ways in which certain groups use rituals and appearance to carve out their own space, let's look at some ways in which larger society creates the common sense world view that all groups are supposed to accept.

hegemony in modern America

Those who experienced American media and everyday American life after the 9/11 attacks could see just what a "common culture" or "common world view" can be – with countless American flags flying and the overwhelming shows of patriotism in the mass media. I can remember a much earlier example of a common view in the television news of the late 70s broadcast on CBS (10) by the recently deceased and very highly renowned broadcaster and news anchorman Walter Cronkite. Cronkite ended each evening broadcast with the famous signoff: "And that's the way it is" followed by the date. During the Iran hostage crisis Cronkite followed the date with the phrase "the … (20th, 45th, 222nd ) … day of captivity for the hostages in Iran." At the time no one seemed to question this as a detail perhaps inappropriately subjective in the evening news.

hegemony in modern Britain

One classic example of hegemony often taken from modern British political life is Margaret Thatcher's election, which was only possible by having large numbers of working-class voters vote for someone who wouldn't normally seem to have their best interests at heart. You could also see aspects of the British educational system as hegemonic in several ways. Aspects such as compulsory schooling, testing, the National Curriculum (🔔 4) could be seen as part of the state or political society since the government has the right to force people to go to school against their will. The belief that education is something positive would be part of civil society since here the family and the media play a role. Education is often part of "cultural capital" as we'll shortly see.

signs of power … in stone

Now that we've seen the kinds of power, met one of the most important figures associated with theories about the special kind of power called hegemony, and seen how groups can express their resistance to a dominant culture through music and fashion, let's look at some expressions of dominant culture and power: architecture, government structures, symbols, education, even clothes again. We'll be ringing bells to remind you of details

**Fig. 13.2**
*Sometimes just the silhouette is enough to convey power: Palace of Westminster.*

covered in Part I of this book, details that we can look at now from another point of view. Sometimes governmental power in architecture is immediately recognizable as in London or Washington (🔔 8) or not as recognizable as in Cardiff (🔔 5). Larger than life statues indicate the importance of individuals who wielded power in the past politically (🔔 2) or otherwise (🔔 8). Power can also be expressed in less "concrete" ways.

... in structures and rituals ...

If you look back at the chapter "Queendom and Republicracy," you can find one example of how power can be shown through political action (🔔 4). You may have asked yourself why I gave you four different long names for the changes in the Department of Education. These examples provide us with another way that power can be represented: through the changing of governmental structures as in "cabinet reshuffling." There are also rituals used in politics that reinforce power – the distance between the two sides of the House of Commons (🔔 4) is the length of two swords, implying the battle between the two parties, a battle that shouldn't lead to bloodshed but often does lead to loud behavior that seems very odd indeed to Germans used to disciplined debates in the Bundestag.

... in education...with "cultural capital"

And yet another instance of power is the status of having attended a public school and thus becoming a member of the "old boys' network." Remember the positive description of the Open University in the education chapter (🔔 4)? One could also describe the Open University as well as the proliferation of universities and degrees and diplomas as a result of those who really have the power, the old boys' network, being willing to grant some of the same status – a university education and degrees and diplomas – to the working class to satisfy the needs of the ambitious. We would have a classic case of hegemony here since the rulers – the old boys' network with the prestigious backgrounds and the proper family ties – were willing to allow the masses a university education but of course not of the same quality as the ruling class. In return the masses then grant the ruling classes a continual recognition of the innate superiority of a public school and Oxbridge education as a prerequisite for positions of power and money. Of course you could also see the growth of universities in Britain more idealistically as an attempt to satisfy basic human needs for intellectual growth or a bit less idealistically as evidence of a society that recognizes the economic needs for a better educated workforce. The expansion of redbrick universities in the 19$^{th}$ century was driven by increased industrialization as we've seen (4).

We can mention here in passing the concept of cultural capital, created by the French sociologist Pierre Bourdieu, as an important aspect of education and an important motivation for the British and especially for Americans to invest huge sums of money in college education from prestigious institutions. The cultural capital that graduates have with a university degree from such institutions is a sign of power as much as wealth is sign of economic power and knowing the "right" people is a sign of social capital.

... the celebrity factor ...

One cultural studies explanation for the political power of entertainment celebrities in the US is the lack of an aristocratic ruling class. We've met perhaps the most famous example of this special American breed of politician in several chapters in Part I: former actor Ronald Reagan as president (2, 5, 6, 8). We can add here other examples like actor and former bodybuilder Arnold Schwarzenegger as California governor, singer (and former husband of Cher) Sonny Bono as Representative of California in the House, actor and director Clint Eastwood as mayor of the beautiful California town Carmel-by-the-Sea, and wrestler Jess Ventura as Minnesota governor.

... in clothes ... and charisma ... and even in things

We can now use the Mark Twain quote which opened this chapter if we remember that Twain's use of "man" should apply to women too. A lot of attention was paid to vice presidential candidate Sarah Palin's dresses compared with presidential candidate Hillary Clinton's pantsuits in the 2008 presidential campaign, and Angela Merkel's décolleté also made back page news at least in summer 2008. And there was a lot of discussion during the 2008 presidential campaign about Barack Obama wearing or not wearing a flag as lapel pin to show his patriotism. Perhaps it's helpful to remember that wearing the wrong color or the wrong material could have resulted in draconian punishment in earlier times and thus to remember that fashion in the broadest possible sense has always been a sign of power. The choice of clothes can be a part of the charisma of politicians – and for that matter of celebrities too. Charisma – etymologically "a divine gift" – is the hard-to-define combination of charm, attractiveness, and persuasiveness that the famous German sociologist Max Weber and the famous French sociologist Pierre Bourdieu, whom we've just met, saw as one important component of power. And what about the power of things? The use of tin cans allowed the extension of the British Empire out across the waves to name just one brief example here.

the role of class

Of course class is also a sign of power. Class played a crucial role in two important books by two of the founding fathers of cultural studies, E. P. Thompson and Richard Hoggart. What wasn't

**biggies in boxes**

Fig. 13.3 | *E. P. Thompson*

**E. P. Thompson**, English-born historian and peace activist, founding father of cultural studies, 20th century

Edward Palmer (often referred to as E. P.) Thompson wrote one of three books always mentioned in summaries of the history of British cultural studies: *The Making of the English Working Class* was important for the development of cultural studies. Thompson's book was "history from below" and included details about the people historians had usually overlooked. Thompson didn't see class as a given structure in society but as the result of people's feelings and experiences of political, economic, and social relationships. With his most famous book Thompson achieved his goal of rescuing British workers "from the enormous condescension of posterity" to use his now famous phrase. Thompson's work hugely influenced studies in social history.

Thompson, also known as a biographer of the socialist and Marxist leader of the 19th-century arts and crafts movement in Britain William Morris, had joined the Communist party as a student but left after the Soviet invasion of Hungary in 1956. Like so many of the other famous names in British cultural studies, Thompson was involved in the adult education of working-class people who had left school but then had the chance to further their education in postwar Britain. Thompson dedicated *The Making of the English Working Class* to these students.

Thompson regarded himself as an academic outsider and scathingly criticized what he saw as a commercialization of higher education in the early 1970s in the book *Warwick University Ltd* before leaving the university altogether to become an independent writer and scholar (he could afford this move financially partly due to his wife's tenured position). In the 80s Thompson became a vocal opponent of nuclear arms, a proponent of a Europe without superpowers, and refused to take sides in the Cold War, criticizing both NATO and the Soviet bloc. He and his wife Dorothy Towers, also a social historian of repute, were well known in intellectual circles in Britain.

Thompson believed passionately that individual human beings through persistent resistance to the arrogance of the powerful can have a positive effect on society. He combined being an academic with also being a public intellectual and activist and exemplifies in the best cultural studies tradition the belief in using knowledge to change the world.

**biggies in boxes**

**Richard Hoggart**, English-born founding father of cultural studies, mid 20th–21st century

Richard Hoggart, just a few years older than Raymond Williams (16), is like Williams known for his turning the study of popular culture, especially the culture of the working classes, into a serious academic pursuit. His semi-autobiographical book *The Uses of Literacy: Aspects of Working-Class Life*, first published half a century ago, praises the sense of community and the value of popular culture among English working-class communities before Americanized mass culture reached England in the late 1950s. Hoggart extended the kind of critical analysis that other scholars (like F.R. Leavis 16) had applied to great works of literature to include cultural products like popular song, working-class rituals connected with pubs, and popular magazines. In the second half of his book, Hoggart harshly criticizes what he considered the bad influence of "mass culture" like the rise of a specifically new British youth culture formed by the influence of American rock and roll music as destroying the genuine culture made by and for the working classes.

In the early 1960s Hoggart was one of the leading witnesses for Penguin Books in trial that determined that D.H. Lawrence's novel *Lady Chatterley's Lover* wasn't obscene and thus could be made widely available in the United Kingdom. Hoggart became a professor of English literature at the University of Birmingham where he founded the Centre for Contemporary Cultural Studies (CCCS) 16 and remained its director until Stuart Hall (12) took over in the early 1970s. Hoggart later worked for the United Nations Educational, Scientific and Cultural Organization (UNESCO) before retiring as head of Goldsmith's College, which has achieved a reputation for producing renowned graduate artists like the YBAs (11) and has also now become one of the centers of cultural studies with distinguished faculty like Angela McRobbie (15). One of Hoggart's sons, the well-known print and radio journalist and prolific writer Simon Hoggart, has criticized the academic discipline of cultural studies as nonsense.

**Fig. 13.4**
*Richard Hoggart*

included in our very brief look at the social class system in Chapter 3 (3) was Thompson's view that politics and conflict were essential parts of the identity of the English working class – and thus one very big distinguishing factor between the English and the American working class. The term "working class," by the way, isn't as common in the US as in Britain – the "middle class" is the most common term used in the US and usually is thought to include the working class. Thompson used the word "class" in the title of his most famous book, and it's time to meet him.

While Thompson decided to leave the university as an institution, another one of the founding fathers of cultural studies remained and founded his own department, which gave the new subject cultural studies its name. For Hoggart too class played a role in his research, but he came from the working class and his origins and upbringing had great influence on his thinking. While *class* isn't in the title of his most famous book, it is in the subtitle.

**biggies in boxes**

**Fig. 13.5** | *Michel Foucault © Bruce Jackson, photograph used by special permission.*

**Michel Foucault**, French philosopher, sociologist, historian, 20th century

We could've put this biggie in any box in any of the chapters in Part II, but since we started with an Italian, why not end the chapter with a Frenchman, especially since one of Foucault's most influential ideas involves how power is used in all aspects of life as this chapter's opening quote was supposed to show: bringing together "power" and "knowledge" and "truth." Foucault's work includes much of what you can find throughout Part II of this book, summarized in keywords like "power-knowledge," the way those in power determine what's true; biopower, the way the bodies and health of entire populations are controlled and regulated; and discourse, a way of trying to show how what people consider to be absolute truths changes through history – for example, how the concept of insanity changed from divine inspiration to a mental illness. In addition to his enormous influence on the academic world, Foucault is also a good example of the connection between academic abstraction and political action, turning personal concerns into scholarly investigation. Foucault not only wrote about how prisons were examples of the power of the state over individual bodies, he also was an activist and founding member of a group that fought to reform the prison system and give prisoners a voice. An openly gay man – and one of the first prominent people to die of AIDS in the mid 1980s – Foucault has become a source of personal and political inspiration for gay activists.

Foucault was a restless scholar, teaching and traveling all over the world, spending time in Sweden, Poland, Germany, Tunisia, Brazil, Japan, Canada, the US, and Iran in addition to the time he spent in his country of origin, France, at the Collège de France, one of the most reputable educational institutions in the country. When asked to define his role within academic disciplines – historian or philosopher or Marxist or "Professor of the History of Systems of Thought," Foucault famously said: "I don't feel that it is necessary to know exactly what I am. The main interest in life and work is to become someone else that you were not in the beginning." His influence on academic disciplines from history to the social sciences including of course cultural studies is enormous with Foucault being the most cited scholar in the humanities and social sciences according to a list published in the *Times Higher Education* magazine at the end of the 2000s. Foucault might have been amused by the connection of knowledge and power that such a list implies – the list was created by the "information company" Thompson Reuters.

Michel will have to be our token Frenchman, but there are many other very important French thinkers who'd also deserve their individual boxes in a much larger edition of this book: Jacques Derrida, Roland Barthes, Jacques Lacan, Jean-François Lyotard, Jean Baudrillard, Louis Althusser, Jean-Paul Sartre, and our token very famous woman Simone de Beauvoir... But at least in passing we heard of Pierre Bourdieu (who made number 2 on the list of the most cited scholars mentioned above) ...

Let's use an example that neither Thompson nor Hoggart covered in their books to illuminate the connection between class and power. Food is also about class both in Britain and in the US, and knowing what is healthy is based on income and education. Food that is high in sugars and fats is often cheaper, and cutting back on money for food is one of the first choices of those caught in poverty. The resistance by many people to Jamie Oliver's plans to revolutionize the way Britain's schoolchildren eat shows how the choice of food is part of identity, even if this choice of food results in poor teeth and disease. The issue remains the same as it was in Victorian times: Does the government have the right or duty to protect its citizens from hunger or to encourage people to eat healthy foods? Or is individual responsibility more important? Should the government have the power to make alcohol illegal (2) or to prohibit schools from making money off soda machines? As with so many questions of power in our lives, those who formulate the questions also determine the answers. And the attention to how our choice of words and concepts determines our protest brings us to our last biggie in this chapter, one who turned the word "discourse" into one of the most popular academic key words of the last and the present century.

Have you noticed what almost all the biggies in this chapter have in common? They're not women. Who's to blame? Certainly there are many important female voices in contemporary cultural studies as well as in the past, but with a few exceptions mentioned in passing they didn't seem to fit into this chapter on power. But maybe that will change with the next generation of up-and-coming cultural studies scholars. Women do fit very well into our next chapter, though.

## Exercises

1. Which very big name has only been mentioned in passing and who would probably deserve the biggest box of all if influence determined size? And who's becoming very popular again now after the economic crisis? Why wasn't he (first gender hint) included although based on the readership of this book he could've been a good pick (second hint nationality)?

2. One of the biggies wrote one of the three books "always mentioned in summaries of the history of British cultural studies," as I claimed. Which three books?
3. Can you interpret the title of this chapter according to the content? (This is a tricky question, so I'll give you a hint: Think of grammar rules you learned at school.)
4. One of the questions from the chapter on political life was about the photograph of the Queen. How can you interpret this photo now in light of the discussion in this chapter? Hint: Think about signs of power.
5. Look briefly at the beginning of the last chapter of the book and find a fitting example of hegemony that you could most likely relate to.

---

Interesting and challenging project:

Make a chart with three columns and list in the first column the powerful people and institutions based on your memories of school life and based on your experiences at university. Now write down in key words in the second column the justification for each of your examples of personal and institutional power and in the third column the ways in which each example exercises power.

And finally the oh-my-god-if-you-can-do-this-you'll-maybe-become-known-as-the-biggest-and-brightest-new-hope-in-cultural-studies tasks:

(not quite serious) Try and explain why three Frenchmen were at the very top of the list of most quoted scholars in the humanities and social sciences and don't refer to their personal biographies but only to their ideas and their role in 21st century academia. Now turn your analysis into a suspense thriller and sell the rights to a movie production company. (But please don't forget to have this book mentioned in the closing credits.)

(serious) Answer the following question based on the "interesting and challenging project" given above: Does the chart you've created mirror justice or the injustices of life?

And finally, further topics not dealt with in this chapter … for those who'd like to know just a little more about the trappings of power (and maybe even come to understand more about those complicated terms like power-knowledge or the original Foucault expression pouvoir-savoir)...

of course a lot lot more about Karl Marx and the power of the proletariat; examples of how hegemony has been achieved through family background and class; the Puritan work ethic from a hegemonic point of view; role of the scholarship boy and girl – those young people admitted to university on merit, not income or family background – in the early history of cultural studies and as a great example of hegemony; Gramsci's analysis of "American Fordism"; the shift from "idols of production" to "idols of consumption"; the role of government in the funding of the arts; a comparison of the discourse on terror used by Bush and his administration after the 9/11 attacks with that of Al-Qaeda; Foucault's technologies of the self with what some would consider a very happy ending to this chapter, namely the belief that people are able to "transform themselves in order to attain a certain state of happiness, purity, wisdom, perfection, or immortality" to close this chapter with another Foucault quote...

# 14 Gender: Wo-Men

"We hold these truths to be self-evident: that all men and women are created equal [...]"
from the Declaration of Sentiments read at Seneca Falls, New York, in 1848

"The emotional, sexual, and psychological stereotyping of females begins when the doctor says, 'It's a girl.'"
Shirley Chisholm

You might have heard the song "Let's Talk about Sex" by the American hip hop group Salt-n-Pepa, which was also very popular in Germany at the beginning of the 1990s. Maybe some of you were very disappointed that hip hop wasn't mentioned earlier in the chapter on the arts although with its mix of youth, race, popular culture, and gender it could be considered a very appropriate topic for cultural studies. I can't make up for this lapse here, but I can promise that we will be talking about sex in this chapter in a connection that you may not have come across before unless you've already done some reading on feminism. In addition to sex, we'll also be looking at gender and women and men and gays and lesbians.

Hopefully you've noticed the strange title of this chapter. "Wo-Men" isn't a typographical error. The title is supposed to get you thinking about the differences between women and men in a new way using new concepts like "gender." I'm tempted to say "manmade" concepts and probably wouldn't be far off base with feminists by using "manmade" in its most literal sense. One of the goals of this chapter will be to get our terminology "straight" ...

When you finish the chapter, in addition to understanding something about the terms "sex" and "gender," you should be able to say something about

- people and issues from the history of the women's movement in the US and the UK
- some examples from contemporary American politics allowing for different roles for women
- the waves of feminism
- important feminist scholars

- some historical and current issues in the struggle for equal rights for gays and lesbians
- a critical analysis of choices relevant to sex and gender made in previous chapters.

women as a minority?

We could've dealt with women and women's rights in our look at minorities (7), especially if we consider the term "minority" as not applying only to those groups in society who are fewer in number than the majority but also to those who don't share the same power or prestige or social standing that other groups do. The focus of chapter 7, however, was on minorities and immigration taken together where gender wasn't as important an issue as race or country of origin. But in this chapter we have the chance to look at women and their fight for equal rights in America and in Britain.

Wollstonecraft's revolutions

The belief in the equality of men and women can be traced back to some extent to a revolutionary book written by one passionate woman at the time of the American and French Revolutions, so let's begin our overview with Mary Wollstonecraft, who lived for a while in Paris with her American lover before returning to England, the country of her birth. Wollstonecraft's *A Vindication of the Rights of Woman* claimed that women were as rational as men – reason being a cardinal virtue at the time of the Enlightenment – and should also have the same rights as men and equal opportunities in education. Women could best serve their families and society not as subservient wives but as intelligent companions in marriage, a truly revolutionary idea at the end of the 18th century. Initially, Wollstonecraft's new ideas didn't survive long – she died soon after giving birth to a daughter who would become the famous author of *Frankenstein*, Mary Shelley, but they were rediscovered a century later. The details of her unconventional life, at first criticized and ridiculed, helped to establish her as an important role model for later feminists.

from suffrage to the Queen

By the end of the 1870s women had gained some control over their own property, which before had been fully in the hands of the husbands. The suffragette movement, which also involved some violent protests, led gradually to most women gaining the right to vote in Britain by the end of the 1920s. As in the US, both World Wars led to a temporary boost for women's rights since women were needed for the workforce while men were away fighting the wars. Afterwards, however, the women were sent back to the kitchen and to their traditional roles as housewives and mothers. The American women's movement of the 60s arrived in Britain, and women in the UK gained similar governmental protection against discrimination and for equal pay as in the US – with the same very mixed results: women in Britain today also earn a third less than men. Who could function as possible role models? Margaret Thatcher, nicknamed the "Iron Lady" because of characteristics like determination or ruthlessness, which aren't considered typically feminine, was the first female prime minister, who however allowed no other women in her cabinet. Princess Diana combined traditional ideals of feminine beauty with a very savvy use of the media. And of course then there's the Queen as Head of State and at the same time a devoted wife and grandmother, whose own children, however, can't be taken as role models with their broken marriages and problematic family lives.

In the 1960s British feminists had looked to America for inspiration, and we'll turn now to the history of women's rights there. An American history appetizer provided us with one place to begin with, a place connected with the reform movements that started in the 19th century, back in the days before the Civil War began (2).

Seneca Falls

The founding mothers of feminism were all there at Seneca Falls, New York, in 1848: the well-off mother of seven children Elizabeth Cady Stanton, who wrote the Declaration of Sentiments, based on the Declaration of Independence, with the belief that all men and women are created equal; Lucretia Mott, an independent Quaker and Abolitionist; Lucy Stone, a hardworking farm girl who became one of the first female college graduates of Oberlin; and Susan B. Anthony, a pioneer who fought for women to gain the right to vote, regarded family as a burden and became the first real woman (as opposed to the symbolic figure of Liberty) to be portrayed on an American coin.

**Fig. 14.1** *Susan B. Anthony. United States coin image*

The right to vote wasn't meant for everyone in spite of the resounding opening words of the Constitution "We the People." The "we" meant white male property owners up until the middle of the 19th century. Enfranchisement – another fancy word like "suffrage" for the right to vote – had first been extended to former male slaves via the Fifteenth Amendment to the Constitution during Reconstruction (2). It took another half a century before the right to vote was extended to the other half of the population.

**Fig. 14.2**
*US postage stamp from 1998 celebrating the 19th Amendment passed in 1920*

Starting in the new western states in the latter part of the 19th century, women gradually gained the right to vote at the state level. They didn't gain the right to vote in all elections until the passing of the 19th Amendment in the year 1920 after all the founding mothers of the Declaration of Sentiments had died. The wording of the 19th Amendment is wonderfully simple: "The right of citizens of the United States to vote shall not be denied or abridged by the United States or by any State on account of sex." Not only did women gain the right to vote, they also began to do other shocking things, like cut their hair, smoke, and dance the Charleston in the age that became known as the Jazz Age (2).

ERA and NOW

The 19th Amendment was the last amendment in the US Constitution to deal specifically with women – so far. An attempt to add an amendment to fully guarantee equal rights for women was originally started just after the 19th took effect, but it wasn't until the 1970s – half a century after women gained the right to vote – that the proposed amendment known as ERA, the Equal Rights Amendment, finally passed Congress and thus at least overcame the first hurdle to becoming part of the Constitution. The text of the proposed amendment was simple: "Equality of rights under the law shall not be denied or abridged by the United States or by any State on account of sex." Who could be against guaranteeing women equal rights? Well, some who opposed the amendment claimed it wasn't necessary, others claimed that women would be obliged to serve in military combat operations. The National Organization for Women (NOW), founded in the mid 1960s by Betty Friedan, author of the famous book exploring the frustrations of modern women in traditional roles, *The Feminine Mystique*, was strongly in favor of the ERA. Phyllis Schlafly, a conservative political activist, became famous through her passionate opposition to the ERA, arguing that passage of the amendment would weaken laws that protect women from working in heavy industry and would also change laws that had favored women in child custody and divorce cases. While the ERA eventually failed to be passed by the required number of states, the women's movement of the 60s made more progress in fighting for women to receive equal pay, in gaining full access for women to higher education, in supporting more women to become elected to the political office, and in the legalization of abortion (3).

modern American contradictions: women

American society can present contradictions that aren't always easy for foreigners or even Americans themselves to explain or to understand. Two aliens from outer space with the task of describing the role of women in American society might come up with two totally contradictory views. The first alien could claim that Americans are in favor of a traditional family with the father as breadwinner and the mother as housewife, that an attempt to guarantee women the same rights as men failed to make it into the much beloved Constitution of the land, that less than one-fifth of the Senators and Representatives in the Congress of the United States at the end of the 2000s are women although women make up more than one-half of the population. The second alien could claim with just as much evidence that American women are liberated and independent with more rights and choices than women in many other countries, could point to an increasing awareness of sexist language, expressed for example in the use of Ms. as a form of address that doesn't reveal marital status, or to famous organizations like NOW, or to internationally known feminists like Betty Friedan and Gloria Steinem, or to women who've been very successful in media and business like Oprah Winfrey, Martha Stewart, and Mary Kay Ash. This second alien could also point to women who have important political roles like Speaker of the House Nancy Pelosi or to former state governors and current members of the Obama cabinet like Janet Napolitano or Kathleen Sibelius.

changing roles

Both aliens from outer space would've taken notice of the political role of American women that made the news not only across the country but also around the world during the very long presidential election of 2008, which began in January 2007 when Hillary Clinton announced that she would be running for president. While there have been dozens of women who have been nominated to run for the presidency by various small political parties and dozens more who were unsuccessful at gaining party nominations, the first serious contender for a major party was Clinton, who came in a very close second to Barack Obama for the nomination to run as the Democratic candidate. The first woman to be nominated by a major party as vice president was Geraldine Ferraro, who ran in 1984 on the Democratic ticket with Walter Mondale as the unsuccessful presidential nominee. The incumbent Republican Ronald Reagan won reelection in one of the biggest landslides ever in American politics. The first woman to be nominated by the Republican Party as vice president was Sarah Palin. Palin's nomination provoked much discussion. The evangelical conservative Christians who very strongly supported Palin because of her strict opposition to abortion and her strong support of the right to bear arms (🔔 3) wouldn't have allowed a woman to serve as a pastor in one of the churches, yet now they were caught in the contradiction of supporting someone who was just a heartbeat away from becoming president. This contradiction may end up liberalizing attitudes towards women among the most conservative Americans. But Palin isn't the first conservative woman who seemingly presents a direct contradiction to the traditional role of women as wives and mothers only. Phyllis Schlafly, whom we've already met, is another, a woman who believes in the traditional role as wife and mother yet who at the same time has expanded this role to include a very public one of conservative activist and outspoken author.

progress for women now or still ahead?

The future of the role of women in US society? Hillary Clinton is the second female Secretary of State in a row, following Condoleeza Rice as the first female African American Secretary of State; Michelle Obama has assumed a prominent role in the media as an independent, and intelligent and stylish First Lady with star power. Sonia Sotomayor is the first female Hispanic Supreme Court justice – and the third female ever. The first female president of Harvard University, Drew Gilpin Faust, was just elected a couple of years after a president was forced to resign partly based on comments he made about the link between biological sex and academic success. In spite of the Equal Pay Act passed in the early 1960s, which was intended to insure that sex didn't play role in income, women in America still only earn between 60 to 80 % of what men do.

waves of feminism

The history of the struggle for equal rights for women is sometimes summarized in waves. The first wave started with Seneca Falls in the US and with Wollstonecraft in the UK and ended with American and British women having fought for and won the right to vote. The second wave started with the changes in society caused by women entering the workforce in World War II in both countries and lasted until the failure of the proposed Equal Rights Amendment in the US. And as you would expect, a third wave usually follows a second. Proponents of third-wave feminism sometimes criticize the use of the word “feminism” itself, which some think puts too much attention on an outdated view of gender being fixed (an important issue in cultural studies as we’ll shortly see). Partly a generational question – third-wave feminists were born after the legal and social successes of the women’s liberation movement of the 60s – younger activists of the third wave have advocated an expansion of the struggle for equality to include other minority groups like African Americans and other economic groups, such as the poor and the working class, and other sexual orientations, like lesbians or transgender individuals.

We began our glance at some highlights in women’s struggle for equality with a white $18^{th}$ century English writer who believed strongly in the role of education as the tool to equality. We’ll end this section with our first biggie, a black $20^{th}$ and $21^{st}$ century American writer, who also strongly believes in the power of education.

**biggies in boxes**

**Fig. 14.3** | *bell hooks*

**bell hooks**, pen name for Gloria Jean Watkins, Kentucky-born feminist philosopher, poet, social critic, and teacher; late $20^{th}$ to $21^{st}$ century

bell hooks created her pseudonym from her grandmother’s name in honor of her family’s female tradition; the small letters are supposed to emphasize more her message and not the person Gloria Watkins. At the same time this double persona points to the performance part of identity that is now a central aspect of discourses on gender. Being both African American and female she provides us with two “minority” groups in one, and it’s exactly this combination that she has used to reveal struggles for power and rights. Thus as with all other biggies in cultural studies she too could’ve been placed in the chapters about identity, power, media, or culture since hooks has also done research on how blacks and women are represented in popular culture. hooks sees black women as being doubly disadvantaged for being black and for being female.

After having enjoyed her school experiences at a segregated school (2, 7) hooks found education at a newly integrated school to be disappointing – her all-white teachers didn’t have the same sense of mission that the black female teachers had been able to inspire her with. After gaining degrees in English literature, bell hooks began a career as a university professor and has emphasized her belief in the liberating aspects of education again and again. She has published on a wide range of topics at the heart of cultural studies like gender, race, media, popular culture, and education. Her highly personal anecdotal writing style might shock some German academics but has not prevented her from becoming one of the best-known and most respected academics in the fields of gender and race studies.

One of the goals of this chapter is to get our terminology "straight" about sex and gender discourse ( 13). The pun here is on "straight" also being a somewhat dated term for heterosexuals and the opposite of "gay" for (male) homosexuals. We started our look at the struggle for equality for women with a famous woman in Britain and a famous event in the US. We can start our look at the struggle for the equality of gays and lesbians at a small bar in lower Manhattan.

straights and gays

More than forty years ago a diverse group of gay men and lesbian women and transvestites (people who dress as the opposite sex) resisted one of the regular raids by the New York City police at the Stonewall Inn in Greenwich Village. The spontaneous protests against arbitrary arrests lasted for several days and are now considered to be the beginning of a revolution in the public awareness of these sexual minority groups. The anniversary of the Stonewall Riots is now celebrated each summer across the country and around the world as Gay Pride or LBGT Pride – LBGT is the acronym for lesbians, bisexuals, gay, and transgender. In Germany these events are named Christopher Street after the location of the Stonewall Inn.

US: Stonewall

American society can present contradictions that aren't always easy to explain or to understand. Those two aliens from outer space now faced with the task of describing sexuality and sexual orientation in America might come up with two totally contradictory views. The first alien could claim that America is number one in the production of hard-core pornography, that America can claim to be one of the birthplaces of gay and lesbian rights, and is obsessed with sex in all its forms. Gays and lesbians today in the US are present in the media, in politics, in the entertainment industry to an extent that those who experienced Stonewall probably wouldn't have dreamed of. In five states same-sex marriage is legal with all the rights and privileges of opposite-sex marriage. The second alien could claim with just as much evidence that America is the most puritanical of all Western industrialized countries with laws prohibiting any kind of nudity, state laws that make not only gay sex but also many forms of heterosexual intercourse illegal. Conservative religious groups condemn homosexuality as a sin and regard sexuality as something that the government needs to regulate and point to the fact that most states restrict marriage to opposite-sex couples.

modern American contradictions: LBGT

UK: Wolfenden to Section 28 to civil partnership

The beginning of the gay liberation movement in the US is often traced back to the Stonewall Riots. In Britain a first tentative step towards equality was made in the late 1950s with the Wolfenden Report, which based its findings on research in the social sciences and recommended that the state avoid legislating morality and sexual behavior. A decade later and a couple of years before Stonewall, private sexual acts between two men older than 21 were legalized. This age of consent between two male sex partners was later reduced to 18, but not until the beginning of the new millennium was the age lowered to 16 and thus made equal for same-sex and opposite-sex partners. A huge setback to the struggle for gay and lesbian equality was the passage of Section 28, a law that prevented local governments from presenting homosexuality as an acceptable family relationship. The British LBGT activist group Stonewall was founded as a response to Section 28, was instrumental in Section 28 being repealed in the early 2000s, and is now one of the largest of such groups in Europe. Civil partnership for gays and lesbians in Britain now includes the same rights and privileges as for marriage between heterosexuals.

After our look at the struggle for equal rights for women and for gays and lesbians in the US and the UK, we now come to the more difficult theoretical part, and we'll have to begin with what was once a relatively easy to understand clear-cut distinction between male and female and between the two concepts of sex and gender. (We'll be looking at other binary contrasts like nature and culture or high culture and low culture at the end of the book and seeing how all these contrasts have turned out to be problematic.)

he and she

As a student of a foreign language, you've probably already come across one meaning of the word "gender" in gender-specific pronouns, which can lead you to some very interesting questions that are relevant for cultural studies. The third person pronoun only allows the possibility of two genders: "he" and "she" ("it" refers to objects). If I want to express male/female distinctions using pronouns, I can do so just by using the third person singular personal pronoun "he" or "she," but which pronoun can I use to describe someone who's not fully male or female or something in between? The third-person pronouns "he" and "she" in English won't help me here. And other languages express male-female distinctions in even more ways. Why is it so difficult to express aspects that go beyond or confuse the seemingly clear-cut male-female dichotomy? Fascinating cultural studies questions that I can at least make you aware of here.

biological sex and gender roles

Anthropologists (16) have always been interested in gender, but old views categorizing men as hunters and women as gatherers have been modified. Cultural studies, as we will see, has come to question other distinctions between men and women. But let's start with some seemingly simple biological facts. Sex is the biological category that divides almost all human beings into either female or male depending on genitals, hormones, or the reproductive system. Individuals who can't be specifically categorized as just male or just female are sometimes referred to as intersex or in older usage hermaphrodite. Gender describes the historical, cultural, and social differences between men and women. Gender roles are taught consciously and unconsciously by parents and by society to babies and children of a very young age. Gender identity doesn't always have to coincide with sex. People can feel male or female or something in between or as neither male nor female. Transgender or transsexual people are individuals who feel that they belong to the opposite biological sex and who then undergo sex reassignment operations so that their gender role and their sex are then the same.

gender = liberation?

I said at the beginning of this chapter that gender was a "man-made" concept, and two of the people who came up with the distinction between biological sex and the social construction gender were indeed men: Alex Comfort, an English physician, poet, novelist, and pacifist who became much better known for his bestselling *Joy of Sex: A Gourmet Guide to Lovemaking* in the early 1970s, described how gender roles were learned at an early age. Robert Stoller, an American psychoanalyst, also did trailblazing research into the distinction between the biological basis of sex and the cultural and social construction of gender. Work done at this time began to shake the common belief that the biological differences between male and female were the root of all other distinctions. This distinction between sex and gender, first used in the 1960s, allowed supporters of the women's liberation movement to argue that inequality between men and women wasn't based on biological facts but on cultural views. With third-wave feminism, the focus changed from a narrow female-male distinction to include race, ethnicity, and class.

sex as a speech act

We've seen how identity could be defined as a kind of action (🔔 12). We could take our opening quotation from Shirley Chisholm (🔔 7) to be a performative speech act like "I now pronounce you man and wife." You may think that it's a bit strange to claim that language has the power to make someone "male" or "female," a distinction that most people would regard as a biological fact independent of language. But from the 1980s onwards under the influence of important French philosophers like Foucault (🔔 13) some people began to question a clear-cut distinction between sex and gender. Maybe sex isn't a given fact outside of our influence; maybe sex too is a social, historical, and cultural category. The person perhaps most associated with these views is one of the most important American female scholars working in cultural studies and our second biggie in this chapter, Judith Butler.

**biggies in boxes**

**Fig. 14.4** | *Judith Butler*

**Judith Butler**, American feminist philosopher and writer, late 20th to 21st century

Many of the personal details you can find about Judith Butler include her illustrious academic career with degrees from the Ivy League Yale University (🔔 4) and her teaching positions at such reputable institutions as Wesleyan, Johns Hopkins, and the University of California Berkeley as well as her academic star status. Butler has become known for questioning fixed identities of any sort and calls herself a gay woman philosopher anti-Zionist American Jew. Butler, though, isn't known just as a feminist philosopher but also as one of the founders of queer theory (🔔 16), which calls into question the idea that certain forms of sexuality like heterosexuality are natural. She's become known for her view that gender and sex aren't given "facts" or "nouns" outside of our culture but come into existence only by being "performed" and thus are "verbs."

Butler's influence hasn't only been academically enormous, with hundreds of books and articles written about her theories in addition to the dozen books she's written herself. In spite of the difficulty and denseness of her writing, which has been criticized as being too far removed from daily life and not political enough, she has a devoted following among graduate students and feminists. Her most famous book *Gender Trouble* even generated a fanzine called *Judy!*, which both took Butler's theory seriously and parodied her star status. I remember attending a conference in Berlin years before I had ever heard of her and being amazed at the level of enthusiasm of those who had gotten seats, enthusiasm I'd more often seen for pop stars than for professors of literature and philosophy.

Those who find her writing inaccessible might try some of her lectures available online, which give evidence of her wit and her passion. And a fascinating documentary film, *Judith Butler: Philosophical Encounters of the Third Kind*, could provide more immediate access for all those interested in identity and gender and power.

masculinities and femininities

Many working in cultural studies support a more complex view of sex and gender than a simple male-female, homosexual-heterosexual distinction. You've already encountered some of the variety of terms used for sexuality and gender-based identities in this chapter. To pick just one more example from popular culture: "metrosexual" has become a common word to describe heterosexual men who have acquired the same interests in personal appearance and consumption that are often stereotyped as being gay male characteristics. While some researchers still see the influence of a biological male-female distinction as important, most people working in cultural studies emphasize plural forms: masculinity and femininity aren't essential characteristics but occur in varying degrees and are matters of representation. Presenting masculinity as a matter of representation and not defining it as an essential characteristic with necessary qualities like success at work or success at war could make life much easier for men. To take just two examples: think of the psychological pain suffered by those men who weren't a success at work during the Thatcher years of union busting in Britain. Or the pain of those Vietnam War Veterans who weren't a success at war when they came home to America. Redefining boundaries between masculine and feminine might be threatening to some but can also be liberating. Making ourselves conscious of where the boundaries are and how they can change can also help us to understand aspects of popular culture. To end with just one example: drag queens or drag kings are men and women who dress and behave like the other sex, which results in calling such gender roles into question while – perhaps – at the same time reinforcing them since drag only works as a parody if the performer and the viewer know what's being parodied.

bodies

And before we finish the chapter on (fe)males, which in spite of all the talk about socially constructed gender still has something to do with biology and the body, we need to mention that body in the very concrete sense of the word has become a popular "subject" or "object" of cultural studies. We can connect bodies to the American ideal of beauty as a driving force behind some of the culture that America has exported to the rest of the world. We can see American ideals of beauty as exemplified in the enormous success of the Barbie doll, which recently celebrated its 50th anniversary, or in Miss America pageants and the popularity of bodybuilding, but also in the problems of obesity, fitness crazes, diets, and anorexia – these are all very hot topics and popular in cultural studies in general. Other examples from the recent past and the present: popular culture products and performers like the enormously popular exercise videos by Jane Fonda in the 1980s, or Oprah Winfrey's publicized battle with weight in her television show. The body is the place for playing out cultural differences and it connects identity and gender and race as in the ironic expression "dead white males" – used to criticize the overemphasis on white men as contributors to European and Anglo-American civilization. We could look at the body's role in Foucault's (🔔 13) studies of executions in the context of changes in the way capital punishment in the US has been applied. We still have time to mention a booklet published in the 1970s by a small group of feminists. With its combination of personal experience and research to help empower women to make decisions about themselves that others – male doctors for example – had made for them, *Our Bodies Ourselves* isn't just a wonderful example of a book for this chapter but one for cultural studies in general.

Cultural studies has also started to study "posthuman" bodies, plastic surgery, and Second Life avatars. And by mentioning avatars, those 3-D objects or icons that computer users choose to represent themselves, we've already moved from sexed bodies to virtual reality, part of the new media, which is the topic of our next chapter.

## Exercises

1. Look back through the history appetizers and through the chapters on minorities, on the media, and on the arts in Part I to find some examples that you could praise as good choices of women.
2. Criticize the content of this chapter from a cultural studies point of view – and keep in mind Part I. Praise the contents of the chapter from a cultural studies point of view – and keep in mind the focus of area studies on "life and institutions."

Challenging questions and interesting projects:

Tell a few friends you're doing a project and you need their help. The friends need to ride the bus or tram or just walk through a crowded store immediately before meeting you. You ask them to describe the people they just saw. Note the categories they use in their descriptions. Maybe they use words like "tall" or "white" or "old" or "beautiful" or even "men" or "women." Then work together and try and come up with definitions for the categories. The goal of this project is to raise your awareness of how subjective and how difficult to define such categories can be. If your friends protest that there's a clear distinction between "men" and "women," then ask them how they know that someone's a man or woman: clothes, behavior, hair, skin?

And finally the oh-my-god-if-you-can-do-this-you'll-maybe-become-known-as-the-biggest-and-brightest-new-hope-in-cultural-studies task:

Using poststructuralist theory explain how academics who write in such a difficult to understand way as Judith Butler or who use such startlingly autobiographical details as bell hooks have managed to become the academic superstars of the early 2000s.

And just a few examples of things we couldn't talk about in this chapter but that are also important in the sex/gender/body/feminist/male studies debates:

gendered subjectivity; the influence of poststructuralist theory on the sex/gender distinction; Freud and the feminists; the feminists and the origins of British cultural studies at the Birmingham Centre for Contemporary Cultural Studies; use of terms like "gendered body" and "sexed body"; pornography as a lightning rod issue for feminists; hip-hop music with its misogynist lyrics; the development of female sexual enjoyment from the advice given to women in the Victorian era who were supposed to bear children but not enjoy sex to "close their eyes and think of England" to the advertisement for the American cigarette brand Virginia Slims "You've come a long way, baby"; analysis of gender bending in describing Madonna's performances; origin of drag kings in British music hall variety shows of the 19th century …

# 15 New Media Was, Is, and Always Will Be the Message?

"...the medium is the message..." and/or *The Medium is the Massage*
famous saying by Marshall McLuhan and the title of a later published book

*We're All Journalists Now*
title of a book by American lawyer and writer Scott Gant

"Someone the other day said, 'It's the biggest thing since Gutenberg,' and then someone else said, 'No, it's the biggest thing since the invention of writing.'"
media mogul Rupert Murdoch describing the internet

The first question we're facing in this chapter deals with terminology. We've already had a more or less traditional chapter on the media in Part I and touched upon some of the big changes taking place in the world of media today. But maybe we shouldn't use the old-fashioned word "media" in the title of this chapter. You may come across the acronym MSM, which isn't the name for yet another American or British television network (10) but instead stands for "mainstream media" and which refers to much of the media that we looked at in Part I. A more appropriate term for the media we'll be covering in this chapter could be ICT for Information Communication Technology or just IT for Information Technology. But if I had decided on that term, the allusion to the famous McLuhan quote above wouldn't have been possible. And new media comprises more than just ICT. In this chapter we'll be looking from the cultural studies perspective at media both new and old by at first using the same distinction as in the previous media chapter: the distinction between newspapers and television. And we'll even take up another topic from Part I – natives and immigrants – but this time from a very different perspective.

When you finish the chapter, you should be able to say something about

- digital natives and digital immigrants
- newspapers and television from a cultural studies perspective
- the role of the audience

- some well-known media critics
- diversity, interactivity, and Web 2.0
- new and old aspects of the new media
- the future of the new media.

digital immigrants and natives

I assume that you already have experience with the brave new world of the web and that you're maybe even a digital native, a term first used appropriately enough at the beginning of the new millennium to describe those who have grown up with the use of digital technology like computers, the internet, and cell phones. And what are the digital non-natives called? Digital immigrants like me who believe in digital technology or who have to believe in it because of their jobs as teachers. The educator, writer, and software designer Marc Prensky, who is said to have coined the terms digital native and digital immigrant, has done research into ways of using the digital world in the classroom. Prensky strongly believes in listening to and learning from student experience, and as a teacher he shares a job with practically all the big names in this chapter: McLuhan, Postman, Hall, Williams. If you transfer Prensky's philosophy of taking students seriously to researchers in cultural studies taking media users seriously, then you already have one of the main topics of the chapter right from the start.

from broad- to narrow- to webcasting

We could summarize some of the changes in media by looking at the word family "casting." Over-the-air broadcasting is the word used when broad audiences share the same television experience as in the pre-digital age, narrowcasting when material is available only to those who must sign up first or pay for programming sent via cable or satellite from the 70s onwards or via limited access areas of the internet. Webcasting is the general word for making any kind of material accessible over the internet, and podcast refers specifically to digital media files – audio or video or both – available online. The means of communication via paper, waves, and bytes that we covered in Part I could be seen as converging to one screen that serves the purpose of newspapers, radio, and television, and that isn't created by the few and directed at the many but created by the many and directed at the many. Computer hackers could be seen as those who fight against powerful institutions threatening to curtail the freedom of the net. In spite of all these changes, let's still begin with the newspaper, familiar to us from the earlier chapter on the media (10), but now with a different cultural studies focus.

print media: aspects of racism and gender

We'll begin with someone you met a few chapters ago. In the late 1970s Stuart Hall wrote a book with several other colleagues from the Centre for Contemporary Cultural Studies (CCCS) (16) entitled *Policing the Crisis*, which analyzed the treatment of crime and race in British newspapers and showed connections between media and racial prejudice in creating moral panic, the sense that a particular minority group had become a threat. Also in the 1970s Angela McRobbie, a graduate of the CCCS, began to look closely at *Jackie*, a weekly British magazine written for girls, in order to see how the readers interpreted what they read and absorbed the ideology that the producers of the magazine and society in general wanted. The print media was being closely read in a cultural studies context to understand how power and identity were expressed. In the earlier media chapter we had already begun to look at newspapers from a cultural studies perspective when we speculated about the future of the newspaper and the increasing online presence of what used to be a medium exclusively on paper.

blogs and citizen journalism

A logbook was – and still is – a written record used for navigation in ships, and I suppose sailing on water and surfing the internet are closely enough related to justify the connection. In any case blogs – or blogs with video clips sometimes called vlogs – have become one of the most important ways of distributing information and opinion and are now an integral part of the old-fashioned newspaper media with both the online articles of journalists being called blogs as well as the contributions of the users. Just check any online article from any of the newspapers mentioned in the traditional media chapter and see how many of them have space at the bottom for readers to record comments. You could say that this kind of participation is little different from the letters to the editor section in the paper editions – with the difference that these readers' comments are easy to send and can reach millions of readers immediately. Another perhaps more marked difference between traditional media and the new online media is the use of audience participation in the form of "citizen journalists" and "I-Reporters," integrating the texts and audiovisual contributions of users – made easy through the widespread use of cell phones – into traditional online media sites. Whether this dramatic increase in participatory journalism is a sign of increased democracy and shared power or indicates a loss in quality journalism is one of the exciting ongoing debates in media studies and in cultural studies.

aggregators, *Drudge Report, Huffington Post*

Another dramatic change that came with online media is the spread of aggregators, websites composed of collections of headlines with links to a variety of other sources – mostly online versions of print newspapers. (The technical word "aggregate" means "to flock or cluster together.") Sometimes the headlines are automatically chosen as in Google News; sometimes human selection plays a role as in Yahoo News. The *Drudge Report* and the *Huffington Post* are two other examples of similar websites with very different American political views (Matt Drudge is conservative, Arianna Huffington liberal) that combine links to articles from the mainstream media with original contributions and blogs. These aggregators may point to the future of the news online. The *Seattle Post-Intelligencer* was one of the newspapers to go entirely online (10) and now has a website that looks like the *Huffington Post*. We've already moved now from paper to bytes, but before we continue our look at online media, we first need to switch to traditional television first.

encoding and decoding

One of the biggest names in cultural studies, Stuart Hall (12), developed in the early 1970s a theory that was to become influential in understanding television audiences: encoding and decoding. Television texts – text in the broadest sense of the word – carry multiple meanings, which Hall categorizes as dominant, negotiated, and oppositional. The producers encode the texts with one meaning, which the audience can accept by using the dominant code, adapt by using the negotiated code, or understand but reject by using the oppositional code. Hall's taking television programs and their audiences seriously led to a series of studies from the 80s onwards that made use of various kinds of American and British television programs and signaled a change from a textual analysis of content to a look at the way audiences create meaning.

soap operas

Television has always been a very popular medium for cultural studies because of the sheer amount of popular culture it produces and for the hugeness of the audience reached. Let's look at one special genre of special interest: the soap opera. What originally began on American radio in the 1930s for a mostly female audience and sponsored by commercials for laundry detergent –

hence the name – made a successful move to daytime American television of the 50s and later expanded to primetime (10) with such internationally successful series as *Dallas*, *Dynasty*, and *Falcon Crest*. If you look at the German title for *Dynasty* (*Der Denver-Clan*) and recall the title of the British television soap opera *Coronation Street* (10) or know of other British soap operas like *EastEnders* or *Emmerdale* or perhaps one of the first American televised soap operas *Peyton Place*, then you can guess from the titles alone one characteristic of soap operas in general: their connection to a specific place, often a small town. Soap operas also have open-ended story lines since they aren't limited like other television series. The content deals with interpersonal relationships and melodramatic incidents.

watching *Dallas, Crossroads, Nationwide*

Cultural studies researchers like Ien Ang, Dorothy Hobson, David Morley, and Charlotte Brunsdon began to look at how audiences understood the popular American and British soap operas *Dallas* and *Crossroads* and the British news program *Nationwide*. They discovered that audiences interpreted what they saw in widely different ways, and that this range could only partly be accounted for by such factors as class, education, and ethnicity. Cultural studies had changed the way audiences were seen and basically discounted the hypothermic model, which had claimed that television audiences were easily manipulated by the producers and "injected" with the meaning and intentions the producers wanted. Researchers began to question the traditional view of television news as a mere reproduction of the hegemonic (13) structures of society through the primary definers of the news, the authoritative sources in government, and the talking heads of the television news presenters.

too much entertainment; sequence and flow

We need to mention some other big and much more widely known names than those above, names of academics connected with important and very critical views of television. During the mid 1980s in his book *Amusing Ourselves to Death* the American cultural and media critic Neil Postman damned television for its emphasis on entertainment, on the image instead of the word, and its oversimplification. Raymond Williams (16), whose words were heard on the opening day of the British Channel 4 (10), irritated by American television with its commercial interruptions, developed a system of analysis based on sequence and flow with emphasis on how television programming was organized with commercial interruptions and contributed to the general flow of the channel (10) with the producers' intention of keeping the attention of the viewer. Of course Williams' analysis was based on old-fashioned television broadcasts on television sets without the help of remote control. Television was for Williams a result of social and economic causes and not a powerful cause of change in itself as Marshall McLuhan, the man whose famous quotes opened this chapter, believed. Although McLuhan died years before the World Wide Web came into existence and thus couldn't be considered a digital native, in many ways he was way ahead of his time.

**biggies in boxes**

**Marshall McLuhan**, Canadian-born scholar and one of the big names in media studies, mid to late 20th century

Marshall McLuhan is known for two catch phrases: the medium is the message and the global village. Like some of the other biggies in cultural studies we've met (Richard Hoggart 13) or will be meeting (Raymond Williams 16), McLuhan was also trained as a professor of English literature. He studied in England as a graduate student under F.R. Leavis (16) and was influenced by what came to be called New Criticism, the belief that great books deserved close reading without taking into account extra-textual sources. One of McLuhan's early books, *The Mechanical Bride*, was published in the early 1950s and analyzed newspaper and magazine advertisements. His *Gutenberg Galaxy*, published a decade later, popularized the term "global village," which McLuhan saw as the result of people being able to see and hear events all over the world as they happen and thus feel more connected to each other and other places. The famous phrase "the medium is the message" comes from his book *Understanding Media* and was later used in the title of the collage book *The Medium is the Massage*, which became something of a cult classic with its collage style of pictures and text. McLuhan believed that the medium influenced the content in a fundamental way and thus content that was conveyed via writing would have a different effect on the reader than content conveyed via images like television. He believed that new technologies were the cause of changes in human cultural life: the print media created a mass audience of readers, electric media created a mass audience of viewers. McLuhan also predicted the importance of networks and in effect described the internet years before it came into existence.

Late in his life McLuhan appeared as himself in Woody Allen's acclaimed romantic film comedy *Annie Hall*. He had already become one of the most famous and most criticized American academics of the late 20th century, appearing in magazines like *Newsweek*, *Life*, *Esquire*, and *Playboy*. McLuhan was a devout Catholic convert and an avid reader of James Joyce's last and most difficult to understand book *Finnegans Wake*. After his death, McLuhan became the "patron saint and holy fool" of the print and online magazine *Wired*.

**Fig. 15.1**
*Marshall McLuhan*

horrors of the global village

While McLuhan's view of technology creating a global village might lead you to think about the positive aspects of increased communication and understanding among people connected via the media, McLuhan himself didn't see the global village created by television to be necessarily a harmonious one. The defining televised experience of the 2000s certainly proved that the inhabitants of the global village experiencing an event live together didn't lead to increased understanding or communication. The attacks on the World Trade Center carried a symbolic force not possible without the media. Those who planned the attacks knew how to use the media to spread their message, and thus the 9/11 attacks are fundamentally different from two other defining moments in American history: Pearl Harbor (6) was a military base and the attack came without the media looking on; the Kennedy assassination was witnessed only in retrospect on videotape by large numbers of people. My personal memory of the 9/11 events is a woman being interviewed on television in New York, who in tears kept asking "What have we done so that some people would hate us so much as to do this?" It remains to be seen if the shared media experience of 9/11 and its aftermaths will result eventually in a deeper understanding of one another within the confines of our networked global village. What seems to be true is about television and the internet that neither television networks nor the new worldwide internetwork has provided the same sort of "social glue" that some media analysts saw in television's golden age.

television – the social glue no longer sticks

As we saw in the media chapter in Part I, cable and satellite television with hundreds of channels provides viewers with an overwhelming choice of programming. Some people regret the loss of the shared experience they had during the 50s and 60s with few major American and British broadcasting companies. In this so-called golden age of television, people at work and in school all had similar experiences to share with one another about the television they watched the evening before – there was little choice anyway about what to watch. This common sharing of experience was sometimes described as a kind of "social glue" that bound people from different backgrounds and classes together and gave them something to talk about. Yet on the other hand the kind of television shown in Britain and America in the 50s and 60s was a reflection only of the majority white middle-class nuclear families. Other groups (immigrant families, African Americans, single parents, gays) weren't shown until the 70s. Now of course there are television networks tailor-made for specific target groups (10), and these target groups can watch television online, making a transition from the old medium of television to the new Web 2.0 easy for us here.

from ARPANET to WWW to Web 2.0

While the age of the internet is global, its roots can be localized, so we can summarize some of the relevant details and still remain with Anglo-American studies. What came to be the internet began in the early 1970s originally as a US military project called the Advanced Research Projects Agency Network – or ARPANET for short – which was supposed to provide a computer network that would allow communications in event of nuclear war. The network expanded among American universities in California and soon included universities across the country and by the mid 80s had reached Germany too (the first email sent to the University of Karlsruhe had the subject line "Wilkommen," a typically American interference spelling mistake). The number of computers connected to this early version of the internet began to increase rapidly. At the beginning of the 90s while working at the European Organization for Nuclear Research (CERN) in Switzerland the British engineer and computer scientist Tim Berners-Lee created what came to be called the World Wide Web, a simpler way of sharing texts, sounds, and images (in effect uniting paper and waves with bytes) that turned the academic internet into a web that would cover the whole wide world and turn the three letters www into the key to a vast amount of information – and commercialization – previously unknown in human history. With the help of programs called browsers, businesses, institutions, and people can advertise and sell products, simplify communication, and share personal information around the world.

Just over a decade later a new term appeared, Web 2.0, often used to indicate interactive audience use via blogging, YouTube, and Wikipedia. While some, including Berners-Lee, see Web 2.0 as nothing more than a different name for the interactivity that was always there, the passive audience of browsers just a decade ago has now turned into an active audience of creators.

Web 2.0 and the user

For those who are puzzled by the name: Using numbers with decimal points is a way of distinguishing various versions of software development. Many of you have probably used the 3.5 or 4.0 version of the browser Firefox; some digital immigrants like me might remember Windows 3.0 before Microsoft stopped using the version numbers and switched to other version names like Windows Vista. Web 2.0 is supposed to represent a further development of the original web: the user is now the focus. The US newsmagazine *Time* named "The User" their Person of the Year for 2006 (the computer was the choice in 1982). And the most popular websites like YouTube or Wikipedia are those created by users for other users.

wikis and *Wikipedia*

Just over a decade ago, an American computer programmer developed software that would allow users to create and edit web pages. Ward Cunningham named his invention WikiWikiWeb from the Hawaiian word for quick and the alliteration with www. With the speed of a digital revolution the most famous wiki, the user-driven *Wikipedia* website, created by the American businessman Jimmy Wales, has grown from a small project to one of the most visited sites on the web. The underlying principle of community responsibility with many contributors has the advantage of a pooling of knowledge and experience by many people and the disadvantage of a lack of personal responsibility since the authors and editors of Wikipedia articles remain mostly nameless in contrast to the expert-driven principle of other encyclopedias. Probably everyone can agree on the uncontroversial fact that Wikipedia is one prime example of Web 2.0. Why, though, do some academics seem to dislike Wikipedia so much? Is it just the chance of finding wrong "facts" or sabotaged descriptions or is it the loss of the power that comes to those who have access to the libraries and the books and the "hidden knowledge"? We could continue here but then we'd be back in our chapter on power (13).

His Master's Voice

As in our chapter on traditional media, let's end this one by going chronologically backwards to the very beginnings of recorded sound, even further back than the medium of radio. It's probably difficult for us as digital natives or digital immigrants to imagine the sense of wonder people must have had when hearing recorded voices for the first time in human history. Perhaps the poignant story behind the famous music trademark "His Master's Voice" visible on American, British, and German record labels can help us understand what hearing recorded voices

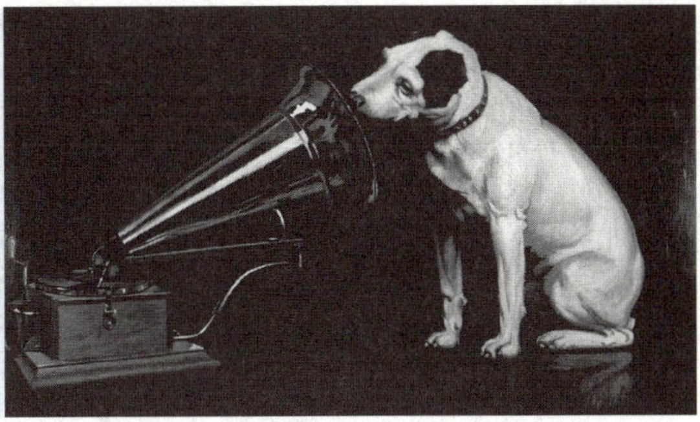

| Fig. 15.2
*Francis Barraud's painting "His late Master's Voice"*

must have been for those who in the 19th century couldn't have even dreamed of a digital future. The image used by the HMV label is based originally on a painting of a dog listening intently to recordings of the voice of his deceased master coming from the loudspeaker (which looked like a trumpet back then).

biggest thing since writing?

Can we believe Rupert Murdoch's (🔔 10) claim at the beginning of this chapter that the internet is the biggest thing since writing? When we look at all kinds of media and their history from the point of view of communication, we can see that for all the talk about the radical innovations of ICT you could also argue that actually not a lot has changed or as the French say: plus ça change, plus c'est la même chose. Using beacons and smoke signals to communicate at a distance is as old as the use of fire itself, the telegraph was invented in the early 1800s, even earlier than the telephone (🔔 2). Thus the first use of technology in the modern sense to bridge distance and shrink time is more than two centuries old. And is there really any big difference between the vinyl recording and the DVD disc – other than the amount of information stored? We could even see the digitalization of society built on the binary code, on just two numbers 0 and 1, like the on and off flashes of beacons in lighthouses thousands of years ago. And Twitter, the latest development in blogging allowing users to send short text messages to anyone or everyone, has the same name as the sounds birds make, a reminder perhaps that the messages carrier pigeons once delivered aren't different in content from those transmitted by the bytes filling the air and cables that connect our world.

virtual utopian world: global or national?

We could continue this chapter with media studies or go even further and mention Virtual Reality as the newest kind of media, but a uniquely Anglo-American component isn't clear. The very idea of national borders seems absurd in the virtual world with social networking sites like Facebook or MySpace, which may have been founded in the US and have their headquarters there but are accessible and popular worldwide. Of course it's still possible for countries to attempt to block parts of the internet from users within certain geographical borders. And national identity can of course still be important to Web 2.0's individual users. Do digitopians – a word combined of "digital" and "utopian" meaning those who believe in a positive future for us all online – have the better arguments? Will boundless internet geography and the virtual space created by the user lead to a digital democracy? The digitopians might believe so, pointing to the origin of the internet with its ideals of free flow of information, knowledge sharing, justice, and community. They would see the end of traditional media as something positive, old media having produced cultural domination and imperialism from the powerful few for the many without a real voice. New media can be seen as bringing a dramatic change from limits in space (paper) and time (TV schedules) to the ability to see what you want when you want it and to create content for the rest of the world to experience, the ultimate in attaining audience empowerment. But will the new media succeed in empowering users in new and exciting ways or are they just a sign of the dumbing down of humankind, of the triumph of the mindless image over the rational word? Stay tuned ... for the next episode on an online platform of your choice...

## Exercises

1. First the easy part. Give a few concrete names that show how different branches of the old and new media have become intertwined today (hint: you'll need to review a bit of Chapter 10 in Part I for this answer) and remember to include one important name from the past too. Now, the more difficult part: criticize the content of your answer by using some of the concepts mentioned in the chapter.
2. Can you give any examples that link paper, waves, and bytes?

3. See how many different meaningful combinations of words you can create from the title of the book *The Medium is the Massage*.

Interesting and challenging projects:

Since the topic of media seems to have morphed from paper and waves and bytes to a unified focus on the portable computer or mobile phone screen, you may ask why this cultural studies chapter on new media is organized along the same lines as the traditional media chapter in Part I? Using the same structure was supposed to help you understand the differences between area and cultural studies more easily, but perhaps a better structure from a purely cultural studies point of view would be to categorize both old and new media in different ways and use categories like production (institutions, organizations, industry), control (government and economic forces), and consumption (audiences) of programs (or texts in the widest possible sense), and the connection between these programs and popular culture. Try and rewrite the chapter using the same content given but with this different structure.

Watch and compare how the news is presented on the Cable News Network (CNN), the Fox News Channel (FNC), BBC News Channel, IT News, or Sky News and determine if the choice of programming or the manner in which the news is presented tends to support or refute a hegemonic model of news.

And the if-you-can-answer-this-question-please-let-me-know-via-email-or-twitter-or-even-carrier-pigeon-as-soon-as-possible-so-that-I-can-put-the-answer-in-the-next-edition task:

Will new media succeed in empowering users in new and exciting ways or is it just a sign of the dumbing down of humankind, of the triumph of the mindless image over the rational word?

And finally, further topics not dealt with in this chapter ... for those who'd like to become a digital native or at least get rid of your digital immigrant accent:

how *The Simpson's* and other cartoon series like *South Park*, *American Dad*, and *Drawn Together* transform an old medium for children into a new one very much for adults with many references to popular culture; the role of minorities and ethnicities in American and British television series like *All in the Family*, *Goodness Gracious Me* (with both Indian Hindu and English stereotypes), and *The Kumas;* the influence of American television series like *All in the Family* on German series like *Ein Herz und eine Seele*; the roots of popular talent shows in the British variety tradition; Hartley's and Fiske's analysis of television and of American television news; examples of the combination of teaching and entertaining on television like the English historian and television presenter David Starkey's series *Monarchy* or the BBC broadcaster David Dimbleby's *A Picture of Britain* and *How We Built Britain*; the blending of audience and text in the reality TV genre; how cultural texts are produced and distributed with the Sony Walkman as a prime example; …

# Culture with a Big "C" and with a Little "c" in Anglo-American Cultural Studies

16

## "What is culture?"

If you're lucky, you could get this question in an oral or written exam. Lucky, because practically any answer you give would be right. You could also claim that trying to answer that question has resulted in many (some might say too many) books and – if you want to drop names – mention that Raymond Williams (name-dropping means you can expect Williams to be a "biggie in a box" later on in this chapter) hated the word. Or that the famous literary critic Terry Eagleton called it a "slippery term." Or you could mention the great pun by David Walton (author of a very entertaining introduction to cultural studies): "difficulture."

If you're unlucky, you could get this question in an oral or written exam. Unlucky, because if the examiners have done their job correctly, the question should be followed with: "Please give specific contexts for your definitions." Culture has been one of the central concepts in the humanities and in the social sciences in the past thirty years, and philosophers have been defining and redefining culture for many a century. We'll be taking two steps towards understanding culture in this final chapter. The first step is to know that "culture" is an extraordinarily vague idea, the second step is to be able to define "culture" in at least a few concrete contexts.

When you finish the chapter, you should not only be able to mention several different definitions of "culture" but also be able to say something about

- the importance of some big names in a modern discussion of culture
- aspects of culture that we've covered in previous chapters
- the founding of the new subject of cultural studies along with
- other subjects that can be compared and contrasted with cultural studies in the UK and the US and
- reasons for the choice of facts in previous chapters combined with a critique of these choices.

In the middle of the $20^{th}$ century two anthropologists named Kroeber and Kluckhohn listed more than a hundred different definitions of the word "culture." We'll be glancing at the discipline of anthropology at the end of the chapter; for now, let's keep it much simpler and ignore most of the definitions of culture and concentrate on just two, "culture" with or without a capital letter.

But first we need to look briefly at what "culture" has been contrasted with as well as some uses of the word in common phrases.

culture vs. nature

If we think about the etymology of the word "culture" and about phrases with "culture," then one basic meaning of the word might become clear: "man-made" as opposed to nature or natural. But one nice or frustrating thing about "culture" and "nature" is that both concepts are so vague, so complicated, and so ambiguous that they've provided many great philosophers and academics in need of a subject to write about with enough work for millennia (nice if you need the job). For our very simple purposes here, we could see "nature" as designating what's already there and "culture" as something that human beings do, often to "nature." Another way to distinguish culture from nature is to ask which one is primarily the cause of human activity: culture (nurture) or biology (nature). Or in other words do we learn through what we do or through what we've been born with? This question presents one dividing line between the humanities and the sciences and has been asked again and again, probably because the answers weren't completely satisfactory, from the last century until the present.

Kultur vs. civilisation

The idea of the noble savage, the ideal of the romantics who saw everything better in its natural state, can be criticized for being just as one-sided as the idea of the savage nobleman, who was corrupted by the civilization he (since women didn't count) grew up in. Speaking of civilization, we can also look at another contrast and use two languages to try and capture the difference: German *Kultur* and French *civilisation*. While the German word came to represent the characteristics that make up a separate nation or a separate people, the French word was thought to be universal, applicable to all humanity. Later "civilization" in the phrase "western civilization" would become a buzzword especially in the US in the culture wars between those in favor of a western (white male) tradition and those in favor of multicultural inclusion of other races and of women.

These binary oppositions have proven not to be very useful once we start thinking about "culture" as being part of human "nature" and "nature" as not being separate from the cultural way in which we see things.

culture with a big "C"

An important British literary critic named Frank Raymond Leavis (commonly known as F.R. Leavis) believed very much in culture with a big "C", the kind of culture to be found in great literary works of the Great Tradition by Jane Austen, George Eliot, Joseph Conrad. Leavis also included more contemporary writers (contemporary for him writing around a century ago) like T.S. Eliot, Ezra Pound, or James Joyce. (I'm dropping lots of names now but no biggies in boxes here since you can find out more about these authors in your literature courses.) Leavis admired the works which merit a close and careful reading and analysis because they reflected a serious moral attitude towards the complexity of life. You can look at culture with a big "C" – which is also sometimes called "high culture" – as the production and consumption of works of art, or in other oft-quoted words of the 19th century English poet and critic Matthew Arnold "the best that has been thought and said in the world." These are things you find in art museums, see performed in theatres, read in introductory courses to English literature, or in words that Arnold certainly wouldn't have used: sometimes those things that we were told we should like and that might have made us feel a little guilty – or uncultured – for not being able to appreciate them.

"c" as in "canon"

And here we have our first problem with culture with a big "C" and culture based on a canon – it can be used to divide us into those who are "cultured" and those who aren't. And we immediately have a second problem connected with the first: Who decides what the really great works of art, great dramas or comedies, great novels are? And do we have to believe what these people tell us? The problem of trying to evaluate this kind of culture has been around at least ever since two of those "great" Greek writers Plato and Aristotle began to tackle the question of defining what's truly great. And you've no doubt had a look at one of those countless lists telling you just which books you need to read as students of English or which places you need to visit if you want to become sophisticated – in other words you've probably already had the need for a canon and hated having to follow it.

one Arnold, two Blooms

We can't summarize the problematic discussion of culture with a big "C" here; but if you want to hear more from some other big Anglo-American names who were very much in favor of the civilizing aspects of this kind of culture, then pick your favorite encyclopedia for detailed information about: Matthew Arnold, whom you've just heard of and who wrote the book *Culture and Anarchy* in the 19th century; or Allan Bloom, 20th century American philosopher known for his defense of the "Great Books" and his bestselling critique of American education, *The Closing of the American Mind*; or Harold Bloom (no relation to Allan), late-20th-century American critic, who wrote *The Western Canon*.

from Culture to culture

As you can imagine, a canon would include great works of culture like great paintings, great plays, great novels, great symphonies, great books in general, maybe great films, great pop songs, ... Great pop songs? What about a very popular Broadway musical like *Cats*? The author of the poems which form the backbone of the musical was the American ex-patriot and poet T. S. Eliot (whom F. R. Leavis admired and who wrote poems that provide much for academics and often bewildered students to analyze). Eliot once claimed that Europe had the highest culture the world had ever known. This view of culture has become known as cultural imperialism and has been out of fashion for the last few decades. But it does point to the role power plays in culture, and the phrase "culture with a big (or *capital*) c" gains a new meaning when we remember another term that links culture with power: "cultural capital" (13). The German sociologist Theodor Adorno (associated with a movement in the second half of the 20th century that became known as the Frankfurt School) thought pop music and all popular mass-produced culture was bad because of its standardization, that its purpose was to provide quick satisfaction, perhaps not unlike the bread and circuses (11, 13) of ancient Rome. (Adorno, by the way, was also a composer, who was influenced by other composers like Alban Berg and Arnold Schönberg – good examples of culture with a capital "C," if we want to refer to works that are "challenging" to enjoy.) Maybe neither T. S. Eliot nor Adorno would've appreciated pop songs, but with pop songs we've arrived now at another kind of culture. As you can imagine, if there's culture with a big "C" or "high culture," then there should also be culture with a "little" c, sometimes also called "low" or "popular" or "mass" culture. And this kind of culture could very well include things like pop songs. (Maybe you even noticed that this book's introduction ended with a few lyrics from a pop song.)

culture with a little "c"

Let's start with one example of culture with a little "c" that many of you may remember from television. Can you guess whose name was missing in the last part of our British history appetizers and whose life and death helped to sell millions of copies of newspapers? One contemporary textbook on cultural studies with "The Basics" in its subtitle starts with the incident in August 1997 that nearly caused the thousand-year-old British monarchy to collapse. The death of the "Queen of Hearts," as she called herself in a famous BBC TV interview, is a good example since it shows clearly two characteristics of popular culture. Popular culture originates from the people: the masses who brought countless bouquets to Kensington Palace, Diana's home in London, the over a million people who lined the route of the funeral procession, and the billions of people who watched the funeral on television. Popular culture is commercial: the pop song by singer Elton John at Diana's funeral "Goodbye England's Rose" became one of the best-selling pop songs ever. Was the media event surrounding Diana's death manipulation by the press in order to sell more papers and Elton John's song commercialized exploitation, or were the media a mirror of genuine expression and the song a sign of real feeling? And how would you evaluate the identification of many people with someone who claimed to be queen not because of her royal roots but because of her public popularity? The answers depend on how you see popular culture, and definitions of popular culture always involve value judgments.

culture with a c – big or little?

If you've been reading along up until now chapter by chapter, then you've already come across quite a few examples of what some would consider culture with a capital "C," so many in fact that if we continued to use bells, the book would be getting really loud towards the end. But since loud noises aren't good for digestion and we're also nearing the end of our evening meal, let's keep most of the bells off the page, save a review of some of these examples for later in the chapter, and turn now to an even broader definition of culture.

culture as pretty much anything and everything

The United Nations Education, Scientific, and Cultural Organization (UNESCO) defines culture in its Universal Declaration on Cultural Diversity: "[...] culture should be regarded as the set of distinctive spiritual, material, intellectual and emotional features of society or a social group, and that encompasses, in addition to art and literature, lifestyles, ways of living together, value systems, traditions and beliefs" and thus includes pretty much everything in this entire book, perhaps appropriately enough for a book entitled Anglo-American Cultural Studies. In a standard book used in cultural studies, *New Keywords* (see the Recommendations for Further Reading at the end of this book for further details), an updated version of *Keywords* by Raymond Williams, one of the "biggies" in cultural studies, "culture" is given as a keyword separately and then in quite a few phrases like "high culture" and "mass culture," which we'll also be dealing with shortly. Other phrases include culture wars, sports culture, cultural landscape, cultural capital (13), national culture, cultural history, cultural evolution, cultural turn (to describe the rise of the importance of cultural studies). And if you haven't had enough, what about "culture shock": either an overexposure to cultural stimulation or what people might feel when they've encountered or experienced a foreign culture.

So that we can recover from culture shock, let's go back to the etymology I mentioned but didn't give you details about at the beginning of the chapter. *Culture* comes from the Latin verb *colere*, which originally meant "inhabit" in the sense of "colonize or protect" or "honor with worship" as in cult. You can also find "culture" in "agriculture" and "horticulture", reminding us of the activity, the doing and making and cultivating that's connected with the word. Culture could include elements of political leadership right down to body language and fashion, including quantitative social data, popular media, music, sports.

The biggie with whom we opened this chapter and who we've just heard a bit about, the one who wished he had "never heard the damned word," Raymond Williams, actually came up with several different definitions of culture during his long academic life. And although he started off in the tradition of F.R. Leavis (you may remember the literary critic who was very much in fa-

biggies in boxes

**Raymond Williams**, Welsh-born founding father of cultural studies, 20th century
Born in south Wales but very close to the English border, Raymond Williams had a Welsh working-class background but became a Professor at Cambridge. He served in the army during World War II but refused to serve in the Korean War. His interest in socialism and Marxism in Britain of the 1930s and 40s as well as his later experience in adult education are important aspects of his academic interests. Williams' book *Culture and Society* examined how definitions of culture have changed through the ages and established him as a pioneer in the study of popular culture, a topic previously thought unworthy of serious academic study. Williams said that the word culture was one of the two or three most complicated words in the English language and also claimed that he hated the word because it was so difficult to analyze, but still Williams' work – he published widely on literature, culture, and media – established him also as one of the important founders of the new discipline with culture in its name: cultural studies. He not only wrote about but also appeared on television. Channel 4's (10) first day on the air included excerpts from Williams' writing. Williams also wrote novels, plays, and short stories. One of his early novels, *Border Country*, had the same setting as his last unfinished work, *People of the Black Mountains*: the area of rural south Wales close to the English border.

Williams was not an academic in an ivory tower with little interest in the real world, he was also eminently political – against nuclear armament and a member of the Communist party as a young man, against the politics of the Thatcher period.

Maybe it's appropriate that one of our last biggies, like the other founders of cultural studies, was a teacher involved in adult education. Certainly it's appropriate from a cultural studies point of view to include Williams as a biggie, as one of the founding fathers, and as someone who can't be categorized according to conventional labels like "sociologist," "professor of drama at Cambridge," "visiting professor of political science at Stanford," or "novelist," "media critic," or "cultural historian" – just as hard to categorize as cultural studies, the discipline he helped to found.

**Fig. 16.1**
*Raymond Williams*

vor of a canon and culture with a capital "C"), Williams came to see the importance of popular culture and produced one definition of culture often quoted in cultural studies: "a particular way of life, whether of a people, a period or a group." Williams also talked about culture as patterns and a "structure of feeling."

from culture to cultural studies

Williams provides us with the bridge to the last part of this chapter and this book. He's considered one of the founders of the new discipline, academic subject, intellectual and political field of interest, which would come to be called "Cultural Studies" or "cultural studies," mostly used with a singular and sometimes with a plural verb. And now that we've had a chance in this chapter to see how culture can be defined and have already begun in the other chapters of Part II to review and criticize some of the content choices in the first part, let's turn our attention to the subject(s) of our book. We're almost at the end and it's about time to mention the title, don't you think? But since we've now waited so long to hear about cultural studies, and although we've been using this term without definition throughout Part II, maybe we could wait just a little longer and first take a quick look at some of the other established disciplines that share some of the same interests and methods.

a for anthropology

We'll begin with "a" for anthropology, literally "the science of humanity," which began in the 19th century and combined new theories about evolution (Charles Darwin's famous *On the Origin of Species* was published in the mid-19th century, Darwin himself was born two centuries ago in 1809) with old practices of archaeology, "the science of ancient things," which had begun a hundred years earlier with excavations of ancient Italian cities like Pompeii and was later revived with passion by men like the German Heinrich Schliemann, who looked for the origins of ancient Greek civilization and for proof that Homer's *Iliad* and Virgil's *Aeneid* (part of the canon of great books of culture with a capital "C") were based on fact. Anthropology now encompasses many specialized areas like physical anthropology, which emphasizes biological differences between human beings and other animals, and cultural anthropology, which shares some of the very same interests as cultural studies such as film, nutrition, work, but also areas where equality and discrimination are important, like feminism. In fact some anthropologists see cultural studies as just one of the later developments of anthropology. Some people working in cultural studies criticize anthropologists for their belief in the scientific objectivity of their findings, especially criticizing the role of anthropologists within a colonial tradition and its latent superior view of the "primitive" peoples anthropologists had studied in the 19th century.

a for area studies

Did you read the titles of the two parts of our book carefully or did you maybe miss a small but crucial distinction? Part I is titled "Specific Topics in Anglo-American Area Studies." Maybe you asked yourself what "area studies" is or are (the term is used in the singular and in the plural, with capital or small letters). In a very simple way area studies has to do with a certain geographical area, like American Studies, Middle Eastern Studies, Romance Studies, Pacific Studies. But as you can see from these examples "area" can take on very different meanings. The discipline can deal with a political entity like the United States (and you might remember the problems with the use of "American" to designate the United States Introduction). It can also be a region with similar cultures (like Middle Eastern Studies) or languages (Romance Studies) or just share an ocean in common (Pacific Studies). And the complexity only starts with trying to figure out just what an "area" is. Let's say we agree that "British Studies" means something. After all, there's a Centre for British Studies as part of Humboldt University in Berlin and also a Center for British Studies at the University of California Berkeley, and Oxford offers a three-term course called British Studies (currently costing £12,000). There's a *Journal of British Studies* published by the North American Conference on British Studies. But what exactly is/are British Studies? History, geography, political life, sociology, languages, literature? Interdisciplinary? Multidisciplinary? Any and all of the above is the answer, and this variety can be overwhelming too, in addition of course to the complexity of the term "British" itself as you might remember (1). Scholars in the field of anthropology have attempted clearer definitions by using "cultural area" or "cultural province" or "Kulturkreis" (the German word is used often without translation). The question remains, however, whether these terms represent real distinctions or are just constructs. As we've already seen, Edward Said (12) uncovered the subjectivity of those who claimed to have objectively analyzed the Orient.

f for film studies

We've already looked at film as an art form in the last chapter of Part I (11). Film studies is one of the many relatively recent disciplines in which you can get a college degree in the US and UK. The actual name of specific degrees may vary from Cinema Studies to Filmmaking, but film studies in addition to a study of film history and theory shares many of the interests of cultural studies with topics like gender, sexuality, class and their representations in film.

g for gender studies

We devoted Chapter 14 in Part II to looking at women's rights and the differences between sex and gender. The latter has given its name to gender studies, which has become increasingly well known due to both American female scholars like Judith Butler and Gloria Jean Watkins (better known under her pen name bell hooks) but also to the French female philosopher Simone de Beauvoir and the occasional French male like Michel Foucault. The term "gender," as we've seen, calls into question those biological differences between men and women that many had taken for granted and looks at maleness and femaleness as constructions. Gender – specifically the connection between gender and power – has become one of the main focuses of cultural studies.

I for Landeskunde

What's the German word doing in this list of disciplines, you may ask. I could've put Landeskunde as one possible translation of area studies as given above. But since the word itself is important and since you've probably all come across this word at some point in your studies at school or at university, Landeskunde deserves a separate entry among the disciplines we're surveying here. Landeskunde as a part of English departments at German universities has been criticized in the past because of its tendency to deal just with "facts" and not be "wissenschaftlich" enough – a typically German academic debate in which "wissenschaftlich" unfortunately can at times seem to mean "too difficult to be understood by those outside the inner circle." Another reason for Landeskunde's role as the less important part of the English curriculum, taught usually by native speakers with temporary contracts, as opposed to literature and linguistics, usually taught by non-native-speaker professors with tenure, lies in Germany's past. From the turn of the 20th century until well after the end of the Third Reich the important goal of learning more about typical Landeskunde topics was to be able to love Germany more. The term Kulturkunde was used in Germany by the Nazis, who weren't very interested in learning about English identity or British history and culture presumably because they feared such knowledge might lead to deeper understanding and to tolerance of other peoples, not the goal of Nazi Germany. British imperialism, however, was seen as something that Germans should copy so that they could become even more imperial. We all know the end of that story… After World War II the purpose of Landeskunde was to provide background information for the study of literature, and even today Anglo-American cultural studies programs are just beginning to flourish, with the advent of new degree programs and new – sometimes in name only – curricula as reform sweeps through Germany's universities.

There are justifiable criticisms of Landeskunde as a subject that just presents facts in categories without providing any justification for the choice of these categories and facts. This lack of justification is often hidden behind the lack of a direct author (the "I" being banned from serious German academic research as if that would magically produce objectivity). I've continually used the "I" throughout this book, which I'm sure you've noticed and may have been a bit surprised by but hopefully not so much that you stopped reading. I use the "I" not only because I've found personal accounts and opinions tend to make an academic subject more relevant and more interesting to the reader but also because this element of explicit subjectivity is an important part of work done in English on Anglo-American cultural studies. There have been some attempts to come up with ways of organizing the material used in Landeskunde differently than the way I've presented it in Part I of this book, which is the way most introductory books present American and British Studies. Some German academics have, for example, tried to organize the material based on abstract entities like "time," "space," "decentring," and the like.

criticism of Landeskunde

We've devoted two chapters of this book to media, from a more traditional perspective in Part I and from a more cultural studies perspective in Part II. Media studies itself has become a name for degree programs in traditional media like television and newspapers as well as in new media like the internet and can cover both the consumption (audience) and the production (journalism) sides. Media studies sometimes includes communication in general. And communication is part of the new field of intercultural communication. One of the first professors of media studies was someone whom you may remember as one of our biggies from a previous chapter, Stuart Hall (🔔 12).

m for media studies

You may remember details about power and identity from earlier chapters in the second part as well as details about Britain's colonial past from the first part of our book. You might remember one of the earlier biggies, Edward Said (🔔 12), whose book *Orientalism* is considered the bible of this new discipline, which looks at many of the same topics that cultural studies – identity, class, gender – but focuses on these topics from the perspective of former colonies of Britain and of other colonial powers. And you might remember another one of the earlier biggies, Homi K.

p for postcolonial studies

Bhabha (12), whose name is closely linked with postcolonial studies and the concept of "third space."

q for queer studies

We've also already encountered this name for the study of sexual orientation, which is sometimes considered a broader field than gay and lesbian studies, in the chapter on gender. While the word "queer" – probably related etymologically to the German word "quer" – was originally used as an insult to designate something odd and later became used in reference to effeminate homosexuals, it has now come to be used as an umbrella term to refer to all kinds of sexual orientations. Queer theory questions the very existence of stable permanent sexual identities. Queer studies has expanded beyond sexuality to include other social categories and to connect sexuality with race, social status, power, and identity.

s for sociology

Like anthropology, sociology, the "science of society," became an academic discipline in the 19th century. We could look at sociology as the study of contemporary human groups in comparison with anthropology's origins in the study of what was then considered "primitive people" in isolated areas of the world. Modern anthropology has since changed, and nowadays it's not always easy to distinguish some forms of anthropology from sociology. Pierre Bourdieu (13) is sometimes considered an anthropologist, sometimes a sociologist. And yet another Frenchman Claude Lévi-Strauss (no, not the German-American who became known for Levi's jeans) developed or applied theories from other disciplines (structuralism is perhaps the most important) that became important for anthropology and for sociology. As we've seen, one central interest of sociology, the concept of class, is also a primary concern for cultural studies. Some sociologists see cultural studies as just one of the later developments of sociology. Some people doing cultural studies see sociology as the non-sexy variety of cultural studies.

Describing cultural studies as sexy sociology is a good way for us now – finally and at last – to turn our attention to cultural studies as a subject, discipline, trajectory, …

And what is cultural studies?

"What is cultural studies?" If you're lucky, you could get this question in an oral or written exam. Lucky, because you could reply that based on what's been written about in the last thirty years it seems as if no one really knows. You could claim that this very question has been used as the title of books and articles, so either no one really knows the answer or it takes a lot of print and writing and reading time to explain the answer. You could also do a little name-dropping along the lines of "Cultural Studies in Britain is of course usually connected with the CCCS and with Stuart Hall"; you could refer to Paul Smith's article "Looking Backwards and Forwards" as a good summary of the history of cultural studies in Britain. You would mention Paul Moore's article "European Cultural Studies" as a good starting point for placing the discipline in a European – including German – context. Within American cultural studies you could drop names like Paddy Whannel and John Fiske (and smilingly say that of course you know that both Whannel and Fiske were born in Britain but were very influential in the US with their studies of popular culture and the media). Mention Henry Nash Smith's work on popular culture in the US and his trailblazing analysis of the American West, long before cultural studies became a name in academia. And of course everyone knows Marshall McLuhan – for those who don't know, here's the 15 – the one who claimed that the medium was more important than the message, a theory which Raymond Williams adamantly disagreed with (you can give your examiner a knowing wink).

cultural studies in the US

Drop Lawrence Grossberg's name with the term "vectors" and regretfully murmur how difficult it is to define what "vectors" are. Mention Grossberg's criticism of British cultural studies as failed attempt since there's no such thing as "culture" or "society" and mention Grossberg's view of the history of the Birmingham School, where he studied at in the 70s. Add that Grossberg is a very big name in American cultural studies with his studies on youth culture and politics and that cultural studies has become a popular subject in the US – with conferences, journals, and degree programs, and with a greater degree of institutionalization than in its home country of Britain. You could mention in passing the reader *American Cultural Studies* published at the turn of the millennium co-edited by an Australian academic, John Hartley, born and educated in Britain and known for his research into television. You could also mention Grossberg's essay "The Circulation of Cultural Studies" or Alan O'Connor's essay "The Problem of American Cultural Studies" or Joel Pfister's "The Americanization of Cultural Studies" for views of the discipline in the US in the 80s and 90s. Or for a more up-to-date discussion of cultural studies in the US cite Toby Miller's introduction to the paperback edition of *A Companion to Cultural Studies* and en passant quote Miller as saying that cultural studies is simply "magnetic." You could add Miller's reference to the "iconic significance" of American food as a wonderful example of what makes cultural studies so interesting.

a liberating intellectual project

You could mention some of the areas that cultural studies is especially interested in: class, race, nation, gender. You could try and make a joke by saying that based on the research done in Britain in the 80s, the more appropriate term should be "subcultural studies" since the behavior and characteristics of certain groups of people from what is commonly called "subcultures" were the main topics of investigation. You could argue that the lack of a clear definition of cultural studies has its advantages – there's an openness and a methodological flexibility that allows academics to respond to everyday life and not just to ivory tower topics, that cultural studies can be seen as a properly liberating intellectual project.

examine the examiner!

You could of course reverse the roles and ask the examiner to explain cultural studies and mention in passing that the hierarchical world of university examinations can be a wonderful example of hegemony (13) with elitist keepers of the gate only admitting those who play the game the way the keepers want. You could argue that education in general and university in particular are among the most powerful hegemonic forces in society (assuming that both your examiner and you have reviewed the content in Chapter 13 about power and hegemony). Giving the exam and having control over the grade gives the examiner a sense of power, which he or she believes is a good product of the system. Passing the exam as an examinee gives you a good feeling – you've achieved your goal – and at the same time you've reinforced the system, if perhaps only unconsciously. But since the results of oral exams are usually very difficult to contest in German courts and since some German academics are not adverse to an authoritarian approach, maybe you'd better pursue another tactic. And although it might seem really difficult to define cultural studies, we can come up with a few characteristics that sound good in oral exams even if they are somewhat contradictory.

Some academics have spent time arguing about what cultural studies is, whether it should be written in capital letters or used in the plural, and we'll be reviewing a few of the characteristics of the subject in a little while. Keep in mind for now that we can't define cultural studies as easily as we can define some of the older disciplines like anthropology or sociology. These disciplines like literature and linguistics have a longer history as institutionalized subjects. Keep in mind too that we've been doing cultural studies in the past five chapters! And the doing is important as you can see from the titles of some of the books on the subject: *Doing Cultural Studies* or *The Practice of Cultural Studies*.

**biggies in boxes**

**Centre for Contemporary Cultural Studies (CCCS)**

Our penultimate biggie isn't a person, it isn't even an institution that still exists, but it just may be the one most important thing in the history of cultural studies – at least in Britain. Those who've been reading carefully enough have already come across the name The Centre for Contemporary Cultural Studies (abbreviated as CCCS) at the University of Birmingham a few times, which as we know was founded by Richard Hoggart (13) in 1964. Some of the biggest names in cultural studies researched and taught at the CCCS. Stuart Hall (12) became Director after Hoggart left a few years after the founding. Hall's decade of guiding the CCCS in effect established cultural studies as a discipline, "guiding" being a better term than "leading" since collaboration was an important principle to offset the typical university hierarchy. Topics of research included popular culture, youth and working-class culture, the uses of power, the role of race and gender, the role of the media – in other words pretty much everything that you've been reading about in Part II (and a lot more besides too!).

If the CCCS was so well known and respected, then why was it closed? This was a question that some intellectuals asked themselves in 2002 when the University of Birmingham decided to close the Department of Cultural Studies and Sociology, the successor to the CCCS. The answer lies partly in different ways of assessing the value of university departments, partly in the competition with other subjects like engineering and the sciences, perhaps too in tensions between the anti-hierarchical leftist or Marxist philosophy behind cultural studies and hierarchical university administration structures.

Another institution that you've already heard of and that is still going strong after forty years is the Open University (4). In the late 1970s a unit in "Popular Culture" was offered that would be an important step in the development of what was becoming known as "cultural studies." And the founding fathers of cultural studies, Raymond Williams and Richard Hoggart, were both involved in adult education; Stuart Hall spent the last two decades before retirement there – as a Professor of Sociology.

But before we continue our practice of cultural studies, let's have a look at its origin and mention some names, almost all of which you've heard before. We can begin with our next-to-last biggie in a box.

origin of British Cultural Studies

Some people trace the beginnings of cultural studies further back than the founding of the Birmingham CCCS in 1964. The Suez Crisis in 1956 (6) could be seen as the beginning of the cultural studies movement in Britain and the end of Britain as a real world power. Maybe you remember some of what we dealt with about minorities and immigration to Britain in the 50s (7). Some people see the social, cultural, and economic changes that this first mass immigration wave brought to Britain as the breeding ground for cultural studies. Some people see the roots of cultural studies in Britain as beginning even before the disintegration of the British Empire after World War II, perhaps beginning with the way English literature came to be taught at English universities like Cambridge in the 1930s. As we've seen, some of the later biggies in cultural studies started out studying and teaching English literature. And some point to the criticism and praise of the Americanization of Britain starting in the 50s as one important motivation in the development of cultural studies.

cultural studies perspective

Now that you've heard something about the history of cultural studies, let's mention a few characteristics of this relatively new discipline by doing a review and critique of some of what you've read in the first part of the book. First of all, cultural studies isn't restricted to a specific culture or to a specific nation-state although the discipline started in Britain and also has roots in the United States. Thus the title of our book, Anglo-American Cultural Studies, points to the fact that we're not dealing with cultural studies in general, which has now expanded around the world with many important scholars in Australia and new exciting research being done in Asia.

choices in Part I

We are now almost at the end of our journey together, so it's certainly high time I made you aware of the process of selecting information – especially the information you found in Part I. First of all, my collecting of data that I've shared with you is by no means original. I've summarized what other writers have considered important about American and British Landeskunde topics and have used my personal experience in teaching American and British Studies at German universities over the past twenty years as an explicit guide. I've kept my background and yours in mind, assuming that Anglo-American Area and Cultural Studies from, say, a French or Muslim perspective would be at least somewhat different than from a German perspective. I've made choices about the narrative, trying to maintain textual coherence to keep you interested in the story and to provide you with as many links as possible. The links (the bells) are an important didactic part of the choices I've made about content – how to present the material in the best possible UTB Basics way. (Some of the choices are based on mundane aspects such as copyright and space and time limitations, too, of course – true for actually everything in life but perhaps not often enough admitted.)

experience cultural studies

You may have been surprised about the personal details, some of them perhaps seeming to be inappropriately personal. Writing and researching in cultural studies is more personal than in some other academic discipline, certainly more so than in typical German academic discourse. By including personal details, I've not only tried to make you aware of the inescapable subjectivity of the discipline but also wanted to give you the chance to experience cultural studies, especially if this is the first book you've read on the subject. Some who work in cultural studies believe that, while it's possible to summarize a view or interpret what others say, you can't speak FOR others although you'll have noticed that I've been doing this throughout this book. For one last example of how personal details can support academic teaching, have a look at the popular film *The Mirror Has Two Faces* (good example of popular culture) in which the main character played by Barbra Streisand, a university professor, mentions personal details of her life and her family in an attempt to indicate some truths about romantic love – and thus makes an abstract topic more pertinent for her students than abstract theorizing would.

Part I as bricolage

In a way perhaps you could look at the choice of material in Part I as a kind of bricolage – remember the word at the very end of Part I, just before your after-dinner drink? Big names in cultural studies like Claude Lévi-Strauss (who you may remember as NOT being the jeans man) and Jacques Derrida used the word in somewhat different ways. The literal meaning of the French word bricolage is making use of the things at hand in whatever way one can choose, a kind of do-it-yourself process. Bricolage has become a very popular word in cultural studies and in the arts too. In music it can refer to the lack of classically trained musicians in punk, in art to the collage. Just surf any of the millions of personal homepages to see examples of the putting together of lots of bits and pieces. Bricolage often has a subversive sense with consumers using what producers created in a different way than the producers intended.

Part I as subversion

Speaking of subversion, cultural studies likes to analyze the way subcultures adapt various things and use them in ways that subvert their original meaning – for example young people "hanging out" in shopping malls and thus using this space not for consumption as intended by shopping mall designers, but as a social gathering place. Just as young people can subvert shopping malls for their own uses, I hope we'll be able to "subvert" Part I for our own cultural studies uses. While I hope you found most if not all of Part I interesting, if you've been reading Part II carefully you've already learned to re-read the "facts" with a critical eye. Let's continue our critical re-reading of Part I from a cultural studies perspective.

start with the cover

What about the cover of our book? We could interpret it from a cultural studies point of view: the Stars and Stripes and the Union Jack as symbols of the two nations covered in the book with the German flag in the corner symbolizing the intended audience – readers in Germany or with a German background. The flags aren't shown fully, an indication that we can't give the full objective picture, but overlap, making us aware that certain aspects will remain hidden because of our subjective viewpoint. We could continue with the chapter titles, which you may have found a bit unusual based on your reading of academic books in a German environment. The creative chapter titles are meant to be typical of research work in cultural studies.

cs perspective: geography

If we were to apply the criteria of cultural studies to the first part of the book, you might now look differently at the selection of information given there. Along the traditional lines of area studies (or Landeskunde) with the emphasis on commonly accepted facts, we learned about several different names for each country. Area studies is after all based on "area" and on geographical boundaries. Have a look again at the first US geography and the first UK geography appetizer. On the one hand I've given you commonly accepted facts about the boundaries of both countries, and on the other I've made you aware (hopefully) of how unclear in a fundamental way these boundaries can be. The cultural studies turn is present in the choice of the terms and the fact that the terms in themselves are contradictory and somewhat confusing. You could find another cultural studies tidbit in the Deutsche Bahn's confusing "England" with "Britain" (1). And now I can use the packaging of the chocolate soccer balls DB distributed for free during the World Cup 2006 also a good example of what a "text" can be in the broader sense of the word as well as an example of popular culture worthy to mention.

Other cultural studies alternatives as examples taken from the geography appetizers: Instead of talking about a few American cities (1), we could've looked at Manhattan's skyline as an assertion of the power of money. We could've mentioned the distinctions between inner cities, suburbs and introduced the term "exurb" (those areas beyond the suburbs) because the exurbs aren't just examples of urban sprawl (9), they also display some of the inequalities in income and power most clearly. Or instead of mentioning some physical features of Britain (1), we could've discussed in what way the rural landscape of England represents a concept of Englishness. Instead of mentioning the traditional Latin and Anglo-Saxon roots of English place names (2), we could've chosen place names as examples of power and representation like using the name Derry or the name Londonderry depending on which political view you have. (We did see how the term British Isles is politically loaded for the Irish, however.)

cs perspective: history

A common view of history in its very traditional sense is that it's able to tell us what happened when. Have a look again at the first US history and the first UK history appetizer. We saw the problems with dates at the very beginning and couldn't even clearly come up with an exact date to start with. A historian could perhaps ask the following questions: Why mention John Hancock's signature if given only three lines to talk about the Declaration of Independence (2)? If you only have five lines to talk about Alfred the Great, why spend half of the space describing a legend (2)? And why include a question about the Spanish Armada (2) but not even mention the disaster the British Navy endured during the War of Jenkins's Ear – in addition of course to the question why include nothing about this war in spite of its original name? The answer in all cases from a cultural studies point of view: because John Hancock's signature and the legend of King Arthur and the defeat of the Spanish Armada are bits of cultural trivia that probably most Yanks and Brits have heard of and that they would consider part of their cultural identity. We're assuming here that the goals of a student of Anglo-American cultural studies are to see how a country and people define their own history, keeping in mind of course that the differences between a national self image and a view from outside could be important. Even though we'd be running the risk of essentialism (12), we could point to Frederick Jackson Turner's frontier thesis as an attempt to define the Americans as a people uniquely shaped by the history of the land, by westward expansion, by Manifest Destiny (6) in a similar way to how the British have liked to identify themselves as seafarers, as islanders (1).

The history chapter contains appetizers based on big names like presidents, queens, and wars and ignores the role of ordinary people although some of those working in cultural studies might like my including somewhat odd autobiographical details and use of popular culture products (movies with Charles I and television series with Henry VIII) in the history appetizers. Maybe some would also approve of my somewhat irreverent retelling of the story of Bonnie Prince Charles involving not only the idea of physical beauty but also involving a woman's help. Or my mentioning the Teddy Bear, a children's toy and product of popular culture, in connection with Theodore Roosevelt. Or my implicit criticism of organizing historical information into clearly defined decades by using a heading like: Choose a few influential events between 1954 and 1969.

cs perspective: education

The "facts" given in the chapters on education and political life are taken from the systems of power that people doing cultural studies criticize. Just giving the facts about institutions without asking important questions about power, gender, race, and class could be an area studies, maybe an American/British Studies way of doing things, but it definitely isn't a cultural studies way. Just to mention one well-known study on British education: Paul Willis's *Learning to Labour* examined the attitudes of working-class boys at an English secondary school and came to the conclusion that their very rebelliousness against the school structure destined them for working-class jobs; the very school structure is able to provoke reactions that reinforce the system –

an ideal example of the hegemonic function of the English education system.

cs perspective: arts, leisure time, fashion

The chapter on the arts is based on big names at the expense of exploring how art represents a particular culture or group. Instead of mentioning some of the great names in painting, we could've discussed English landscape painting from the perspective of the landowner and included class (those with property vs. the working class) and gender (situation of the dependent wife). Probably no one would disagree that specific operas – depending of course on which canon you choose – are culture with a big c. But is going to the opera culture with a big c? What about leisure time activities in general (11)? We could look at all leisure time activities including buying expensive theatre tickets or traveling to the South Seas or just to the seashore (which, as we might remember from British geography (2), is never far away) as examples of the importance of consumption in the shaping of our lives and cultures. Maybe fashion in the sense of beautiful designs or extraordinary articles of clothing or jewelry could be considered as culture with a big c. What about buying fashionable clothes or shopping in general as a cultural activity or as a cultural institution? Interest in fashion from a cultural perspective isn't as new as you might think. One of the first scholars in the new discipline of sociology, Georg Simmel, wrote an essay on fashion in the 19th century. Great works of architecture could be culture with a big c – depending of course on … which list (11) you prefer as you've probably already guessed. But what about looking more closely at the architecture of the shopping mall, especially in America with comparisons to castles and gated communities showing the power relationships between those inside and outside, between those at the center and those at the margin, between the culture and the subculture?

cs perspective: film and television

You may have recognized some or many of the works and artists referred to in the first part of our book – I chose some of the most highly acclaimed – but from the point of view of culture with a little c these works aren't necessarily more worthy of study than many other examples from what's sometimes called "popular" or "mass culture." But you could also criticize choices I made from the popular cultural perspective. I chose Roland Emmerich as a representative of popular culture for several (hopefully convincing) reasons, and his films would of course be a fitting example of popular culture. Yet I only mentioned in passing another emigrant to America from the German-speaking world, Billy Wilder, whose films critically analyzed American hypocrisy and were not only box office successes but also acclaimed and thus possible candidates for culture with a big c. His film noir *Double Indemnity* deals with adultery and murder, *The Lost Weekend* was the first major film to address the issue of alcoholism, *Sunset Boulevard* and *The Apartment* both deal with exploitation. Another example – this one from television – of a combination of popular and high culture could be the TV series *Civilisation* (🔔 10); at least it certainly includes lots of indisputably culture-with-a-really-big-capital-C works of art. But what about other TV series like *Coronation Street* or *All in the Family* (🔔 10)? What about watching television itself? The role of the audience?

cs perspective: food and drink

By looking at "culture" as an important part of the word "agriculture," you shouldn't be surprised at all by the last part of the chapter "Bread and Circuses"; and food is indeed one of the hot topics in cultural studies. Did you notice a couple of facts tied in with economic and identity issues? Look at the claim that Marmite is typically British, the Jewish origin of fish 'n chips, the economic aspect of mass-produced foods … We heard about Prohibition in our history survey, but did you know that Prohibition in the US was needed to keep men sober for industrial labor and that pub closing times in the UK were intended to keeping men fit for the next day to work in the factory or in armaments production during wartime? We can thus see how food and drink aren't just part of a nation's "culture" but can also be seen as elements of power (🔔 13). Those who see Anglo-American Studies through the cultural studies perspective would certainly approve of our look at leisure time activities and at food at the end of Part I because both topics are popular in current cultural studies research. And what better way to end Part II than to remind ourselves of the importance of the leisure time we need to read (and write) books like this and the food and drink we need to sustain us while doing so!

## Exercises

**1.** Give one example of culture with a big "C" and one example of culture with a little "c."

2. When was the term "cultural studies" first used?
3. Name three or four founding fathers of cultural studies and three pioneering books. (Hint: you may need to skim through chapters 12 and 13 to jog your memory if you don't recognize this trivial pursuit question already from another chapter).
4. Skim through Part I and note all those aspects where I indicated that my choice was based on my personal preferences. Do you find the use of such personal details convincing or not "scientific" enough?

---

Challenging questions and interesting projects:

Pick any of the suppositions I've given in this chapter and try to prove – or disprove! – them. Concrete example: I've tried to justify in this last chapter my inclusion of John Hancock's signature, the Spanish Armada, and King Arthur in the first part of this book. But have contemporary Asian Americans or African Americans or Americans from the Dominican Republic really heard of John Hancock? What about British people of Indian descent or Black British people in reference to the Spanish Armada? Do the Scots claim King Arthur as part of their heritage? And – perhaps more importantly from a cultural studies point of view – how could you go about trying to answer the questions? Questionnaires? Analysis of television programs? Critical look at the National Curriculum? Survey of online Hispanic newspapers?

And finally the oh-my-god-if-you-can-do-this-you'll-maybe-become-known-as-the-biggest-and-brightest-new-hope-in-cultural-studies-task:

Design a curriculum that gives undergraduate students the necessary factual background found in Landeskunde combined with some of the critical views of power, class, gender, and of race found in cultural studies so that within one module students not only have learned more about the United States and the United Kingdom but also have come to see in what ways their knowledge is limited.

And finally further topics not dealt with (or not dealt with in enough depth) in this chapter… for those who just can't get enough of culture or of cultural studies:

Some of the other hundred different definitions of culture; a look at the subjects history, linguistics, and literature (not given in the list from "Anthropology to Sociology") in comparison with cultural studies; how the origins of the American school of comparative literature has foreshadowed the development of cultural studies; how the term "text" has changed in the last hundred years and its current meaning in cultural studies; criteria to distinguish between good and not-so-good examples of high culture and popular culture; lots of other important figures in the history of cultural studies – including a lot of foreigners with mostly French-sounding names …

# Conclusion

We've now come to the end of our day together after appetizers, lunch, and dinner, and we've come to the end of this book. Hopefully you've enjoyed the meals and are now well nourished to continue with your explorations of all things American and British. Hopefully the many bells that should ring when you come across some of the topics that you've read about here won't result in a cacophony but rather in a grand symphony. Or to change metaphors: I hope you're able now to see Anglo-American Area and Cultural Studies as a diamond that sparkles from many different angles.

Since cultural studies always contains personal experience and motivation for action beyond the ivory tower and outside of hallowed academic walls, I feel that I can include a bit of my personal experience as well as my wish for action here at the very end of our time together.

My curiosity as a young American exchange student about all things German involved travelling from Flensburg to Garmisch, going to see *Faust* and finding it excruciatingly boring, being astonished at the nudity on the front covers of magazines, eating Wurstsalat, and observing the (to me seemingly rude) behavior of the natives in crowded subways and pedestrian zones or being surprised by the fashion fact that the majority of German women wore earrings. And there were also many things which convinced me to stay – the beer, the coffee (in a pre-Starbucks world), the bread, buildings made of stone (instead of plastic), the public transportation system, the social security system, the history (it took me years to get used to the fact that I could touch human artifacts older than the country I was born in), the admirable way in which Germany confronted its own past. I've tried to keep my original curiosity about the Old World in mind when planning and writing this book. I hope I've been able to make you curious about the two cultures hyphenated together as Anglo-American, but in ways very distinct from each other. And I hope I've been able to answer some of your questions and to satisfy some of your curiosity, but I especially hope I've been able to whet your appetite for even more Anglo-American Area and Cultural Studies.

Since cultural studies often contains a call to action, please let me express my own fascination and reservations about cultural studies here and now.

In cultural studies you can do anything you want, can explore areas that have to do with what it means to be human, explore topics that are probably immediately interesting to students. The beloved teacher and cultural researcher Vicki Galloway came up with my favorite list of four old-fashioned approaches to learning about another culture, which I'll adapt slightly here for our purposes (Galloway was writing from the perspective of Americans learning about Spanish culture) including a last look at some of the tidbits I've shared with you.

- The Frankenstein Approach: a look at American attitudes towards abortion, a glance at British resistance to adopting the metric system, a bit of history of the special relationship between the US and the UK.
- The 4-F Approach: folk dances (at least I mentioned square dancing and ballet), festivals (Last Night at the Proms, of course), fairs (circus was part of the chapter title on the arts), and food (bread as part of the title of the area studies chapter on the arts, and food as a factor of identity – and the whole narrative was framed as a meal!).
- The Tour Guide Approach: monuments (count those in geography and the arts and don't forget the national identity monuments in Part II), rivers (count the number in chapter 1), cities (even included some touristy photos), etc. (the etc. is my favorite part of this approach).
- The By the Way Approach: sporadic lectures or bits of selected behavior (you can find enough of this in Part I and maybe even some in Part II).

Galloway criticized these haphazard approaches for good reason. At the end of the day after creating your Frankensteins, doing the obligatory 4-Fs, going on the obligatory tour, and taking in all the "oh-by-the-way-did-you-happen-to-know" tidbits, do you really understand everything you need to know about the Americans and the British? Hopefully not! The critical cultural studies view that you've gained by reading this book should have made you cautious.

But on the other hand we have to start somewhere, and knowing a bit about festivals and food, rivers and cities, strange customs and attitudes can lead to a deeper critical understanding both of things on the other side of the Channel and on the other side of the ocean, critical understanding being infinitely better than blind awe. And a critical understanding of the Americans and the British can lead to a better understanding of our own cultural environment and of our own personal identity.

I've felt uncomfortable with the breadth and depth of cultural studies, at times near drowning in the ocean of theories, books, journals, names both big and little. I've also felt uncomfortable with the relativism that at times seems to pervade the field. I can sometimes sympathize with the critics who claim that cultural studies busies itself too much with reading cereal boxes instead of Shakespeare, looking at Brillo boxes instead of Bauhaus. My undergraduate education was at St. John's College, the "Great Books" school, with a curriculum that at first glance anyway is as far from cultural studies as you can get. We had a canon, a rather strictly defined one, and read each and every week some of the most inspiring and at times the dullest and most complicated books written in western civilization. (I could put a bell here with a reference to what you read about in the last chapter – remember the issue of canon and Allan Bloom? Allan Bloom was a popular person at St. John's. But no more bells at the end of our time together since we'll have more beautiful music in just a few paragraphs…)

But there is one connection between my St. John's education and the spirit of cultural studies that I find inspiring. Even with the Great Books canon as a guide, we weren't able to latch on to one right way of thinking since the authors we read as part of the Great Conversation were busy contradicting one other – and sometimes themselves. And we students learned quickly to question the wisdom and even the competence of our "tutors" (there was no professorial hierarchy at St. John's).

I hope that you've found what you hoped to find in this book – an introduction to things American and British that you can use in your courses, in exams, and perhaps in later life too. I also hope that what you've read will encourage you to increase your critical awareness of the world in general and of the German university in particular with its persistently and sometimes startlingly feudal structures – especially disturbing so many years after "Unter den Talaren, der Muff von 1000 Jahren."

Cultural studies should create a more emotional response than other disciplines in academia. Some fear and hate cultural studies for its potential to change power systems or for its taking popular culture seriously. But I hope that you won't be discouraged – neither by those who hate cultural studies nor by some of the incomprehensible stuff written by poor academics in cultural studies both here and abroad (remember the publish-or-perish principle of university education?). While I hope you've enjoyed reading this book, I also hope that you were at times just a little bit annoyed with me and perhaps asked: "Why didn't he just come out and give us the facts? If Part II criticizes so much of what was in Part I, why didn't he write Part I differently?" Part of my honest response to these reactions would include deadlines and space limitations, but the much more important reason is my attempt to encourage you to think critically yourselves, to accept no given answers or selection of details or choice of facts just because someone – even someone with a title – claimed

**last biggie in a box**

**YOU**, future scholar in Anglo-American Area and Cultural Studies, born in Germany, late 20th and 21st century

Perhaps because cultural studies is a young discipline (or more accurately an anti-discipline), or because of its emphasis on the study of power and its inherent criticism of institutions, or because so much research in cultural studies is driven by personal and political interests, or most probably because of all these things and others too, you the reader, the interested student, the future scholar have the opportunity to shape the future of cultural studies. Even as cultural studies has become more institutionalized with new degrees, with university departments, with journals, anthologies, books, professorships, conferences, those who do cultural studies continually and consistently question the value of this institutionalization (sometimes from a comfortable tenured chair). Even while trying to define cultural studies, those who do cultural studies are resisting and wrestling with definitions, arguing strongly against a canon while publishing anthologies of articles by the big names of the past, resisting prescribed guidelines for research while trying to write clear introductions for students telling them how to do cultural studies.

the authority to provide them. I've kept our last biggie in mind throughout this book.

Barbra Streisand started her concert in Berlin in summer 2007 with an old song which some of you have perhaps heard. In 1966 she closed her second highly praised television show "Color Me Barbra" with the same song.

**Now take my hand**
**For the greatest journey**
**Heaven can allow**
**Starting love**
**Starting here**
**Starting now**

May our journey continue …

# Recommendations for Further Reading (a partly annotated bibliography)

In the hope that this book has made you curious to find out more about the topics mentioned, here are some recommendations for further reading integrated within the general bibliography. I've given annotations only on books in English that I can recommend. I've decided not to provide what others do: hundreds of titles and name-dropping with no information as to what's readable, which would scare me off as a student. The recommendations below are intended to do exactly the opposite – not scare you off but to whet your appetite. Although at the end of the day and the end of this book and the end of our meal together, you're hopefully no longer hungry, tomorrow is another day …

Unfortunately all books published on both American and British Studies especially for students of English at German universities are either out of print, out of date, or written in German (except for the book you're reading now). You can find, however, some books about the United States and the United Kingdom combined, as well as about each country separately, mostly written with an international student audience in mind as well as some excellent introductions to cultural studies in general.

You can find my brief annotations on the following books in the alphabetical bibliography below:

- One book about American and British studies: Oxford Guide.
- Four books about American studies: Breidlid, Campbell, Datesman, Mauk.
- Six books about British studies: Christopher, McDowall, Oakland as writer, Oakland as editor, O'Driscoll, Storry.
- Four books about British cultural studies: Bassnett, Morley, Tönnies, Turner.
- Seven general introductions to cultural studies (with almost exactly the same titles but with very different ways of presenting the content): Barker (2008), Lewis, Longhurst, Sardar, Storey, Walton, Williams.

- Eight cultural studies anthologies and dictionaries: Barker (2004), Burgett, Bennett, Hartley, Miller, Radway, Ryan, Storey.

You can stay on the cutting edge of cultural studies by browsing the online catalogs of three important publishers with Blackwell, Routledge, Sage Publications. And you can find some recommended websites on the companion website to this book.

utb-mehr-wissen.de

## Bibliography

**Anderson, Benedict:** *Imagined Communities* (2006 revised edition) Verso

**Ang, Ien:** Watching *Dallas: Soap Opera and the Melodramatic Interpretation* (1985) Routledge

**Barker, Chris:** *Cultural Studies: Theory and Practice* (2008 third edition) Sage Publications

A popular comprehensive introductory volume now in its 3rd edition.

–: *The SAGE Dictionary of Cultural Studies* (2004) Sage Publications
You can find short and clearly written articles about some of the key words of cultural studies from B for "body" to H for "hegemony" to Y for "youth culture" and also biographical details about some of the biggies, both those in boxes in this book like Bhabha or Williams as well as some who didn't fit in this book but who are still important in cultural studies like Bakhtin or Bourdieu or Freud or Marx.

**Bassnett, Susan** (editor): *Studying British Cultures* (2003 second edition) Routledge
short articles and essays on a variety of topics are edited by a well-known scholar in translation and cultural studies

**Bedau, Hugh and Paul Cassell** (editors): *Debating the Death Penalty* (2004) Oxford University Press
A superb collection of eight essays representing serious thinkers on both sides of this controversial issue. If you thought you were clearly for or against capital punishment, then reading this book may cause you to doubt your certainty.

**Bennett, Tony and Lawrence Grossberg, Meaghan Morris** (editors): *New Keywords. A Revised Vocabulary of Culture and Society* (2005) Blackwell
Based on Raymond William's *Keywords*, edited by three well-known academics in the field of cultural studies: Tony Bennett (not the American singer or football player or basketball player; this one is an Australian who's published on such things like the cultural use of museums), Lawrence Grossberg (an American scholar who studied at the CCCS and is known as one of the importers of cultural studies to America), and Meaghan Morris (an Australian who teaches in Hong Kong).

**Bradley, Ian:** *Believing in Britain* (2006) I.B. Tauris
An interesting look at British identity especially from a religious perspective, extending from Druids to New Age and including of course the Church of England. Bradley sees common history and tradition as a way to create a sense of identity that transcends national English, Irish, Scottish, and Welsh differences and that strongly contrasts with American religious characteristics.

**Breidlid, Anders and Fredrik Chr Brogger, Oyvind T. Guliksen** (editors): *American Culture: An Anthology* (2007 second edition) Taylor & Francis
Edited by a team of Scandinavian-sounding academics with excerpts from literature, journalism, history, and politics; good to read some of the famous and not so famous in their own words.

**Bromley, Roger:** Interview with Stuart Hall in Munns (1995)
**Burgett, Bruce and Glenn Hendler** (editors): *Keywords for American Cultural Studies* (2007) New York University Press
Includes both words associated with classic life and institutions perspectives like "democracy," "immigration," and "religion." The emphasis is on the cultural studies perspective, however, in the brief and at times challenging articles entitled "border," "class," "diaspora," "gender," "identity," "queer," and "sex."
**Buttjes, Dieter** (editor): *Landeskundliches Lernen im Englischunterricht* (1981) Ferdinand Schöningh

**Campbell, Neil and Alasdair Kean:** *American Cultural Studies. An Introduction to American Culture* (2006 second edition) Routledge
Two academics working at the University of Derby in England with experience in cultural studies, including follow-up work and assignments and areas for study with discussions of many of the cultural studies aspects. Lots of examples taken from literature and movies.
**Christopher, David P.:** *British Culture: An Introduction* (2006 second edition) Routledge
Covers theatre, movies, art and architecture as well as topics connected with media like newspapers, magazines, television, and radio in contemporary Britain. Christopher also looks at pop music and fashion as well as some classic cultural studies topics like ethnicity and feminism.
**Cooke, Alistair:** *Alistair Cooke's America* (1977) Random House and the DVD version of the 1972 television series published by the BBC (2004)
Now more than a generation old but still a fascinating personal look at American history from a Brit who came to visit and decided to stay and ended up helping the British understand the Americans for a longer period of time than probably anyone else. You can either get the book or the DVD version of the award-winning series.

**Datesman, Maryanne Kearny and JoAnn Crandall, Edward N. Kearny:** *American Ways: An Introduction to American Culture* (2005 third edition). Longman Pearson Education
Three authors with experience in teaching English as a foreign language, includes very interesting chapters on American attitudes. Don't let some of the rather simple-looking language exercises mislead you – this book is fully suitable for university students too.
**Dimbleby, David:** *A Picture of Britain* (2005) BBC television documentary series
–: *How We Built Britain* (2007) BBC television documentary series
The well-known BBC commentator David Dimbleby hosted a BBC series, *A Picture of Britain*, on British regions and the art and music they have inspired. From a cultural studies point of view it's especially interesting since he talks about how landscape has been used to mold national identity. He also wrote and presented the series *How We Built Britain*, a chronological look at British architecture from churches and castles to a medieval barn. From a cultural studies point of view it's especially interesting since he covers not only the grand country houses of the Elizabethan Age but also black houses on the outer islands and tenements and highrises in the big cities. Both series are available as DVDs and both are examples of typically lavish BBC cinematography with lush orchestration.
**DuGay, Paul and Stuart Hall, Linday James, Hugh Mackay, Keith Negus:** *Doing Cultural Studies: The Story of the Sony Walkman* (1997) Culture, Media and Identities series. Sage Publications

**Eagleton, Terry:** *After Theory* (2003) Basic Books
–: *Idea of Culture* (2000) Blackwell
Probably many – even university-educated! –people wouldn't flock to read books on literary theory, but Terry Eagleton is able to package theory in a way that's interesting and witty. For a supportive and a very critical look at cultural studies, try his either of these.
**Easthope, Antony:** "But What *Is* Cultural Studies?" in Bassnett (2003)

**Ellis, Hattie:** *Eating England. Why We Eat What We Eat with Over 500 Special Places to Eat and Shop* (2002) Mitchell Beazley

**Foucalt, Michel:** *Technologies of the Self: A Seminar With Michel Foucault.* Editors: Luther H. Martin, Huck Gutman, Patrick H. Hutton (1988) University of Massachusetts Press

–: "Truth and Power" in *Power/Knowledge. Selected Interviews and Other Writings 1972–1977* (1980) Pantheon

**Galloway, Vicki:** "A Design for the Improvement of the Teaching of Culture in Foreign Language Classrooms" (1985) ACTFL Project Proposal.

**Gant, Scott:** *We're All Journalists Now* (2007) Free Press

**Giles, Judy and Tim Middleton:** *Studying Culture. A Practical Introduction* (2008 second edition) Blackwell

**Grossberg, Lawrence:** "The Circulation of Cultural Studies" in Storey (1996)

**Hall, Stuart:** "Encoding/Decoding" in Hall *Culture, Media, Language*

– **and Dorothy Hobson, Andrew Lowe, and Paul Willis:** *Culture, Media, Language* (original edition 1980) Routledge

**Hartley, John and Roberta E. Pearson** (editors): *American Cultural Studies: A Reader* (2000) Oxford University Press

An anthology of many articles by well-known (Tom Wolfe, Susan Sontag, Marshall McLuhan, Umberto Eco) and not as well-known writers on a wide-variety of cultural studies topics.

**Hartley, John:** *A Short History of Cultural Studies* (2003) Sage Publications

Not particularly short at around 200 pages nor always particularly easy to read nor uncontroversial (Hartley himself is a controversial figure), but those who already know some of the many allusions Hartley makes or are willing to look up the names and ideas he mentions will be rewarded by a witty look at past and present cultural studies by one of the academic biggies in the field.

**Hobson, Dorothy:** *"Crossroads": Drama of a Soap Opera* (1982) Menthuen

–: *Soap Opera* (2002) Blackwell

**Hubbard, Phil and Rob Kitchin, Gill Valentine** (editors): *Key Thinkers on Space and Place* (2004) Sage Publications

**Johnson, Richard and Deborah Chambers, Estelle Ticknell:** *The Practice of Cultural Studies* (2004) Sage Publications

This introductory looks at cultural studies from interesting and slightly different perspectives and forms a nice comparison to our book. A good task would be to read our chapters 1 on geography and compare the contents with chapter 6 entitled "Make space! Spatial dimensions in cultural research" or to compare our look at history with chapter 7 "Time please! Historical perspectives". Chambers and her colleagues (Richard Johnson was a former director of the Birmingham Centre for Contemporary Cultural Studies) also provide some more or less helpful and more or less concrete tips on writing research papers of all types.

**Jones, Steven:** *Antonio Gramsci* (Routledge Critical Thinkers series) (2006) Routledge

**Kohl, Stephan:** *Anglistik Research Paradigms and Institutional Policies 1930–2000* (2005) WVT Wissenschaftlicher Verlag Trier

For information about the history of Landeskunde in Germany: Stratmann's article has details about how the study of British culture was (ab)used during by the Nazis for their own purposes. Weimann's article mentions some of the ways in which cultural studies has influenced Anglistik in Germany.

**Kramer, Jürgen:** *British Cultural Studies* (1997) UTB für Wissenschaft Wilhelm Fink Verlag

**Lewis, Jeff:** *Cultural Studies: The Basics* (2008 second edition) Sage Publications
Well-received introduction to cultural studies divided into two sections, "Forming Culture/Informing Cultural Theory" with a look at the history of culture studies and "Cultural Locations" with an examination of some of the "hot" topics of contemporary cultural studies like "the body" and "terrorism."
**Longhurst, Brian and Greg Smith, Gaynor Bagnall, Garry Crawford, Miles Ogborn, Elaine Baldwin, Scott McCracken:** *Introducing Cultural Studies* (2008 second edition) Pearson Longman
Written by a team of academics from various universities in Britain with many excellent concrete examples.

**Mauk, David and John Oakland:** *American Civilization* (2005 fourth edition) Routledge
This book provides a detailed look at the classic life and institutions topics with the same strengths and weaknesses as Oakland's book *British Civilization*.
**McDowall, David:** *Britain in Close-up* (1999 second edition) Longman
Pleasantly written and beautifully illustrated obviously for students learning English. Shame that there's still no new edition.
**McLuhan, Marshall:** *The Gutenberg Galaxy: The Making of Typographic Man* (original edition 1962) University of Toronto Press
–: *The Mechanical Bride: Folklore of Industrial Man* (original edition 1951) Gingko Press
–: *Understanding Media: The Extensions of Man* (original edition 1964) Gingko Press
**– and Quentin Fiore:** *The Medium is the Massage* (original edition 1967) Penguin
**Miller, Toby** (editor): *A Companion to Cultural Studies* (2006) Blackwell
In a revised paperback edition one of the leading Blackwell's Companion Series with mostly very readable contributions by some of the big names in the field. You can get an overview of the hot topics in cultural studies just by glancing at the titles in the series: A Companion to ... Television Studies; Museum Studies; Gender Studies; Asian American Studies; Lesbian, Gay, Bisexual, Transgender, and Queer Studies; and a dozen others.
–: "What It Is and What It Isn't: Introducing ... Cultural Studies" in Miller (2006)
**Moore, Paul:** "European Cultural Studies" in Miller (2006)
**Moran, Joe:** *Queuing for Beginners. The Story of Daily Life from Breakfast to Bedtime* (2007) Profile Books
A witty and illuminating look at many aspects of everyday in life in Britain from the mid 20th century until today and including popular cultural studies aspects like power and food.
**Morley, David and Kevin Robins** (editors): *British Cultural Studies: Geography, Nationality, and Identity* (2001) Oxford University Press
Short articles and essays on a great variety of cultural studies topics.
**Munns, Jessica and Gita Rajan, Roger Bromley** (editors): *A Cultural Studies Reader. History, Theory, Practice* (1995) Longman
A nice selection of classic excerpts going back to Matthew Arnold and Marx/Engels and ending with Bromley's fascinating interview of Stuart Hall. Each chapter has a wonderfully readable overview introduction.

**Newcomb, Horace** (editor): *Encyclopedia of Television* (2004 second edition) Routledge

**Oakland, John:** *British Civilization: An Introduction* (2006 sixth edition) Routledge
Although a bit heavy on facts and figures and at times densely impersonal, it obviously fulfills a need on the international market. There's unfortunately no key to the exercises, and the promised online additional material is very limited.
– (editor): *Contemporary Britain: A Survey with Texts* (2001) Routledge
Provides a wide range of excerpts from original sources and includes helpful notes on some of the unfamiliar terminology.

**O'Connor, Alan:** "The Problem of American Cultural Studies" in Storey (1996)
**O'Driscoll, James:** *Britain* (2009 second edition) Oxford University Press
The new edition is beautifully illustrated with many wonderful asides about all aspects of British life. A workbook and website activities are also available especially designed for foreign students.
*Oxford Guide to British and American Culture* (2005 second edition), (1999) Jonathan Crowther (editor), Kathryn Kavanagh (assistant editor) Oxford University Press
Both the first edition (published in 1999) and the most recent edition (published in 2005) are explicitly intended for "learners of English" and provide compact descriptions of hundreds of words and are very useful as a quick reference guide. There's a CD version with a good search function available as well as a free online guide for use in the classroom.

**Pfister, Joel:** "The Americanization of Cultural Studies" in Storey (1996)
**Postman, Neil:** *Amusing Ourselves to Death* (1985) Penguin
**Prensky, Marc:** *Digital Game-Based Learning* (2000) McGraw-Hill
–: *"Don't Bother Me, Mom – I'm Learning"* (2006) Paragon House

**Radway, Janice A. and Kevin K. Gaines, Barry Shank, Penny Von Eschen** (editors): *American Studies: An Anthology* (2009) Wiley-Blackwell
A challenging anthology of articles about many different aspects of American Studies mostly from a cultural studies perspective and for those who already know the basic facts about American life and institutions and want to see what's being done now.
**Ryan, Michael** (editor): *Cultural Studies: An Anthology* (2008) Blackwell
A truly huge (more than 1300 pages) and weighty anthology of a wide variety of essays grouped according to the classic cultural studies interests like gender, consumer culture, power, music, ethnicity, identity. While many of the essays deal with global cultural studies, you can also find interesting Anglo-American topics with typically creatively provocative titles about cultural geography like "Hegemony, Ideology, Pleasure: Blackpool" and "City of Quartz: Excavating the Future in Los Angeles" or about those classic cultural studies topics like "An Ontology of Everyday Distraction: The Freeway, the Mall, and Television" or classic minority studies like " 'Why Don't You Act Your Color?': Preteen Girls, Identity, and Popular Music" and "The Riot of Englishness: Migrancy, Nomadism, and the Redemption of the Nation" or aspects of environmentalism and consumerism like "Constructing Purity: Bottled Water and the Commodification of Nature."

**Sardar, Ziauddin:** *Introducing Cultural Studies* (2004) Icon Books
Written in a fashion that tends to worry "serious" German academics, Sardar uses comics and illustrations to give the reader an entertaining and illustrative introduction to the discipline.
– **and Piaras Mac Éinrí, Zrinka Bralo, Csilla Hős:** *What is British?* (2004) Birthday Counterpoints series. British Council, available online <http://www.counterpoint-online.org/download/388/What-is-British.pdf>.
**Schrey, Helmut** (editor): *Anglistik – quo vadis?* (2000) Die Blaue Eule
The most readable, charming, entertaining, and highly critical account of Anglistik in Germany, written by a Grand Old Man of Anglistik.
**Sellar, W.C. and R.J. Yeatman:** 1066 and All That: The History Book to End All History Books *(2005 edition, first published in 1930) Methuen*
Has since become a classic of English humor. Even for those who really hate history – you can't help learning and laughing throughout, and even if you really learn nothing about English history from the book, you'll discover a lot about the English sense of humor and their own sense of history. Now available in a special 75th edition.

**Smith, Paul:** "Looking Backwards and Forwards at Cultural Studies" in Miller (2006)

**Sommer, Roy:** *Grundkurs Cultural Studies/Kulturwissenschaft Großbritannien* (2003) Uni-Wissen series Klett Verlag

**Storey, John:** *Cultural Theory and Popular Culture: An Introduction* (2009 fifth edition) Longman
Now in a revised and expanded fifth edition with a companion website.

– (editor): *Cultural Theory and Popular Culture: A Reader* (2009 fourth edition) Longman
Contains excerpts from what some would call the canon of cultural studies, serves as a companion to his popular textbook of the same name.

**Storry, Mike and Peter Childs** (editors): *British Cultural Identities* (2007 third edition) Routledge
Provides much information on a great range of area and cultural studies topics: from education, politics, and religion to youth culture, gender, and leisure, written in an entertaining and enlightening fashion with great examples from the worlds of movies, music, TV, and radio for each topic.

**Stratmann, Gerd:** "'Das Engländertum'" – Discursive Mechanisms in German Writings on 'British Culture' 1933–1945" in Kohl (2005)

**Strunz, Gisela:** *American Studies oder Amerikanistik* (1999) Leske & Budrich

**Teske, Doris:** *Cultural Studies: GB* (2002) Studium kompakt series. Cornelsen Verlag

**Tönnies, Merle and Claus-Ulrich Viol:** *Introduction to the Study of British Culture* (2007) Narr Studienbücher series. Gunter Narr Verlag
The only introduction written in English aimed at German university students, which takes Oxford as a central focus to reveal methods and theories in the British cultural studies tradition.

**Turner, Graeme:** *British Cultural Studies: An Introduction* (2003 third edition) Routledge
A focus on the British tradition but also contains general main topics in cultural studies organized into categories like "texts and contexts" and "audiences" and "politics". Lots of namedropping, but those with patience can get a good overview of what's being going on from the beginnings of British cultural studies until the beginning of the new millennium.

**Walton, David:** *Introducing Cultural Studies: Learning through Practice* (2008) Sage Publications
Doesn't just have many of the basic ideas about cultural studies (mostly from the British perspective), it's also wonderfully fun to read with creative dialogues, excellent exercises, and interesting tasks, proof that Walton is able to make good use of background as an English teacher in Spain.

**Wasko, Janet** (editor): *A Companion to Television* (2005) Blackwell

**Weimann, Robert:** "Towards a History of Twentieth-Century Anglistik" in Kohl (2005)

**White, Mimi and James Schwoch** (editors): *Questions of Method in Cultural Studies* (2006) Blackwell

**Williams, Noel:** *How to Get a 2:1 in Media, Communication and Cultural Studies* (2004) Sage Publications
Includes clearly, interestingly, and briefly written summary articles of "50 key ideas" and "40 key thinkers" and some useful tips for writing papers and taking exams too. What I found especially helpful were the tips for further reading about the 40 key thinkers.

**Williams, Raymond:** *Television: Technology and Cultural Form* (original edition 1974) (2003) Routledgeclassics

**Willis, Paul:** *Learning to Labour. How Working Class Kids Get Working Class Jobs* (1977) Saxon House

– **and Nadine Dolby, Greg Dimitriadis:** *Learning to Labor in New Times* (2004) Routledge

**Wood, Eric S.:** *Historical Britain* (1995) Harvill Press

**Zadjermann, Paule** (director): *Judith Butler. Philosophical Encounters of the Third Kind.* Icarus Films. 2006

# Index

This is a very selective index; please also use the Contents given at the beginning of the book to direct your search. A fully detailed index is available online. The number next to the symbol 🖱 indicates that the entry is to be found in the online parts of chapters 1 and 2 or in the online chapters 3 or 10. More information at www.utb-mehr-wissen.de

*$64,000 Question* 215
1st Amendment 158, 166, 🖱 10
2nd Amendment 🖱 3
8th Amendment 🖱 3
10th Amendment 105
13th Amendment 41, 42
14th Amendment 42, 134
15th Amendment 42, 258
19th Amendment 46, 259
22nd Amendment 🖱 2
26th Amendment 106
*2001 A Space Odyssey* 206, 208
51st state 31, 96, 117, 141
9/11 attacks 204, 246, 255, 276
Aaron, Hank 218
ABC 🖱 10
Aberdeen 74, 119
Abolitionist 258
Abts, Tomma 214
Acadia 190
AccuWeather Channel 🖱 10
Act of Settlement 58
Act of Supremacy 53
Adorno, Theodor 286
adult education 238, 250, 289, 297
affirmative action 138
African Methodist Zion Church 160
aggregators 273
agribusiness 111
*All in the Family* 282, 304
Allen, Woody 208, 275
Alli, Lord Waheed 179
alma mater 82, 84
alphabet agencies 🖱 3
Althusser, Louis 252
Alton Towers 215
alumni 82, 84
"America the Beautiful" 184
American dream 128, 143, 171, 🖱 3
American Indian Movement (AIM) 133
American party 131
American Revolution 33, 34, 186, 🖱 10
American Virgin Islands 118
Amin, Idi 147, 153
Amman, Jakob 163
*Amusing Ourselves to Death* 274
Anderson, Benedict 230
Ang, Ien 274
*Angels in America* 163
Anglesey 187
Anglo-Saxon 27, 48, 49, 144, 236, 301
animated films 208
Annapolis 14
Anne I 58, 61, 174
*Annie Hall* 208, 275
anorexia 268
another bloody church 156
Anthony, Susan B. 258
Apaches 133
*Apartment, The* 304
Appalachian Mountains 7, 12, 190
Appomattox Court House 41
Arbroath Smokies 221
archaeology 290
Archbishop of Canterbury 50, 172, 174
Archbishop of York 172
Archers 🖱 10
aristocracy 🖱 3
Aristotle 285
Arizona 9, 134, 140
Arnaz, Desi 142
Arnold, Matthew 285–86
ARPANET 277
Articles of Confederation 101
Ash, Mary Kay 260
Ashe, Arthur 218
Asian as name for British immigrants 147
*Aspects of Working-Class Life* 251
Asquith, H.H. 65
assembly line 44
assimilation 143, 155, 180
Associate of Arts (A.A.) 82
Association of National Parks Authorities 192
Astor 44, 109, 126
Atlanta 🖱 1
Atlantic Ocean 7, 21
Atlee, Clement 66, 🖱 2
Auntie Beeb 🖱 10
Austen, Jane 285
Austin 14, 🖱 10
avatars 268
Avebury 47
Awakenings 168
Aziz, Lisa 152
bachelor's degree 74, 81, 83, 202
Bad Writing Contest 239
Badwater 9
Baez, Joan 212
bald eagle 186
Baldwin, Stanley 173
ballet 214, 308
ballgame 201
Banglatown 152
Barbados 138, 145, 147
Barbie doll 267
Barnum and Bailey 216
baron 🖱 3
Baron Ahmed 🖱 3
Barry Lyndon 185
Barthes, Roland 252
baseball 217–19
basketball 217–18
Bath 🖱 1
Battle Hymn of the Republic 38
Battle of Bosworth Field 52
Battle of the Boyne 58
Baudrillard, Jean 252
Bay of Pigs 142
Beakers 47
Beatles 211, 🖱 10
beauty 186, 198, 258, 267, 302
Beauvoir, Simone de 252, 292
Beaverbrook, Lord 🖱 10
Becket, Thomas 53
Beckham, David 218
Belfast 95, 🖱 1
Bell, Alexander Graham 44
Belleville Three 🖱 1
Ben Hur 208, 216, 234
Ben Nevis 23
*Bend It Like Beckham* 148, 178
Berg, Alban 286
Bering Bridge 130
Berlin 213, 218, 266, 311
Berners-Lee, Tim 277
Bernstein, Carl 🖱 2
Bernstein, Leonard 141
Beveridge, William 🖱 2

Bhabha, Homi K. 239, 243, 294
Big Apple 9
Big Three 🖱10
bilingual education 86
Bill of Rights, American 88, 101, 105, 158, 166, 🖱3
Bill of Rights, British 58, 88, 93
*Billy Bud* 211
*Billy Eliot* 209
*Billy Liar* 209
bindi 148
binge drinking 82, 162, 🖱3
biopower 252
bird watching 215
Birmingham 28, 73, 151–53, 179, 🖱1
*Birth of a Nation* 207
Bismarck 🖱3
Black Death 52
Black Mountains 185
Blackpool 215, 🖱1
Blair, Tony 88, 90, 92, 126, 175, 238, 🖱10
blogs 272–73
Blood, Sweat, and Tears 212
blood, toil, tears, and sweat 66
Bloody Mary 54
Bloom, Allan 286, 309
Bloom, Harold 286
Blue Laws 112
blue-collar workers 111, 194
Blunt, Anthony 128
Blur 211
body 267, 269
bodybuilding 218, 268
Bollywood 148
Bonnie Prince Charles 59, 302
Bono, Sonny 249
Book of Mormon 161
Border Country 289
boroughs 27
Boston 15, 🖱1, 🖱10
BosWash 15
Boulder Canyon Project 193
Boulton, Matthew 61
Bourdieu, Pierre 249, 250, 252, 294
Bowie, David 212
Bowles, Camilla Parker 174
*Bowling for Columbine* 79, 🖱3
Bradford 28, 🖱1
Brady Bill 🖱3
Bralo, Zrinka 229
*Braveheart* 51
bricolage 223, 225, 299
Bridge (card game) 216
Brigham Young University 162, 168
Brighton 215, 🖱1, 🖱2
Bristol 28, 121, 174, 🖱1
Britain's Imperial Century 122
BritArt 202, 212–13
Britcoms 211, 🖱10
British Airways 119
British Chinese 151
British Gas 119
British Indian 148
British invasion 211
British Nationality Act 145
British Nationality and Status of Aliens Act 144
British Steel 119
British Telecom 119
British-born Chinese 151
Britpop 211, 212, 220
Britten, Benjamin 202, 211
broadcasting 271, 276, 🖱10
broadsheets 🖱10
Brooklyn Museum of Art 213
Brown v. Board of Education 136, 🖱2
Brown, John 38, 40
Brown, Gordon 90
Brown, Lancelot "Capability" 189
Brunsdon, Charlotte 274
BSE 119
Buckingham Palace 89
Buckinghamshire 48
*Buddha in Suburbia, The* 150
Buddhism 176
Burgess, Guy 128
*Bury My Heart at Wounded Knee* 132
Bush, George W. 100, 103, 110, 126, 169, 194, 255, 🖱3
*Butch Cassidy and the Sundance Kid* 208
Butler Education Act 68, 85, 🖱2
Butler, Judith 239, 243, 266, 269, 292
cabinet reshuffling 248
Cablinasian 218
Cadillac 33
Caesar 47
Caine, Michael 73
Caines, Michael 222
Calder Hall 196
Cambridge 72–73, 🖱1
Cambridge Cluster 121
Cambridge University 203, 230, 289, 298
*Camelot* 49
Campbell, Naomi 152
canon 285, 286, 289, 290, 303, 309, 310
capital punishment 105, 268, 🖱3
Capra, Francis 208
captains of industry 44, 109, 🖱3
Cardiff 51, 65, 95, 153, 179, 248, 🖱1, 🖱2
Carlos, John 218
Carlsbad Caverns 190
Carmel-by-the-Sea 249
Carnegie Hall 110
Carnegie 44, 109
Carson, Rachel 186, 199
Carter, Jimmy 102, 169
caste system 155
Castro 142
Cat Stevens 180 see Islam, Yusuf
Catherine of Aragon 54, 172
Catholic Emancipation Act 62, 175
*Cats* 286
caucuses 98, 99
Cavaliers 56
Caxton, William 🖱10
CBeebies 🖱10
CBS 246, 🖱10
CCTV 197, 🖱3
cell phones 271, 272
Celtic Fringe 29, 30
Celtic Sea 21
Celtic 236
Celts 47, 49
Census Bureau 44, 117, 135, 139, 142, 237
Central Pacific 43
Central Plains 194
Chadha, Gurinder 148, 178
Chamberlain, Joseph 63, 65
Chamberlain, Neville 65
channel 🖱10
Channel Four 274, 289, 🖱10
Channel Islands 18–20, 29, 124
Channel Tunnel 21
Chaplin, Charlie 208, 234
*Chariots of Fire* 209
charisma 249
Charles I 56, 57, 59, 302
Charles II 57, 59
Charles, Prince of Wales 172–74, 187, 198, 🖱3
Charleston 40, 46
Charter schools 78
Chavez, Cesar 141
checks and balances 87, 101, 103, 105
Chedworth Roman Villa 199
Chelsea 27
Cher 249
Chernobyl 194
Cherokees 134
Chester 47, 🖱1
Cheyenne 133
Chicago 15, 204, 🖱1
Chicano 140

chicken tikka masala 120, 220
Child, Julia 222, 🖱 10
Chinatowns 151, 155
ChiPitts 15
Chisholm, Shirley 137–38, 256, 266
chosen people 113, 170
Christian Coalition 169
Christian Methodist Episcopal Church 160
Christian Science Monitor 🖱 10
Christopher Street 263
Crown in Parliament 90
Chrysler 🖱 1
Chunnel 21
Church of Christ 161
Church of the Nazarene 160
Churchill, Winston 62, 63, 66, 70, 126, 🖱 2
cinema 206–09, 🖱 10
Circus Maximus 216
circus 216, 223, 308
Cirencester 47
citizen journalists 272
*Citizen Kane* 208
*City Lights* 208, 234
City of Angels 9
city on the hill 158, 171, 182
civil partnership 264
civil religion 159, 169–71
Civil Rights movement 38, 42
civil society 243, 247
*Civilisation* 211, 304, 🖱 10
Clayton, Jack 209
Clinton, Bill 103, 110, 128, 🖱 2, 🖱 3
Clinton, Hillary 128, 138, 249, 260, 261, 🖱 3
*Clockwork Orange* 206
Clooney, George 115
CNN Cable News Network 281, 🖱 10
Cocker, Joe 212
coffee 221, 223, 246, 307
Colchester 47
Cold War 66, 115, 131, 250, 🖱 2
Collins, Phil 212
Cologne 214
Colorado River 9, 10, 193, 194, 196
Columbus 31, 32, 130, 🖱 1
Comfort, Alex 265
commander-in-chief 102
commonwealth status (US) 117, 118
Commonwealth (Cromwell) 56
Communal Family 161
communism 115, 116, 128
Communist party 115
community colleges 80, 81
compact form 🖱 10
Compromise of 1850 40
Congestion Charge 197
congressional districts 12, 15, 26, 104, 230
Conrad, Joseph 285
constituency 26, 91, 105
constitutional monarchy 91, 93, 94
continental US 6, 11, 18
conurbations 27
Conwy Suspension Bridge 198
Cooke, Alistair 🖱 10
Cooperative Baptist Fellowship 160
core subjects 69
Cornish clotted cream 221
Cornish 30
Coronado 32
*Coronation Street* 274, 304, 🖱 10
Costner, Kevin 134
Cotswolds 185
counties 26, 64, 106
Coventry 178, 211
Crathes Castle 199
Creationism 76
Creedence Clearwater Revival 212
Creole 222
Crèvecœur, J. Hector St. John de 229, 240
cricket 217, 219
Cromwell, Oliver 53, 56, 57, 59, 62
Cromwell, Thomas 53
Cronkite, Walter 246
Crosby, Stills, Nash and Young 212
*Crossroads* 274
Crown Dependency 18, 20, 124
C-Spann 🖱 10
CTN 🖱 10
Cuba 115, 118, 131–32, 142, 🖱 2
Cuban Missile Crisis 115
Cukor, George 208
Culloden 59, 61
cultural capital 247–49, 286, 288
cultural turn 288
culture shock 288
culture wars 284, 288
Cuyahoga Valley 190
Cwm Silicon 121
DA (Defense Advisory) 🖱 10
*Daily Courant* 🖱 10
*Daily Express* 🖱 10
*Daily Mail* 🖱 10
*Daily Mirror* 🖱 10
Daldry, Stephen 209
Dallas 🖱 1
*Dallas* 274
*Dancing with Wolves* 134
Dartmoor 184
Darwin, Charles 290
DDT 186
De Cadillac 33
De Soto 33
*Death in Venice* 211
Death Valley 7, 9, 10
decimalization 235–36, 🖱 10
Declaration of Sentiments 256, 258–59
Decorated style 203
Defender of Faith 172
Delius, Frederick 210
DeMille, Cecille B. 201, 207
Democratic party 97–99, 102–03, 🖱 3
Democratic-Republican party 97
DeNiro, Robert 208
Dent, Matthew 236
Derrida, Jacques 252, 299
Derry 301
Desmond, Nora 201
Detroit 33, 🖱 1
devolution 87, 94, 95, 121, 🖱 2
Devon 26
Diana, Princess 89, 173, 233, 258, 287
Dickens, Charles 🖱 3
diets 268
digital immigrants 3, 271, 278
digital native 3, 270–71, 275, 278, 281
Disneyland 205, 214
Disraeli 63, 64
District of Columbia 14, 100
divine right of kings 243
Diwali 177
Dix, Dorothea 37
Docklands 🖱 10
Dolaucothi Gold Mines 199
Domesday Book 25, 50
dominion 64, 122
domino theory 116
donkey 97
Dorset blue cheese 221
Douglass, Frederick 38–40
Dover 184
drag queens/kings 267
Drake, Francis 54
DreamWorks 208
Dred Scott decision 39, 42
drinking 215, 221, 223
Drudge Report 273
Druids 183
DuBois, W. E. B. 136
due process of law 🖱 3
duke 🖱 3
Duke of Cornwall 🖱 3
Duke of Edinburgh 🖱 3
Duke of Wellington 62

Dunblane school shooting 🖱 3
Dunn, Baroness 151
Dust Bowl 10, 196
DVD disc 279
*Dynasty* 274
Eagleton, Terry 283
Earl of Sandwich 221, 🖱 3
East African Asians 147, 151, 153
*EastEnders* 274
Eastwood, Clint 208, 249
Edinburgh Castle 232
Edinburgh 74, 94, 205, 🖱 1
Edison, Alva 44
*Educating Rita* 73
Edward I 51, 62
Edward III 52
Edward VI 53
Edward VII 65, 210
Edward VIII 65, 172–73
Egypt 235
Eisenhower, Dwight D. 195
electives 78
Electoral College 98, 99, 100
electors 100
elephant 97
Eleven Plus 68
Elgar, Sir Edward 201, 210–11
Eliot, George 285
Eliot, T.S. 285, 286
Elizabeth I 33, 52–55, 58, 87, 172, 174, 🖱 3
Elizabeth II 63, 88, 173, 174, 179, 196, 232, 🖱 10
Elk v. Wilkins 134
Elton John 212, 287
Emancipation Proclamation 40
Emin, Tracey 213
*Emmerdale* 274
Emmerich, Roland 208, 234, 303
Empire State Building 204
encoding decoding 273
Endangered Species List 186
Engels, Friedrich 🖱 10
English Channel 21
English Gothic 203, 224
English Navy 49
Enlightenment 257
Environmental Protection Agency (EPA) 193
Ephron, Nora 208
Episcopal Church 160–61, 167, 174–75
Equal Pay Act 261
Equal Rights Amendment (ERA) 259
equal rights 42, 135
ESPN 🖱 10
*Esquire* 275
essentialism 235, 237, 239, 241, 302
Essex 26, 48, 73
Esteban, Gloria 142
*ET* 208
ethnicity 146, 176, 179, 218, 238, 265, 274, 🖱 3
Eton 70, 72
euro 125
European Convention on Human Rights 🖱 3
European Economic Community (EEC) 108
evangelical 261
Evans, Harold 🖱 10
*Evening Standard* 🖱 10
Everglades 190
evolution 76, 183
evolving standards of decency 🖱 3
*Excalibur* 48
exceptionalism 128, 157
executive 🖱 10
Exeter Cathedral 203
Exodus International 167
expansionism 36, 109, 113–14, 128
extracurricular activities 78, 79
Fabian Society 64
Facebook 280
Fair Deal 136, 216
Fair Isle 199
*Fairy-Queen* 210
*Falcon Crest* 274
Falkland Islands 88, 124
Falwell, Jerry 168
fan vaulting 203
fantasy film genre 208
Farm Credit Administration (FCA) 🖱 3
farming 188, 216
farthing 236
fascist 244, 🖱 10
fast food 201, 222, 223
Faust, Drew Gilpin 261
*Fawlty Towers* 🖱 10
Federal Communications Commission (FCC) 🖱 3, 🖱 10
*Feminine Mystique, The* 259
feminine 258, 267
feminism 256, 258, 265, 290
Fens 23
Ferraro, Geraldine 260
fidei defensor 172
filibustering 104
film studies 291
first-past-the-post 91, 92, 95, 97
fish 'n chips 120, 220
fishing industry 26
Fiske, John 295
Fitzgerald, F. Scott 44
Fleet Street 🖱 10
floods 195, 198
*Florida Suite* 210
florin 236
follies 202, 204, 215, 224
Fonda, Jane 218, 268
foot and mouth disease 119
football 201, 217–19
Ford, Gerald 🖱 3
Ford, Harrison 164
Ford, Henry 44, 109
Ford, John 208
Foreman, George 218
Fort Sumter 40, 41
Foucault, Michel 242, 252, 255, 266, 268, 292
Foundation Stage 68
foundation subjects 69
Founding Fathers 34, 101, 106, 158, 🖱 3
Fourth Estate 🖱 10
Fourth of July 170
Fox Broadcasting 281, 🖱 10
fox hunting 187, 188, 215
Frankfurt School 286
Franklin, Benjamin 106, 186, 🖱 10
fraternities 79, 82
Frears, Stephen 209
Free Methodist Church 160
Freedom of Information Acts 🖱 10
Friedan, Betty 259–60
frogs 201
frontier thesis 302
Frontiers of the Roman Empire 48
*Full Metal Jacket* 206
Furman v. Georgia 🖱 3
*Gandhi* 209
Gant, Scott 270
*Garfield* 🖱 3
gated communities 303, 🖱 3
gay marriage 105
Gay Pride 263
*Gender Trouble* 266
General Certificate of Secondary Education (GCSE) 68
General Educational Development (GED) test 79
general election day 98, 99
General Synod 172
Genesis 168
genetically modified (GM) crops 119
Geordie 230
George I 58, 210
George II 59, 210
George III 34, 52, 88
George IV 62

George V 144, 173
George VI 173
George, David Lloyd 65, 66
Georgia 17, 33, 159, 166, 🖱 3
German-American 137, 225, 231, 294, 🖱 10
Gerry, Elbridge 104
gerrymandering 104
Gettysburg Address 41
Ghana 138, 145, 153
Giant's Causeway 24, 198
Gibson, Mel 51
Gilded Age 44, 109
Gilmore, Gary 🖱 3
Gilroy, Paul 232
give me liberty or give me death 33
Gladstone, William 64
Glasgow 28, 60, 179, 🖱 1
Glen Canyon Dam 9, 193, 194
global village 275, 276
Glorious Revolution 57, 60, 93, 🖱 2
Gloucestershire 27
Glyndwr, Owen 51
Goldsmith's College 251
golf 218
*Gone with the Wind* 208
Good Friday Peace Talks 95
*Good Night, and Good Luck* 115
Google News 273
Gore, Al 100
Gothic Revival 203, 204
grade point average (GPA) 78
graduate school 80
Graham, Billy 168
grammar schools 68, 71
Gramsci, Antonio 243–45
Grand Canyon 9, 10, 32, 190
Grant, Cary 208
Grant, Ulysses S. 41, 189
Grateful Dead 212
Gray, Eileen 206
Great Books 286, 309
Great Famine 64, 146
Great Fire 57
Great Lakes 7, 9, 15, 16, 33, 34
Great Plains 7, 10, 12, 185
Great Seal of the United States 186
Great Smoky Mountains 190
Great Society 136, 139, 🖱 3
Great Tradition 285
*Greatest Show on Earth* 207, 216
Greeley, Horace 43, 🖱 10
green-collar workers 194
Greenland 6, 8, 22
Greenwich Village 263
Gregg v. Georgia 🖱 3
Grenada 123, 126
Griffith, D.W. 207, 208
Grossberg, Lawrence 295
Groundhog Day 208
Guam 8, 117
Guantanamo Bay 118
*Guardian* 🖱 3, 🖱 10
Guernsey 18, 20
Guildhall 174
guinea 236
Gulf of Mexico 10
Gulf Stream 26
gun control 79, 105, 🖱 3
Gutenberg 🖱 10
Guthrie, Arlo 212
Guthrie, Woody 185
gymnastics 217
hackers 271
Hadrian's Wall 48, 185
haggis 221
Hail Mary pass 217
Hall, Stuart 238, 240, 251, 271–73, 293, 295, 297
Hallelujah Chorus 210
hamburger 201, 222
Hamilton, Richard 214
Hammer of the Scots 51
Hancock, John 34, 301, 302, 305
Handel, George Frideric 210
Hanovers 57, 60
harp 236
Harrisburg 14, 194, 🖱 10
Harrison, George 211
Hartley, John 295
Harvard 80, 81, 138, 235, 239, 261
Harvey, Marcus 213
Hastings 50
Hawaii Volcanoes 190
Hawaii 6, 8, 10, 13, 114, 117
Hayes, Rutherford B. 42
HBO 🖱 10
health insurance 🖱 3
Hearst Castle 205, 209, 215
Hearst Corporation 🖱 10
Hearst, William Randolph 205, 209, 215, 🖱 10
Heath, Edward 88
Hebrides 18
hedgerows 184, 188
hegemony 223, 242–44, 246–48, 254–55, 296
helicopter parents 81
Hendrix, Jimi 137, 212
Henry II 50, 51, 53, 56, 62, 87
Henry III 51, 52
Henry VII 52, 53
Henry VIII 53, 54, 62, 171, 175, 302
Henry, Lenny 152
Henry, Patrick 33
Hepburn, Katharine 208
hereditary peers 90, 🖱 3
Hereford 119
hermaphrodite see intersex
heterosexuals 263, 264
high culture 264, 285, 287–88, 304, 306
Highlands 23, 184–85
hip hop 256
Hiroshima 108, 114
Hirst, Damien 213
*His Master's Voice* 278
Hitchcock, Alfred 206, 234
Hitler 218, 🖱 10
Hobson, Dorothy 274
Hoggart, Richard 238, 250–51, 253, 275, 297
Hoggart, Simon 251
holiday 34, 170
holidays 112, 120, 166, 170
Holiness Churches 160
Hollywood 206–07, 234
Holst, Gustav 210
Holy Grail 48
Home Rule 64
Homer 290
homeschooling 77
Homestead Act 43, 111, 131
Homestead Strike 110
homosexuality 167, 169, 263, 294
Hong Kong 151, 215, 🖱 2
hooks, bell 262, 269, 292
hooliganism 219, 🖱 3
Hoover Dam 9, 192–94
Hoover, Herbert 192–94
Hossain, Nina 152
hotdog 201, 222
Houston 🖱 1
Howe 38
Hs, Csilla 229
HSN 🖱 10
Huang, Ching He 151
*Huffington Post* 273
Huffington, Arianna 273
Huguenots 144
Humbard, Rex 168
Humboldt University 291
Humboldt, Wilhelm 83
Hundred Years War 52
hung parliament 88, 92
Hungary 250, 🖱 10
hunting 188, 215, 216, 🖱 3

hybridity 239, 241
hyphenated identities 96
hypothermic model 274
Idaho 189
Iliad 290
Illinois 17, 161, 🖱 3
imagined community 229, 231, 239
impeach 103
Imperial Measurement System 236
In God We Trust 165
*Independence Day* 208, 234
*Independent* 🖱 10
independent schools 68, 70, 71, 72
infant school 68
Intelligent Design 76
internet 270–72, 275–80, 293, 🖱 10
intersex 265
Interstate Highway System 195
*Intolerance* 207
Inverness 59, 🖱 2
investigative journalism 🖱 10
Iowa 98
Iran hostage crisis 247
Iraq 88, 116, 126
I-Reporters 272
Irish as minority group in Britain 146
isolationism 36, 109, 113–14, 128
IT News 281
ITV 🖱 10
ivory tower 289, 296, 307
Ivy League 80
Jackson, Andrew 36, 97, 133–34, 🖱 3
Jackson, Glenda 53
Jackson, Michael 215
Jacksonian Democracy 36
Jacksonville 210
Jaguar 121
James Bond 128
James I 54–55, 61
James II 57–58, 151
James 36, 59
James, Henry 211
Jamestown 🖱 2
Jamestown 33
Jamie's Ministry of Food 222
Jazz Age 44, 46
*Jazz Singer* 207
jeans 205
Jefferson Airplane 212
Jefferson Memorial 171, 204
Jefferson, Thomas 34, 97, 165, 171, 🖱 10
Jehovah's Witnesses 167
Jersey 18, 20
Jim Crow laws 135
John I 34, 38, 40, 51, 87, 109
Johns Hopkins 266
Johns, Jasper 214
Johnson, Boris 201
Johnson, Lyndon B. (LBJ) 136, 🖱 3
Joplin, Janis 212
Journal of British Studies 291
*Joy of Sex* 265
Joyce, James 275, 285
Judaeo-Christian tradition 169
Judaism 183
judicial 🖱 10
Jurassic Coast 23–24
jus soli 230
Kansas 14
Keep Britain White 149
Kennedy, John F. (JFK) 115–16, 176, 276, 🖱 2, 🖱 3
Kennedy, Robert 🖱 3
Kensington 27
Kent State University 🖱 2
Kent 26
Kentucky 192, 262
Kenya 137, 147–48, 153
Kerry, John 100
Key Stages 68–69, 72
Khan, Amir 150
Khan, Nazim 150
Khrushchev 115
kindergarten 75, 83
*Kind of Loving, A* 209
King Andrew 36
*King Arthur* 210
King James Bible 210
King Kong 208
King, Coretta Scott 138
King, Martin Luther 137, 138, 🖱 2, 🖱 3
King's College 203
Kingsley, Ben 148
Kissinger, Henry 🖱 2
KitKats 220
Know Nothings 97, 131
Korean War 114, 115, 🖱 2
Kroeber and Kluckhohn 284
Ku Klux Klan 207
Kubrick, Stanley 206, 208
Kultur 284
Kulturkreis 291
Kulturkunde 292
Kureishi, Hanif 150
Kushner, Tony 163
La Raza 140
Lacan, Jacques 252
Lackland 51
*Lady Chatterley's Lover* 251
laissez-faire 110
Lake District 190, 196
Lake Erie 9
Lake Huron 9
Lake Mead 8, 9
Lake Michigan 9
Lake Ontario 9
Lake Powell 9
Lake Superior 9
Lakota Sioux 132
Lambeth Conference 172
lame duck 102
Lancaster 47, 52
Land of Opportunity 🖱 2
Land Rover 121
Land's End 18
Landau 97
Las Vegas 8, 194
Last Night at the Proms 211, 308
latitude 11–12, 25
law lords 91
Lawrence, D.H. 251
Lawrence, Stephen 149, 180
Lazarus, Emma 129
League of Nations 45, 114, 128
Leavis, F.R. 251, 275, 285–88
Lebowitz, Fran 201, 223
Leeds 28, 🖱 1
Leicestershire 27
Leigh, Mike 209
Leitkultur 234
Lennon, John 211, 🖱 3
lesbian 256–57, 262–64, 294
lethal injection 🖱 3
*Letter from America* 🖱 10
Lévi-Strauss, Claude 294, 299
Lewis, Carl 218
liberal arts 202
Liberty University 168
Lichtenstein, Roy 214
life peers 91, 🖱 3
*Life* 275
Lifetime Real Women 🖱 10
Lincoln Memorial 🖱 2
Lincoln, Abraham 38–43, 165, 170, 🖱 2
Lineker, Garry 201, 219
*Lion King* 208
Little Italy 155
Littleton 79
Liverpool 28, 60, 151, 179, 🖱 1
Livingstone, Ken 197
Loach, Ken 209
Local Education Authorities (LEA) 70

*Local Hero* 209
logbook 272
Londinium 24
London Assembly 96
London bombings 180
Londonderry 301
longitude 25
Lopez, Jennifer 141
Lord Alli 🖱 3
Loreley 232
Lost Colony 33, 54
*Lost Weekend, The* 304
Lough Neagh 24
Louisiana Purchase 34–35, 140
Love Canal 193
lower 48 6, 11
Lowlands 23
Lucas, George 208
Lusitania 45
Luther, Martin 171
Lutherans 160, 161
Lyotard, Jean-François 252
Maastricht Treaty 125
Mac Éinrí, Piaras 229
MacArthur, Douglas General 114–115, 127, 🖱 2
Macmillan, Harold 126
Macquarie Mausoleum 198
Magna Carta 51, 87, 93
magnet schools 78
mainstream media 270, 273
Malcolm X 🖱 3
Malik, Shahid 150
Mallet, Elizabeth 🖱 10
Maltby 4
Manchester United 218
Manhattan 204, 263, 301
Manifest Destiny 35, 113, 132, 140, 231, 302, 🖱 10
Mann, Horace 37, 75
Manx 30
Manzoor, Sarfraz 150
Mariana Island group 118
Marks and Spencer 156
Marmite 220, 304
Martin, Ricky 141
Marxist 238, 244, 250, 252, 297
Mary I, Tudor 53–55, 58
Mary II 57–59, 61
Mary Stuart, Queen of Scots 53–55
Maryland 14
masculinity 267
mass tourism 215
Massachusetts Bay Colony 33, 157
master's degree 74, 83
*Masterpiece Theatre* 🖱 10
Maxwell, Robert 🖱 10
McCarthy, Joseph Senator 115, 127, 🖱 2
McCartney, Paul 211
McDonald, Trevor 152
McKinley, William 🖱 3
McPaper 🖱 10
McRobbie, Angela 251, 272
Medicaid 🖱 3
Medicare 🖱 3
Mediterranean 26
megalopolises 15, 27
*Melting Pot, The* 143
Melville, Herman 211
Member of Parliament (MP) 91, 105
Members of Scottish Parliament (MSP) 94
Mercury, Freddie 148
meritocracy 🖱 3
Merkel, Angela 249
*Messiah* 210
Methodism 159–61
Methodist Episcopal Church South 160
metrification 235, 236
Metropolitan Community Church 168
metrosexual 267
Mexican-American War 35, 140
militia 🖱 3
Millennium Bridge 🖱 2
Millennium Centre 95, 🖱 2
Millennium Cities 🖱 2
Miller, Toby 296
Milton Keynes 🖱 1
Minnesota 10, 249
Miralles, Enric 232
*Mirror Has Two Faces, The* 299
Mississippi River 33–34
Missouri Compromise 40
Mittal, Lakshmi 148
*Model of Christian Charity, A* 156
*Monarchy* 287
Mondale, Walter 260
Monroe Doctrine 36, 113, 125, 126
Montana 8, 189
*Monty Python and the Holy Grail* 49
Moore, Michael 79, 118, 🖱 3
Moral Majority 168
Moravians 159
Morill Act 80
Moroni 161
mortgages 120
mosque 176, 179
Motown 🖱 1
Mott, Lucretia 258
Mount Saint Helens 10
Movieum 209
*Ms* 260
muckrakers 🖱 10
Muir, John 190, 200
Murrow, Edward R. 115
*Music for the Royal Fireworks* 210
My Lai Massacre 🖱 2
*My Son the Fanatic* 180
*Myra* 213
MySpace 280, 🖱 10
Nagasaki 108, 114
*Naked Chef, The* 222
Napolitano, Janet 260
narrowcasting 271, 🖱 10
Nast, Thomas 97
national anthem 36, 166, 170
National Cathedral 203
*National Enquirer* 🖱 10
National Forest 192
National Health Service (NHS) 🖱 3
National Monument in Edinburgh 205
National Organization for Women (NOW) 259–60
National Parks Service 192
National Rifle Association (NRA) 🖱 3
National Trust 24, 184, 198
National Vocational Qualification (NVQ) 68
nation-states 240–41
NATO 250
nature vs. nurture 284
Navajos 133
NBC 🖱 10
NDA 197
Nebraska 43
Negro 136
Neverland Ranch 215
*New England Courant* 🖱 10
New Forest 25
New Netherland 33
New Orleans 10
New Universities 72
New World 30
*New York Post* 🖱 10
*New York Times* 🖱 10
Newcastle 28, 🖱 1
News Corporation 🖱 10
*Newsweek* 275
NHS 148, 🖱 3
Niagara Falls 10, 193
Nicols, Mike 163
Nielsen Ratings 🖱 10
Nigeria 63, 123, 145, 153
Nigerian British 153

Nixon, Richard 🖱2, 🖱3
No Child Left Behind Act 86
no taxation without representation 33
Nobel 45, 66, 114
Normans 144
North Sea oil 120
Northcliffe, Lord 🖱10
Northern Ireland Assembly 95
Northern Mariana Islands 118
North-South Divide 29
Notting Hill Carnival 149, 152
*Nova* 🖱10
nuclear power 192, 194, 196
Nuclear Regulatory Commission 194
O'Connor, Alan 295
O2 Dome 🖱2
Oasis 211
Obama, Michelle 261
Oberlin College 258
obesity 223, 225, 268, 🖱3
*Observer* 🖱10
Ochs, Adolf 🖱10
Ofcom 🖱10
*Office, The* 🖱10
Office for National Statistics 29, 🖱1
Ofsted 70
Official Secrets Act 🖱10
Ofili, Chris 153, 213
old boys'network 248
Old Faithful 190
Old Pretender 59
Oliver, Jamie 221–22, 253
Olympics 218, 219
*On the Origin of Species* 290
organic farming 120
organic intellectual 245
Orientalism 235, 293
Orkneys 18, 199
Osborn, John 209
Otis, Charles 44
*Our Bodies Ourselves* 268
Owens, Jesse 218
Oxbridge 72, 80, 248, 🖱3
Palestine 235
Palin, Sarah 249, 261
palm trees 26
Paramount 208
Parekh Report 238, 241
Parent teacher associations (PTAs) 77
Paris 215, 257
Parks, Rosa 138
parliamentary democracy 94
Parry, Sir Hubert 201, 210
participatory journalism 272
party affiliation 99, 105
party conventions 98, 99
Patriot Act 107
PBS 🖱10
Peak District 22
Pearl Harbor 114, 116, 131, 276
Pelosi, Nancy 103, 260
Penn, William 163
Pennine 22
penny press 🖱10
Pentecostal Family 161
performative 237, 266
Perpendicular 203
Pfister, Joel 295
PhD 74, 86, 138
*Philadelphia Story* 208
Phillip II of Spain 54, 55
Pilgrims 33, 157
*Planet Earth* 🖱10
*Planets, The* (suite) 210
Plantagenet 50, 233
plastic surgery 268
plate glass universities 73
*Playboy* 275
Pledge of Allegiance 166, 170
Plessy v. Ferguson 45, 135, 136
Plymouth 🖱1
podcast 271
polytechnics 73
Poor Laws 🖱3
pop art 202, 214
*Pop Idol* 🖱10
pornography 263, 269
Portland 🖱1
Portsmouth 🖱1
Postman, Neil 271, 274
Poundbury 198
Powell, Enoch 150
power-knowledge 252, 255
Prensky, Marc 271
Presbyterians 160, 161
presidential coattails 102
Presidents Day 170
Presley, Elvis 212
primaries 98–99, 117
primetime 274, 🖱10
Prince Harry 70
Prince of Wales 51, 62
Prince William 70
printing press 🖱10
*Prison Notebooks* 244
pro-choice 🖱3
Prohibition 46, 207, 304
pro-life 🖱3
Promontory Summit 43
property tax 77
Protectorate 56
publish or perish 83
Pulitzer Prize 🖱10
punks 245
Purcell, Henry 202, 209–12
Puritan work ethic 🖱3
push and pull factors 144
Quaker Oats 164
Raleigh, Sir Walter 33, 54
rampant lion 236
Rauschenberg, Robert 214
*Reader, The* 209
Reaganomics 110
reception 67–68
Red Scare 115
red tops 🖱10
redbrick universities 73, 80, 249
Redford, Robert 208, 216
Reformation 157, 171
reggae 246
Reisz, Karel 209
Reith, John 🖱10
Remember the Alamo! 140
Remember the Lusitania 45
Remember the Maine 45
reservations 134
Rhossili Bay 199
Rice, Condoleeza 261
Richard I 50
Richard III 52
Richardson, Tony 209
Ringling Brothers 216
Rio Grande 185
Rizzi, James 214
RKO 208
Roanoke Island 33
robber barons 44, 109
Roberts, Oral 168
Robertson, Pat 169
Robin Hood 25, 27
robin 187
rock music 211, 225
Rockies 7, 12
*Rocky Mountain News* 🖱10
Roe v. Wade 🖱3
Rogers, Richard 🖱2, 232
Rolling Stones 211, 🖱10
Rolls Royce 121
Roman conquest 47
romantic film comedies 208
*Room at the Top* 209
Rothermere, Lord 🖱10

rounders 217
Roundheads 56
Royal Academy of Arts 213
Royal Assent 88
Royal Coat of Arms 236
royal prerogative 88
Royal Shield 236
rugby 217
Runnymede Trust 238, 241
Rushdie, Salmon 148, 179
Rust Belt 16, 29, 112, 🖱 1
Ryan, Meg 208
S4C 🖱 10
Saatchi, Charles 213
Sacajawea 35
Sacramento 14, 🖱 10
Said, Edward 235, 237, 291, 293
Salisbury Cathedral 203
Salt Lake City 162
Salt-n-Pepa 256
same-sex marriage 263
*San Francisco Examiner* 🖱 10
San Francisco 15, 205, 🖱 1, 🖱 10
San Jose 🖱 1
SanSan 15
Santana, Carlos 141, 212
Sartre, Jean-Paul 252
Sarwar, Mohammad 150
*Satanic Verses, The* 179
*Saturday Night and Sunday Morning* 209
Savannah 159
Schengen 125
*Schindler's List* 208, 234
Schlafly, Phyllis 259, 261
Schlesinger, John 209
Schliemann, Heinrich 290
Schlink, Bernhard 209
Schmitz, Oscar 210
Scholastic Aptitude Test (SAT) 80
Schönberg, Arnold 286
school boards 76, 77
school prayer 166, 167
Schuller, Robert 168
Schurz, Carl 75, 189, 🖱 10
Schurz, Margarethe 75
Schwarzenegger, Arnold 218, 249
science fiction films 208
Scientology 167
Scilly 18, 21, 26
Scorcese, Martin 208
Scotch beef and lamb 221
Scott Trust 🖱 10
Scottish Farmed Salmon 221
Scottish Gaelic 30
Scottish Parliament Building 232
*Searchers* 208
Seattle 🖱 1
*Seattle Post-Intelligencer* 273, 🖱 10
Section 28 264
Sellafield 196
Senedd 95
Sentamu, John 153
*Sesame Street* 🖱 10
Severn Bore 24
Severn River 24, 🖱 1
shadow government 92
shamrock 233
Shaw, George Bernard 64, 125
Sheffield 28, 🖱 1
Sherwood Forest 25
Shetlands 18, 199
shilling 236
shires 4, 26
shopping malls 246, 300, 🖱 1
*Sicko* 118, 🖱 3
Sierra Club 190, 193, 200
Silicon Glen 121
Simmel, Georg 303
Simpson, Wallis 173
*Simpsons* 🖱 10
sixth form 71, 72
Sky News 281
skyscrapers 195, 204–05
*Sleepless in Seattle* 208
Sly and the Family Stone 212
Smith, Henry Nash 295
Smith, Joseph 161
Smith, Paul 295
Smith, Tommie 218
Snowdon 23
soap opera 273–74
soccer 217–18, 301
social class 🖱 3
social glue 276
Social Security 165, 🖱 3
Social Security Administration (SSA) 🖱 3
socialism 63, 64, 128
sociology 2, 238, 291, 294, 297, 303
Sojourner Truth 138
Solitaire 216
Somali 153
Sondheim, Stephen 141
sororities 79, 82
Sotomayor, Sonia 141, 261
speech act 237, 266
Spivak, Gayatri 245
sports films 208
squirrel 186, 198
St. Andrew's Cross 232
St. David's Day 232
St. George's Flag 19
Stamp Act 🖱 10
Stanford 289
Stanton, Elizabeth Cady 258
*Star Wars* series 208
Starbucks 221, 223, 307
Starr, Ringo 211
Stars and Stripes 232, 300
Statue of Liberty 129, 131, 143
Statute of Westminster 123
Steinem, Gloria 260
Stewart, Martha 260
Stoller, Robert 265
Stone of Scone 231
Stone, Lucy 258
Stonehenge 47–48, 185
Stonewall 263–64
Streep, Meryl 163, 222
Streisand, Barbra 4, 299, 311
structuralism 294
Stuart 56, 59, 🖱 3
Stuyvesant 33
subaltern 243, 245
subcultural studies 296
subjects of the monarch 91
suburbs 187, 195, 301
Suez Crisis 126, 298
*Sun* 🖱 3, 🖱 10
Sun Belt 16, 29
*Sunday Times* 🖱 10
Sunset Boulevard 201, 207, 304
superclass 🖱 3
Supreme Court, British 91
Swansea 🖱 1
swing states 98
tabloids 🖱 10
Tagalog 18
Tallahassee 14
Tata Motors 121
Tate 213
Taylor, Elizabeth 206, 208
TBN 🖱 10
tea 221, 240
Tebbit test 219
technical schools 68
techno 🖱 1
teddy bear 302
teddy boys 245
*Telegraph* 201
televangelism 168
Tennessee Valley Authority (TVA) 192–93, 🖱 3
tennis 218

tenure 83
thalidomide (Contergan) 🖱 10
Thames 24, 210
TheatroZinZanni 216
third culture/place/space 239, 294
third wave 262
Thompson, E.P. 250–51, 253
Three Mile Island 193, 196
Tillmans, Wolfgang 214, 233
*Times, The* 🖱 3, 🖱 10
Toddlers' Truce 🖱 10
Tokyo 215
Topeka 14
tourism 185, 190, 216
Towers, Dorothy 250
track and field 218
traffic light labeling 222
Trail of Tears 132
trajectory 294
transcontinental railroad 43
transgender 262–63
Triangular Lodge 204
Troubles 95, 176
Tudor dynasty 53, 57
Turner Prize 213, 233
Twain, Mark (Samuel Clemens) 242, 249
TWC 🖱 10
Tweed 24
Twenty One 215
Twiglets 220
tycoons 🖱 10
Tyson, Cicely 137–38
Uddin, Baroness 179
Ulster 64
underclass 🖱 3
Union Army 🖱 10
Union Jack 62, 96, 232, 300
Unlock Democracy 93
Untied Kingdom 96, 🖱 2
unwritten Constitution 93
upper class 🖱 3
urban sprawl 195, 301
*USA Today* 🖱 10
User, The 278
Ustinov, Peter 70
vacation 112, 120, 127, 145, 214
Vanderbilt 44, 109, 110
vectors 295
Ventura, Jess 249
Victoria 62–66, 88, 174
Vietnam Veterans Memorial 🖱 2
Virginia Tech massacre 79
Virtual Reality 279
vlogs 272
vouchers 77
Wakehurst Place Garden 198
Waldorf-Astoria 109
Wales, Jimmy 278
wall of separation 158
*Wall Street Journal* 🖱 10
Walpole, Robert 58
Walters, Julie 73
Walton, David 283
War of Jenkins's Ear 301
*War of the Worlds* 🖱 10
War Powers Act of 1973 103
*War Requiem* 211
Warhol, Andy 214
Warner Brothers 🖱 10
Wars of the Roses 52
*Warwick University Ltd* 250
Washington 🖱 2
*Washington Post* 🖱 2, 🖱 10
Washington, Booker T. 138
*Water Music* 210
Watergate Scandal 🖱 2, 🖱 10
Watkins, Gloria Jean see hooks, bell
Watt, James 61
waves of feminism 261
Weather Channel 198, 🖱 10
webcasting 271
weightlifting 218
Weir, Peter 164
Wells 🖱 1
Wells, H.G. 🖱 10
Welsh dragon 62
Wesley, John 159
Wesleyan 266
Wessex 48, 49
West Indies 219
West Lothian Question 96
western (film genre) 208
*Westliche Post* 🖱 10
Westminster Cathedral 123, 175
*Westside Story* 141, 143
Whannel, Paddy 295
whiskey 221, 240
White Anglo-Saxon Protestant (WASP) 159
white-collar workers 111, 194, 🖱 3
Who, The 212
*Who Wants to Be a Millionaire?* 215
Wikipedia 277, 278, 🖱 10
Wilder, Billy 201, 304
William III 61, 88
William III (of Orange) 57–61, 88, 233
William the Conqueror 25, 49–50
Williams, Raymond 274–75, 288–89
Williams, Robbie 212
Williams, Roger 158, 164
Williams, Rowan 174
Willis, Paul 302
Wilshire 48
Wilson 45
Wilson, Woodrow 114
Windrush 145, 152, 232, 238
Windscale 196
Windsor 64, 174
Winehouse, Amy 212
Winfrey, Oprah 260, 268
Winthrop, John 156, 157, 171
*Wired* 275
Wisconsin 115
*Witness* 164
*Wizard of Oz* 208
Wolfenden Report 264
Wollstonecraft, Mary 257, 261
Wolverhampton 🖱 2
Woods, Tiger 218
Woodstock 212, 🖱 2
Woodward 🖱 2
Worcestershire 27, 48, 221
Wordsworth, William 190
working class 244, 248, 251, 252, 262, 303, 🖱 3
workshop of the world 60
World Cup 2006 301
World Heritage Site 23
World Trade Center 116, 204, 276
World Wide Web 275, 277
Wounded Knee 44, 132
Wrangell St. Elias 190
Wren, Christopher 57, 174
Wyler, William 208
Wyoming 140, 189
X-Files 🖱 10
Yale 80
Yellowstone 189, 190
YMCA 217
Yoong, Alex 151
Yorkshire 150, 179
Young British Artists (YBA) 213
Young, Brigham 162
youth culture 243, 251, 295
YouTube 277, 278, 🖱 10
Zimbabwe 123, 145, 153
Zimmermann 45
Zion 190
Zugspitze 7, 23
Zuni 133

# List of Illustrations


1.1: Continental US (National Atlas of the United States)
1.2: Population density (National Atlas of the United States)
1.3: Population change (National Atlas of the United States)
1.4: Outline map UK (Jody Skinner)
1.5: Witch on a pig (Jody Skinner)
1.6: Exeter palm (photo: Anero)
1.7: Westminster sign (photo: Anero)
1.8: Population urban density UK (Jody Skinner)

2.1: Fort San Marcos in St. Augustine, Florida (photo: Anero)
2.2: Sacajawea dollar coin (United States coin image from the United States Mint)
2.3: Territorial expansion map (National Atlas of the United States)
2.4: Dorothea Dix postage stamp (© United States Postal Service. All rights reserved)
2.5: Harriet Tubman postage stamp (© United States Postal Service. All rights reserved)
2.6: Harriet Beecher Stowe postage stamp (© United States Postal Service. All rights reserved)
2.7: Frederick Douglass postage stamp 1 (© United States Postal Service. All rights reserved)
2.8: Frederick Douglass postage stamp 2 (© United States Postal Service. All rights reserved)
2.9: Planta genista: from Handbook to English Heraldry (http://www.gutenberg.org/files/23186/23186-h/23186-h.htm#fig21)
2.10: Owen Glyndwr at Cardiff City Hall (photo: Seth Wales, http://en.wikipedia.org/wiki/File:Owain_Glynd%C5%B5r_at_Cardiff_City_Hall.jpg)
2.11: Armada Portrait of Elizabeth I by George Gower, 16th century (http://de.wikipedia.org/w/index.php?title=Datei:Elizabeth_I_(Armada_Portrait).jpg&filetimestamp=20041215182752)
2.12: Portrait of Bonnie Prince Charlie (National Portrait Gallery, London)
2.13: Statue of David Lloyd George, Cardiff (photo: Anero)
2.14: Statue of Winston Churchill (photo: Anero)

4.1: American education (courtesy of U.S. Department of Education. Institute of Education Sciences, National Center for Education Statistics)
4.2: Sacred Heart High School, London (photo: Anero)
4.3: Dover College in Dover, England (photo: Anero)
4.4: City of London School (photo: Anero)
4.5: St. John's College in Annapolis, Maryland (photo: Anero)

5.1: The Queen on her way to work (photo: Anero)
5.2: Sovereign's Entrance to Parliament, London (photo: Anero)
5.3: Visitor Entrance to Parliament, London (photo: Anero)
5.4: Ministry of Justice, London (photo: Anero)
5.5: Senedd Cardiff, Wales (photo: Anero)

6.1: Puerto Rican flag
6.2: Map of the British Empire at its greatest extent after World War I. (http://en.wikipedia.org/wiki/File:BritishEmpire1919.png)
6.3: Map of the Commonwealth of Nations in 2008 (http://en.wikipedia.org/wiki/File:Commonwealth_of_Nations.svg)
6.4: Flag of the Commonwealth of Nations
6.5: Commonwealth Cemetery Cologne (photo: Anero)

7.1: DuBois postage stamp (© United States Postal Service. All rights reserved)
7.2: Chavez postage stamp (© United States Postal Service. All rights reserved)

**7.3:** "Old English Gentleman" next to "Iranian Cuisine" in London just off Edgeware Road in the City of Westminster (photo: Anero)

**8.1:** Wesley statue (photo: Anero)
**8.2:** American Eagle gold bullion (United States coin image from the United States Mint)
**8.3:** Church in Maryland (photo: Anero)
**8.4:** Washington Presidential Dollar Coin (United States coin image from the United States Mint)
**8.5:** Lincoln Silver Dollar Coin (United States coin image from the United States Mint)
**8.6:** Capitol Building, Washington DC (photo: Anero)
**8.7:** Jefferson Memorial, Washington DC (photo: Anero)
**8.8:** Gold coin with Edward VIII (http://www.garyphelps.co.uk/edward%20viii%20half%20sov%20obv.jpg)
**8.9:** Gold Britannia coin (Royal Mint image)
**8.10:** Islamia Primary School (photo: Muslim Council of Britain)

**9.1:** Great Seal of the United States (http://en.wikipedia.org/wiki/File:US-GreatSeal-Obverse.svg)
**9.2:** Hedgerows in the countryside near Exeter (photo: Anero)
**9.3:** National Parks in the UK (Crown Copyright. All rights reserved 2009 LDNPA)

**11.1:** Interior of Exeter Cathedral (photo: Anero)
**11.2:** Eileen Gray Table (photo: Otto)
**11.3:** Movieum London (photo: Anero)
**11.4:** American pop artist James Rizzi on German stamps (Deutsche Post, http://en.wikipedia.org/wiki/File:James_Rizzi_Danke.jpg )
**11.5:** American pop artist James Rizzi on German stamps (Deutsche Post, http://en.wikipedia.org/wiki/File:James_Rizzi_Gr%C3%BC%C3%9Fe_EUROPA.jpg)
**11.6:** Starbucks (photo: Anero)

**12.1:** Flag of England
**12.2:** Flag of Scotland
**12.3:** Flag of Wales
**12.4:** Edward Said (photo: Jerry Bauer)
**12.5:** Royal Mint image
**12.6:** Stuart Hall (National Portrait Gallery, London, © Dawoud Bey)
**12.7:** Homi K. Bhabha (photo: Bruce Williams)

**13.1:** Antonio Gramsci (http://de.wikipedia.org/w/index.php?title=Datei:Gramsci.png&filetimestamp=20070426110453)
**13.2:** Palace of Westminster (photo: Anero)
**13.3:** E.P. Thompson (photo: Photoshot.com/UPPA)
**13.4:** Richard Hoggart (© Mark Gerson/National Portrait Gallery, London)
**13.5:** Michel Foucault (© Bruce Jackson, used with Special permission by the photographer)

**14.1:** Susan B. Anthony (United States coin image from the United States Mint)
**14.2:** US postage stamp from 1998 (© United States Postal Service. All rights reserved)
**14.3:** bell hooks (photo: Photoshot.com/UPPA)
**14.4:** Judith Butler (photo: Jreberlein, http://en.wikipedia.org/wiki/File:Judith_Butler.jpg)

**15.1:** Marshall McLuhan (photo: Photoshot.com/UPPA)
**15.2:** Francis Barraud's painting "His Late Master's Voice" (http://de.wikipedia.org/w/index.php?title=Datei:His_Master%27s_Voice.jpg&filetimestamp=20070629155107)

**16.1:** Raymond Williams (photo: Gwydion Madawc Williams, http://en.wikipedia.org/wiki/File:Raymond_Williams_in_1972.jpg)